Gentlemen and Poachers

The English Game Laws 1671–1831

Gentlemen and Poachers

The English Game Laws 1671–1831

P. B. MUNSCHE

CAMBRIDGE UNIVERSITY PRESS

Cambridge
London   New York   New Rochelle
Melbourne   Sydney

Published by the Press Syndicate of the University of Cambridge
The Pitt Building, Trumpington Street, Cambridge CB2 1RP
32 East 57th Street, New York, NY 10022, USA
296 Beaconsfield Parade, Middle Park, Melbourne 3206, Australia

First published 1981

Printed in Great Britain at the
University Press, Cambridge

British Library Cataloguing in Publication Data

Munsche, P.B.
Gentlemen and poachers.
1. Game-laws – England
I. Title
343'.0769   SK505   81-6168

ISBN 0 521 23284 8

TO J. M. BEATTIE

Contents

List of illustrations

All illustrations are courtesy of the Trustees of the British Museum.

Graph

A note on dates

All dates before 1752 are Old Style, except that the year is taken to begin on 1 January.

Preface

A decade ago, I was a graduate student at the University of Toronto searching around for a thesis topic. 'Why don't you write something on the game laws?' someone suggested. 'Because I'm not that desperate', I replied. Although the intervening years have not been entirely free of desperation, it was not that which prompted me to write the present volume. Rather, it was a deepening awareness that the game laws were the vehicle by which I, and others, might enter the world of rural England in the eighteenth century. It is a world about which we know surprisingly little – less because of any dearth of evidence, I suspect, than because we tend to assume that we already know a great deal. The pictures drawn by Fielding, Trevelyan and the Hammonds are so clear and powerful that it has seemed that there was little left for the modern historian to do except fill in a few details and tie up a few loose ends. I hope that the following pages will indicate that, in fact, the world of rural England has yet to be adequately explored – and that those who venture into it will be well rewarded for their efforts.

As with any historical study these days, this book could not have been written without the assistance of many friends, colleagues and institutions. Since money provides the sinews of scholarship as well as war, it seems only fair to mention first the Government of Ontario, the University of Toronto and, most importantly, my parents. Their financial assistance enabled me to research and write the thesis upon which the present volume is based, and I shall always be grateful for their confidence in me.

I am also indebted to the archivists and staffs of the various record repositories listed in the Bibliography. In addition to fulfilling patiently my requests for documents, they often directed me to sources which I might otherwise have overlooked. In this regard, I am particularly grateful to the staffs of the Cumberland, Norfolk and Wiltshire Record Offices. I also wish to express my appreciation to the Marquess of Salisbury, the Earl of Aylesford and the Earl of Leicester for generously permitting me to examine and quote from manuscript collections in their possession. Mr R.

H. Harcourt Williams, Librarian at Hatfield House, was especially kind in searching through the Salisbury MSS for me and xeroxing the relevant documents. Finally, it is my pleasure to acknowledge the assistance of the staffs of the following institutions: the Bodleian Library; the Reference Department of the British Library; the British Museum Department of Prints and Drawings; the British Library of Political and Economic Science; the Cambridge University Library; the Goldsmiths Library at the University of London; the Institute of Historical Research; the Kress Library at Harvard University; the Library of the Law Society of Upper Canada; the National Register of Archives; the Norwich Public Library; the Salisbury Public Library; and the University of Toronto Library.

As the notes will indicate, I have also had the assistance of a number of fellow historians who have taken time out from their own work to send me references which I otherwise would have missed. In this regard, I wish to give special thanks to Robert Malcolmson of Queen's University who, in addition, made many helpful comments and criticisms on an earlier draft of this book. My greatest debt, however, is to John Beattie. As a teacher and scholar, he has always been an inspiration; as a colleague and friend, he has always been a cheerful and loyal supporter. I will not embarrass him by recounting his many acts of kindness, nor will I tarnish his reputation by neglecting to point out that any faults and errors in the following pages are entirely my own responsibility. I will simply note that this volume is dedicated to him with the deepest respect and affection.

Toronto   P.B.M.
May 1980

Introduction

The game laws are both familiar and obscure. Most students of English history have come across them at one time or another, usually in discussions of 'life under the squirearchy' in the eighteenth and nineteenth centuries. From these brief summaries, they learn that the game laws, by imposing a property qualification on sportsmen, effectively gave the landed gentry the exclusive right to hunt game in England.[1] They also learn that this monopoly was enforced by the gentry themselves in their capacity as justices of the peace by means of summary trials and severe punishments. As a consequence, the game laws were bitterly resented and, in many cases, violently resisted, but it was not until the dawn of the age of reform that their repeal was finally achieved. Given these facts, it is hardly surprising that historians have unanimously condemned the game laws as harsh, unjust and generally indefensible. To the Webbs, the game code was 'an instrument of terrible severity, leading, not infrequently, to cruel oppression'. The Hammonds also denounced the code, charging that it spilt 'the blood of men and boys . . . for the pleasures of the rich'. More recently, B.A. Holderness has pointed to the game laws as a 'classic example . . . of class selfishness'.[2] Even historians sympathetic to the gentry have judged the game laws harshly. J.D. Chambers, for example, thought their enforcement was 'tyrannical' and went on to assert that 'it was largely owing to the universal indignation which the Game Laws aroused that the squirearchy were so ruthlessly stripped of their powers' in the early nineteenth century.[3] Yet, despite the confidence with which these judgements have been rendered and repeated, we actually know very little about the game laws. Why, for example, were the gentry awarded this privilege? Was it strictly enforced? Who violated the game laws, and why? If the game laws were so damaging to the gentry's authority, why did it take so long to secure their repeal? These rather elementary questions have never, in fact, been satisfactorily answered. Until they are, judgements about the iniquity of the game laws would seem to be premature.

To be fair, these questions probably could not have been satisfactorily

1

answered before 1945. Until that time historians interested in the game laws were almost entirely dependent on printed sources: parliamentary papers and debates, pamphlets and periodicals. While extensive, these sources had important defects. They were, on the whole, dominated by the opponents of the game laws and were therefore apt to concentrate on the negative aspects of the laws' operation. In addition, the bulk of this material dates from the early nineteenth century; thus, it is of limited use in studying the enforcement of the game laws in earlier periods. For a picture of the laws' enforcement in the eighteenth century, the Hammonds were forced to rely on works of fiction, notably the novels of Henry Fielding. Whatever the virtues of the latter, they certainly were no substitute for documentary evidence of the day-to-day operation of the game laws. Fortunately, that evidence began to become available after the end of World War II with the development of the county record offices. In these offices the judicial records of local government were consolidated and, in some cases, dusted off and calendared. Equally helpful was the increasing use of the county record offices as depositories for family and estate papers. Once the gentry's own archives were made available to historians, it became possible to test the charges against the historical record, and thus move a little closer to the truth about the game laws.

Historians, it must be noted, have not exactly jumped at this opportunity. There are probably several reasons for this, but one of the most important, no doubt, is simply the difficulty of such an undertaking. There is no central body of manuscript material for the history of the game laws. Evidence is scattered throughout the holdings of several dozen county record offices, as well as in collections still in private hands. This evidence, moreover, consists of a wide variety of documents. While it might be expected that the centre-piece of any modern study of the game laws would be a table of statistics revealing conviction rates and the like, no such table can in fact be compiled. The surviving judicial records permit, at best, only an estimate of the number of persons convicted under the game laws before the nineteenth century; in most counties even that is not possible. This lack of a statistical core increases the historian's dependence on other sources of information: estate correspondence and account books, personal correspondence and diaries, provincial newspapers and gaol calendars. The interpretation of these sources leads, in turn, to other areas of historical research, such as the impressment of seamen, the economics of the poultry trade and the operation of the poor law. To write a history of the game laws, then, is a formidable task; in order to prevent it from becoming an impossible one, I have found it necessary to impose certain limitations on the subject.

The first limitation is temporal: the following pages will concentrate on the years between 1671 and 1831. The reason for this is fairly straightforward. Although there were game laws in force before 1671, they did not make hunting the exclusive privilege of the landed gentry. The Game Act of 1671 did, and thus marked the beginning of a new era for both the gentry and the game. Similarly, the passage of the Game Reform Act in 1831 brought that era to an end; thus, that seemed to be an appropriate point to conclude this study. The second limitation is geographic: the game laws under examination in the following pages are 'English' rather than 'British'. In our period, the British Isles consisted of three kingdoms, and while they had all been assimilated into a single realm by 1801, each continued to have its own legal code, including its own set of game laws. The English, Scottish and Irish game codes were similar – all, for example, imposed a property qualification on sportsmen – but each had its peculiarities and, more importantly, its own separate development.[4] While a comparison of these codes would have been interesting, I have decided to confine the present study to England, primarily because the game laws appear to have had a more profound impact there than in the other two kingdoms.[5]

There is one final limitation on the scope of this study – one which, at first glance, might seem curious. It concerns the definition of 'game'. Generally speaking, game might be defined as all animals which are pursued for sport. In the period 1671–1831 this would include a wide variety of animals: deer, rabbits, hares, partridges, pheasants, moor fowl (grouse, black game, etc.), wild ducks, foxes, otters and badgers. In the following pages, however, the term 'game' will refer only to hares, partridges, pheasants and moor fowl. The simple explanation for this is that only these animals were accorded protection under what eighteenth-century Englishmen called 'the game laws'. There was no operative property qualification for hunters of deer or rabbits, and there was no property qualification at all for hunters of wild ducks, foxes, otters or badgers. Thus, the definition of game adopted for this study is the one used by Parliament when it passed laws 'for the preservation of the game'. If that is the simple explanation, however, it is not an entirely satisfying one. There were, for example, statutes in force during this period which made the taking of deer or rabbits in certain circumstances a crime. Were not these 'game laws' also? And why was there a distinction between one type of sportsman's prey and another? Why, in particular, should there have been one set of laws for taking rabbits and another for taking hares? Indeed, the closer one looks at the multitude of statutes governing the pursuit of animals for sport in this period, the more confusing they become. Some further explanation, therefore, is obviously necessary.

One might begin by considering those animals which were not protected by any statute: badgers, otters and foxes. Although often pursued for sport, they were classified as 'vermin' rather than game. They tended to prey upon domestic fowl and, as a result, their destruction – by anyone, at any time – was considered to be a service to the community. That, at least, was the attitude of the common law. Some sportsmen, not surprisingly, took a different view and sought to preserve these animals, despite the threat which the latter posed to the chickens, geese and ducks in the neighbourhood. This was particularly true of foxes, the pursuit of which became an increasingly popular sport in the eighteenth and nineteenth centuries. Nevertheless, whatever protection these animals received was effected without legal sanction, and thus can reasonably be considered outside the scope of a study of the game laws. The preservation of wild ducks can also be excluded from the following study, albeit for a slightly different reason. Mallard, teal, widgeon and the like were accorded some protection under the law in the form of a defined 'season', outside of which no person was permitted to kill them. In 1711, Parliament forbade anyone to take wild ducks except in the period between September and June, under pain of a five-shilling fine or one month in prison at hard labour; in 1737, the 'season' was reduced to October through May.[6] The law, however, was rarely enforced. Much more effective, it seems, were the duck 'decoys' – preserves specially created to attract wild ducks to an area – which could be found all along the English coast in the eighteenth century. Decoys were private property and, if need be, trespassers on them could be prosecuted in the courts.[7] In practice, then, wild ducks, like foxes, badgers and otters, were preserved without resort to the criminal code; for this reason, they do not come within the scope of this study.

The same argument, however, cannot be made with regard to deer and rabbits. Parliament did pass a number of laws for the preservation of these animals, and these laws were enforced. Nevertheless, neither deer nor rabbits in our period were 'game' in the same sense that hares, partridges, pheasants and moor fowl were. The explanation for this rests on a concept which will be referred to repeatedly in the following pages: 'enclosure'. In essence, enclosure was a process by which wild animals were confined to a specific area where they were bred and nourished until the landowner permitted them to be hunted and killed. While such animals were never fully domesticated, they did cease to be wild – and that altered the approach of the law to their protection. A wild animal, by definition, had no owner; thus, if it was captured or killed, no person suffered a loss. An intruder who took a wild animal on another man's land could, of course, be sued for trespass, but restitution could not be claimed for the destruction of the animal itself since it was not the plaintiff's property. After enclosure, however, the animal ceased to be wild and acquired, in at least a limited sense, an owner. If the latter was deprived of his property, he could under common law seek restitution in the courts. If, moreover, that property was specifically protected by a provision of the criminal code, then the owner – or anyone else, for that matter – had the right to demand that the offender suffer the penalty prescribed by statute. In order to understand the eighteenth century's definition of game, therefore, it is necessary to ask not only whether an animal was protected by law but also whether it was enclosed.

Nothing, perhaps, illustrates this point more clearly than the changing status of deer and rabbits in the seventeenth century. Ever since the Middle Ages, there had been a property qualification for hunting these animals, and early in the seventeenth century Parliament moved to reassert it. Under the Game Act of 1605, no person was permitted to take deer or rabbits unless he had at least £40 a year from land or goods worth at least £200. By that time, however, deer and rabbits were no longer as free to roam about the countryside as they once had been. On an increasing number of estates, there were fenced-in parks where deer were kept and hunted, in some cases for sport, in others for venison which was then sold in market towns or in London. There were also a growing number of warrens in which rabbits were bred, both for their meat and their skins.[8] The enclosure of deer and rabbits continued throughout the century and gradually the law began to reflect this fact, confirming Lord Chief Justice Willes' observation that 'when the nature of things changes, the rules of the law must change too'.[9] In 1671, Parliament passed a new Game Act redefining the property qualification for sportsmen, but this time deer were omitted from the list of animals which came under the Act's protection. Rabbits were still included, but in 1692 they too were dropped from the list. Thereafter, deer and rabbits were protected by statutes which forbade anyone, qualified or not, to hunt or take these animals without the permission of the person on whose land they were found. Deer and rabbits might still be pursued for sport, but they were no longer 'game' in the eyes of the law. As a result of enclosure, they had become a type of private property and were entitled to legal protection as such. While the property qualification for taking deer and rabbits remained on the statute books for another century, it was no longer enforced. Instead, those who unlawfully took these animals were treated as thieves, which is to say very harshly indeed. A 'game poacher' in the eighteenth century usually risked no more than a £5 fine or three months in prison; a 'deer stealer', on the other hand, risked transportation for seven years.

The concept of enclosure is central not only to the definition of game but also to the development of the game laws in the eighteenth century. Hares, partridges, pheasants and moor fowl were still wild animals in 1671, but over the course of the next century and a half they (with the exception of moor fowl) also became enclosed. As they did, the tendency to view game as property – and poachers as thieves – became increasingly apparent. In contrast with the experience in the seventeenth century, however, the law did not reflect this change in perception. Far from falling into disuse, in fact, the property qualification for sportsmen was enforced with increasing vigour in the late eighteenth and early nineteenth centuries. The reasons for this arrested development of the game laws will be examined in detail in the following pages. What is important to note here is that the attempt to ignore the legal implications of the enclosure of the game was ultimately unsuccessful. In 1831, Parliament repealed the property qualification and declared game to be the property of the person on whose land it was found. Thus, with the passage of the Game Reform Act, the legal distinction between various types of animals pursued for sport disappeared and a general designation of all such creatures as 'game' became possible.

As the character of these limitations of time, place and subject matter should indicate, the primary concern of this study is to examine the game laws, not poaching. The latter, of course, cannot be completely ignored, but it must be admitted that no great effort has been made in the following pages to detail either the backgrounds or the methods of poachers. Instead, I have chosen to focus on the poachers' antagonists, the landed gentry, for it is through them, I believe, that the true significance of the game laws can be discovered. The gentry's identification with the game laws was complete. They wrote the game laws, benefited from them, defended them, enforced them – and they led the fight for their repeal. An investigation of the game laws, therefore, is likely to reveal a great deal about the men who ruled England between the Glorious Revolution and the Great Reform Bill. This by itself is sufficient justification for taking a new look at the game laws. Considering the gentry's dominant position in eighteenth-century society, we know very little about the character of their rule, particularly in their own neighbourhoods. The Webbs and others have outlined the structure of local government in our period, but there are few works which examine how it worked in practice. We know it was a system which gave enormous discretionary power to country gentlemen, both individually and collectively, but how effectively did they use this power? What were the practical limitations on its use? Did discretionary power lead inevitably to arbitrary and unjust rule?

The following pages will give the reader an opportunity to watch the gentry at work in their own communities. It is, however, more than a simple case study, for the game laws operated in a very sensitive area of the law: at the point where legislative will ran into direct conflict with popular belief. The vast majority of Englishmen did not believe that poaching was a crime. The game laws, in their view, were patently unjust because hares, partridges, pheasants and moor fowl were, as one Bedfordshire farmer put it, 'ordained from the beginning free for anyone who could over take them'.[10] Needless to say, the gentry disagreed, and this divergence of views greatly complicated the task of law enforcement. Public hostility toward the game laws was important for another reason as well. Country gentlemen believed that the game laws were concerned with more than just securing adequate sport for themselves and their friends. Society, they argued, was the true beneficiary of the laws since the latter kept the poor from developing habits of idleness, while at the same time rewarding men who gave freely of their time and fortunes in the service of the community. In other words, the game laws were measures designed to preserve a stable society, one which was rural-based, hierarchical and paternalist. Accordingly, country gentlemen tended to regard any opposition to the game laws with alarm. The question, in their view, was less the preservation of game than the preservation of the social order, and on the latter they were unwilling to compromise. Indeed, it was only when the gentry were finally convinced that the game laws themselves were endangering the social order that they agreed to some measure of reform.

What follows, then, is really a study of the values of the landed gentry and the manner in which they tried to impose these on eighteenth-century society. We shall begin by surveying the game laws themselves and the environment in which they were enforced. We shall then turn to poaching and how the law dealt with those who challenged the gentry's monopoly on game. Finally, we shall examine the long campaign against the game laws and the circumstances which finally forced the passage of the Game Reform Act of 1831. Inevitably, the game laws' reputation as an instrument of oppression will never be far in the background, but the real subjects of this study are the men who defended and enforced these laws. From them we should be able to gain a deeper insight into the world of eighteenth-century England – and what made it so different from our own.

1

The game laws

'The statutes for preserving the game,' Blackstone noted in his *Commentaries*, 'are many and various, and not a little obscure and intricate.'[1] Their number was indeed prodigious. Between 1671 and 1831, Parliament passed no fewer than two dozen acts designed to regulate the hunting of game.[2] Since Parliament was reluctant to repeal these even when they were superseded and since the laws were often poorly worded in the first place, the game laws soon became a legal thicket in which it was very easy to get lost. Sir Roger de Coverley might have been able to explain 'a passage in the Game Act', but others were less gifted. When, for example, Sir William Ashhurst of the Court of King's Bench was asked in 1782 to perform a similar feat, he could only reply that 'the act, as it stands, is nonsense'.[3] Historians have also experienced some difficulty in comprehending the game laws. However understandable their confusion, it has contributed greatly to the game laws' reputation for 'savagery'. The Hammonds, for example, noted that an act passed in 1770 made hunting at night an offence punishable by three to six months in prison and a public whipping. They apparently overlooked the fact that this statute was replaced by a milder one only three years later.[4] Another historian has written that 'the game laws provided punishments of seven years' transportation for unarmed poaching, even for a first offence'. He seems to have been unaware that the act which permitted this was repealed within a year of its passage.[5] Yet another historian has claimed that 'illegal shooting' was a capital crime in the eighteenth century, although in fact no offence under the game laws was ever punishable by death.[6]

If, however, the exact meaning of the game laws is sometimes difficult to establish, their intent is not. The purpose of the game laws was to ensure that the hunting of game – particularly hares, partridges and pheasants – was the exclusive privilege of the landed gentry. Initially, the device employed to achieve this was a property qualification: those who did not possess enough property to meet the requirements of the law were forbidden to hunt, even on their own land. The first such qualification was enacted in the fourteenth century, but it was the Game Act of 1671 which was the cornerstone of the eighteenth-century game laws. With a few exceptions, the Game Act forbade all persons to hunt game unless they had freeholds worth £100 a year or leaseholds worth £150 a year. This qualification remained unchanged for the next 160 years. During the same period, however, the game laws grew in number and complexity. New legal devices – civil prosecution, sporting licences, Night Poaching Acts – were grafted onto the game code in order to help protect the gentry's privilege. In the process they caused a great deal of confusion. It is the purpose of this chapter to unravel the game laws and make them understandable, and perhaps the best place to start is with the Game Act itself.

The restriction of field sports to a small minority of the population was not a seventeenth-century innovation. Aside from previous qualification laws, there were three other types of sporting privilege in existence in 1671. The most ancient of these was embodied in the forest laws. Following the Norman invasion, William the Conqueror had set aside vast tracts of land in England as sporting preserves, within which no person might hunt without his permission. His successors expanded these 'forests' and established a code of laws to protect the trees and wild animals within their boundaries. Administered by royal officials and enforced in prerogative courts, the forest laws were harsh and unpopular. Their scope and severity were first checked by the Forest Charter of 1217, and as the power of the monarchy declined in the later Middle Ages the effectiveness of the forest laws was weakened even further. Forest offices grew into sinecures and the sittings of the forest courts became ever less frequent. This process of decay was not halted by the resurgence of the monarchy under the Tudors. By the end of the sixteenth century, in fact, the forest laws had almost ceased to be enforced at all.[7] Charles I attempted to revive the forest laws in the 1630s as a source of revenue, but his efforts were cut short by the Long Parliament and the outbreak of the Civil War.[8] In 1660, the forest laws were restored along with the other institutions of monarchy, but by then, after centuries of neglect and two decades of virtually uninterrupted plundering, the royal forests were no longer the impressive preserves of timber and deer that the Normans had created. Nevertheless, the forest laws remained – as a valuable source of Crown patronage and a reminder of the power which the monarchy had once wielded in the field of game preservation.

Another reminder of that power could be found in the rights of park, chase and free warren claimed by landowners in every part of the country in the late seventeenth century. Granted by monarchs since the Middle Ages, these were franchises to hunt deer and game within certain areas. Parks and chases were, respectively, enclosed and unenclosed sanctuaries for deer, while free warrens protected hares, rabbits, partridges, pheasants and other types of wild fowl.[9] No one was permitted to hunt in these areas without the permission of the holder of the franchise, and the similarity between franchises and royal forests did not end there. A franchise could be inherited and its privileges retained even if some of the land within its boundaries was sold.[10] Unlike the king, however, the holder of a franchise could not punish offences against his privilege on his own authority: he had to seek redress from the common law courts.

Similar to franchises were appointments as royal gamekeepers. First awarded by James I, these were warrants 'to preserve the King's game' within a given area. Royal gamekeepers were permitted to hunt – and to prevent others from hunting – within this area, but their privilege differed from that of the franchise-holder in several important respects. Unlike a franchise, a royal gamekeepership could not be inherited. Even within the royal gamekeeper's own lifetime, retention of his privilege was not guaranteed. In the warrant granting them their office, royal gamekeepers were admonished to prevent 'persons of meane qualitie' from taking the king's game; such persons were to be relieved of their guns, dogs and nets and their names were to be reported to the Privy Council. Non-performance of these duties – or, more likely, loss of royal favour because of political opposition – could result in the loss of the right to hunt. Even if retained, the royal gamekeeper's privilege was not as exclusive as that of the franchise-holder. The area assigned to him was usually the neighbour-hood around his country seat. Some noblemen, however, were made gamekeepers for entire counties; where this happened, the right to hunt obviously had to be shared. Another complication was the existence of franchises, which the Stuarts still continued to grant. It was unclear whether a royal gamekeeper could forbid someone with the right of free warren from hunting within its boundaries.[11] Compensating for these limitations, however, was the fact that, unlike a franchise-holder, a royal gamekeeper was not restricted to his own land, but could hunt over a much wider area confident in the knowledge that he had the king's warrant to do so.

It was, indeed, the king's warrant which was the common element in all three of these types of sporting privilege: forest law, franchises and royal gamekeeperships. The reason for this was that the Crown claimed that all the game in England was the property of the king. The forests were great monuments to this claim, but the granting of franchises was, if anything, more audacious, since it implied that royal hunting rights were not confined to specific areas however large, but rather extended into every corner of the kingdom.[12] It was, typically, the Stuarts who made this claim explicit. James I and his successors referred to hares, partridges and pheasants as 'the king's game' and, as the appointment of royal gamekeepers for entire counties indicated, they did not mean only that game which was found on royal estates. Under the Stuarts, unauthorised hunting of game anywhere in the kingdom was viewed as an offence against the royal prerogative and therefore a matter important enough to warrant the attention of the Privy Council.[13] Like so many of the Stuarts' assertions of prerogative rights, their claim to all the game in England had a much sounder basis in legal precedent than contemporary practice. Although franchises of park, chase and free warren had their origin in the royal prerogative, by the end of the sixteenth century they had become a type of property, one which could be sold or inherited and which was closely associated with being a gentleman. As Elizabeth I had observed in a proclamation issued near the end of her reign, game 'belongeth to the men of the best sort and condition'.[14]

Supporting such a view were the qualification acts, by which men with a certain amount of property were given the right to hunt game. The first act of this kind was passed in 1389. In the wake of the Peasants' Revolt, Parliament had been disturbed to learn that on days 'when good Christian people be at church hearing divine service', servants and labourers were often out hunting and 'sometimes under such colour they make their assemblies, conferences, and conspiracies for to rise and disobey their allegience'. To prevent such seditious gatherings, persons with lands worth less than 40s. a year were forbidden, under pain of a year's imprisonment, to keep hunting dogs or to use ferrets, nets, hare-pipes or any other 'engine' to take deer, rabbits, hares or 'other gentlemen's game'.[15] In the first decade of the seventeenth century, the qualification was both increased and sub-divided. After 1610, there were different qualifications for hunting deer and rabbits, for hunting partridges and pheasants and for possessing dogs or nets to take game; all were substantially higher than the qualification of 1389. To hunt partridges and pheasants, for instance, a person had to possess freeholds worth at least £40 a year, leaseholds worth at least twice that amount, or goods and chattels valued at £400 or more. Those with right of free warren and lords of manors were also deemed qualified to hunt game. The property qualification was higher for hunting deer and rabbits and slightly less for possessing hunting dogs and nets[16] but, on the whole, it can be said that the Jacobean game laws probably granted sporting rights to most gentlemen and noblemen in England – and did so without any reference to the monarch's prerogative.

It was ironic that these acts should have been passed in the reign of a monarch who had a particularly exalted view of the royal prerogative, but, in fact, they did not really infringe on the prerogative. By virtue of the latter, the king essentially claimed the right to do two things: to hunt wherever he pleased and to take such measures for the preservation of the game as he thought fit. It was from the latter right that the forests, franchises and royal gamekeeperships derived their legality. The qualification acts did not deny these rights; indeed, to the extent that the acts gave justices of the peace the power to punish poachers, the king's prerogative had been strengthened. The problem – and, of course, it was not confined to the matter of sporting rights under the Stuarts – was whether the king's warrant was superior to parliamentary statute. Could a royal gamekeeper, for example, legally forbid a qualified person from hunting on his own land or confiscate his dog and nets? While the courts tended to shy away from the issue, some sportsmen were less cautious about expressing their opinion. In Kent, for example, one Henry Grey of Deptford refused to obey a royal gamekeeper's warrant and surrender his setting dog and nets until he had consulted a justice of the peace: 'for aught he knew,' Grey said, 'the warrant was made under a hedge'.[17] A Cambridge man expressed similar sentiments when he was interrupted in his pursuit of a hare by the deputy of another royal gamekeeper, Sir John Cotton. 'He cared not for Sir John Cotton's authority nor for the king's,' the man said, 'and . . . he would course in spite of their teeths.'[18] Such defiance was not typical, but it probably reflected a general hostility to the privileges of royal gamekeepers. Certainly when Lord O'Brien applied for a royal gamekeepership, he was reluctant to do so publicly. 'I would come up [to London] to ask for it,' he wrote to Sir Joseph Williamson, 'but consider that, if any of my brethren should find me soliciting for it, it might prevent my future services.'[19] It boded ill for the Crown that its favours were treated with such caution.

The Game Act of 1671 did not overtly challenge the Crown's prerogative in matters concerning game. It did, however, make changes in the law which had that effect. First, it raised the property qualification once again. After 1671, all persons were forbidden to hunt game unless they (a) had freeholds worth at least £100 a year, (b) had leaseholds (for 99 years or longer) or copyholds worth at least £150 a year, (c) were sons and heirs apparent of esquires or other persons 'of higher degree', or (d) held franchises of park, chase or free warren. Secondly, the Act authorised all lords of manors 'not under the degree of esquire' to appoint gamekeepers who would have the power to search for and to seize all guns, dogs, nets and other 'engines' kept on the manor by unqualified persons.[20] In themselves, these were major innovations. The basic qualification was raised from £40 to £100, the latter amount being fifty times the electoral franchise. Moreover, in contrast with previous qualification statutes, the Act of 1671 excluded those with non-landed wealth from the ranks of qualified sportsmen. Income, however large, from trade, stocks or offices was no longer in itself sufficient to qualify a man to course a hare or shoot a partridge. Such a man, indeed, ran the risk of having his gun and his hounds confiscated by the lord of the manor's gamekeeper.

In the context of sporting privilege in the late seventeenth century, however, these were more than major innovations. They signalled the transfer of the game prerogative from the king to the landed gentry. The monarch, as we have already noted, claimed the right to do two things: to hunt where he pleased and to take whatever measures he thought necessary to preserve the game. After 1671, he still had those rights – but now the gentry had them also. Previous qualification acts had permitted qualified sportsmen to hunt only on their own land, but the Game Act of 1671 contained no such restriction. The qualified sportsman could, therefore, hunt where he pleased. He was, of course, still subject to the law of trespass, but by another law passed in 1671 plaintiffs in trespass cases could not be awarded full costs unless the damages were found to exceed 40s. Since the latter was unlikely to occur in a case of simple trespass by a sportsman, suits against qualified gentlemen were effectively discouraged.[21] One reason why damages were likely to be low in such suits was that the aggrieved could seek redress only for the invasion of his land, *not* for the destruction of game found on his land. Game was not the property of the person on whose land it was found. Instead, it belonged to all qualified sportsmen.[22] In short, 'the king's game' had become 'the gentry's game' and the right of country gentlemen to hunt it where they pleased was limited only by the weak provisions of the law of trespass.

By the Game Act of 1671, the gentry also took over the other half of the royal game prerogative: they assumed responsibility for preserving the game. Prior to the Act's passage, this had manifestly been the responsibility of the Crown. Both franchises and royal gamekeeperships were, at least in theory, granted to preserve the game. In addition, royal proclamations and Privy Council orders were periodically issued to emphasise the king's interest in the game and to encourage greater vigilance by the local authorities against the activities of 'mean and base' people.[23] As with the king's right to hunt where he wished, the Game Act did not prevent the monarch from continuing to take measures to preserve the game, but it extended this right to most of the principal landowners in England.[24] By allowing lords of manors to appoint their own gamekeepers and by giving the latter powers previously exercised by royal gamekeepers, the Game Act vested a large portion of the gentry with an authority in the field of game preservation which was – with one exception – equivalent to the king's. The exception was the authority to empower other persons to hunt game. Gamekeepers, unless they were qualified in their own right, were not permitted to hunt. A lord of the manor, therefore, lacked the king's power to confer sporting privileges simply by virtue of his own writ. It was not until 1707 that this final part of the royal game prerogative was surrendered.[25]

Even though it stopped short of awarding the gentry the full powers of the game prerogative, the Game Act effectively overthrew the Crown's claim to all the game in England. This was certainly the understanding of the committee of the House of Lords which considered the legislation in April 1671. Such were the implications of the bill that the Earl of Northampton proposed that the following proviso be added to it:

> And because all liberties, privileges, franchises, and royalties whatsoever now claimed by any Lords of manors or other of his Majesty's subjects, were originally derived from the Crown; it is therefore declared and enacted that nothing in this Act contained shall in any way extend to the diminishing or weakening of his Majesty's sovereign power and authority to hunt and hawk in any part of this realm when it shall please him, or to give orders or directions for the preservation of such game. Nor shall this Act abridge, change, or alter any part of the Forest Laws of this realm.[26]

A shorter and less explicit clause was eventually adopted; it claimed only that the Act should not be construed as 'taking away or abridging any royalty or prerogative royal of his Majesty'.[27] In the immediate aftermath of the Game Act's passage, even this proviso might have seemed unnecessary. The forest laws remained untouched, and the Crown continued to grant franchises and appoint royal gamekeepers. Gradually, however, the changes wrought by the Game Act began to be felt. The forest laws, of course, were already a hollow shell. The organisation of the forests, with their rangers, keepers and courts, might remain intact for another century and a half, but those who unlawfully hunted in the forests were, for the most part, tried in the common-law courts for offences against parliamentary statute, not prerogative law.[28] After 1671, franchises also began to drift into obsolesence. Like any ancient right, they had a certain amount of prestige which would continue to be valued,[29] but the Game Act had given most country gentlemen rights which were at least equal to those associated with free warrens and, in 1692, the remaining privileges of franchises were extended to every manor in the kingdom.[30] Franchises, therefore, soon ceased to have any practical value, and by 1700 the Crown had stopped granting them. By the turn of the century, royal gamekeeperships had also begun to die out.[31] Their privileges were now claimed by all qualified sportsmen, and the powers of the office were being exercised by all lords of the manor. The Crown, in short, had ceased to be the source of sporting privilege; in its place stood the Game Act of 1671. The change was not merely a theoretical one. As Blackstone was to observe a century later, 'the forest laws established only one mighty hunter throughout the land, [but] the game laws have raised a little Nimrod in every manor'.[32]

II

The reasons for the passage of the Game Act are obscure. The parliamentary
diarists of the time, Anchitel Grey and Sir Edward Dering, make no
mention of it and contemporary newsletters give only terse bulletins of the
bill's progress through Parliament.[33] The Commons' *Journal* does not even
record who introduced the bill. Nevertheless, it is clear that the Game Act
was not passed in a fit of absent-mindedness. As we have already noted,
the House of Lords showed itself aware of the bill's implications, and there
are indications that the Commons also gave the measure close scrutiny.
All the county members for Yorkshire, Nottinghamshire, Suffolk, Wiltshire,
Dorset, Hampshire and Kent were invited to attend the Commons'
committee which considered the bill, and out of these deliberations came
a number of amendments which were apparently major enough to
warrant changing the bill's title.[34] The details have not survived, but
enough is known of the period and of the Cavalier Parliament to suggest
reasons why the latter should want to raise 'a little Nimrod in every
manor', even as it took from those with non-landed wealth the sporting
privileges they had previously enjoyed.

At first glance, it might seem likely that the Game Act was passed in
reaction to destruction of game by the common people. During the Civil
War years, parks and warrens as well as royal forests had been regularly
plundered. 'Since the beginning of the late Unhappy Rebellion', wrote
one royalist gentleman soon after the Restoration, deer and game had
been 'Excessively & outragiously Spoyled & destroyed by base p[er]sons of
Mean & Lowe condition with Gunns Netts doggs snares & other
Engines'.[35] The preamble to the Game Act also complained of 'disorderly
persons, laying aside their lawful trades and employments' in order to
hunt game, 'to the great damage of this realm, and prejudice of noblemen,
gentlemen and lords of manors and others'. This, however, was the theme
of all game law preambles, and its indignation was in sharp contrast to
Parliament's leisurely consideration of the problem. Soon after the
Restoration, Parliament had tightened up the laws against deer-stealing,[36]
but it showed little concern for other varieties of illegal hunting. In 1665, a
bill 'to restrain Artificers, Labourers, and other Persons from destroying
Hares, Pheasants, Partridges, and other Game' was introduced, but it died
in committee and was not re-introduced in the following session.[37] No
other bill was introduced until 1671; nor are there any indications of a
sharp increase in poaching during these years. Parliament's apparent
complacency suggests that there were other more important factors
involved in the passage of the Game Act.

One of these may have been the attitude of the king. As the Exclusion
Crisis would demonstrate, Charles II could be quite firm when defending

the essentials of monarchy. On less fundamental aspects of kingship, however, he showed a willingness to compromise, especially when it would cost him money to do otherwise. In 1660 he had traded away wardship and purveyance in return for a guaranteed income from the excise, and a similar calculation of interest may have coloured the king's attitude toward the game prerogative. Writing to his Master of the Hawks in 1667, Charles ordered that, in the interests of economy, salaried gamekeepers should be employed only on the five principal royal estates; game in the rest of England, he suggested, could be preserved by giving appropriate powers to 'gentlemen of quality'.[38] It is likely that he envisaged no more than an expansion of the corps of royal gamekeepers, but the provisions of the Game Act were not inconsistent with a policy of giving 'gentlemen of quality' more responsibility for the preservation of the game. As long as his own rights were not disturbed, Charles does not seem to have minded sharing them with the landed gentry. More important than the king's acquiescence, however, was the attitude of the gentry themselves, since it was they who initiated the Game Act and decided its form.

The outlook of most country gentlemen in the 1660s was dominated by their memories of the Civil War and the Commonwealth; few would have described these memories as pleasant ones. As individuals, some had suffered physical wounds, others the pain of exile. As a class, the gentry had seen their estates heavily taxed and, in some cases, confiscated. Added to these injuries was a deep sense of social humiliation, for during the Interregnum the commanding position which the gentry had held in their communities was successfully challenged by 'new men' of lower rank and shorter pedigree.[39] In 1660 country gentlemen were restored to their former place in English society, but it was a restoration just as ambiguous as that of the king or the Church: the ability of all three to dominate their respective spheres was not nearly as complete as they had remembered it to be. Especially galling to the Restoration gentry was the continued prosperity and influence of the very people whom they held to be responsible for the Civil War. Dissenters were their principal *bêtes noires*, but country gentlemen also exhibited a deep hostility toward the urban bourgeoisie. 'There is not any sort of people,' wrote one observer in 1671, 'so inclineable to seditious practices as the trading part of a nation . . . And, if we reflect upon our late miserable distractions, 'tis easy to observe how the quarrel was chiefly hatched in the shops of tradesmen.'[40]

The increasing affluence of such men contrasted painfully with the indebtedness of so many country gentlemen, and there were those who thought that this was far from a coincidence. After all, it was to the urban bourgeoisie that the gentry had been forced to mortgage their lands, both before and after the Restoration, in order to pay off their debts.[41] In such circumstances, it was perhaps only natural that country gentlemen should come to look upon merchants, lawyers and bankers as parasites. Indeed, long before the founding of the Bank of England, the gentry's fear and resentment of the 'moneyed interest' was evident. In the years after the Restoration, for example, there was a determined campaign by country gentlemen to lower the legal maximum rate of interest.[42] In Parliament, the gentry's dislike of bankers found frequent expression, and the session which passed the Game Act was no exception. That session, in fact, was the occasion of some particularly vituperative attacks on moneyed men. There was 'no fraud like banking', declared Sir William Coventry in 1670, while another M.P. assured the Commons that bankers, by their very nature, were 'commonwealthsmen'. The best Sir Thomas Clifford could say about bankers was that they were 'necessary evils'. The high rate at which the Commons voted in 1670 to tax bankers' holdings suggests that the House was far from convinced that this was so.[43] In light of this attitude, it is perhaps not very surprising that four months later the Commons also voted to exclude possessors of non-landed wealth from the ranks of qualified sportsmen.

As a discriminatory measure the Game Act had its weaknesses. Most merchants, for example, owned or could have easily purchased enough land to qualify under the Act.[44] The same was probably true of the despised bankers and of many lawyers as well. For the upper ranks of the urban bourgeoisie, then, the Game Act was not a formidable barrier to sporting privilege. But to surmount it would cost them something more than the purchase price of a small manor. The Game Act's property qualification forced them to concede the superiority of land over other forms of wealth – and for country gentlemen that was the important point. Resentment of the 'moneyed interest' was only one side of the coin: the other was the self-esteem of the gentry themselves.

The superiority of rural over urban society was not, of course, an idea peculiar to Restoration England. Both classical and feudal culture had exhibited a suspicion of cities and a corresponding enthusiasm for the countryside. If the gentlemen of seventeenth-century England were particularly antagonistic toward urban society, it was probably because they were uncomfortably aware of the latter's growing power. Between 1500 and 1700 the population of London rose from approximately 60,000 to 550,000 persons, the latter figure representing 10 per cent of all the inhabitants of England and Wales.[45] In the same period, the wealth of the metropolis also increased enormously. As the remaining feudal constraints on its commerce were thrown off, London rose to pre-eminence as a port and as a capital market, not only in England but in Europe as well.[46] This massive growth of the capital posed a very real threat to the traditional patterns of life in the rest of the country. At the very least it necessitated an 'agricultural revolution' so that the metropolis might be fed, but its impact on rural England was not limited to that. The ideas, fashions, arts and scandals of London filtered out into the countryside, upsetting the orthodox and attracting the young.[47] The reaction of the rulers of the countryside to the influence of London was predictably hostile. From Elizabeth's reign onward, there were sporadic attempts in Parliament to limit the growth of London, and after the Great Fire destroyed much of the city in 1666 these efforts were renewed. Although futile, they were nevertheless significant as a reflection of the unease with which country gentlemen viewed the steady advance of urban England. Sir Robert Howard spoke for many when he told the Commons in 1670 that 'the greatness of London . . . would be the ruin of the country'.[48]

This tension between urban and rural England was as much cultural as it was economic. In the countryside, landownership was the basis of social organisation; status, privileges and personal relationships were all determined by the amount of land owned and by the length of tenure. The city, on the other hand, valued liquid assets; position in the urban hierarchy depended on the amount of 'ready cash' one could produce and how quickly.[49] As the eighteenth century would demonstrate, the two societies were not incompatible, but to country gentlemen in the decades following the Restoration this was far from obvious. They looked upon London as an alien, unstable, even disloyal place: it was the gathering place of dissenters and papists, the home of luxury and indebtedness. The gentry eagerly applauded the crude caricatures of urban men which dramatists wrote for them in these years. In 1671, for example, they were enjoying the humiliation of Alderman Gripe – 'a covetous, lecherous, old Usurer of the City' – in Wycherley's *Love in the Wood*.[50] Although willing enough to marry their sons to City heiresses for the sake of a handsome dowry, the gentry were notably less enthusiastic about alliances between their daughters and urban men, since that might imply a degree of social equality. Even the purchase of an estate was not always enough to wash away the odour of 'trade' from the hands of an urban man. When, for example, Thomas Papillon, a Kent landowner as well as a London merchant, tried in 1684 to marry his son to Lady Cartwright, he was rebuffed. His friend, Sir Joseph Ashe, sympathised but noted 'how little esteeme[d] marchantts are in the opinion of some Gentry touching their estates in money'.[51]

Contempt for the merchant, however, went beyond mere snobbery. It was an important factor in moulding the self-image of English country gentlemen. Just as anti-Catholicism had helped seventeenth-century Englishmen to form a sense of national identity, so a deep prejudice against urban men and their ways helped the gentry to define their social identity. The process of definition is difficult to trace, but by the second half of the seventeenth century certain characteristics had emerged which both the gentry and the rest of society tended to associate with country gentlemen. Whether embodied in the 'booby squire' of Restoration comedy or in the more admirable Sir Roger de Coverley, these character-istics were distinctly anti-urban. The most prominent of them, perhaps, was a staunch Anglicanism, which reacted to the doubtful orthodoxy of urban England with legislation like the Clarendon Code. Another trait was a scorn for 'fashion', that thoroughly urban preoccupation with appearances which seemed to value manners and dress more than rank or property. 'The fashion's a fool', thundered Sir Wilfull Witwoud, the booby squire in *The Way of the World*.[52] More to the point, fashion was subversive of the order of rural society, which had only recently been restored. Yet another characteristic was a passion for field sports. By the turn of the century if not earlier, 'fox-hunter' had become a synonym for a country gentleman – and not necessarily a mocking one. As Christopher Hill has noted, the rustic squire's enthusiasm for 'cakes and ale, hunting and open-air virtues' was often approvingly contrasted with 'the book-keeping sordidness and petty-fogging plutocracy of London'.[53] Hunting, in fact, was recommended as an antidote to the influence of the city. 'The Exercise of Hunting,' wrote one enthusiast in the 1670s, 'neither remits the Mind to Sloth nor Softness, but rather inclines men to good Acquaintance, and generous Society.'[54] Field sports, then, were more than a recreation. They were a symbol to English country gentlemen of the virtues of their class.

Such, then, was the context in which the Game Act of 1671 was passed. In the decades following the Restoration, the gentry watched the growth and prosperity of the urban bourgeoisie with feelings of anger and frustration. The consequence was not only a number of discriminatory measures against the bourgeoisie, but also an enhanced feeling of self-esteem among the gentry themselves. The Game Act combined both elements. It withdrew the right to hunt game from any person who could not prove himself to be a substantial member of landed society. It also added to the prestige of the gentry by giving them privileges which were not dependent on royal favour, but which rather could be enjoyed simply by virtue of being a landed gentleman. As we have already noted, there is no direct evidence of the motives behind the passage of the Game Act, but it seems likely it was the desire of country gentlemen to redefine and enhance their own social position *vis-à-vis* the urban bourgeoisie, rather than to punish the activities of 'disorderly persons', which lay behind its enactment. The Game Act itself tends to support this interpretation, for while it made great changes in the qualification for hunting game, it did not alter the punishment to be imposed on the unqualified person who snared a hare or netted a partridge. The punishment of such persons, in fact, was not mentioned at all.

III

Whatever the motives behind its enactment, the effect of the Game Act was to prohibit the vast majority of the population from hunting game. To make such a prohibition effective was obviously not an easy task. Game animals were in essence wild animals. It was their unfettered existence, not their food value, which made them valuable to sportsmen. The principal excitement of hunting, after all, lay in the pursuit of a prey capable of escaping. Wild animals, however, could not be trusted to respect the will of Parliament and confine themselves to the lands of those who met the requirements of the Game Act. Game was just as likely to be found on commons and lands occupied by labourers and farmers as on the property of country gentlemen. Nor was it certain that the unqualified would pay any greater heed to the Act than the game did. It was, indeed, a safe assumption that most would ignore it, and that some would deliberately set out to violate it. How was it possible to 'preserve' – or rather, 'reserve' – the game for country gentlemen without at the same time compromising the game's freedom and thus its value to sportsmen?

The problem was not, of course, a new one. William the Conqueror and his successors had attempted to solve it by setting aside vast tracts of land on which the game could be protected without becoming domesticated. The very size of the royal forests, however, worked against game preservation: even if the forest officers had been efficient and honest, areas like the New Forest were simply too large to be policed effectively. The parks and warrens of the nobility and gentry were, on the whole, more easily secured. The smaller the enclosure, however, the less wild the game inside was apt to be. The deer parks, which from the sixteenth century onwards were a common feature in the English countryside, were better suited to provide food than sport for country gentlemen. Stags were, on occasion, 'carted' out to be hunted, but, as with 'bagged' foxes, the price of convenience was artificiality. As one sixteenth-century gentleman observed, hunting parked deer 'serveth well for the potte. . . . But it contayneth therein no commendable solace or exercise' for the sportsman.[55] Warrens took the process a step further by abandoning all pretence that the rabbits within its boundaries were being preserved for sport. Rabbit warrens were really farms, and the crop of meat and skins which they yielded were sold on the open market.[56] In addition to rendering animals less attractive to sportsmen, enclosure had another serious drawback: it erected barriers in the countryside which inhibited a hunter's free pursuit of his prey. These barriers were legal as well as physical, since enclosure of a previously wild animal transformed it into the property of the person on whose land it was found. It was a change more likely to enrich lawyers than please sportsmen, and to the gentry in the late seventeenth century that was a compelling argument against it.

If game was not to be preserved by enclosure, however, country gentlemen would have to limit the number of persons who were permitted to hunt and back this up with legal sanctions. The most obvious type of sanction, of course, was a severe penalty for hunting without legal qualification, but Parliament did not show much enthusiasm for this. In 1671, it forbade the unqualified to hunt but was silent about the punishment which was to be inflicted on those who disobeyed. It apparently assumed that the penalties prescribed by the previous qualification act – a fine of 20s. per head of game killed or three months' imprisonment – would also apply to offenders against the new act.[57] In 1707, the penalty was changed to a blanket £5 fine or three months' imprisonment;[58] thereafter, it was left unchanged until 1831 when the qualification itself was repealed. There were, however, other types of deterrents. One was to prevent the crime from occurring by forbidding the unqualified to possess the means to hunt. The Game Act authorised the confiscation of dogs, nets and other 'engines' kept by the unqualified to take game. Under later statutes, unqualified possessors of these items were liable to a fine or imprisonment; by 1707, the penalty for possessing a snare or a hunting dog was the same as that for killing game, a £5 fine or three months in prison.[59] In addition, Parliament forbade unqualified persons to possess killed game; after 1711, this too was punishable by a £5 fine or three months' imprisonment.[60] For unqualified persons, therefore, an offence against the game laws did not necessarily involve hunting at all. They were equally liable if found with a greyhound or a dead partridge.

This was what we shall call 'the old game code', and there are three points which should be made about it. The first is that it was class legislation. The actions which it punished were crimes only because of the social class of the offender, not because hunting or possessing game were in themselves dangerous or offensive to society. The second point is that the penalties prescribed were relatively mild ones. While the unqualified hunter of a hare faced a £5 fine or three months in prison, a 'deer-stealer' at the beginning of the eighteenth century was liable to a year's imprisonment plus an hour in the pillory if he was unable to pay a fine of £30.[61] The final point to be made about the 'old game code' is that both of these characteristics were absent from game legislation passed after the beginning of the eighteenth century. Between 1711 and 1831, there were no additions to the list of what unqualified persons were forbidden to do or possess; nor were the penalties attached to this list increased. The 'old game code' was not repealed or superseded, but it was augmented by new laws, which limited the actions of *all* persons and imposed harsher penalties than the 'old game code' did. The purpose of the game laws – to ensure that the landed gentry had a monopoly on the hunting of game – remained the same, but the means by which Parliament sought to achieve it underwent a fundamental change.

This shift in tactics was the result of two developments, the effects of which began to be felt around the middle of the eighteenth century. One was a change in the character of field sports, particularly those involving game birds. As the gun began to replace the hawk and the net as the principal means of taking pheasants and partridges, sportsmen came to be judged by their marksmanship, the popular measure of which was the quantity of game that they were able to kill. One consequence of this change was an increased demand for game, a demand which was met by breeding and maintaining large numbers of game birds in preserves on the gentry's estates. Thus, game gradually became enclosed and, like deer and rabbits in the previous century, it soon began to assume the character of private property.[62] In contrast to their treatment of deer and rabbits, however, the gentry did not then proceed to ignore the property qualification and treat poachers as thieves.[63] Parliament did enact several measures designed to protect the game in the new preserves, but the property qualification was nevertheless retained, and indeed was more rigorously enforced in the second half of the eighteenth century than it had been previously. The explanation for this can be found in the other development which shaped the game laws in this period: the commercialisation of poaching.

Game in the eighteenth and early nineteenth centuries was not just a target for sportsmen; it was also a culinary delicacy – or, as one writer put it, 'an essential ingredient in every entertainment that has the slightest pretensions to elegance'.[64] Such entertainments were quite common, not only in country houses but also in fashionable spas, provincial towns and, of course, in London. The inhabitants of these places were quite willing to pay for game, and the demand was eagerly met by innkeepers, victuallers and poulterers. As Crabbe noted in his *Tales of the Hall*,

> The well-known shops received a large supply,
> That they who could not kill at least might buy.[65]

A profitable market for game was obviously an inducement to poachers; accordingly, from the sixteenth century onwards there had been periodic attempts to outlaw its sale. These had not been noticeably successful,[66] but in 1707 Parliament made another attempt, forbidding any 'higler, chapman, carrier, innkeeper, victualler or alehousekeeper' to buy, sell or possess game under pain of a £5 fine (per head of game) or three months in prison.[67] The game trade, however, continued to thrive and, in 1755, Parliament responded by imposing a total ban on the trade. Thereafter the sale of game by any person, qualified or unqualified, was illegal and subject to the penalty prescribed in the Act of 1707.[68]

The Act of 1755 was no more successful than its predecessors in halting the game trade, but its effect on poaching and game preservation was profound. Denied a legal source of game for their customers, the poulterers, innkeepers and victuallers became totally dependent on poachers for their supply. This was soon reflected in the scale and character of poaching activity in the countryside. The second half of the eighteenth century saw the emergence of a highly organised and profitable black market in game. It was supplied by poaching gangs which energetically threw themselves into the business of providing London and the provincial towns with hares, patridges, pheasants and grouse. 'I never remember this country so much over run with Poachers as it is at present', wrote one East Anglian gentleman in 1780, adding that 'upon the Coast of Norfolk they [the poachers] are still worse for they pay no Regard even to Appearances, for game they say they must and will have, for Norwich must be supplyed'.[69] The gangs were understandably attracted to the game preserves which began to appear on the gentry's estates after mid-century. To protect these, country gentlemen expanded their corps of gamekeepers and, in addition, demanded that harsher measures be enacted against 'the present most insolent method of the common people in destroying the game of this kingdom'.[70] This, however, was not as simple as it seemed. The 'old game code' was a blunt instrument at best. It did not distinguish between commercial poaching and the occasional coursing of a hare for sport. Yet, it was precisely this distinction that game preservers now wished to make. One alternative to increasing the standard penalty against hunting by any unqualified person was to treat game as a type of private property, similar to deer and rabbits. This would have allowed the gentry to punish severely the gangs which invaded their preserves, but it would have also meant the abandonment of the property qualification, that symbol of the gentry's special position in English society. Indeed, if the treatment of deer and rabbits was to be the model, it would have meant permitting the sale of 'gentlemen's game' to the bourgeoisie in London and other cities. That would have been a bitter pill to swallow. To avoid taking it, the gentry began to supplement the 'old game code' with several new penalties which might be applied at the discretion of country gentlemen to commercial poachers and to other persons deemed to be in particular need of chastisement.

The first such penalty came in the form of civil prosecution.[71] Almost all game laws directed that the fine (if paid) should be divided equally between the overseers of the poor of the parish in which the offence took place and the person who had laid the accusing information before the justice of the peace. An act passed in 1722 did not interfere with this division but gave the informant a choice of means by which he could obtain his half of the fine. He might, as before, lay his information before a J.P., who on the oath of one witness could convict the defendant and distribute the fine. Alternatively, the informant might sue for his portion of the fine by initiating an 'action of debt' in any court of record. If successful in his suit, he was then entitled to recover not only his half of the fine but also double the costs of the prosecution from the defendant.[72] The advantage of a civil suit over ordinary criminal prosecution was obvious: the defendant was faced with a much larger penalty which, if it could not be paid, might consign him to a debtors' prison for a period much longer than that which the statute required in such circumstances. Indeed, as will be seen in a later chapter, the mere threat of such proceedings was often sufficient to reduce a defendant to submission. The disadvantage of civil prosecution, however, was equally obvious. The unsuccessful plaintiff had to pay the costs himself, and this risk tended to limit the popularity of the option among country gentlemen. Nevertheless, civil prosecution could be an important weapon in the hands of game preservers determined and rich enough to use it.[73]

The second type of special penalty originated in a revenue measure. In 1784 the ministry of William Pitt proposed a number of new taxes, among which was a tax on hunting. Every person who wished to hunt was required to take out an annual licence, the stamp duty on which was two guineas. The requirement applied to all persons, whether they were qualified or not, and to gamekeepers as well, although the keeper's licence cost only half a guinea.[74] The penalty for hunting without a valid licence was a £20 fine or three months in prison. Parliament was, in effect, setting up a new qualification system, one which was based on the payment of an annual fee. The new system operated independently of the Game Act,[75] but its effect was to support the old system. The unqualified hunter was now liable to a fine four times the amount previously imposed; indeed, the fine might be five times as large, since conviction under the Game Duty Act did not preclude conviction under the 'old game code' for the same offence. The effect of these heavier fines was to make it more likely that the offender would be unable to pay the penalty and thus suffer imprisonment. It was, of course, possible for an unqualified person to escape the snares of the Game Duty Act by taking out a licence, but after 1785 the names of all licence-holders were published in the provincial press and few would-be poachers were bold enough to issue so public a challenge to the gentry.[76] It should be emphasised, however, that the imposition of the heavier fine was not mandatory. It was left to the discretion of the prosecutor whether the defendant was to be charged under the old or the new qualification system, or both. Like civil prosecution,[77] the Game Duty Act could be used selectively. In that, much more than in the severity of its penalties, lay its principal value to game preservers.

The third and final type of selective penalty arose out of the laws against hunting game at night. Since the late sixteenth century, it had been illegal to hunt after dark,[78] and an act passed in 1711 made the taking of game at night subject to the standard penalty of £5 or three months in prison.[79]

The rationale behind these laws was fairly clear. Game, specifically partridges and pheasants, was quiescent at night and therefore extremely vulnerable. It could be safely assumed that those who hunted after dark were not interested in sport, but rather in taking as much game as they could, either for food or for profit. As commercial poaching increased in the second half of the eighteenth century, Parliament's attitude toward 'night poaching' became much stricter. In 1770 it passed an act which made imprisonment and public whipping mandatory punishment for all night poachers.[80] For reasons which will be explained in a subsequent chapter, the Act of 1770 aroused fierce opposition and in 1773 it was replaced by a new Night Poaching Act.[81] The new law reinstated fines for night poaching, but at a much higher level: the fine now ranged from £10 to £50, depending on the number of previous convictions. The term of imprisonment in default of the fine was three months, unless the offender had two or more previous convictions, in which case he could be imprisoned for up to twelve months and, if the court thought proper, be publicly whipped as well.[82] The Act of 1773, then, did not so much repeal the Act of 1770 as simply reserve the latter's harsh penalties for habitual offenders.

The severity of these Night Poaching Acts was due, at least in part, to the gradual enclosure of the game which was occurring at this time. As game assumed more and more of the character of private property, the same principle of the law which judged theft at night to be more heinous than theft during the daytime came also to be applied to game.[83] But as the century drew to a close, there was another factor influencing game legislation: the changing character of poaching itself. As has already been noted, the ban on the game trade gave poachers an effective monopoly on the supply of an expanding and profitable market. Poachers responded by organising themselves on an impressive – and, to many, a frightening – scale. Their practice, wrote a Yorkshire J.P. in the 1780s, was 'to assemble together *in the night*, *in companies*, armed with *firearms*, *clubs*, and other *offensive weapons*' and proceed to a local wood where they would take large quantities of game.[84] Poaching gangs naturally concentrated on areas where game was intensively preserved, and their raids were often attended by violence. On the night of 23 December 1781, for example, a gang of sixteen men with guns and 'large Clubs, armed with Iron Spikes' invaded the Earl of Buckinghamshire's preserves at Blickling in Norfolk. When challenged by his gamekeepers, 'the said Poachers threatened their Lives, swearing [that] they would shoot them'. A 'terrible battle ensued', resulting in the death of one assistant keeper and the serious wounding of another.[85] Such incidents punctuated rural life in the decades after 1770 or so, and it was not only obsessive game preservers who found them alarming.[86]

In 1782 the Norfolk quarter sessions asked Parliament to enact more stringent measures against night poachers, particularly those who operated in armed gangs. 'Combinations have been formed in [Norfolk] against the execution of [the game] laws, and some lives have been lost', explained Thomas Coke of Holkham, as he introduced a bill which proposed to classify night poachers as 'incorrigible rogues', thus permitting them to be pressed into the armed forces.[87] The bill was subsequently withdrawn,[88] but the idea of applying the penalties of the Vagrant Act to the problem of night poaching surfaced again in 1800. Under the Night Poaching Act of that year, poaching gangs (defined as two or more persons found hunting at night) could be punished under the Vagrant Act; if not pressed into the army or the navy, offenders were liable to imprisonment at hard labour for up to two years.[89] The penalty for night poaching became even harsher in the years after the end of the Napoleonic wars. Under the Night Poaching Act of 1817, any person found at night with firearms, bludgeons or other 'offensive weapons' could be transported for a period of seven years, although the courts were given the option of imposing some other punishment.[90] In 1828, however, this too was repealed, and in its place Parliament passed a more durable Night Poaching Act. Not surprisingly, perhaps, the Act of 1828 contained elements from most of its predecessors. Under its provisions, night poachers were liable to mandatory terms of imprisonment at hard labour, the length of which varied from three months to two years, depending on the number of previous convictions; for those with two or more convictions, transportation for seven years was permitted as an alternative punishment. For night poaching gangs (defined as three or more persons found hunting at night), any *one* of whose members was armed, the Act of 1828 prescribed either imprisonment at hard labour for up to three years or transportation for seven to fourteen years.[91] There the penalties stayed for the rest of the century.

The number and severity of the Night Poaching Acts have tended to so awe (and outrage) modern historians that the Acts' position in the game laws has been distorted. Anyone reading the Hammonds' *Village Labourer*, indeed, might be forgiven for thinking that the Night Poaching Acts *were* the game laws. In reality, only a small minority of poachers were tried under these acts. Even in the early nineteenth century, most continued to be charged under the 'old game code' with its standard penalty of a £5 fine or three months in prison. The Night Poaching Acts – like civil prosecution and the Game Duty Acts – were only invoked when the prosecution thought the accused deserving of particularly harsh punishment. Indeed, the real significance of these three types of special punishment under the game laws lay less in their severity than in the large amount of discretionary power which they placed in the hands of the gentry. The game laws permitted the authorities to treat poachers harshly but did not force them to do so. It was up to the prosecutor whether a labourer found taking partridges at night in the late eighteenth century would be charged with hunting without legal qualification (a £5 fine), hunting at night (a £10 to £20 fine), hunting without a licence (a £20 fine), or some combination of these offences. On the level of the fine, of course, depended the accused's chances of avoiding imprisonment. Even if he was able to pay £20, there still remained the possibility that the prosecutor would proceed by means of a civil suit, in which case the defendant might be required to pay two, three or even four times that amount. When, in 1816, Parliament introduced the penalty of transportation into the game laws, yet another weapon was added to the gentry's arsenal – to be used or not, as circumstances and inclination dictated. In this sense, it was not the severity of the game laws which was increasing in the late eighteenth and early nineteenth centuries: rather, it was the gentry's power to decide the poacher's fate.[92]

The discretionary power of country gentlemen, indeed, pervaded the entire operation of the game laws. In addition to their role as prosecutors, the gentry also commanded a corps of gamekeepers whose duty it was to prevent the unqualified from hunting or even possessing the means to hunt. How strictly a keeper enforced the Game Act depended, to a large degree, on the attitude of his master. A number of country gentlemen were also able directly to affect the administration of the game laws in their capacity as justices of the peace. It was they who issued search warrants, reached verdicts and imposed sentences. The eagerness – or lack of it – with which they performed these duties could obviously be of great consequence not only to poachers but to the entire rural community. The game laws, in short, were not simply the acts passed by Parliament for 'the preservation of the game'. Those statutes could be rendered mild or harsh, meaningless or oppressive according to the wishes of those who enforced them. The administration of the game laws, indeed, could vary not only from J.P. to J.P., but also from defendant to defendant. For, as we have seen, it was an established principle of the game laws that some persons were more deserving of punishment than others. The factors which entered into the determination of who those persons were will be the subject of the next two chapters.

2

Field sports and game preservation

Under the game laws, only the landed gentry had the right to hunt game. The vast majority – perhaps as high as 99 per cent – of the population was not even permitted to own a gun or keep a lurcher.[1] That was the law. When, however, we turn from the statute books to the diaries and correspondence of the period, it becomes clear that many unqualified persons did in fact hunt game – and, moreover, did so with the knowledge and approval of country gentlemen. After Thomas Smith, a Wiltshire gentleman, went coursing one winter's day in 1721, for example, he recorded in his diary that 'we had my Tenant Gibbs with us and tarry'd out till Night'.[2] Joseph Page, an Essex yeoman at the end of the eighteenth century, was worth approximately £80 a year. Yet he often shot with the local gentry and, like them, sent gifts of game to his friends.[3] Nor were farmers the only unqualified persons who engaged in field sports. A justice of the Court of Common Pleas observed in 1756 that 'it generally happens that near every great town in England some gentleman keeps a pack of dogs, and it is well known that he never goes out without being accompanied by many tradesmen as well as others not qualified'.[4] Even servants were to be found pursuing game. Nicholas Blundell, a Lancashire squire at the beginning of the eighteenth century, and James Woodforde, a Norfolk parson at the end of it, both allowed their servants to go out coursing hares; indeed, these gentlemen lent their own dogs for the occasion. The Rev. William Cole proudly recorded in his diary in the 1760s the sporting exploits of his servant, Tom, who hunted regularly with his father (the parish clerk) and the local blacksmith.[5]

Nor were these simply examples of personal friendship overriding the technical requirements of the law. Allowing unqualified persons to sport was, in many cases, an openly avowed policy. 'I doe not desire that you take Guns from any sufficient Tennants altho they may not be Quallify'd by Law', a Kentish gentleman instructed his gamekeeper in 1708. Lord Dunkellin announced in the *Salisbury Journal* that his Hampshire tenants had his permission to 'kill game on their own premises in a fair manner'.[6]

In the early nineteenth century, Lord Stafford allowed his tenants 'occasional coursing parties' as well as 'a few days shooting' on their farms.[7] Even the Derbyshire Association for the Preservation of Game, one of a number of such organisations formed in the eighteenth century to combat poaching, disclaimed any intention of preventing 'Gentlemen Farmers, or substantial Tradesmen, (tho' Unqualified) from Sporting, in a fair and reasonable Manner'.[8]

Clearly, then, the impact of the game laws on rural society was less clear-cut than the Game Act of 1671 would lead one to assume. Not only was there widespread evasion of the Act, but this evasion was tolerated and even publicly condoned by the very men whose privileged position the game laws sought to preserve. Their behaviour may, at first sight, appear strange, but it becomes less so when the nature of rural society in the eighteenth century is recalled. It was a society based on landownership; those who owned large amounts of land were acknowledged to be superior to those who possessed little or none. With few exceptions, however, the owners of large estates did not have the power to dictate to rural society: they only had the power to *lead* it. The smaller freeholders, farmers and tradesmen in their neighbourhoods formed the gentry's natural constituency. Like most constituencies, however, they had to be cajoled, petted and occasionally bribed if they were to remain a dependable source of support. The cultivation of one's 'interest' was a type of husbandry with which most country gentlemen were familiar, and they knew that a bountiful harvest depended on a liberal distribution of favours. Church livings, alehouse licences and myriad other marks of favour were regularly deployed in order to maintain and advance a gentleman's 'interest'. Among those marks of favour was game. Not only was it part of the massive meals which country gentlemen were expected to provide at their tables, game was also packed into baskets and sent off to friends, dependants and neighbours, even though they might not be legally qualified to possess it. At Holkham, more than half of the game killed in the 1797–8 season was given away; the recipients ranged from Charles James Fox, Mrs Fitzherbert, and the headmaster of Eton, to the local brewer, butcher, grocer, postman and a multitude of farmers.[9] In the West Country, approximately one third of the game killed on Sir Richard Colt Hoare's manors went to farmers in the area.[10] Like all forms of patronage in the eighteenth century, gifts of game served to define social relationships. A brace of partridge delivered by a liveried servant reasserted the bonds of deference and obligation which bound individuals, and classes, together. So did the conferring of sporting rights.

Under the game laws, responsibility for the preservation of the game was entrusted to every lord of the manor 'not under the degree of an esquire'. This, generally speaking, included all country gentlemen of any substance, as well as a number of institutional landowners, such as colleges, municipal corporations, cathedral chapters and even some almshouses.[11] They were authorised to appoint gamekeepers, whose powers after 1707 included taking game on the manor of their deputation.[12] Although the wording of the Act was unclear, it was generally assumed that this permission was not confined to the lord's own land but instead applied to the entire manor.[13] Thus, gamekeeperships became a kind of currency by means of which sporting rights could be given, traded and accumulated. When, for instance, Thomas Benet rented his Wiltshire estate to the Earl of Corke in 1771, the latter was also granted a deputation as gamekeeper for the manor, so that he might hunt over it without legal challenge.[14] The rector of Wath in Yorkshire, Benjamin Newton, and his neighbours switched gamekeeperships in 1818 by mutual agreement, the terms of which Newton recorded in his diary: 'Settled with Mr Askwith that he should have the deputations of Norton and Melmerby and I would try to get those of Wath and Middleton and Mr Allanson who met Mr Askwith on the road very kindly said he would give me the deputation of Middleton.'[15] Lords of manors themselves were often anxious to become gamekeepers, since this extended the area over which they could hunt without competition from other sportsmen. On occasion this could result in some rather startling juxtapositions. In Wiltshire, Lord Pembroke was enrolled as gamekeeper to Lord Chedworth, while in Essex, the Rev. Joseph Arkwright, an avid sportsman, negotiated to become the gamekeeper to Robert Chatham, a Holborn tavern keeper by trade.[16]

Deputation as a gamekeeper was one of the principal ways the gentry conferred sporting rights on those who were otherwise unqualified to kill game. The practice, indeed, was so widespread in the early eighteenth century that in 1717 Parliament complained that it had

> become usual and frequent in several parts of the kingdom,
> for lords and ladies of manors to grant powers and
> deputations to farmers, tenants, and occupiers of the lands
> and estates lying within the precincts of their respective
> manors, to be gamekeepers, with the power to kill and destroy
> the game; which practice is a very great abuse of the powers
> . . . granted.

Accordingly, it passed an act which required that gamekeepers be either servants of the lord of the manor or qualified to kill game in their own right.[17] Nevertheless, farmers continued to be appointed as gamekeepers. Writing in 1784, Richard How, a Bedfordshire squire, expressed surprise that such a law even existed. 'Gamekeepers,' he wrote, 'were formerly appointed in this parish without any regard to Qualifications – two of my Tenants successively and afterwards either

F. Moore or Chapman without any objection being made, but how . . . the legality of the appointment could be defended, I will not presume to determine.' From the numbers of yeomen, tradesmen and even innkeepers listed in the surviving deputation rolls, it would appear that many gentlemen exercised their power of appointment in a similar fashion.[18] The supply of gamekeeperships, however, was limited. In 1711, Parliament had restricted the number of gamekeepers to one per manor, and this greatly reduced the ability of country gentlemen to confer legal sporting rights on all those whom they wished to favour.[19]

The solution to this problem was simply to ignore the Game Act and allow at least some unqualified persons to hunt game illegally. Since the gentry were responsible for enforcing the game laws, this was not difficult to do. It was, indeed, common practice in the eighteenth century for landowners to grant certain local sportsmen – whether qualified or not – permission to hunt over their manors. 'Leave' to hunt over a great estate was a favour highly prized in the rural community, both in its own right and as a mark of status. As such, it could be used to win 'friends' for a country gentleman. When, for instance, the Duke of Marlborough was trying to lure the borough of Marlborough away from Lord Bruce's 'interest', he offered to give the gentlemen of the corporation permission to hunt over his manors.[20] There were dangers, however, in distributing such favours with too free a hand. If granted carelessly, they could just as easily lead to a loss of support. In 1753, for example, the Whig 'friends' of the Duke of Dorset were extremely upset when they discovered some Tories coursing hares at Knole, apparently with impunity. 'We who are [the Duke's] staunch Friends,' they protested, '. . . who amuse ourselves sometimes with a few beagles on His Grace's manors in a very modest way, think it is hard that We should be interrupted by His Grace's avow'd enemies.' As a general election approached, one of the Duke's 'friends' warned that 'If their [the Tories'] insolence is to go uncorrected, our Friends are like to have a bad time o' it, nor can I possibly do His Grace's business here on such terms.'[21] Even more dangerous was the fact that once leave to sport had been granted, it could not be revoked without causing a great deal of ill feeling. 'A forbidding to shoot,' observed Benjamin Newton in his diary, 'is always a closing of intercourse between the forbidder and the forbidden.'[22] It was no consolation to the latter to realise that he had no legal right to hunt game anyway. On the contrary, that fact made the loss of the privilege all the more galling.

The great difference between a qualified and an unqualified sportsman, then, was not that one hunted game while the other did not: it was that one hunted by right while the other hunted by sufferance. There were a great many small freeholders, tenants and tradesmen in rural England who coursed hares and shot pheasants in the eighteenth century, and as long as they did so 'with proper leave' they were not prosecuted under the game laws. It would be incorrect, however, to conclude, as did one observer in 1784, that 'the qualified and unqualified associate and pursue the pleasure [of sporting] together with as little distinction, as if such laws were obsolete in *spirit*, as they are in *effect*'.[23] On the contrary, the 'spirit' of the game laws – that only the gentry should have the right to hunt game – was very much alive in the eighteenth century. Indeed, as the century progressed, that 'spirit' seemed to grow stronger. The willingness of country gentlemen to 'indulge' their tenants and neighbours with sporting rights slackened noticeably after 1750. There were exceptions to this, of course, but it is clear that by the end of the century, 'indulgences' were being granted far less frequently than they had been fifty years earlier. Unqualified sportsmen who had been accustomed to ranging all over the countryside in search of game now increasingly found themselves confined to their own land – or even forbidden to hunt altogether – under pain of the gentry's displeasure. This change was to have profound consequences for the game laws, and, for an explanation of it, we must turn from the sportsmen to the sports themselves.

II

Field sports in the eighteenth century included a variety of methods of taking game: hawking, netting, shooting, coursing. In addition, there was 'hunting' in the strict sense of the word: the pursuit on horseback of a wild animal with the aid of hounds. The latter activity had a long tradition behind it even in the early seventeenth century, when Gervase Markham in his survey of rural recreations gave it precedence over all other types of field sports.[24] Its eminence arose from its association with royalty (and, by inference, with the noble, manly qualities which royalty were thought to possess) and also from the expense involved in keeping horses and hounds, a practical consideration which greatly limited the number of people who could engage in the sport. Within hunting itself, there was a hierarchy arranged along similar lines. The pursuit of stags, for instance, was deemed superior to the pursuit of hares since 'none but Persons of Estate and Quality have the Privileges and Convenience of Forests, Chases and Parks; but Men of lower Rank may sometimes divert themselves with the Hare'.[25] In the eighteenth century, 'Men of lower Rank' seem to have done so with great enthusiasm. Hare-hunting may have been less prestigious than either fox- or stag-hunting, but it could be just as exciting as the hare led hunters and hounds over miles of countryside at great speed until finally the exhaustion of the quarry brought an end to the chase.[26] As late as 1835, there were still more packs of harriers than of foxhounds in England, a testament to hare-hunting's reputation as 'the freest, readiest, and most enduring pastime'.[27]

There was another, less formal way of pursuing hares: this was coursing. It too was an ancient sport, and all that was necessary to engage in it was to possess a greyhound and find a hare. The latter was often discovered by chance and this lent an element of spontaneity to the sport which hunting sometimes lacked. 'Found 2 hares . . . so after dinner we went after them . . . but killed neither', ran a typical entry in the diary of Thomas Isham, a Northamptonshire youth in the 1670s.[28] Several decades later, Nicholas Blundell in Lancashire recorded one day that he had 'found a Hare & sent for John Farer to see it coursed, it led us such a Round that I lost both Men & Dogs'.[29] At the end of the century, Parson Woodforde in Norfolk noted in his diary that 'a hare being found near here, Mr. Cross and myself went out and coursed it before breakfast . . . and a good course it was'.[30] Finding a hare, in fact, brought both recognition and reward in the countryside. Squire Blundell scrupulously recorded in his diary the names of those who had 'found a hare setting'; Parson Woodforde gave such persons six pence or a shilling for every hare found, 'as is always customary'.[31] Not all coursing, however, was of the informal, spontaneous kind engaged in by these gentlemen. Since coursing was a test of a greyhound's skills, there were inevitably disputes over whose dog was best and these naturally led to matches in which two greyhounds chased a hare under controlled conditions. It was these competitions which attracted the attention of the more affluent gentry and turned coursing into an organised field sport.

The rules for coursing matches had been set down in the late sixteenth century, but it was not until the last quarter of the eighteenth that the occasional meets between greyhound owners developed into a regular, organised sport with a popular following.[32] The first clear sign that this was happening came in 1776, when Lord Orford and twenty-five other gentlemen established a coursing club which sponsored annual meets at Swaffham in Norfolk. Within a few years, coursing clubs were being formed in other counties and before long they began to compete with one another. In 1780, for instance, the gentlemen of Wiltshire matched their greyhounds against those from Norfolk on Salisbury Plain. 'Ld. Orford, & half Bedlam are to attend', grumbled the Earl of Pembroke before the event. Three years later, 'The Annual

I. Coursing hares in Hatfield Park

Coursing Meeting' between the two counties drew an estimated crowd
of five hundred gentlemen.[33] In other areas, there was a similar
enthusiasm for coursing. Riding through Lincolnshire in 1791, John
Byng noted that the area around Louth was famous for coursing,
'which brings in winter a society to this place'.[34] In Yorkshire, annual
meets were held at Flixton in the early nineteenth century, and when
Benjamin Newton 'went coursing at Norton' in 1817, he found '200
people assembled and 8 brace of hares killed'.[35]

Coursing owed its popularity in the late eighteenth century to a number
of factors. One was the improvement in dog breeding which, in addition
to producing a faster foxhound in this period, also had a positive effect on
the performance of greyhounds.[36] Another factor was probably that
coursing matches did not require much exertion on the part of those who
attended them. In contrast to hunting, it was possible to share the
excitement of the event without actually engaging in it, something which
may have appealed to the middle class who inhabited the growing towns of
provincial England. Allied with this was the attraction which these
matches had for the betting man. There had always been, it is true, a strong
link between coursing and gambling; indeed, the original rules of
coursing had touched on the subject.[37] But the regular meetings of the
coursing clubs, and the clash of personal and regional pretensions which
they encouraged, undoubtedly strengthened that link. It was reported that
there were 'considerable sums' at stake in the match between Norfolk and
Wiltshire in 1780; several years later, a Yorkshire meet resulted in the

reallocation of 'much money, as well as sporting fame'.[38] Certainly it seems likely that heavy betting did nothing to reduce attendance at these events.

The pursuit of partridges, pheasants and moor fowl never became a spectator sport like coursing, but the change which this sport underwent in the eighteenth century was, in fact, more profound. Before the Restoration, the principal methods of taking these birds were hawking and netting, the latter being the less expensive – and thus, the less prestigious – of the two. Although the flintlock – shorter, safer and more accurate than its predecessor, the matchlock – had been used in England since the beginning of the seventeenth century, it was not until after the royalist gentry returned from their exile on the Continent in 1660 that it seems to have been employed to any great extent in the taking of game.[39] Hawking was the first to feel the competition. Traditionalists like the Earl of Bedford would continue to hunt with falcons and goshawks until the end of the century, but as early as 1686 the author of a sportsman's guide was advising his readers that 'It is now the mode to shoot flying [game], as being by experience found [to be] the best and surest way.' By the beginning of the eighteenth century, hawking had all but disappeared from sporting guides.[40] The triumph of the flintlock over netting was less rapid, perhaps because the lesser gentry were less susceptible than the aristocracy to the arguments of fashion. In 1711, Sir Roger de Coverley observed with some annoyance that one of his neighbours with an income of £100 a year 'shoots flying',[41] but for other modest sportsmen acceptance of shooting as a sport took longer. Nicholas Blundell, for example, had a gun by 1703 if not earlier, but for over a decade and a half he seems to have used it only to shoot pests like blackbirds and kites. To catch partridges, Blundell continued to go out with his setter, 'Tory', and a net. It was not until 1718 that he recorded in his diary: 'Mr Percy went a Parteridg shooting, [and] I went with him.'[42] Even then, he was probably only being polite.

There was prudence as well as conservatism in Squire Blundell's reluctance to embrace the future, since the eighteenth-century flintlock was prone to explode, fire of its own accord or otherwise endanger the lives of those in its immediate vicinity.[43] It was, however, the game which had the most to fear from the flintlock. The bullet was faster than the hawk and, unlike the hunter with his net, it did not distinguish between cocks and hens and release the latter so that the species might continue to propagate itself. With the introduction of the flintlock, the balance between hunter and prey was altered in the former's favour, and the effects of this were soon felt in the countryside. 'The Art of shooting flying,' complained one writer in 1750, 'is, within a few Years, come to such a Degree of Perfection, that few Fowls escape.'[44] The improvements which continued to be made in the design of the flintlock during the century served to facilitate even greater destruction of game. As the accuracy of the rifle increased, sportsmen came to be judged by their marksmanship, the popular measure of which was the quantity of game which they were able to kill. Game books, in which this information was meticulously recorded, were being kept by sportsmen even before 1750.[45] It was in the second half of the eighteenth century, however, that the competitive slaughter of game came to dominate the sport. In 1762, for example, Lord Bath was looking forward to 'killing [an] abundance of Patridges on the first of Septr. We will be as early after them as any of our Neighbours.' By 1790, John Byng was lamenting that 'all the world issue out to destroy, calling it sporting; and game being thus sought and pursued, makes every one adopt the vile principle of committing what destruction he can, for he judges that what escapes will never again be seen by him'.[46]

As with coursing, this competitive element helped to make shooting very popular. Some gentlemen, indeed, dedicated their lives to the sport. Colonel Peter Hawker, for instance, killed game season after season with a fierce, single-minded devotion: between 1810 and 1830 he alone shot 3732 partridges.[47] In the same two decades, Lord Malmesbury killed 6737 partridges, to say nothing of 4113 pheasants.[48] Enthusiasm for shooting was reflected in other ways as well. In East Anglia the renting of sporting manors for the season became a common practice. Culford manor in Suffolk, for example, was rented in 1823 for £300 'with a restriction of not shooting more than 700 Pheasants' during the season.[49] Other sportsmen travelled north to shoot grouse and other types of moor fowl. As early as 1773, 'vast Wastes' in Yorkshire were being rented 'for the purpose of shooting Moor Game'.[50] By the early nineteenth century, some moors had been taken over by grouse-hunting clubs, whose members paid for tickets permitting them to shoot over the area.[51] The effect of these seasonal invasions on the local economies of these areas must have been very great. The shooting season in Yorkshire, observed John Byng in 1792, was 'ardently wished for' by the innkeepers. They were not the only ones. Gunmakers, tailors, victuallers, purveyors of flints, powder, shot and game bags – even the government, through its game duty – all took their profit.[52] Of even greater consequence to the countryside, however, was the introduction in the 1790s of a new method of shooting, the battue.

For most of the eighteenth century partridges and pheasants were shot 'over a dog'. Having located the game with the aid of a setter or pointer, the sportsman took aim and fired at his prey, sometimes not even waiting for it to take flight.[53] The battue, which was imported from the Continent in the last decade of the century, relieved sportsmen of the trouble of having to search for the game by forcing the latter into the air – and into the line of fire. This was done in one of two ways: either the game took flight to escape

II. Pheasant Shooting

being trapped between a wall of nets and an advancing line of shooters, or it was frightened into the air by 'beaters' who, at a given signal, drove the game out of its covert and into the range of a stationary party of sportsmen. In the latter case, the birds flew higher and faster than in the former and thus provided a more difficult test of the shooter's skill, but in either type of battue the number of birds likely to be shot was much larger than that which could be expected from a day's solitary sport with a favourite setter.[54] It was this promise of an impressively full game bag which lay behind the battue's popularity, but there are other reasons as well. One of these was undoubtedly the fact that the battue was well suited to the entertaining of large numbers of house guests, some of whom had neither the skill nor the patience to take game in the traditional manner. It is not surprising, indeed, that the battue was first introduced at Holkham, already famous for its huge house parties, nor that it soon became an established part of the social routine on many aristocratic estates.[55]

Around the battue was constructed an establishment whose function was to shield sportsmen from the rigours of shooting. In addition to the beaters, there were servants to reload the guns and count the number of shots, as well as gamekeepers to provide advice and support. 'Do not forget the sandwich cases,' admonished one gamekeepers' guide, 'and the flask of brandy, to hand to the gentlemen, when their nerves get a little affected . . . [After they have fired,] let them stand as still as possible till they get quite cool and collected. The trembling being quite off, proceed very deliberately.'[56] In this protected atmosphere, game was slaughtered on an unprecedented scale. At the beginning of the eighteenth century, one of Sir Roger de Coverley's 'exploits' had been to take 'forty Coveys of Partridges in a Season'.[57] At a grand battue a century later, that number could easily have been taken in a single day. In 1796, the Duke of Bedford and six other gentlemen shot eighty pheasants, forty hares and an unknown number of partridges, all in a few hours. In 1810, the same number of guns killed 107 pheasants and 100 hares in a day.[58] In only thirteen days Lord Uxbridge and his friends shot 1298 pheasants and 648 hares.[59] These were extraordinary accomplishments, but the norm against which they were judged tells the same story. At Holkham in the 1790s, the average number of pheasants shot in a season was 359; two decades later the average had risen to 825, and in at least two seasons more than 1200 pheasants were killed.[60] This wholesale destruction of game and the ease with which it was accomplished met with the contempt of some traditionally minded sportsmen. 'The *feeds* given on these occasions are generally capital', sniffed one critic, but 'to a real Sportsman, there is but little amusement'.[61] For many sportsmen in the early nineteenth century, however, the amusement offered by the battue was more than sufficient. In the pageantry of dozens of liveried servants, the comradeship of their fellow shooters and the satisfying mound of game which was the result of their labours, they found a congenial and exciting pastime. It became part of their world and they were not likely to treat those who threatened it very kindly.

There was, then, a fundamental change in the character of field sports between 1660 and 1830. Some traditional sports, like hawking and netting, virtually disappeared in this period, while others, notably coursing and shooting, were transformed. In the late seventeenth century, field sports were generally spontaneous affairs, involving a small number of participants and little preparation. A hundred years later they tended to be scheduled, highly structured events, which drew as many spectators as sportsmen.[62] In addition there was a certain artificiality about field sports after the middle of the eighteenth century, and this was not confined to the battue. In the early eighteenth century, for instance, sportsmen had had 'much adoe to gett clear of the Blackthorns' and other undergrowth when searching for game. By the 1780s, however, paths were being cut through the woods on some estates in order that sportsmen might be spared the discomfort.[63] Behind these changes in form and style, there was an alteration in the very nature of field sports. In the seventeenth century they had been contests between a hunter and his prey, and in hare-hunting and the old-fashioned coursing of a Parson Woodforde these contests continued throughout the eighteenth century. The newer and more fashionable sports, however, tended to be competitions between one sportsman and another.[64] Coursing matches tested the greyhounds, and shooting parties the marksmanship, of gentlemen. The game on these occasions was little more than a moving target.

As a target, however, game was in much greater demand than it had ever been as a prey. The appetite of the battue for partridges, pheasants and hares was insatiable; even on estates where the battue was not a regular feature, the hunger of sportsmen for game was not easily satisfied. On the manors of Sir Richard Colt Hoare, for example, the average head of game shot in the 1790s was 760; three decades later it was 1270.[65] Coursing matches did not require a great number of hares, but they did need a reliable supply. It would have been intolerable in the late eighteenth century for several hundred gentlemen to have gathered for a coursing match only to discover that, as happened a century earlier, 'the beaters could not find a hare'.[66] It was essential for all these sports that large quantities of game be found and kept in readiness for the pleasure of sportsmen. It is not surprising, therefore, that around the middle of the eighteenth century, gentlemen began to take measures to ensure that the supply of game was sufficient.

III

Game preservation basically involves three different types of activities: the breeding of game, the destruction of 'vermin' and the concentration of game in protected areas. All three had been practised in England long before the gentry became game preservers in earnest. Enclosure of game in protected areas was, of course, practised by the owners of deer parks and rabbit warrens. By the end of the seventeenth century, the hare population in some parts of the kingdom was also beginning to be enclosed. Thomas Baskerville, riding through Hertfordshire soon after the Restoration, 'saw a hare-warren late made and railed in by the present Earl of Salisbury'. In Wiltshire at the same time, there were hare warrens at Everleigh and Wilton; in 1682, another was created at West Lavington.[67] Destruction of vermin was also well established in the countryside by the end of the seventeenth century. The common law permitted the destruction of all 'noxious' animals, and in some parishes the church wardens paid a bounty for every fox or badger brought to them.[68] As for the breeding of game, it had been practised in at least some areas since the early sixteenth century.[69] By the end of the seventeenth century, a mews in which partridges and pheasants were raised appears to have been a standard feature of many estates.[70]

Although the principal elements of game preservation were established by the beginning of the eighteenth century, implementation of them was neither systematic nor, in fact, always very helpful to sportsmen. The Earl of Pembroke's hare warren at Wilton, for example, was not popular with his neighbours. 'The gentlemen,' reported Defoe, 'complain that it marrs their game, for that as soon as they put up a hare for their sport, if it be any where within two or three miles, away she runs for the warren, and there is an end to their pursuits.'[71] Nor was sport greatly enhanced by the breeding of game birds in mews. The partridges and pheasants raised in this manner were tame birds, bred for the table not the field.[72] Although the technique of 'planting' a covert with game (specially reared for the purpose or attracted by strategically placed heaps of grain) was known by the early part of the century, it was, as one gentleman wrote at the time, 'generally thought to be so difficult and expensive that but few will undertake it'.[73] It was not until field sports themselves had been transformed that game preservation came to be systematically practised. As coursing matches became more popular, hare warrens began to be viewed as guarantors of, rather than threats to, sport. And as the passion for ever larger 'bags' took hold of country gentlemen, the planting of coverts with game became an absolute necessity.

The beginning of systematic game preservation on the gentry's estates cannot be precisely dated, but evidence of it begins to appear after the middle of the century, particularly in the south and east of England. In the 1750s and 1760s, 'pheasantries' were built and existing mews adapted to answer the needs of sportsmen. In these structures, game eggs found on the estate were hatched and the resulting brood of game protected until it was ready to be planted in the coverts.[74] In the 1770s, buckwheat began to be placed in fields and woods to attract game, particularly pheasants.[75] In the following decade the actual breeding of game birds on some estates was transferred from the pheasantry to the coverts. John Byng, walking about Blenheim in 1787, saw 'in various parts of the park . . . clusters of faggots around a coop, where are hatch'd and rear'd such quantities of pheasants that I almost trod upon them in the grass'.[76] After the 1790s, the rearing of pheasants in coverts was probably an established practice on all estates where battues were held. Hares also came under the protective arm of the game preserver in these years. The breeding of hares, of course, needed no encouragement, but the concern of country gentlemen to secure an adequate supply can be seen in the creation of additional hare warrens, in restrictions on the trimming of hedgerows and in payments for hares 'brought in by Harvestmen' and other labourers.[77] Such measures evidently achieved their aim. At Netherhaven in Wiltshire, William Cobbett saw 'an acre of hares' (whose movement he compared to a flock of sheep), and on large sporting estates the evidence was, if anything, more dramatic. Lady Shelley, visiting Holkham for the first time in 1807, described it as 'a veritable oasis surrounded by the dreary Norfolk landscape, swarming with partridges, and other winged game, which seemed to rise out of the wastes of sand bearded with stunted corn'.[78]

Such concentrations of wild life were not, however, solely the products of intensive breeding. Equally important was the protection which the game found on preservers' estates. Crows, stoats, weasels, hawks, owls, kites, polecats, magpies and other predators of game were proscribed animals on these estates after mid-century and landowners handed out liberal rewards to those who destroyed them. Indeed, vermin-catching developed into a relatively lucrative occupation in the second half of the eighteenth century. At Longleat, for example, William Bishop, the son of one of Lord Weymouth's grooms, earned more than £10 a year in the 1780s killing vermin.[79] There were also efforts to check the activities of the game's human predators. The measures enacted against poachers have been outlined in the preceding chapter, but equally significant were the curbs placed on qualified sportsmen. In 1762 Parliament passed the first of a series of statutes establishing seasons in which game could be legally killed. By 1773 these had assumed their now-familiar form: grouse shooting began on the twelfth of August, partridge shooting on the first of September and pheasant shooting on the first of October. This legislation gave each year's crop of game birds time to grow without disturbance before being harvested by the gun.[80]

In addition to these restrictions, barriers were erected to prevent country gentlemen from exercising their right to hunt game where they pleased. Some game preserves were actually fenced in,[81] but most lords of manors depended on persuasion to prevent their expensively reared game from being plundered by neighbouring sportsmen. Beginning in the 1770s, advertisements were placed in the provincial press which, in addition to uttering the usual threats against poachers, 'requested' qualified gentlemen not to sport on certain manors.[82] Such requests lacked the force of law, but they carried the clear implication that, should the request be ignored, it would soon be followed by a formal notice not to trespass. After such notice had been given, further invasions of the manor could be answered with legal action. Although some gentlemen continued to believe that the law of trespass, 'when enforced against a sportsman, is generally reprobated by an English jury', the appearance of such an advertisement amounted to the *de facto* enclosure of the game on the manor concerned. Qualified gentlemen might still sport on it, but if they were to avoid the threat of prosecution, they first had to secure the permission of the lord of the manor.[83] In this respect, at least, the difference between a qualified and an unqualified sportsman was beginning to disappear by the end of the eighteenth century.

By implementing these measures, country gentlemen hoped to ensure that there would be an ample supply of game for their sports. Their hopes, of course, were not always realised. Like all crops, much depended on the weather. An unusually dry or wet or cold spell could have a ruinous effect on the game. The severe winter of 1813–14, for example, was said to have killed some 20,000 head of game at Holkham alone.[84] Aside from the weather, though, the most important factor in any programme of game preservation was the gamekeeper. It was he who bred the game, destroyed vermin, caught poachers and 'warned off' sportsmen who hunted on the manor without permission. On his ability to perform these duties rested his master's hopes for an abundance of game, and, as demand for the latter grew in the eighteenth century, so did the importance of the gamekeeper in rural society. The authority of the gamekeeper's office had been set out in the Game Act: he could search for and seize all guns, dogs, nets and other 'engines' kept by unqualified persons on the manor. After 1707, he was also empowered to kill game on the manor.[85] There is little evidence, however, that the office was a very demanding one in the early eighteenth century. On some estates, 'gamekeeper' was just an additional title given to a gentleman's park-keeper or warrener; on others, deputations were bestowed on tenants and stewards.[86] Where a full-time gamekeeper was employed, it was usually at a comparatively low wage; the norm seems to have been about £5 a year in the first half of the century.[87] In some instances, a keeper was simply paid according to the quantity of game he was able to kill for his master's table.[88]

Such practices could not last long in an era of strict game preservation. The breeding of game and its protection from predators required the attention of at least one full-time servant. During the summer months, care had to be taken to 'rescue' young hares and game eggs from the mowers in the fields, procure hens to hatch the eggs and rear the resulting brood. 'I am in Hopes I shall have A good Maney [game birds] Brought ought in theair wild state and thay will Be Much Better than those Brought up tame', reported Samuel Whitbread's gamekeeper in June of 1816. 'I have had 13 Nests Mowed ought in the Parke woods and Plantations. I have 9 Broods of Pheasants in My worren that I [k]now of and 6 Large coveys of Partridges . . . all in the wild state.'[89] During the hunting season, the keeper was kept busy assisting sportsmen, destroying vermin and shooting game, both for the table and for gifts. In addition, he spent many a winter's night watching for poachers, a duty which some gamekeepers found particularly onerous. Whitbread's keeper, for instance, complained that he had 'Laid ought Many cold Nights in your Woods and Plantations Wen the Rest of your servants Ware a Bed and By doing so I have Decayed My Concitration for the Percivation of your Game.'[90] The gamekeeper, in short, was required to have a variety of skills – and it is worth nothing that among these, as described in advertisements and letters of recommendation throughout this period, the detection and capture of poachers is rarely mentioned. Much more important to country gentlemen, it seems, was an applicant's ability to shoot game, train dogs, raise pheasants and kill vermin.[91] It was as guardians of game and assistants to sportsmen, more than as enforcers of the game laws, that gamekeepers came to be valued.

The compensation which gamekeepers received varied, of course, even within estates, but generally the level was well above that given in the first half of the eighteenth century. In 1772, William Taplin estimated the average wage of a gamekeeper to be £20 a year,[92] and estate account books tend to confirm this, although head gamekeepers on great estates undoubtedly earned more. John Chapman at Audley End and Robert Mills at Longleat both had salaries of £40 or more, while at Holkham, in the 1790s, two of Coke's gamekeepers received £50 a year. Most of the gamekeepers on the estates, however, received wages in the area of £20 a year.[93] To these sums, of course, must be added the perquisites of the office – usually livery and a cottage – plus the benefits which often came to valued and trusted servants, such as allotments of coal or free medical care. 'Poor Brown [the gamekeeper] has been dangerously ill,' reported the steward of Castle Rising to his master in 1786, 'and as You desired he might not want any Medical Assistance, and finding he cou'd not afford it, I sent for a Physican from [King's] Lynn, from whose Directions he found Relief. Otherwise, I think he wou'd have died.'[94] Other keepers received care in their old age. Robert West of Longleat, for instance, was retired at full pay in 1786, and, when he died ten years later, he was buried at Lord Bath's expense, as was West's widow five years after that.[95]

Not all gamekeepers, however, were blessed with such financial security. On some estates, game preservation was actually contracted out to the keepers: for a given sum he agreed to provide both his services and the materials necessary to maintain a sporting establishment. On the Yorkshire estates of the Duke of Norfolk, for instance, the gamekeeper agreed to employ one under-keeper and two warreners, to maintain one horse, twenty-one sporting dogs, and all the necessary guns and nets and to perform his own duties as gamekeeper – all for a flat sum of £500 a year.[96] Even on estates where this was not the practice, gamekeepers often had to absorb the expense of purchasing powder and shot or of maintaining pointers and greyhounds, on the understanding that they would be reimbursed at a later date. These methods of financing a game establishment obviously put a strain on the gamekeeper's personal resources and, not surprisingly, there was a tendency for gamekeepers to be in debt, some temporarily, some chronically. 'The Keepers with all their emoluments have much ado to make matters meet at the end of the year', observed Lord Ailesbury's steward in 1779, of all your lordship's Servants, their Lott is by much the hardest – Their expences are Necessarily great, they certainly have a Maintenance, but they can Save Nothing'.[97]

It was probably for this reason that gamekeepers clung so tenaciously to their customary right to keep the skin of every rabbit killed on the manor. The sale of these skins obviously helped ease the strain on the keeper's budget.[98] There were many persons, however, who were convinced that gamekeepers did not confine themselves to dealing in rabbit skins. Throughout the eighteenth century, there were charges that keepers supplemented their incomes by selling game to innkeepers, coachmen and poulterers. John Mordant noted that they had 'the knack of pleasuring market towns, &c. . . . with game for lucre, by which unjustifiable practice, [they] may make as near as much *per ann.* as their wages.' William Taplin charged that 'the extensive Game Trade that is carried on by those plush-coated, black-capp'd Gentry with Road Waggoners would, to those unacquainted with it, surpass Belief'.[99] Such accusations were rarely specific, and understandably so. Part of the gamekeeper's job was to kill game and deliver it to various places, including coaching inns. It was therefore difficult to distinguish between a keeper who was supplying the black market and one who was simply following his master's instructions.[100] For some persons, however, lack of evidence was the most convincing form of proof, and the image of the gamekeeper as poacher par excellence became deeply embedded in the popular imagination. It would, of course, have been surprising if some keepers had not succumbed to the temptation to supply the black market, but it is likely that other, less questionable activities of gamekeepers led to many of these accusations. The gamekeeper was both the agent and the symbol of game preservation and this alone was enough to make him unpopular with many sectors of rural society. As we shall see, farmers anxious to protect their crops did not look kindly on large concentrations of game near their land; nor did fox-hunters enjoy the prospect of their favourite prey being systematically destroyed as vermin. Added to these irritants were others arising out of the game laws themselves, notably the right of the gamekeeper to sport over an entire manor while farmers were denied the right to shoot a hare even when it was eating their crops. Small wonder, then, that gamekeepers were resented and abused, but, for that very reason, the charges levelled against them should be viewed with a certain amount of scepticism.

By the end of the eighteenth century, then, a new element had been introduced into English rural life. Responding to the pressure of sportsmen for large and conveniently located concentrations of game, country gentlemen began systematically to preserve hares, partridges and pheasants on their estates. This was not necessarily an easy thing to do. First of all, it was expensive, since it required not only a staff of keepers and assistant keepers, but also fairly substantial quantities of barley and buckwheat. At Audley End in the 1780s, expenditure on the game amounted to almost £150 a year. At Longleat in the same decade, the pheasantry alone cost over £200 a year, while at Goodwood, the Duke of

Richmond spent an average of £385 a year on his game establishment.[101] For this reason it was wealthy landowners who first engaged in systematic game preservation. Not until the 1790s, when high corn prices and rents brought general prosperity to landowners, did game preservation come to be practised by gentlemen of more modest means. The introduction of game preservation was also partially dependent on the spread of new agricultural methods. The cultivation of turnips and the accompanying increase in the number of wheat fields provided a particularly congenial environment for partridges and pheasants.[102] It was probably for this reason that game preservation was first practised in southern and eastern England and only gradually spread to the Midlands and to Yorkshire. The greatest obstacle to effective game preservation, however, lay in the rural community itself. It was on the latter's co-operation that the success of the scheme would ultimately depend; yet, that co-operation was far from assured. Even as they were increasing the availability of game, the gentry were trying to restrict the number of people who might hunt it. This was bound to provoke resentment and even resistance. It was the task of country gentlemen somehow to reconcile the rural community to these two contradictory developments.

IV

Friction resulting from the gentry's seemingly boundless love of field sports was not, of course, something peculiar to the eighteenth century. 'Is hee a Christian,' William Harrison had asked in 1577, 'that liveth to the hurt of his neighbour in treadinge and breaking downe his hedges, in casting open his gates, in tramplinge of his corn, and of otherwise annoying him, as hunters doo?'[103] Two centuries later, the grievances of yeomen had changed little. Sportsmen, it was said, continually broke fences, beat down unharvested corn, trampled turnips, disturbed sheep 'big with lamb' and generally pursued game with little concern for the damage they caused.[104] The quantity and volume of these complaints suggest that such conduct was common and deeply resented. Country gentlemen, however, were not completely indifferent, particularly when it was their own tenants who suffered. The Holkham accounts, for example, include payments to local shepherds for sheep 'worried by His Lordship's Dogs'.[105] Similarly, in the late 1770s, both the Earl of Pembroke and the Duke of Queensbury, complaining of 'great abuses' to their tenants' crops and flocks, forbade coursing on the manors adjoining their hare warrens before the first of November, when both sheep and corn were still vulnerable.[106]

Even more revealing, perhaps, were the efforts made to delay the start of the shooting season. As has already been noted, in 1762 Parliament established seasons during which game might be legally killed. Although grouse and black game could be taken in August, for most sportsmen 'the season' began with partridge shooting on the first of September. In many areas the harvest was not finished by that date; consequently, shooters and their dogs caused a great deal of damage to the corn. In some northern counties, this problem was alleviated by private agreements among local sportsmen not to begin shooting until the end of September,[107] but following the bad harvest in 1795, the situation seemed to call for some national remedy. As Lord Belgrave later recalled, 'every twig had been caught hold of' in that year to relieve the scarcity of corn. Early in 1796 Parliament voted to postpone the start of partridge shooting until the fourteenth of September.[108] Predictably, once the crisis had passed, sportsmen began to agitate for a return to the previous date. 'The lawful sportsman,' it was argued, 'should at least be allowed to start fair with the encroaching poacher, who was now permitted to sweep away whole coveys *en masse*, from which the country gentlemen in vain would look for recreation.' In 1799 the first of September was restored as the opening day of the season, and thereafter gentlemen were legally entitled to a 'fair start' against the poacher.[109] Many sportsmen, however, did not take advantage of it. In the following decades, whenever the harvest was expected to be late, gentlemen in Hampshire, Bedfordshire, Lincolnshire and other counties would gather at quarter sessions or assizes and agree to postpone their sport until the corn was in.[110]

The gentry, then, were not totally insensitive to the problems which their sports created for the farmers in their neighbourhoods. This would continue to be true even after the introduction of systematic game preservation, although the latter did impose new limits on what the gentry were willing to do to accommodate their neighbours. One of the most common complaints of farmers after the middle of the eighteenth century concerned the damage done to their crops by large concentrations of game, particularly hares, near their land. 'Numberless are the places and parishes of the kingdom,' claimed one writer in 1757, 'which have at least one third part of their wheat crop devoured and eat[en] up by hares.' In addition to wheat, hares also had a fondness for barley, clover and turnips, the latter being particularly vulnerable to damage. 'The quantity [of turnips] they *eat* is considerable,' reported William Marshall from Norfolk in 1787, 'but small in comparison to the waste they create. Before a hare will make a meal of turneps, she will taste, perhaps, ten, without meeting one to her tooth.'[111] Pheasants were, if anything, even more destructive, especially where wheat and clover were planted. 'In order to judge of the Damage they do the Farmer,' wrote yet another observer, 'you must look at the Corn Fields, and see it with your own Eyes, or you would think it incredible.'[112] In some cases, the farmer received no compensation for this loss, but in general it seems to have been the practice of game preservers to offer some kind of restitution. This usually took the form of rent reductions, and, where the damage to crops was great, these could be substantial. In the case of one of Lord Suffield's Norfolk tenants, the reduction amounted to 20 per cent of the original rental of the farm. It was, indeed, said of Lord Suffield that 'the whole of his lands were let an average of ten shillings per acre less than they would have brought, had not the game been reared to so inordinate a head'.[113] Other landowners probably sacrificed less than Lord Suffield to the cause of game preservation. Edward Littleton, for example, simply permitted his Staffordshire tenants to course and keep all the hares found on their farms between 15 November and 15 January. But whatever the form of compensation, there can be little doubt that the granting of it was widespread by the beginning of the nineteenth century, if not earlier.[114]

Game preservers proved to be less conciliatory, however, when it came to the matter of foxes. They viewed the fox as their natural enemy, and with good reason, since it fed on their expensively reared pheasants, as well as on chickens and other domestic fowl. Where foxes were, asserted Lord Pembroke, 'there can never be any thing else'.[115] Consequently, most gamekeepers had standing orders to destroy all foxes found on their manors.[116] Such orders were, needless to say, unpopular with the fox-hunting fraternity. While the latter was dominated by country gentlemen, it was not limited to that class. There was no property qualification for fox-hunting, and as the sport became established in the second half of the eighteenth century it attracted considerable numbers of farmers, trades-men and urban gentlemen to its ranks.[117] Like squires, they could become quite passionate on the subject of foxes. There was 'a pretty free conversation about you at one of the hunting dinners', Lord Herbert reported to his father in 1787, after it had become known that the keeper at Wilton was killing foxes. Similar talk was heard in Somerset when Sir Richard Colt Hoare's gamekeeper was caught transporting foxes out of the county.[118] In both cases, there were threats of retaliation against the game, but the most common response seems to have been a discreet bribe to the gamekeeper. Hoare's gamekeeper, in fact, defended himself to an irate fox-hunter by saying (so the latter claimed) that 'as he [the keeper] had never seen the colour of my money, I could not expect & should not have any Fox of his catching'.[119] Bribery, however, was not effective in every case, and some fox-hunters were actually forced to give up their packs for lack of sport. In the great 'war between the Pheasant and the Fox', one observer concluded in 1826, 'the former has generally been victorious'.[120]

The rancour which this caused, however, was minor when compared with that which resulted from the denial of 'indulgences' to those who were accustomed to receiving them. A game preserver might have been able to conceal his efforts to exterminate foxes, but it was impossible to refuse secretly a request to sport on his manors. Refusals, however, could not be avoided if the game preserver and his friends were to have the enjoyment of bringing home a full game bag. 'Considering the Scarcity of Game,' advised Lord Bruce's steward in 1770, 'and the great demand your Lordship has for it for yourself and your Friends, I should think your Lordship might reasonably excuse yourself from giving leave [to sport] to any but persons of some consequence.'[121] There were a number of different ways in which a gentleman's neighbours could be informed of their lack of consequence. Some simply received a printed notice, warning them that if they persisted in sporting on a given manor they would 'be deemed a wilful Trespasser' and be prosecuted accordingly.[122] This, however, could not be done in all cases, since the lord of a manor could not legally forbid a qualified person from hunting on his own farm; nor could a lord file suit for trespass on land which had been leased to a tenant.[123] As a result, other stratagems were employed. One of these was to hold out the prospect of some reward in return for deference to the game preserver's wishes. In 1770, for example, John Neate, a farmer's son much given to coursing hares on Barton Down in Wiltshire, received a sharp rebuke from Lord Bruce's steward: 'His Lordship [the steward explained] had promised Mr Craven & Other Gentlemen that the Hares should be preserved in that part of the Country for Hunting, and therefore it is no longer a question between Mr Liddiard and you, but whether his Lordship is to have it in his power to oblige his Friends.' To soften the blow, Bruce's steward promised Neate that he and his father would continue to receive the 'civility' of gifts of game and venison.[124] Such trade-offs were quite common, but increasingly in the late eighteenth and early nineteenth centuries game preservers came to employ a more formal device. This was a clause inserted into the tenant's lease which reserved for the landlord (and his appointees) the exclusive right to hunt over the tenant's farm; in some cases the tenant was also required to file suit for trespass against any person who sported on his farm without the landlord's permission.[125] With his rights thus secured, the game preserver was in a position to reserve the game for 'persons of some consequence'.

Inevitably, the enclosure of the game was greatly resented by those who had previously been indulged by the gentry. 'Tis . . . hard, I think', wrote one farmer as early as 1735, 'that we who have bred up a good Store of this Game must be wholly denied a little Recreation at some of our leisure Times, which are not many'.[126] As the number of 'indulgences' granted to farmers and tradesmen diminished, there was growing indignation about the activities of the gamekeeper, who 'if he meets a curate, or an apothecary, or a reputable tradesman, or even a neighbouring lord of the manor, boldly insults them, [and] threatens to shoot their dogs or seize their fowling pieces'.[127] Indignation and resentment soon developed into defiance. 'I have', reported William Taplin in 1772,

> visited many Farmers, and never saw one that could not take
> me into his Pantry, and produce a Hare or more, and two or
> three Brace of Birds. I may be believed, when I assert, that the
> Farmers will (in Opposition to all Game Laws that are, or may
> hereafter be in force) by some Means or other, take that share
> of Game, that they are justly and beyond any Doubt entitled
> to.[128]

Such attitudes threatened to cost the game preserver more than just a few head of game: alienation of farmers and tradesmen could endanger his 'interest' as well. Eighteenth-century stewards were well aware that by taking a generous approach to sporting privilege, a gentleman could acquire 'not only the esteem of his tenant or tenants at home, but [also] a popular name for affability and good nature' in the rural community at large.[129] A gentleman risked losing that reputation when he introduced strict game preservation on his estate. In 1787 the young Earl of Darnley was pointedly advised 'not so closely [to] imitate his Father's example in the preservation of game, as to deprive himself of that influence in the country [i.e. Kent] to which he was justly entitled by his rank and fortune'.[130] The gentry were expected to show 'liberality' toward their neighbours and dependants. If they did not, the bonds of deference would weaken and their position in the rural community would be brought into question.

It is probably for this reason that the withdrawal of 'indulgences' was never complete. Anxious to preserve their 'interest' as well as their game, a number of gentlemen continued to permit farmers to sport on their estates, albeit in a restricted fashion. The 'very liberal' landowners of Wiltshire in the early nineteenth century, for example, allowed their tenants to hunt game, though only 'to a certain extent, and upon certain lands'.[131] The chorus of complaints heard in the countryside after 1750, however, testifies to the fact that this was no longer the common practice it once had been. 'A gentleman who preserves an inordinate quantity of game upon his estate,' observed William Marshall in 1787, 'is . . . perpetually in hot water, with the yeomanry and minor gentlemen of his neighbourhood.'[132] In part, this was due to the damage to the crops and the threat to fox-hunting which accompanied the introduction of game preservation. The principal grievance of farmers and tradesmen, however, was the systematic attempt to exclude them from field sports. Both as recreations and marks of status, coursing and shooting were just as important to yeomen as to gentlemen. The bitterness which resulted from the attempt to curtail their participation in these sports did not soon die away.

V

Historians, if they mention game preservation at all, tend to treat it as part of the game law 'system'. This view is mistaken and has distorted our perception of the game laws and their impact on rural society. While not unconnected with the game laws, game preservation was nevertheless a separate development. Intensive breeding of game, destruction of vermin and concentration of game within guarded coverts were all carried out independently of the Game Act. Indeed, far from being a product of the game laws, game preservation had, by the end of the eighteenth century, begun seriously to undermine the gentry's game prerogative. The enclosure of game obviously inhibited the freedom of country gentlemen to hunt where they pleased, but beyond that it called the *raison d'être* of the game laws into question. Because hares, pheasants and partridges were still wild in the late seventeenth century, Parliament sought to secure their preservation by limiting the pursuit of game to a single class, the landed gentry. Yet, within a century of the passage of the Game Act, game had come to assume the characteristics of private property. On many estates, it was bred by the landowner and could be hunted only with his permission. Game, in short, was coming to resemble deer and rabbits, but its legal status did not reflect this change. As one gentleman remarked in 1817, 'when wild animals were chased over wild country by wilder men', the game laws were explicable, but this ceased to be so when the object of their protection was 'a valuable, half-tame, and exotic bird . . . guarded in its coverts by legions of gamekeepers'.[133] It was not surprising, therefore, that after 1750 it came to be questioned whether the gentry's monopoly on game was just – or even necessary.

More damaging to the game laws, however, was the alienation of farmers, small freeholders and tradesmen which followed the enclosure of the game. These men constituted the natural constituency of country gentlemen. They followed the latter's lead, and in return expected rewards appropriate to their place in the rural hierarchy. No matter how clearly the Game Act might draw the line between qualified and unqualified sportsmen, the nature of a deferential society demanded that there be a gradation of privilege. By means of gamekeeperships and 'indulgences' country gentlemen were able to distribute sporting rights to a large number of persons who had no legal right to hunt, or even to possess, game. After 1750, however, this type of accommodation became rarer. Having planted their coverts with game, the gentry were reluctant to allow 'any but persons of some consequence' to share in the harvest. Naturally, this was resented by those who had previously been indulged, and it was not long before they began to question the legitimacy of the laws which allowed the gentry to deny them a recreation – and a mark of status – to which they felt entitled.

The signs of discontent could be seen as early as 1750, but the gentry made no move to alter the Game Act. On the contrary, they clung to the property qualification and defended it passionately. In the light of their repeated evasions of both the spirit and the letter of the Game Act, this conduct might seem inconsistent. Country gentlemen, however, did not find it so. When repeal of the property qualification was first seriously debated in 1796, Sir Richard Sutton, a Nottinghamshire gentleman, explained why he opposed the proposal. He was, he said,

> one of the last persons in the country who would prosecute the lower class of people for pursuing Game sometimes. He was also entirely against prohibiting farmers the sport of following Game now and then, especially if they had anything like a decent substance to live upon. He thought it would be improper to prosecute such persons for killing Game, even though they should not be qualified to do so by law; but with regard to any measure . . . tending to favour poachers, he was entirely against [it]: they were a class of person much too insolent already.[134]

But who, then, were 'poachers' and why were they so insolent? This will be discussed in the next chapter.

3

Poachers and the black market

Who was a 'poacher'? In common usage, he was a person who unlawfully took game. A more precise definition, however, depends on the context in which the word was used. In the sixteenth century, for example, those who took deer from a gentleman's park or chase were called 'poachers', but two hundred years later they were not. Instead, the term 'deer-stealer' was used. In the early eighteenth century, 'poaching' still encompassed the taking of rabbits out of a warren, but later in the century it did not. With that exception, however, most people in the period 1671–1831 understood a poacher to be someone who unlawfully took hares, partridges, pheasants or grouse. What, however, did 'unlawfully' mean? As we have seen in the previous chapter, the gentry's interpretation of the Game Act could be quite elastic. Was the unqualified tenant who coursed a hare with his landlord's permission a poacher? Most country gentlemen would have agreed that he was not. On the other hand, they did sometimes apply the term to those who were legally qualified to hunt game. The young scholars of Eton, for instance, carried out frequent (and successful) 'poaching' raids on the royal game preserves at Windsor, and in the early nineteenth century there were angry complaints about 'the host of patrician poachers' who sported over manors without permission.[1] 'Poacher', in fact, was not a legal term at all. Rather, it was an epithet applied to those who violated certain established conventions of sporting. Like all epithets, it was sometimes used too loosely, but in the minds of most eighteenth-century country gentlemen there was no doubt that a poacher was a distinct and easily recognisable type of person. 'Give me Leave to tell you, Sir,' wrote one irate sportsman to a Derbyshire game preserver in 1780, '. . . that if you will take Care to preserve your Game from *Poachers*, and behave with a little more civility to the *Gentlemen Sportsmen*, you will not have so much reason to complain.'[2] As this letter itself indicates, poachers were not the only ones to run afoul of the game laws, but they were the principal targets of those laws. Thus, if the administration of the game laws is to be understood, it is important to know what the characteristics of a poacher were and why these were so abhorrent to the gentry.

To most country gentlemen, the primary characteristic of a poacher was simply that he was not a sportsman. Whereas the latter revelled in the excitement of the chase, the poacher did not, but instead snared game when it was most vulnerable. As one Restoration playwright expressed it:

> So Poachers basely pick up tir'd Game,
> Whilst the fair Hunter's cheated of his Prey.[3]

It followed from this that a poacher usually hunted at night. Indeed, remarked one police officer in the early nineteenth century, 'I should hardly call the men that go out [hunting] by day poachers; they are little tradesmen, and unqualified persons.' Sir John Shelley agreed: a poacher, he told the House of Commons in 1824, was simply a 'thief who snared his game by night'.[4] Game was also vulnerable when it was breeding; thus, hunting out of season was deemed to be another trait of a poacher. In 1713, for example, John Mordaunt warned his bailiff in Warwickshire against netting partridges in early April, since 'ye Sportsmen will condemn you for a Poacher'.[5] Those who hunted at night or out of season, the gentry felt, could have only one motive: to destroy as much game as possible, even if that meant the extermination of the breed. This conviction was clearly revealed in the middle of the eighteenth century, when it was discovered that some gentlemen themselves were regularly 'destroying five or six Hares, and twenty or thirty Partridges a Day'. To the traditionally-minded, destruction of game on such a scale was a shocking breach of the sportsman's code. '*A poacher,*' lamented one observer in 1757, 'was once a term of disgrace, but now *poacher* and *sportsman* are synonymous.'[6]

But, of course, they were not. For even when their 'bags' reached awesome proportions, sportsmen did not sell their game. Poachers, on the other hand, did, thus violating one of the cardinal rules of sportsmanship in the eighteenth century. The gentry professed to hold the 'mean rascal who kills game and sells it' in great contempt,[7] but there was more to their attitude than simple indignation. Fear was also involved. The fact that 'the vulgar sort, and men of small worth, [were] making a trade and a living' by killing game was seen as a serious threat to social order.[8] Most country gentlemen in the eighteenth century believed that the only thing which stood between the poor and 'immorality' was the necessity of having to work for a living. Without the discipline of constant labour, they agreed, the lower classes would soon sink into lives of crime and debauchery, and that would inevitably lead to their own – and society's – ruin. This was the usual justification for imposing a property qualification on sporting. If labourers, apprentices and other 'men of small worth' were allowed to hunt game, it was argued, they would soon begin to neglect their trades and, shortly thereafter, lose all sense of morality. The poor injured themselves by sporting, Giles Jacob contended in 1705, since by 'neglecting their honest Callings, [and] wasting their Time not only Unprofitably, but Wrongfully', they soon contracted 'such an Idleness (the Mother of all Vices) as inclines them afterwards to Robberies and Burglaries'.[9] This argument was so often repeated and embroidered upon that by the early nineteenth century it was an article of faith among country gentlemen that poaching was 'the first step toward the gallows'. 'The habit of nightly plunder,' explained one writer in 1815,

> by depriving the poor man of the conscious integrity of his conduct, deprives him of more than half [of] his motives to abstain from crime. He acquires the feelings, the fears, the suspicions of the thief: he considers himself as in a state of warfare with all the honest part of the community . . . Failing his success in the wood, the field, and the forest, he resorts to the hen-roost or the sheep-fold . . . What principle of restraint can . . . prevent him from . . . the extremes of burglary and murder? The whole process is as simple and natural as it is in most cases inevitable.[10]

The 'inevitability' of this process was, of course, open to challenge, but many country gentlemen were convinced that poachers were, at the very least, potential felons. Some, indeed, were far less cautious in their judgements. Poachers, one Surrey J.P. told a Commons committee in 1823, 'are all poultry stealers, and sheep stealers also'.[11]

In the minds of country gentlemen, then, a poacher was not simply someone who took game without being legally qualified to do so. All such persons might technically be poachers, observed a gentleman in 1770, but those who were 'commonly understood to deserve' the name were 'common fowlers, or fellows who kill Game privately, with an intention to sell it'.[12] The crucial elements in this definition were the covert nature of the poacher's activities and the monetary reward he received. When seeking to discourage poaching, therefore, Parliament tended to concentrate on these two aspects of the 'common fowler's' trade. It forbade all but country gentlemen to possess dogs, guns, nets, snares or other 'engines' which could be employed to take game 'privately', and it also imposed heavy penalties on anyone who hunted at night. The commercial aspect of poaching was combated by an act which outlawed the sale of game. While this measure was notoriously unsuccessful in halting the game trade, its passage was nevertheless a significant event in the history of the game laws, for it had a profound effect on the nature of poaching in the eighteenth century. Far from cutting the poacher's links with his customers, the ban on the game trade actually strengthened the connection. The expanding urban market became increasingly dependent on poachers for its supply of game; as it did, the character of the poacher's activities began to change. Poaching became both more organised and more violent. Armed gangs began to make regular raids on the gentry's preserves, and when they encountered resistance, the woods echoed with the sounds of battle and death. In order to understand this transformation, it is first necessary to examine the development and organisation of the game trade in the eighteenth and nineteenth centuries.

II

Ever since the reign of James I, the game trade had operated in a legal twilight. Outlawed in 1603, the sale of partridges, pheasants and hares nevertheless continued throughout the seventeenth century with little interference from the authorities.[13] In London, Winchester, Oxford and other cities, game was bought openly and 'in quantities large enough,' as one historian has observed, 'to indicate . . . a supply which could not have come from any but professional fowlers or country folk'.[14] Some of these suppliers may have been legally qualified to kill game, but it was clearly suspected at the time that most were not. In 1680, for example, Richard Newcombe, a Stratford-on-Avon carrier, was ordered to appear before a local J.P. 'to make known [from] where he hath the hares that he carries to London'. In 1688 Christopher Matson, when applying for a patent for his device to hatch eggs by 'artificial heat', argued that it would be 'serviceable to the public, especially by supplying the Town with sufficient partridges and pheasants at cheap rates, whereby the game belonging to all gentlemen within fifty miles of London will be much preserved'.[15]

Country gentlemen, however, did not want the urban market supplied: they wanted it shut down. Blaming 'the multitude of higlers and other chapmen', who by trading in game 'give great encouragement to idle loose persons to neglect their lawful employments', Parliament in 1707 forbade any higgler, chapman, carrier, innkeeper, victualler or alehousekeeper to buy, sell or possess game under pain of a £5 fine (per head of game) or three months in prison.[16] In London, the Poulters' Company at first took fright and promised to give up the trade. The Master and other members of the Company declared that they would no longer buy or sell game, and furthermore 'would Informe against them that acted to the contrary'.[17] Their resolve did not last very long, however. Selling game, as they admitted, formed 'A very considerable Part of their Trade'; if they refused to provide what their customers wanted, they risked losing all of their business to those with fewer scruples. So, instead of informing on those who dealt in game, the poulterers were soon helping to pay the costs of their defence.[18] In the provinces as well, the trade seems to have gone on relatively undisturbed. Writing in 1742, one gentleman professed it 'quite shocking at Bath to see at the poulterers at least twenty brace of hares daily, [and] partridges and pheasants without number'. In Nottingham, it was reported a decade later, 'Our great Inns are seldom in want of this Sort of Dainties to supply their Customers with.'[19]

The poulterers obviously could not be expected to enforce a law which diminished their trade; nor could innkeepers, victuallers and other suppliers of 'Dainties'. The only persons, in fact, who had any interest in enforcing the Act of 1707 were the gentry themselves, and in the 1740s they began to form associations for that purpose. In 1748, for example, the Nottinghamshire game association threatened to prosecute not only poachers but also 'every victualler, Innkeeper or other person exposing to Sale any Game, and all Higlers and Owners or Drivers of any Stage Coach or Waggon who shall be found carrying Game within the said Country'.[20] If enforcement was to be effective, however, it would have to extend beyond county boundaries; in particular, it would have to include the markets of London and Westminster. In 1752, therefore, several hundred game preservers – including the Dukes of Marlborough, Beaufort, Ancaster and Kingston, the Marquess of Rockingham, the Earls of Orford, Litchfield, Egremont and Lincoln, as well as the heirs of several other prominent landowners – agreed to establish an association 'for the Preservation of the Game All Over England'. In one of its first pronouncements, the Game Association warned those engaged in the game trade that 'the Laws will be strictly put in Execution'.[21]

Like its provincial predecessors, the Game Association was a subscription society. Members contributed an agreed amount (initially it was two guineas a year) and the resulting fund was used to pay for the prosecution of offenders against the game laws – chiefly civil prosecutions, since the high legal costs involved were thought to be a more effective deterrent than the standard fine. In addition, the Game Association offered to pay a reward of £5 for information leading to the conviction of a poacher or someone dealing in game.[22] By enriching informers and ruining game traders, the Association hoped to shut down the game trade completely, and at first it seems to have been successful. Within a week of the Association's establishment, it was reported that over fifty prosecutions had been initiated in London, 'so that in the Market, which used to abound [with game], there is not any to be seen'. Apparently encouraged by their success in the capital, the gentlemen of the Association then announced that they would 'keep Agents in their Service in all the great Towns in England' as well as persons 'to watch the several Markets and Carriers within the Liberties of London and Westminster'. By late July 1752, it was reported that one hundred and fifty persons were in its employ.[23]

It was not long, however, before the Association began to encounter resistance. Its promise of stricter enforcement of the game laws was denounced in newspapers and pamphlets, in coffee shops and even in the streets.[24] In addition, the game traders, once they had recovered from the initial shock of prosecution, decided to challenge the Association in the courts. They were aided in this by an ambiguity in the game laws. Since the Act of 1707 did not specifically mention 'poulterers' in its list of those forbidden to buy, sell or possess game, the London poulterers had been prosecuted as 'chapmen' – that is, as common traders. But was a poulterer with £100 a year from land truly a 'chapman' and thus forbidden to possess what he was qualified to kill? Faced with the disruption of their trade, some qualified poulterers decided to find out. In the autumn of 1752, they resolved 'to buy and sell Game as usual . . . All unlanded Merchants, and all Ladies, Gentlemen, and Tradesmen, whose Misfortune it is to have 99 l. per Annum, may depend on being served at the lowest Prices.' As a final provocation, they promised 'the most Ready Money' to those who would supply them with game.[25]

The issue was decided, at least to the satisfaction of the lawyers, in 1755. Benjamin Boulter, a qualified poulterer, had been charged in 1753 with selling a hare for four shillings. After two years of complicated legal proceedings, the Court of King's Bench finally ruled in the defendant's favour. The Act of 1707, concluded the Lord Chief Justice, Sir Dudley Ryder, was directed against loose, idle persons: 'it never could be the intention of the legislature to prohibit every trader from having game in his custody or possession'.[26] The legislature, however, was soon to prove him wrong. Within days of the decision, a bill was introduced in the House of Commons 'to explain and amend' the Act of 1707; two months later, it received royal assent. Under the new Act, all persons, 'whether qualified or not qualified to kill game', were forbidden to sell game, and the mere possession of it by any 'poulterer, salesman, fishmonger, cook or pastry cook' was declared to

III. A London poultry stall

be sufficient evidence for conviction.[27] Although the game trade was now obviously illegal, the poulterers fought on for a while longer. When prosecuted under the Act of 1755, they argued that they possessed game only in order to dress and pack it for qualified gentlemen, but in 1763 this defence was dismissed by the courts, and the poulterers were left without a case.[28]

They still had their trade, however. As the Association itself admitted, poulterers and their agents continued to buy and sell game, albeit 'in a clandestine Manner'.[29] In the latter decades of the century, even that precaution was dropped, as it gradually became evident that the Game Association had all but given up trying to enforce the ban on the game trade. The Association's decline as a threat to poulterers is difficult to document, but it seems clear that within a decade of its founding it was beginning to lose both members and income. Citing the death of some of its members and the fact that 'several others have neglected to pay their Subscription-money', the Association announced in 1761 that it would have to double its subscription fee to four guineas a year and tighten its rules governing expenditure.[30] Later in the 1760s, regular announcements of its meetings disappeared from the newspapers, as did reports of its prosecutions. Even more revealing, perhaps, was the re-emergence of provincial game associations: in Hampshire in 1769, Devon in 1773, Wiltshire in 1787,

Norfolk in 1789, Dorset in 1791, and so on.[31] The evidence is mostly negative, but it suggests that after the 1760s the Game Association was no longer the scourge of poachers and poulterers it claimed to be. Its members continued to meet until at least the beginning of the nineteenth century, but their activities were probably more social than legal. 'What do they execute after all their pompous Advertisements?' jeered William Taplin in 1772. 'Why they *Meet, Dine, Drink, Game,* and *Depart* . . . Even the major Part of their own Society are sorry that they ever embarked [on] so barren a scheme.'[32]

Why did the Game Association go into decline? Since its records have almost completely disappeared, it is difficult to answer the question with any certainty. It is possible that internal dissension had something to do with it. In 1754, for instance, the Warwickshire branch of the Association split into two factions. The reasons for the split are not very clear, but they seem to have been more concerned with personalities than policy. In 1755 one of the factions made its own membership in the Association conditional on the exclusion of Sir Roger Newdigate; when 'the rest of ye Gent. insisted' that he should remain a member, the faction 'struck out their names' from the subscription list.[33] There may have been other such incidents, but in view of the fact that the Association continued to meet for the rest of the century, it seems unlikely that internal quarrels were the principal reason for the organisation's decline. It appears much more probable that the Association's reduced membership and vitality was due to frustration at its apparent inability to shut down the black market in game. Certainly, the provincial game associations formed in the second half of the eighteenth century all pointed to the flourishing game trade as the chief object of their concern. 'The great destruction of the Game,' declared the Wiltshire association in 1787, 'has arisen from the encouragement held out by Innkeepers, Alehousekeepers, Stage-Coach Drivers, Carriers and Higlers, who receive such game, and convey it in large quantities to London, Bath, Salisbury, Southampton, Romsey, and other Places'. The purpose of the Norfolk association, wrote Lord Townshend a year later, was 'to check ye grand Receivers & Supporters of ye audacious Gangs which have infested ye whole County'.[34] But why had the Association been so unsuccessful in its efforts to end the game trade? To answer that question, it is necessary to take a closer look at the operation of the black market in game.

In the first half of the eighteenth century, the central figure in the game trade was the higgler. He was an itinerant poultry dealer who bought eggs and fowl in the countryside and sold them in the cities and market towns, mostly to poulterers but sometimes directly to the public. Because he was able to transport large numbers of birds quickly and without attracting attention, the higgler was the natural link between the poacher and the urban market. After the middle of the century, however, there were others who could also provide this service. Improvement in the quality of the roads had encouraged the development of a network of stage coaches which reached into even the most remote parts of the kingdom. With the commencement of the mail coach service in 1784, most provincial towns were brought within a day's travel of London.[35] In addition to passengers and mail, coaches also carried perishable agricultural produce, including game. Stewards sent game to their masters; gentlemen sent it to their friends; and higglers sent it to their customers – all through the agency of the stage coach. For the drivers and guards of these vehicles, it was only a short step from carrying game for others to dealing in game on their own. Assisted by the keepers of the inns where they stopped, coachmen soon became as important in the operation of the game trade as the higglers themselves.[36]

By the latter half of the eighteenth century, then, game reached the London market via two principal routes. At certain points these routes overlapped, but they were nonetheless distinct. The first route was the higgler's. He and his agents bought game from poachers and sent it by coach to poultry 'salesmen' – that is, to wholesalers – in Leadenhall and Newgate markets. The salesmen then sold the game, on commission, to the poulterers who, in turn, sold it to the public. What was left over was sold to hawkers, who peddled it in the poorer districts of the metropolis. The other route was the coachman's. He received his game, it seems, principally from innkeepers and gamekeepers.[37] When the coach arrived in London, he sold the game through the porters at the coaching inns to poulterers and innkeepers in the capital, who then supplied their customers. The surplus, once again, went 'to the lower sort of the people'. The higgler's route was an orthodox marketing network, linking the producer and the consumer by means of a middleman, a wholesaler and a retailer. It was, in fact, the same structure as that of the legitimate poultry trade and as such was susceptible to certain forms of control. Higglers were licensed by justices of the peace, for instance, and poulterers were at least nominally under the jurisdiction of the Poulters' Company. Had such controls been employed to their fullest extent, it might have been possible to make continued participation in the legitimate part of the trade contingent on a promise not to deal in game. The entrance of the coachmen into the trade, however, destroyed whatever slight chance there was of this happening. The coachmen were commercial buccaneers. Operating outside of the established structures of the poultry trade, they were subject to no regulatory authority other than their own employers, and the latter were not, perhaps, as devoted to the preservation of the game as they might have been.[38] In the absence of any real supervision of their activities, the coachmen and their allies were able to bring game to market at little risk to themselves. Their obvious success served to undermine whatever scruples higglers and poulterers might have had about trading in game.

The scruples of higglers and poulterers were probably not very strong to begin with, for the game trade was a lucrative one. What evidence we have from the late eighteenth and early nineteenth centuries indicates that dealers were well compensated for breaking the law. In the 1820s, for example, a hare bought by a higgler for 2s. could be sold by a poulterer for 5s. 6d.; a brace of pheasants, bought in the countryside for 3s. 6d., might fetch 7s. or even 10s. in London. The prices quoted before parliamentary committees in that decade indicate that, in general, poulterers sold game for two or two-and-a-half times the amount paid to the poacher.[39] On the coachman's route, the mark-up was probably higher, since there were more middlemen, all of them intent on making a quick profit. Henry Zouch in the 1780s mentioned the 'very exhorbitant rate' at which innkeepers sold game, and William Daniel at the turn of the century described the prices charged by porters at coaching inns as 'astonishing': '*four* and *five* shillings (sometimes as high as *eight*) [for] a brace of *Partridges*; *twelve* to *sixteen* for *Pheasants*, and from *five* to *seven shillings and sixpence* for a *Hare*'. The shillings quickly added up to hundreds of pounds a year.[40]

For some game traders, admittedly, the profits were accompanied by a certain amount of anxiety. Even after the decline of the Association, there were still occasional prosecutions, like that of a Suffolk higgler who in 1803 was fined £100 for buying game from poachers.[41] A more common danger, however, was blackmail. The profitability of the game trade, combined with its illegality, made game traders attractive prey for extortionists and in the early nineteenth century, if not before, the payment of blackmail to them does not appear to have been unusual. The porter at one London inn complained in 1823 that 'informers run away with a great sum of money; the informers have cost me £100'. Six years earlier, the poulterers of the capital had acknowledged that they 'sometimes judged it most prudent to compound with their prosecutors, rather than run the risque of being ultimately ruined by the law charges'.[42] If making accommodations of this sort was the price game traders had to pay in order to protect their profits, it was a good bargain. Not only did it cost them less than a prosecution, it also gave the informers a vested interest in the operation of the game trade, and thus prevented the formation of any alliance between the informers and organisations like the Game Association. The extent of the informers' attachment to the continued prosperity of the black market was strikingly revealed in 1817, when the House of Commons was considering a bill to legalise the sale of game. 'The persons who generally make it their business to live by' extorting money from the London poulterers, the latter complained to Parliament, 'have lately . . .

commenced a vast many Actions [under the game laws] . . . from an apprehension that the said Acts, or some of them, are about to be repealed'.[43]

Their panic was premature. Parliament did not lift the ban on the sale of game until 1831. The poulterers were then free of the attentions of both the Association and the informers, but their relief may have been touched with regret. For the laws which made the game trade illegal had also made it highly profitable. It is impossible to say whether the ban actually increased the demand for game, but it certainly allowed traders to demand a higher price for their services. The poultry salesmen of Leadenhall market, for instance, charged twice the rate of commission on game as they did on chickens and rabbits.[44] The prices quoted above suggest that other traders calculated the value of their services in a similar fashion. Certainly the prospect of a large and easy profit was what attracted the coachmen to the trade; their enthusiasm for the marketing of wild fowl declined noticeably after the ban on the sale of game was lifted. By making the game trade illegal, Parliament had, in effect, ensured that the poacher would easily find someone who would purchase his game – and, indeed, would encourage him to kill more. It was not long before poachers responded to the invitation.

III

The higgler's shilling was not, of course, the only reason why men went out to take game in defiance of the law and the squire's wishes. Some did so simply for sport. Adam Arrowsmith, for example, was the son of an Essex farmer in the early nineteenth century. He was reputed to be 'one of the first shots in the kingdom', and seems to have lived off the wagers he won performing feats of marksmanship. He was also 'an out Law in the Game way'. One day he was shooting near the manor house of one Mr Abdy, a justice of the peace. When the latter went out to find out who was shooting on his land, Arrowsmith shouted, 'Stand back, stand back! Don't you see my Dog pointing a Pheasant?' After he had shot the bird, Arrowsmith turned to Abdy and told him that 'if he had not behaved so ungentlemanly, He [Arrowsmith] would have given him the Pheasant'.[45] Those were the words of a man with a full stomach. Many were not so fortunate, and some of them probably hunted in order to feed themselves and their families. How common this was, however, is far from clear. Certainly 'a hare in the pot' was a welcome addition to the diet of most rural labourers, but there is little evidence to support the traditional image of starving peasants snaring game in order to keep body and soul together.[46] The absence of such evidence, of course, does not rule out the possibility that this actually happened, but it should encourage scepticism about how frequent such occurrences were. The principal element in the labourer's diet, it should be remembered, was bread, not meat. In times of dearth, game was more valuable to him as a source of money with which he could buy bread, than as an alternative source of nourishment. Even when this distinction is made, hunger still does not seem to have been a primary motivation for poaching, for, as we shall see in a later chapter, there was no direct correlation between the price of wheat and violations of the game laws.[47]

More tempting than the taste of a hare, perhaps, was the excitement which surrounded a foray into the squire's woods. This comes through clearly in songs like 'The Lincolnshire Poacher', which first became popular in the second half of the eighteenth century:[48]

> When I was bound apprentice, in famous Lincolnshire
> Full well I served my master for more than seven year,
> Till I took up with poaching, as you shall quickly hear:
> Oh! 'tis my delight of a shiney night, in the season of the year.
>
> As me and my comrads were setting a snare,
> 'Twas then we seed the gamekeeper – for him we did not care,
> For we can wrestle and fight, my boys, and jump o'er everywhere:
> Oh! 'tis my delight of a shiney night, in the season of the year.
>
> As me and my comrads were setting four and five,
> And taking on him up again, we caught the hare alive;
> We caught the hare alive, my boys, and through the woods did steer:
> Oh! 'tis my delight of a shiney night, in the season of the year.

Taking a hare on 'a shiney night' with one's comrades was undoubtedly the stuff of high adventure for many a labourer – an adventure made all the more exciting by the possibility that it would end in a brawl with the gamekeeper and his assistants. Daniel Bishop, a Bow Street officer who infiltrated a number of poaching gangs in the early nineteenth century, observed that 'they take a delight in setting to with the gamekeepers, and talk of it afterwards, how they served so and so'.[49] For some, even the tedium of lying out at night waiting for a snare to do its work (or for a keeper to stop doing his) could have its satisfactions. 'Sir, I have been out in the coldest nights in winter – on nights when I heard of persons being frozen on top of the coach, but I have never felt it cold', one veteran poacher told the Governor of the Bury St Edmunds gaol. 'I have always been very comfortable, and have felt as much pleasure as the Marquis himself.'[50]

One thing which undoubtedly increased this sense of satisfaction was the poacher's unshakeable conviction that he had a God-given right to take game. Poachers 'consider the game which they take not to be private property', reported one Bedfordshire J.P.; 'they say God has made the game of the land free and left it free'. This was not simply the rationalisation of thieves. Most observers acknowledged that there was consensus among the lower classes that, as one observer put it, 'Game is the property of those who can take it.' Thus, as the Governor of the Bury St Edmunds gaol admitted, there was 'a general understanding amongst the lower orders of people that there is no crime in [poaching]'.[51] This general understanding was occasionally translated into a personal protest. When, for example, the constable of Folkestone came to call on Daniel Underdowne in 1720 to search his house for nets, Underdowne admitted that he possessed them. 'But flipping in of ye Door, he fasten'd it upon us,' reported the constable, 'And refus'd to let us enter saying he thought he had as much Right to keep Guns and Netts as any Others.'[52] More often, however, popular feeling found expression in a wink exchanged in the village alehouse or in a handful of stones shattering the window of the gamekeeper's cottage. As much as the game laws themselves, the widespread conviction that poaching was no crime formed the context in which the poacher operated.

Crime or not, poaching was a trade. By killing game a man could maintain a modest existence and that, for some persons at least, was justification enough. In 1678, for example, one George Knitstall told a Hertfordshire landowner that if the latter 'would not give him leave to take game in his manor, he would take leave; that he preferred to serve him with partridges in his [public?] house at 8*d*. per piece, and that he did not care a straw for all the justices'.[53] It was probably from men like Knitstall that higglers in the seventeenth and early eighteenth centuries obtained the game they sent to market. Their names are mostly forgotten, but they must have included Thomas Holden, a Hertfordshire labourer who, in 1685, was caught with twenty-five partridges. They must have also included the Warwickshire 'Tunneler' who, Lady Aylesford informed her husband early in the next century, 'makes £20 a year by that trade'.[54] While transportation remained difficult, these poachers probably supplied only the town or city nearest them, but with the advent of the stage coach, they were brought into contact with a much larger market. Gentlemen, like those in the Derbyshire game association, gradually became aware that 'great Quantities . . . of Game is [*sic*] Weekly, and oftner, taken to London, and other Places'. By the 1770s, game from as far away as the Scottish border was finding its way to the cities of the south.[55]

With both higglers and coachmen now competing to supply an expanding market, the poacher's trade became a more attractive one. The two or three shillings which the Norwich higglers were offering for a pheasant, wrote William Marshall in 1787, were for most men 'a temptation . . . too powerful to be withstood'. He feared that there were as many as 500 men in Norfolk 'whose principal dependence, for their own and their family's support, is on poaching'.[56] A great deal more than mere 'support' could, in fact, be acquired with a little application. The Broadways, a poaching family living near Marlborough, were said to have had an income of nearly £100 a year. The estimate may well have been accurate, as it came from a knowledgeable source: the local publican.[57] A poacher, of course, had to be very skilled at his trade to reap substantial rewards, and this required a lengthy apprenticeship. The delicate arts of setting snares, netting hares and evading gamekeepers were not quickly learned, and many poachers spent part of their childhood absorbing the wisdom of their fathers and uncles on such subjects as the nocturnal habits of pheasants and the proper use of gate-nets.[58] This apprenticeship tended to produce poachers who preferred to work alone, who went to great lengths to avoid attracting attention and who generally looked upon poaching as a craft. Poachers of this sort were resident in many villages during the eighteenth and early nineteenth centuries and were major suppliers of game for the black market. After 1750, however, a new species of poacher began to appear in the English countryside. Unlike the traditional practitioners of the trade, these new poachers were neither solitary nor silent. Instead they poached in gangs and were not particularly shy about making their presence known.

There had, of course, been 'poaching gangs' of one type or another since the Middle Ages. Royal forests, deer parks and rabbit warrens had all along been the targets of raids by bands of armed men and would continue to be in the eighteenth century. Rabbit warreners in Sussex, for example, complained bitterly in the early years of the eighteenth century about the losses which they sustained from such raids. The gangs responsible for them were 'so impudent as to beat the said Warreners Doors, bidding them Defiance, and fetch a Justice of Peace's Warrant, saying, *They do not value it*'.[59] Not until the middle of the eighteenth century, however, do we hear of similar tactics being used to take game. One of the first reports of a change came from a correspondent to the *Gentleman's Magazine* in 1749. 'Those gentlemen that now endeavour to preserve their game, do it at the risque of their servants' lives', he complained after a raid 'by many poachers'. A gamekeeper, he added, 'is become of almost no use, for if he tells of any of them [i.e. the poachers] they threaten to kill him'. In the 1760s, Lord Bruce's steward had the same complaint. 'Those rascals,' he wrote, 'go out together with arms of some kind, and they know very well how dangerous it is for any equal number to apprehend 'em if they should be seen, which makes 'em bold.'[60] However exaggerated such reports might have been, it is clear that after the middle of the century game preservers were faced with a challenge quite different from that offered by the traditional poachers. The latter depended on their knowledge of the land, the game and the gamekeeper to shield them from detection. The poaching gang, on the other hand, depended on force – both of numbers and of arms – to avoid capture. Members of these gangs may have had some of the traditional skills of a poacher but, as we shall see, this was not essential. Given adequate leadership and some measure of solidarity, a poaching gang could be successful even if its members knew little more, than how to shoot a gun or wield a bludgeon.

It seems likely that the appearance of poaching gangs was closely related to the creation of game preserves in the second half of the eighteenth century. When game was spread all over the countryside, there was little reason for poachers to band together: four men hunting together were not likely to bring back much more game than one hunting alone. The concentration of large quantities of game in small areas changed all this. Poachers, like sportsmen, quickly learned that in a well-stocked preserve the more guns there were, the larger the 'bag' was likely to be. It is not surprising, therefore, that poaching gangs first appeared in those parts of the country where game preservation was most intensively practised: in the south and east, particularly in East Anglia with its vast and well-stocked sporting estates. There was, however, another factor which encouraged the formation of poaching gangs at this time. The Act of 1755 banning the game trade had, in effect, given poachers a monopoly on supplying game for the urban market.[61] This market was growing in the second half of the eighteenth century, and, in order to satisfy its appetite for game, poachers were forced to become organised and systematic in their operations. Nathaniel Smith, a Norfolk poacher in the 1780s, actually 'employed and paid a regular set of men as deputies, and consigned his game to a London trader, on whom he has drawn bills of exchange to a considerable amount'.[62] Although in some respects exceptional, Smith symbolised the change in poaching after 1750: from a craft, it was turning into a business – one which occupied large numbers of men and was capable of yielding large rewards.

Aside from reports of their raids, there is little surviving information about poaching gangs in the late eighteenth and early nineteenth centuries. They had no constitutions, no account books, no membership lists. It is, however, possible to make a few general observations about them. First of all, not all poaching gangs were made up of rural labourers. In the 1770s, for example, gangs of 'journeymen weavers, and other low mechanics' in Norwich went out into the surrounding countryside to kill game for the market. Industrial workers continued to be active in the trade in the early nineteenth century. The labourers of Sheffield regularly raided the neighbouring manors of the Duke of Norfolk in the 1820s, and in 1828 the chairman of the Warwickshire quarter sessions testified that most of the poachers he encountered were stocking-makers, ribbon-weavers and watch-makers.[63] Another group prominent in the trade were the miners.

They were, wrote one observer in 1828, 'upon the whole, moral and orderly in their habits, honest and industrious, with the exception of being most of them poachers'.[64] The miners' solidarity made them particularly formidable opponents. When, in 1820, a constable was sent into the Northumbrian mining village of Garrigill to serve some summonses, 'he was oblig'd to return without serving them, [since] about 40 of the Poachers assembl'd as soon as it was known he was there, & he was glad to make his escape'.[65]

For miners and urban workers as well as for rural labourers, the game preserves of the gentry acted as a powerful magnet, drawing them from many miles around. Henry Zouch noted that the gangs in the West Riding would 'frequently wander to a great distance, the distance of many miles from their respective homes, where they can have a more convenient opportunity of succeeding in their nightly excursions'. It was, indeed, not unusual for a poaching gang to travel up to ten miles in order to raid a well-stocked preserve. In 1777 one gang made what was, in effect, a grand tour of the sporting estates in Norfolk, including the Earl of Buckinghamshire's 'repositorys' of game at Blickling. 'They travel without horses,' Buckinghamshire was informed by his steward, 'and no person as yet has made them out.'[66] In the early nineteenth century, such exploits became common, and they highlight one of the principal functions of the poaching gang: protection for its members from the dangers, known and unknown, of trespassing on unfamiliar territory in the dead of night. For the apprentice weaver out for game and adventure in a strange wood filled with gamekeepers and spring guns, this kind of protection was, indeed, essential.

To game preservers and gamekeepers, then, poachers were often strangers. In some of the large gangs which operated after 1815, they may even have been strangers to one another, but in general the members of these gangs seem to have been neighbours. The gentry, indeed, were convinced that the recruiting centre for most poaching gangs was the village alehouse. It was there, charged Henry Zouch, that 'ill-disposed persons of every complexion do frequently collect themselves, and from whence they can conveniently issue forth at any hour *in the night*, in the prosecution of their unwarrantable designs'.[67] Country gentlemen, of course, were traditionally hostile toward alehouses, but there was probably some foundation for their suspicions in this case. The alehouse was the principal social centre for the lower classes, and there was no safer place where poachers could meet, particularly if the house was run by someone involved in the game trade. The justices of Hampshire, in fact, complained in 1778 that it was the practice of some public houses to sponsor shooting matches, 'whereby the servants in husbandry, and the other lower sorts of people, learn and are taught to shoot and destroy the game, and are seduced from their respective labours and employments'.[68] Gambling debts incurred at these houses may have also been an effective inducement to poaching. At the alehouse in Nunburnholme in the East Riding, complained Sir Joseph Pennington in 1780, 'they have frequently Cockfights and Carding all Night, during which time some of the party go out, Shooting by Night in the Snow and I hear the Guns all round my House'.[69] Even if it did not actively encourage poaching, the alehouse was nevertheless a place where poachers could meet with their comrades. There, remarked one police spy, they met 'just like a club'.[70]

Just how permanent or organised these 'clubs' really were is almost impossible to say. It seems likely that most were informal, transitory associations, composed of friends and relatives, led perhaps by one or two veteran poachers. In the early nineteenth century, however, there is some evidence of more formal organisation. Some gang members in this period wore white handkerchiefs on their hats in order to recognise one another in the dark.[71] Others swore oaths not to inform on their comrades.[72] In these and other cases, the gangs had acknowledged leaders. In 1823, for instance, a parliamentary committee was told of a Dorset village, all of whose men – including the constable – belonged to a poaching gang, the 'head' of which was 'a baker who kept a good shop there'. The 'head' of the Gloucestershire gang which murdered the gamekeeper at Berkeley Castle in 1816 was a farmer named Allen.[73] Just how someone became the leader of a gang is unclear, but from what little evidence we have, the position commonly seems to have been filled by a person with some degree of social authority; often he was a farmer. One reason for this may be that the 'head' of a gang was usually responsible for disposing of the game after a raid. An ordinary labourer might have found it difficult to convey large quantities of game to a higgler or innkeeper without attracting attention, but for a substantial farmer or tradesman with a horse and waggon, this was a relatively easy task. This may have been the reason why in Wiltshire farmers were commonly thought to be 'the master poachers'.[74]

Valuable as such leadership was, the real strength of the poaching trade lay in the willingness of ordinary labourers, both in the countryside and in the cities, to go out and kill game. That willingness, as we have already noted, was not solely the result of the incentives offered by the black market. The love of sport and adventure undoubtedly drew some men into the trade, as did the widespread conviction that poaching was not a crime. Nevertheless, poachers were not slow to grasp economic opportunity when it presented itself. As the demand for game increased in the second half of the eighteenth century, so did the incidence of poaching. Game preservers, not surprisingly, responded to this challenge. They began to employ large numbers of men to guard their preserves; in some districts they installed spring guns and man traps. The result was the 'poaching war', an extraordinarily bitter conflict which would last well into the nineteenth century.

IV

On Christmas night in 1775, at about midnight, six men entered 'Mossims', a wood owned by Lord Walpole at Itteringham in Norfolk. The men began to shoot pheasants, and the sound of their guns soon alerted the gamekeeper, Sebastian Daniel, to their presence. With several assistants he went into the wood after them. Upon their approach, one of the poachers levelled his gun and fired. Daniel dropped to the ground, severely wounded in the thigh, and the poachers fled. Three years later, five men were committed to Norwich Castle in connection with the assault. All came from Oulton, a small village near the wood, and among their number were 'a small farmer' and a weaver ('a very old offender'). The man charged with the actual shooting was Thomas Bell, a shoemaker who had recently gone to live in East Dereham, a small market town about twelve miles away from Oulton. Only two of these men were eventually tried at the assizes, and only one was convicted. Thomas Bell was sentenced to death, and, on 3 April 1779, he was hanged before a crowd said to have numbered 20,000 people.[75]

The affray at 'Mossims' was unusual only in its final outcome. Normally, poachers were not hanged unless they were found guilty of murder or manslaughter. Bell was, no doubt, a victim of that periodic impulse of eighteenth-century judges to 'make an example' of a criminal in order to deter others. With that exception, however, the incident was typical of many which occurred in game counties in the late eighteenth century. They began with a nocturnal raid on a game preserve by a band of armed men, which led to an altercation with the gamekeeper and his men, which in turn usually ended in the flight of one or other of the parties. These incidents became a staple item in the provincial newspapers during these years, and were convenient occasions to moralise about the 'demoralising' effects of poaching on the lower classes. They were also occasions of very real pain and loss, as can be seen in the ballad about the death of 'poor Bill Brown', a Yorkshire poacher shot in 1769:

> When we got to the woods our sport begun,
> But I saw the keeper present his gun.
> I called to Bill to climb the gate,
> To drop the buck, but it was too late,
> For there he met his untimely fate.
>
> Then dying he lay upon the ground,
> And in that state poor Bill I found.

IV. Poachers and constables fighting outside the village alehouse

> And when he saw me, he did cry:
> 'Revenge my death!' 'I will', said I,
> 'For many a hare we've caught hard by.'[76]

Gamekeepers too risked their lives in these affrays. Following one in Norfolk in 1785, Parson Woodforde wrote in his diary: 'Poor Tom Twaites of Honingham who was beat by Poachers at Mr [Charles] Townshends the other day is lately dead of the Wounds he received from them. His Skull was fractured in 2 Places.'[77] Twaites was not the only one to suffer so. In 1779, one of the Duke of Richmond's grooms, assisting the gamekeepers at Goodwood, was strangled to death by poachers. Two years later, the gamekeeper at Blickling was killed following an affray in the Earl of Buckinghamshire's preserves.[78]

Such incidents should, of course, be kept in perspective. Not all poachers went around shooting and beating gamekeepers; many took game silently and rarely went out in groups of more than three. Nor had brutal assaults been unknown in the countryside before the arrival of game poaching gangs. In January 1671, for example, three men were coursing over John White's farm at Little Workington in Warwickshire. White, being in his barn a threshing, came out to them [and] asked them why they would break down his hedges. Upon this, they called him the son of a whore & fell upon him, knocked him down, and beat him very much. At last his wife saw and came; they fell upon her, flung her down and trod on her . . . and hurt the woman very much.

As a final outrage, they said that 'they would beat White till he would forgive them for what they had done to him'![79] Violence remained a part of rural life in the following century. What was significant about poaching gangs was that violence was part of their *trade*: they depended on it, more than on silence or skill, to protect them from capture. Sometimes, the threat of violence was sufficient. When, for example, a Wiltshire gang raided the Earl of Ailesbury's woods at Burbage in 1787, they first visited the cottage of Robert Blundy, one of his gamekeepers:

the ringleader, after presenting his gun, and threatening to shoot the said Robert Blundy if he offered to interrupt the party in the night's sport, which he declared they came purposely for, and were determined to have, left two of the party as centinels [sic] over the said Blundy for the greatest part of the night, and then, with the others, proceeded to shoot in the same wood.[80]

More often, though, gangs simply employed their weapons to save themselves. On being discovered taking game on a manor near Birmingham, one gang 'stopped, challenged their pursuers, and set them at defiance, calling them to come on, for they were ready'. At Blickling in 1787, a gang of fourteen poachers first threw 'vollies of stones' and then fired their guns at the gamekeeper and his assistants, wounding several. In another affray, a member of an Essex gang was rescued by seven of his comrades, who 'rushed upon the keeper and his men with bludgeons and beat them in so unmerciful a manner' that they were left for dead. When the servants of a Dorset landowner came upon five men shooting pheasants, 'the villains said, d—m you, have at you! when they immediately fired all together, and most dangerously wounded the three servants'.[81]

The response of the game preservers was predictable. 'Nothing but a much superior force would strike any terror into 'em', wrote Lord Bruce's steward, echoing the conventional wisdom on such challenges to rural order,[82] and in the second half of the eighteenth century there was a determined effort to assemble just such a force. Gamekeepers, naturally enough, composed part of it, although it is difficult to identify any large increase in the numbers of gamekeepers in this period, much less to link such an increase to the emergence of poaching gangs.[83] More significant, perhaps, was the deployment of 'watchers' in these years. These were labourers hired, usually at the rate of one shilling per night, 'to watch for poachers' during the hunting season. Payments to them begin to appear in estate accounts in the 1770s, but it was in the following decade that watchers became a common – and, on some estates, a major – expense for game preservers. At Longleat, Lord Weymouth spent an average of £20 a year on watchers in the 1780s; in the autumn of 1786, the Duke of Richmond paid more than £100 for their services.[84] Expenditure on watchers declined in the following decades, but in the early nineteenth century bands of watchers were again very much in evidence. Robert Haldane Bradshaw, a Lancashire M.P., claimed command of 'a little army, who assist my keepers and go out at nights'. Sir Robert Peel had five assistants for every one of his gamekeepers. They and most game preservers seem to have agreed with William Dyott's observation that the preservation of the game was dependent on 'having a force sufficient to awe Poachers'.[85]

But armies, even little ones, were expensive to maintain – and were just as capable of feeling terror as of inspiring it. Some country gentlemen, therefore, deployed man traps and spring guns on their estates instead. The former were pairs of iron jaws with sharp teeth, which when sprung caught and held the leg of their victim. The largest known man trap weighed eighty-eight pounds and had teeth one-and-a-half inches in length. In addition, there were variations on this basic design with evocative names like 'thigh-crushers' and 'body-squeezers'. A spring gun was a gun mounted on pivots and controlled by wires which extended out into the area around it. When one of these wires was pulled, the gun would swing around in the direction of the disturbance and fire its charge.[86] John Mayer thought that man traps and spring guns were 'the best gamekeepers', and it was not difficult to see their attraction.[87] They could be used to guard a preserve with minimal expenditure. Some gentlemen, in fact, did not bother to install them at all, but simply put up notices saying that they had.[88] Perhaps some game preservers also thought that a spring gun would be more trustworthy than a watcher whose nightly wage was only half the amount a poacher could receive for a pheasant.

Spring guns and man traps appear to have been first used to protect game preserves in the late 1770s in East Anglia. Within a few years of the raid on 'Mossims', Lord Walpole had had them installed in his woods, and in the following decade Lord Townshend, Lord Buckinghamshire, Lord Walsingham and a number of lesser landowners followed his lead.[89] Outside of East Anglia, however, the introduction of these devices seems to have come later. To judge from the notices appearing in the *Salisbury Journal*, man traps and spring guns were not used by game preservers in Wiltshire and western Hampshire before the 1790s. Robert Thistlewayte, for example, waited until 1793 before announcing that 'STEEL TRAPS and SPRING GUNS will be set in all the Covers' on his estate, although he had been plagued by poachers for more than a decade.[90] Perhaps this was simply a reflection of the advanced state of game preservation in East Anglia in the eighteenth century, but there were, in fact, good reasons for being cautious about installing such devices. The legal liability of the landowner for injuries inflicted by man traps and spring guns set on his grounds was uncertain. In addition, there was the nature of those injuries to consider. In 1785 a Hampshire gentleman gave this description of what happened when 'thigh-crackers, body-squeezers, spring guns, and man traps' were set in a Suffolk wood frequented by poachers:

> This hardened banditti disregarding the notice that was given of what was prepared for their destruction, ventured in the night, as had been their usual custom, into the wood, where no less than four of them were found in the morning caught in these terrible engines; three had their thighs broke by the crackers and traps, and the fourth was found dead in a body-squeezer . . . I saw the poor wretches immediately after they were taken out of these destructive engines.

It was, he said, 'the most shocking [scene] I ever beheld'.[91]

There was a certain grim irony in using wires and traps to capture poachers, but in fact they do not seem to have been very effective. Poachers gradually learned how to disarm the 'engines'. One gentleman in the early nineteenth century, in fact, was forced to booby-trap his spring gun to prevent its being stolen! As Lord Suffield wryly observed in 1825, 'poachers are almost the only persons who escape being shot by spring guns'.[92] Among those who were injured were several game preservers themselves. 'Archer, the fat & busy attorney of Mildenhall, was wounded in the legs by some of his own [spring] Guns,' Sir Thomas Callum informed his son in 1825, '& is I believe confined to his bed & not likely to recover; & within these few days, the great squire of Bildeston . . . Mr Wilson have [sic] been shot in the legs by one of his own Guns, but how dangerously I have not heard.'[93] In spite of such incidents, many country gentlemen continued to insist that the setting of man traps and spring guns was essential to the preservation of the game. After these devices were

V. Cartoon depicting the dangers of mantraps and spring guns

outlawed in 1827, there were protests, particularly from the less affluent gentry, that they had been left defenceless. 'My fortune,' complained Sir William Bryan Cooke, a Yorkshire baronet, 'does not authorize my keeping up an army of keepers to resist and to meet at all times an army of poachers.' In spite of all evidence to the contrary, he and other country gentlemen continued to believe that the only alternative to spring guns and man traps was the abandonment of game preservation altogether.[94]

The real significance of the setting of man traps and spring guns was actually more symbolic than practical. In one sense, of course, it could be seen as a reflection of the gentry's determination to preserve their game, even if that meant killing a few of their fellow men. Historians who have presented spring guns and man traps in this light, however, tend to overlook the fact that some of those who defended the setting of these 'engines' did so on humanitarian grounds. The leader of the game law reformers, James Stuart-Wortley, for example, opposed the abolition of spring guns, arguing that they 'prevented scenes which would be ten times more fatal than any which could result from [using] them'.[95] However questionable the argument, it contained a kernel of truth: that spring guns and man traps were a reaction to the deadly affrays between poachers and keepers which had become an established part of rural life by the end of the eighteenth century. As another defender of spring guns noted, these 'engines' were of little use against traditional poachers, who as men with an intimate knowledge of the local terrain 'might [still] go into the covers, and kill pheasants, without accident'. Spring guns and man traps could only be 'a protection against large bodies of poachers', who were often strangers to the area in which they were hunting.[96] In another sense, therefore, spring guns and man traps were a reflection of the gentry's fear of poaching gangs – and also of their sense of desperation. A few days before writing to the Home Secretary to appeal that spring guns be made legal once again, William Dyott wrote in his diary: 'If Gangs of Armed Men are to commit depredations close to your Door, & from their numbers to intimidate resistance, it is full time that the Government of the Country took some means to put a stop to these lawless proceedings, prejudicial alike to Individuals as well as [to] Social Order.'[97] Considering its source, Dyott's cry was a particularly poignant one. For well over a century Parliament had been giving him and his fellow J.P.s extraordinary summary powers to deal with poachers. Yet, at the very height of their power, they claimed to be helpless to prevent poaching gangs from operating right on their doorsteps. If the game laws were instruments of 'terrible severity', why were they so ineffective? The answer to this question requires a closer examination of how the game laws were actually enforced.

4

The enforcement of the game laws

The enforcement of the game laws, like the pursuit of wild game, was the prerogative of country gentlemen. As prosecutors, as justices, as grand jurors and as employers of the gamekeepers who appeared as witnesses, the gentry dominated the legal system which determined the poacher's fate. It was, in fact, possible for a gentleman to perform several of these roles at the same time. In one celebrated case in the 1820s, a Hampshire farmer named Richard Deller was convicted by the Duke of Buckingham on the information of the latter's gamekeeper and the testimony of another of his servants – all in the Duke's own drawing room. If he 'uttered one impertinent word', Buckingham warned Deller, 'there was a constable in the room to take him to "gaol or to the stocks" '.[1] Even where the J.P. was not directly interested in a case, the suspicion remained that he was far from impartial. 'There is not a worse constituted tribunal on the face of the earth, not even that of the Turkish cadi,' charged Henry Brougham in 1828, 'than that at which summary convictions on the Game Laws constantly take place; I mean a bench or a brace of sporting justices.'[2] Historians have, on the whole, agreed with Brougham's harsh verdict. Even the sympathetic J.D. Chambers concluded that in their administration of the game laws the gentry 'were undeniably guilty of gross, indeed, tyrannical abuse of power'.[3]

There are, however, some problems with this judgement. The most obvious is that it is based, not on an examination of the evidence, but simply on the accusations of men who were openly hostile to the power and influence of the landed gentry. Brougham's denunciation of 'sporting justices' is quoted in almost every discussion of game law enforcement, but, in fact, there is no reason to think that he knew much more about the activities of J.P.s than he did about those of the Turkish cadi. Deller's case – which was probably the chief inspiration for Brougham's remarks – is a revealing episode, but was it, as one recent historian has claimed, 'typical'?[4] No effort has been made to find out. Instead, it has been assumed that the case must have been typical – principally because of a supposed weakness in the characters of country gentlemen. It was, wrote the Webbs, the gentry's 'overmastering desire to maintain their field sports and protect the amenity of their country seats' which rendered them incapable of administering the law justly. 'In their ardour . . . the Rulers of the County sometimes lost sight of every consideration of personal delicacy and natural justice.'[5] That many justices of the peace were passionately devoted to field sports cannot be denied, but it does not necessarily follow that their enthusiasm was translated into vindictive enforcement of the game laws. Certainly game preservers do not seem to have thought so. When they wanted to 'make an example' of a poacher, they almost always ignored the local magistrate and instead proceeded against the culprit in a higher court.

Summary trial of poachers before a justice of the peace was, in fact, a comparatively late development in the history of the game laws. Although the Game Act of 1671 had allowed individual J.P.s to convict poachers on the oath of one 'credible witness',[6] they do not seem to have exercised this power until the beginning of the eighteenth century. Before then, enforcement of the game laws was primarily in the hands of the quarter sessions.[7] Occasionally, a J.P. would issue a warrant to seize the gun or dog of an unqualified person, but the actual punishment of poachers was usually reserved for the justices' quarterly meetings. When, for example, the Sussex quarter sessions was informed in 1692 that 'John Skinne of Barnham . . . did in the night time take and destroy eight partridges', it ordered that he be apprehended and bound over to appear at its next meeting.[8] The only major exception to this rule seems to have been those cases which were tried at the assizes. Just why some game cases were treated in this manner is unclear since the offences involved do not appear to have been more serious than those which were dealt with at quarter sessions. At the Warwick assizes in 1696, for example, two men were convicted of hunting hares illegally; in 1727 a Sussex man was 'forced to go to the assizes at Lewes for catching partridges'.[9] Perhaps trial at the assizes was an early form of 'making an example'. If so, it is worth noting that gentlemen did not seek to do this by denying the accused a trial by jury, but rather by transferring the case to a higher court where the delays and expense involved could be more painful than the penalty prescribed by law.

After 1700 the enforcement activities of J.P.s 'out of sessions' gradually increased. Justices began to record convictions as well as warrants in their diaries and notebooks. Some, like William Emmett in Kent, heard cases only in the presence of a fellow J.P. Others were less cautious, if not always very enthusiastic about their duties. 'Mr Gayer sent me to Convict Farmer Mason of setting Snares,' wrote one Berkshire J.P. in his diary, 'which I was obliged to do and fined him £5.'[10] By the middle of the century, the transfer of jurisdiction was almost complete. Thereafter, the vast majority of game cases were decided by J.P.s acting singly or with another justice. If, in the late eighteenth and early nineteenth centuries, poachers appeared at quarter sessions, it was because they were charged with night poaching[11] or with a related offence such as assaulting a gamekeeper. As for the assizes, its role in the enforcement of the game laws after mid-century seems to have been confined to hearing the cases of poachers charged with serious assault or homicide.

Over the course of the eighteenth century, then, there was a fundamental alteration in the way poachers were tried. Cases which had previously been heard by a jury at quarter sessions were, by the second half of the century, generally decided by one or two J.P.s. Although this was only part of a much larger redistribution of judicial responsibility taking place at this time,[12] the introduction of a more summary mode of proceeding against poachers obviously suited the convenience of game preservers. Quarter sessions, like any court, had its established rules and procedures which, in the right hands, might be turned to the advantage of the accused. When, for example, Thomas Eves, a Kent victualler, and several other men were indicted in 1739 for poaching and resisting a constable, a concerned gentleman wrote to the Clerk of the Peace to ask for his assistance with the case. 'Mr Franklin of Gravesend is Attorney for the Indicted,' the gentleman explained, '& promises them Success.' Even where acquittal was unlikely, a defendant might still be able to bargain his way out of paying the full penalty.[13] Thus, it is understandable that the gentry did not object when, in the first half of the eighteenth century, an increasing proportion of game cases came to be tried before a court whose rules were few and whose judgements were swift. Gentlemen undoubtedly hoped that poachers would find it more difficult to escape punishment in such a setting. It should be remembered, however, that an individual J.P.'s powers of punishment were limited. Under the game laws he could usually do no more than fine a poacher or, in default of payment, consign him to the house of correction for a few months.[14] For more severe penalties, the game preserver had to look elsewhere: either to quarter sessions or to the courts at Westminster. In either case, that meant exposing himself, as well as the poacher, to the expense and uncertainty of a jury trial. The convenience of summary proceedings, then, had to be weighed against the relative mildness of the penalties imposed. It is worth noting that most country gentlemen opted for convenience.

In the following pages we shall examine the enforcement of the game laws by all these different tribunals. Beginning at the manorial level, we shall outline the gentry's use of their power to seize guns, dogs, nets and other 'engines' from the unqualified. We shall then turn to the quarter sessions' enforcement of the game laws in the late seventeenth and early eighteenth centuries, after which the use of civil suits against poachers will be discussed. Next, we shall look at the summary trial of poachers by justices of the peace and, finally, there will be an examination of the quarter sessions' enforcement of the Night Poaching Acts in the early nineteenth century. It should then be possible to arrive at some conclusions about the treatment of poachers in the century and a half between the passage of the Game Act and its repeal.

II

The game laws, as they developed in the first half century after 1671, were concerned with preventing two things: the hunting of game by unqualified persons and the possession of dogs, nets, guns and other 'engines' by the unqualified. The two offences were obviously related and, in prescribing penalties, the game laws made little distinction between them. Before 1707 both could be punished by a £1 or £2 fine or a month's imprisonment; after 1707 the penalty for either offence was fixed at a £5 fine or three months in prison.[15] In the actual enforcement of these laws, however, there was a great difference between hunting and having the means to hunt. The former was a deliberate act; once performed, all that was required to bring it before the courts was a prosecutor and a 'credible' witness. The crime of illegally possessing a dog or an 'engine' to take game was, on the other hand, more difficult to deal with. The game laws listed various types of dogs and 'engines' which the unqualified were forbidden to possess, but it was not always easy to establish ownership. In addition, the law was less than clear about possession of firearms. Under the Game Act, guns might be seized by the lord of the manor, but subsequent statutes did not say whether an unqualified person could be prosecuted simply for having a flintlock or a pistol in his possession. The authorities were also faced with the problem of how the law should be enforced. Was every house in the kingdom to be searched for greyhounds, lurchers, nets, snares and guns, or should only those suspected of poaching be required to surrender these possessions?

Such questions were of more than passing interest to Englishmen in the late seventeenth century. Memories of the Civil War and the Protectorate were still fresh; indeed, the spectre of arbitrary rule would continue to haunt Englishmen well into the eighteenth century. Their anxiety expressed itself in a variety of ways: in harsh treatment of dissenters, in an anti-Catholicism which sometimes bordered on hysteria – and in the formation of a militia. The purpose of the latter was to make the establishment of a 'standing army' unnecessary, and thus prevent the Crown from acquiring the means to govern without Parliament.[16] In practice, the militia failed to supplant the regular army, but the conviction

persisted in many quarters that English liberty was dependent on the
existence of an armed and vigilant yeomanry. This obviously ran counter
to the spirit of the Game Act, and it was not long before opposition to the
latter was voiced in Parliament on the grounds that it constituted a threat
to the liberties of Englishmen. In 1693 an amendment to the Game Act
was proposed 'to enable every Protestant to keep a musket in his House for
his defence'. Several speakers supported it, arguing that the measure was
necessary for the protection of the new government from Jacobite attack,
but Sir John Lowther accused them of trying 'to arm the mob' and the
amendment was defeated.[17] Opposition to the 'disarming of the people'
continued to be heard in the next century. In 1739, for example, *The
Craftsman* declared that 'it would be better for Us, that there was not a
Pheasant, a *Partridge*, or an *Hare*, in the whole Kingdom, than that they
should be preserv'd at . . . the imminent *Hazard* of our *Liberties*'.[18] Not
everyone agreed with such sentiments, of course, but while the threat of a
foreign invasion or a papist *coup d'état* remained, some gentlemen were
clearly reluctant to enforce all the provisions of the Game Act to their
fullest extent. Indeed, in 1704 the Devon quarter sessions ordered that,
while the houses of unqualified persons should be searched for dogs, nets
and other 'engines', no Protestant was to be deprived of his gun.[19]

The law was less ambiguous and the authorities less hesitant when it
came to dogs, nets and 'engines', but even so, there were factors working
against a wholesale confiscation of these items. Although the evidence is
admittedly incomplete, the records of quarter sessions and of individual
J.P.s strongly suggest that the search-and-seize provisions of the game laws
were invoked only when and where the local gentry demanded it. Few
search warrants appear to have been issued on the magistrates' own
initiative. Usually, they were granted in response to a specific complaint,
and the authority which they conferred was confined to a specific area. In
1675, for example,

> On complaint by the agents of John, Lord Pawlett, that divers
> idle persons in the hundreds of Crewkerne, Houndsborowe,
> Coker, Southpertherton, and Kingbury East [all in Somerset]
> keep dogs, nets and engines to destroy gentleman's game,
> having no estates to justify their doing so; the Court [of
> quarter sessions] orders that Lord Pawlett, or any servant or
> agent appointed by him, do forthwith seize and destroy all
> such dogs, nets and engines.[20]

The issuing of a warrant did not, of course, guarantee that these items
would in fact be seized. 'Before any warrant Can be had from any
Justice of ye Peace,' complained some Yorkshire magistrates in 1718,
'. . . The Parties offending Convey [the dogs, nets and 'engines'] to

such obscure places That there can nothing be found Against them.'[21] Still, a warrant was necessary, since the courts were unwilling to sanction the confiscation of private property without one. In the early eighteenth century, therefore, it became the practice in some counties to issue general warrants for the seizure of any gun, dog, net or 'engine' kept by an unqualified person. In the North Riding of Yorkshire, this practice led to the creation of an office of county gamekeeper (also called a 'General Searcher'), who had the authority to seize guns, dogs and nets from the unqualified. He was paid between £4 and £10 a year, and in the 1720s there were often two such country gamekeepers employed by the North Riding quarter sessions.[22] How much more effective they were than their privately employed counterparts it is impossible to say, but the Yorkshire justices' periodic threats throughout this period to prosecute those who continued to keep guns, dogs, nets and 'engines' in defiance of the game laws would suggest that neither kind of gamekeeper was very effective in keeping the unqualified from possessing the means to hunt.[23]

There is, in particular, little evidence that Englishmen as a whole were 'disarmed' by the game laws. Some undoubtedly had their guns taken from them; others may have been forced to hide theirs temporarily. But the fears of *The Craftsman* and others are belied by the large proportion of game cases heard by the quarter sessions in this period which involved the use of firearms. They are belied as well by the known popularity of shooting matches at this time and by the openness with which unqualified men acknowledged their possession of firearms. When, for example, Ralph Willis, an Oxfordshire labourer ('very poore havinge a wife and six small Children to maintaine'), applied to the quarter sessions in 1687 for relief, he apparently saw no reason to lie about the cause of his distress: 'in discharging of a gunne your Petitioner hath lost his thumbe'.[24] Indeed, given the haphazard system of law enforcement which existed in the late seventeenth and early eighteenth centuries, disarmament of the population was a remote possibility at best. It became an impossibility after 1739, when the courts decided that possession of a gun by an unqualified person was not in itself an offence against the game laws, unless it could be proven that the gun had been used to kill game.[25] The law still permitted the authorities to seize guns, and some continued to do so. 'Met Mr Wyndham at Mr St Johns on Acc[oun]t of Guns taken there', Richard Lee, a Berkshire J.P., wrote in his diary in 1743; 'gave Bullet Gun & Bullets & 12 wires to Mr St John, br[ough]t one Gun home'.[26] But without the prospect of profiting from a criminal prosecution, gamekeepers had little incentive to inform on those who illegally kept guns. Instead they waited for more lucrative opportunities to enforce the game laws. After the middle of the eighteenth century, the summary seizure of guns became increasingly rare.

But if a man's gun was relatively safe, his dog was not. Country gentlemen did not see the keeping of setters, lurchers and greyhounds as necessary for the defence of English liberty. On the contrary, the dogs kept by farmers, labourers and tradesmen were regarded as a standing threat to the gentry's game. Among the 'lower orders', thought Robert Buxton, a Norfolk squire, 'dogs were only . . . useful to poachers . . . no industrious man would wish to keep a dog'.[27] Industrious or not, many unqualified men did keep dogs and were very unwilling to part with them, for sentimental as well as economic reasons. Just after the Game Act of 1671 became law, for instance, young Thomas Isham recorded in his diary that a man had 'threatened to kill Mr Saunders [a local J.P.] for taking his dog from him'.[28] Others contemplated less dramatic forms of revenge. 'Sir John Bridgeman took two greyhounds from [some] Birmingham men', Lady Aylesford reported to her husband in a letter, 'and they were so civil [as] to send [to] Sir John to restore them or they would course in his garden, upon which he hanged the dogs'.[29] Sir John's reaction was not unique. In 1725, for instance, the Earl of Cardigan ordered that every dog on one of his Northamptonshire manors be destroyed. Later in the century, the Duke of Devonshire issued a similar decree for his estate in Yorkshire. 'I have . . . given Notice to the Duke's Tenants', wrote his steward in 1778, that 'if any of them keep any Dogs that destroy Game, unless they dispose of them immediately, I have ordered the Keeper at Londesborough to shoot them'.[30] Not all gentlemen, of course, resorted to such sweeping measures; most, indeed, probably limited themselves to occasionally destroying the dogs of 'notorious' poachers.[31] Nevertheless, the century following the passage of the Game Act of 1671 was a particularly hazardous one for dogs unlucky enough to have unqualified masters.

By the late eighteenth century, however, many observers had come to the conclusion that the summary execution of dogs was not a very effective way of preventing poaching. They agreed that 'being allowed to keep Dogs is what seduces so many young Labourers and Artisans to engage in the Business of Poaching', but pointed out that the law prohibiting the unqualified from owning sporting dogs was in danger of becoming 'a dead Letter', because 'when even the poorest Houses contain several Dogs, it is impossible to establish the Fact of Ownership'. As a remedy, they suggested that every dog, whatever the status of his owner, be subject to a tax. This would have the laudable effect of discouraging the poor from keeping dogs, while, at the same time, raising revenue which could be used to offset the escalating poor rates.[32] Something like this had been proposed as early as 1735, but it was not until the second half of the eighteenth century that the idea began to receive serious attention in the press and in Parliament. A bill to enact 'this reasonable and equitable Tax' was first introduced in 1755, supported by over a dozen petitions from farmers and freeholders in various parts of the country. It was defeated, however, as was another attempt in 1776.[33] 'Oh, for a dog tax,' moaned John Byng fifteen years later, 'and yet its first unpopularity will prevent what every one wishes!'[34] In 1796, in response to another flood of petitions as well as the financial demands of the war with France, the government of William Pitt finally persuaded Parliament to accept a tax on dogs. The duty, at first, was a modest one (five shillings on sporting dogs and three shillings on others), but by the end of the war it had risen to almost three times its initial level. In one case, the increase was even greater: after 1812 every greyhound was subject to an annual tax of £1.[35]

For those who hoped that it would reduce both poaching and the poor rates, the dog tax proved to be a disappointment. The revenue which it produced – £145,000 in 1816 – was used instead to meet the costs of the war; moreover, the poor (at William Pitt's insistence) were exempted from most of the tax.[36] The government had wanted a tax on 'luxury', not a new game law, and that it what it got. Nevertheless, the agitation for a dog tax was significant. It acknowledged the ineffectiveness of the search-and-seize provisions of the Game Act. More importantly, perhaps, it offered an alternative to the heavy-handed paternalism to which those provisions were a monument. The Game Act had split society into two sections – the qualified and the unqualified – and had given the former the power to supervise the activities and possessions of the latter. The advocates of a dog tax argued that such a division was unnecessary: poachers could, they felt, be deterred more effectively by the promptings of their own self-interest. 'If the Instruments of Poaching were rendered more expensive, or, in other Words, [if poachers] were compelled to pay for their Dogs,' reasoned one petition to Parliament in 1791, 'they might be reclaimed to the Habits of Industry.'[37] The argument was not a new one: Pitt had used it several years earlier when defending the introduction of game licences. Nor was it necessarily correct. William Windham was not alone in thinking that 'if a poacher wanted a dog . . . he could afford to pay for it'.[38] But to many in the age of Smith and Bentham, the argument was appealing, and as they embraced the dog tax the paternalistic controls of the Game Act fell into disuse. After 1800 or so, the seizure of dogs seems to have been largely confined to the cases of those who had already been caught poaching.[39] Instead of taking every man's dog away from him, the gentry looked increasingly to the courts to punish those who actually used their dogs – or guns, or nets – to take game.

III

Until the second quarter of the eighteenth century, most game cases were tried at quarter sessions. These, in theory, were meetings of all the J.P.s for a county, but attendance always fell short of that ideal, particularly in the larger counties. Even if every justice had attended, the assembly would not have necessarily included every man of wealth, rank and influence in the county, for the commission of the peace in the late seventeenth and early eighteenth centuries was subject to periodic purges. The most drastic of these occurred in the 1680s, when Charles II and James II removed almost every J.P. opposed to their policies, but well into the next century the commission continued to reflect changes in the balance of power at Court and in Parliament. The purge of the Tories from the bench in 1715 was executed just as vigorously as that of the Whigs in the 1680s.[40] These sudden shifts in the composition of the bench could affect the administration of justice, for although the J.P.s did not directly decide whether a person should be indicted or convicted – those decisions were made by grand and petty juries composed of lesser freeholders – they did have considerable influence over how strictly the laws were enforced. It was the J.P.s for instance, who decided what punishment should be inflicted on the convicted offender. The laws prescribed the maximum penalty which could be imposed, but the quarter sessions had the power to mitigate this and often did so. Even more important, perhaps, was the justices' power to initiate prosecutions. Ordinarily this was left to the individual citizen, but occasionally the quarter sessions would order the constables to present the names of all those in their parish or hundred who violated a certain law or set of laws. The result, needless to say, was the prosecution of persons who would have otherwise escaped the notice of the court. At various times during this period the J.P.s used this device to combat such social evils as Catholicism and gambling.

The extent to which violators of the game laws were prosecuted and punished in the half century following passage of the Game Act of 1671 is difficult to determine. The surviving records of quarter sessions vary enormously in quality, and even in the best of them there are ambiguities which conspire against attempts at statistical analysis.[41] Nevertheless, an examination of quarter sessions records for four counties, supplemented by information from three others,[42] suggests that there was a common pattern to game law enforcement during this period. To judge by this evidence, passage of the Game Act was not followed by an immediate increase in the number of game cases heard at quarter sessions. Only in the late 1670s and early 1680s did prosecutions begin to increase. In Warwickshire, for example, there were rarely more than two prosecutions a year under the game laws in the 1670s, but in 1681 thirteen persons were presented for game offences, and in the following year the number climbed to nineteen.[43] The same type of increase can be found at this time in the North Riding and, a little later, in Hertfordshire and Buckinghamshire. In none of these counties, however, was it a sustained increase. On the contrary, after a few years the number of prosecutions declined to a level equal to, or even below, that of the 1670s. In the 1690s, the quarter sessions of these counties appear to have heard, on average, one game case a year, and after the beginning of the next century, there seems to have been a further decline. By the late 1730s, few if any violators of the game laws were prosecuted at quarter sessions.

The eventual disappearance of game cases from the quarter sessions' docket was, of course, primarily due to the transfer of jurisdiction over these cases to J.P.s 'out of sessions', but this in no way helps to explain the curious pattern of enforcement in the late seventeenth century, particularly the sudden but short-lived surge in prosecutions in the 1680s. This surge may, of course, have been nothing more than a reflection of the incidence of poaching in the countryside, but there is good reason to suspect that it was actually created by the justices themselves. As we have already noted, the quarter sessions had it within their power to promote the prosecution of certain types of offenders, and there is evidence that this power was used against violators of the game laws. In the autumn of 1687, for example, constables in Oxfordshire were ordered by the justices to report the names of all those who violated the game laws in their respective divisions. At the next quarter sessions, sixteen men were presented, most of them for nothing more than keeping – or being suspected of keeping – dogs, guns or nets to take game. This was in sharp contrast to the previous four sessions when no presentments for game offences had been made.[44] In Warwickshire, there is no evidence of a direct order from the bench, but the character of the prosecutions suggests that they were abnormal. More than three quarters of those presented in both 1681 and 1682 came from Birmingham, and without exception they were charged, not with actually taking game, but simply with keeping dogs in defiance of the Game Act. A similar concentration on crimes of unlawful 'possession' can be seen in the cases heard by the North Riding quarter sessions at this time.[45] In some counties, the justices' attitude was also reflected in the penalties they imposed. Although the law prescribed a forty shilling fine for illegal possession of dogs or nets, most convicted offenders in the late seventeenth century were ordered to pay only a fraction of that amount – at most no more than five shillings. In Buckinghamshire, however, the justices departed from this practice on several occasions in the 1680s. In 1686 and again in 1689, certain offenders were fined twenty shillings for keeping dogs, nets and other 'engines' to take game; in another case, a poacher was fined twenty 'nobles' (£6 13s. 4d.) and imprisoned until he could pay it.[46] During the same decade, the Warwickshire quarter sessions ordered several offenders to pay amounts ranging from ten to thirty shillings.[47] Although such fines were exceptional, they lend support to the view that in the 1680s J.P.s were suddenly much more intent on enforcing the game laws than they had been previously – or would be in the succeeding decades.

Why should this have been so? No obvious explanation presents itself, but it seems possible that the sharp increase in the number of prosecutions for game offences was related to the purge of Whigs from the commission of the peace in the wake of the Exclusion Crisis. There was not, of course, an identifiably Tory (or Whig) attitude toward the game laws. On the whole, the gentry in the late seventeenth century seem to have been united in the belief that field sports were inappropriate, and even harmful, diversions for the lower classes. Nevertheless, a sudden preponderance of Tory squires could have affected the enforcement of the game laws. For example, the Tories might have been tempted to use the game laws as a means of harassing their political enemies. It was, perhaps, more than sheer coincidence that in Warwickshire most of those presented for possessing dogs came from Birmingham, whose relative freedom from the constraints of the Clarendon Code had made it a haven for dissenters. It might also be noted that among those fined for keeping dogs, was a Birmingham gentleman named Henry Matthewes, who eventually became a J.P. himself – after the Revolution of 1688 had once more made the bench safe for Whigs.[48] But more important than partisan rancour, perhaps, was the Tories' passion for social order. For men whose overriding concern was to prevent a repetition of the 1640s, the Exclusion Crisis – with its direct challenge to the royal prerogative, played out amid scenes of popular hysteria and mob violence – must have been a frightening experience. Little wonder that they should seek to remind the lower orders and the urban bourgeoisie of the superior position of the landed gentry in English society. And what better instrument for this was there than the game laws, under whose provisions the mere possession of a sporting dog could be conveniently turned into a punishable offence?

Like the laws against forestalling and regrating, the game laws in the late seventeenth and early eighteenth centuries seem to have been vigorously invoked only when events forced the authorities to assert the values of a paternalistic social order. When pressure of this kind was missing, enforcement was left to individual country gentlemen, and to judge by the number of cases appearing before quarter sessions, they do not appear to have been very active in this period. But as game preservation came to be practised more intensively around the middle of the eighteenth century, gentlemen started to show a greater interest in enforcing the game laws. This can be seen not only in the increasing number of informations which their gamekeepers began to lay before J.P.s after mid-century, but also in their use of several alternative methods of enforcement, most notably the civil prosecution of poachers.

IV

By the middle of the eighteenth century, the transfer of jurisdiction over game cases had been completed. The formalities and delays of a trial at quarter sessions were replaced by a summary hearing before one or two J.P.s who, on the oath of one 'credible' witness, had the power to imprison an offender for three months if the latter could not pay the fine imposed by the court. The procedure was fast, simple and relatively cheap. It is hardly surprising, therefore, that after 1750 most offenders were prosecuted in this manner. But there were some poachers who did not end up in a J.P.'s parlour. They were, instead, proceeded against in a variety of other ways, all of them legal, if not necessarily just. Before the significance of summary conviction of poachers can be understood, it is necessary to consider these alternatives.

The aim of all game preservers was to keep poachers from poaching, and the basic premise of the game laws was that this could be done by inflicting a sufficiently severe punishment. In the view of more than a few country gentlemen, however, the best way to stop poaching on their estates was to expel known poachers to other parts of the kingdom – or, better still, to other parts of the planet. In attempting to do this, they were aided by the Settlement Act of 1662, which permitted local authorities to 'remove' poor persons from a parish if they had not established legal residence there. Some suspected poachers were vulnerable on this point. 'Remov'd W. Harvey the Poacher', ran one entry in Sir Roger Newdigate's diary, and there were undoubtedly removals by other J.P.s which were less candidly recorded. It seems unlikely, however, that the authorities in Harvey's new home were very happy about this use of the poor laws. Certainly the Rev. Patrick St Clair was not when, in 1739, his Norfolk parish was ordered to receive a new parishioner. 'If the fellow had been a working man, we [would have] not appealed [the order],' St Clair explained, 'but he is thievish, and lazy, and always out a nights a poaching, which makes me desirous to get rid of him.'[49] 'Removal', in short, was a double-edged sword: the parish which 'got rid of' one poacher might soon find itself the recipient of another. It was, perhaps, for this reason that some game preservers sought instead to have their poachers impressed into the armed forces.

The impressment of the able-bodied and the unlucky into the navy had been going on since the Middle Ages, but the pressing of men into the army was of more recent origin. It was first authorised by Parliament during the War of the Spanish Succession, when J.P.s were told to hand over men without 'any lawful calling or employment or visible means for their livelyhood' to the local recruiting party.[50] Wars later in the eighteenth century produced similar opportunities to get rid of poachers. During the invasion scare of 1779, for instance, it was reported that orders had been issued to apprehend 'all idle young fellows (as well 'prentices, journeymen, lawyers clerks &c. not qualified) who shall be found with dogs, nets. &c'. Assurances were given that everyone reporting the names of such persons to the nearest recruiting party 'will be handsomely rewarded . . . and [have] their names concealed'.[51] To what extent game preservers availed themselves of press gangs and recruiting parties is, of course, difficult to say, but estate records do reveal occasional instances. In 1756, for example, Lord Weymouth reimbursed a certain John Francis for the latter's expenses 'in searching for George Eyres for poaching and having him impress'd for a Soldier'. Two decades later, John Grimston, a Yorkshire J.P., was asked to help get rid of William and Thomas Burton, both of whom were 'suppos'd to live by killing Game'. 'One of the Brothers,' wrote a neighbouring game preserver, 'has declar'd that in Spite of me He will kill a hare when he can – would not a Reccommendation from You to the Capt[ain] of the press Gang at Hull, put those young men in a way of beccoming usefull subjects?'[52]

How often letters of this sort were written – or acted on – one can only guess, but it should be remembered that the vulnerability of poachers to impressment varied considerably. The activities of recruiting parties and press gangs were limited to times of war, and, until the end of the eighteenth century, naval impressment was largely confined to the coastal areas of the kingdom. It was, indeed, only during the Napoleonic wars that the impact of impressment seems to have been widely felt. Under the Quota Acts of 1795, inland counties as well as coastal ones were required to provide men for the fleet. Every county was given a quota – Yorkshire's was 1081, Rutland's 23 and so on – and these were filled in the time-honoured manner. Vagrants, felons and other undesired characters were alternately bribed and bullied into enlisting; among these there were undoubtedly some poachers. As a contemporary critic wrote,

> For his Majesty's Service, we'll press
>   The Felon who steals but a Hare;
> For his Brats, the whole *Parish* assess:
>   All poachers and Anglers, *beware*.[53]

With the defeat of Napoleon in 1815, however, the danger of impressment virtually disappeared. Voluntary enlistment proved sufficient to meet the needs of a much-reduced military establishment after the war, and, in some quarters at least, this was a matter of regret. 'The punishment of compulsory service on board a man-of-war,' claimed one Dorset gentleman in 1825,

> was ever that which most terrified a poacher in his contem-
> plations, and most subdued him when it was inflicted; it forced
> him into Habits of laborious and regular activity, and from the
> wild haunts and licentious liberty, and evil society in which he had
> delighted . . . he could not then, as now, reappear after the
> absence of a few months, to boast of manly constancy in a well
> regulated gaol, or [of] his fortitude under prison allowances . . .
> The Example of one sent to sea . . . effected more toward the
> discouragement of crime, than twenty instances of commitments
> to gaols or to houses of correction.

Peace, he regretfully concluded, had greatly inhibited the ability of magistrates 'to dispose suitably' of those who preyed on the gentry's game.[54]

Both 'removal' and impressment of poachers, then, were of only limited value to game preservers. Most eighteenth-century poachers were simply not vulnerable to such proceedings: either they had established legal residence, or they were beyond the reach of the press gang, or they poached during peacetime. Every poacher after 1722, however, was vulnerable to another type of proceeding: civil prosecution. Under an act passed in that year, game preservers could choose between two ways of prosecuting an offender against the game laws. They could (as before) lay an information before the local J.P. and, upon conviction of the accused, collect half the fine, or they could sue for their portion of the fine in a court of record (usually King's Bench or Exchequer) and, if successful, recover not only half of the fine but double the costs of prosecution as well.[55] The Act of 1722 may have been intended as a rebuke to the quarter sessions, whose fines, as we have already noted, tended to be well below the amounts prescribed by law. Certainly the Act was an invitation to game preservers to inflict ruinous financial penalties – and possibly a spell in a debtors' prison – on poachers. The costs of prosecution alone would have been enough to impoverish most defendants: one (admittedly hostile) observer estimated in 1753 that these costs ranged from £50 to £80. And, if that was not sufficient, the plaintiff was permitted to sue for half of *several* fines. In 1736, for example, an unqualified man was charged with two separate instances of using a gun to kill game, as well as with exposing six hares for sale. At £5 per offence, the plaintiff was able to sue for half of £40. It was, perhaps, fitting that the defendant in this case was an attorney.[56]

The option of civil prosecution was open to anyone who wished to enforce the game laws, but it seems that game associations, rather than individual preservers, most actively availed themselves of it. The reason for this is not hard to fathom. The same element of expense which made civil prosecution such a powerful weapon against the poacher also made it a dangerous one for the plaintiff, for if the suit was unsuccessful the financial burden became his own. The Act of 1722 went to some pains to prevent cases being thrown out on technical grounds, but civil suits were decided by juries and they continued to exercise their own very independent judgement. One jury, for example, chose to believe Nathaniel Mayhew, a Norfolk farmer, when he denied killing a hare, saying that, on the contrary, 'it was only a Coney that sat under a Turnip, which he knock'd on the Head with his Walking Stick'. In 1786 an Oxford jury not only awarded Alexander Willis treble costs following his acquittal on a charge of hunting without a licence, but also let him off lightly when he was convicted of assaulting his accuser, Robert Smith. 'The Jury,' it was reported, '. . . not thinking Mr Willis had done more than the ungentleman-like conduct of Mr Smith justified, gave only 20s. damages, and each party [was ordered] to pay their own costs.'[57] The risk of receiving decisions of this sort probably would have discouraged many country gentlemen from engaging in civil prosecution of poachers had it not been for the establishment of game associations to help absorb the costs.

Game associations were first formed in the 1740s. In 1742, for instance, eight gentlemen in the Peak district of Derbyshire subscribed a guinea each for 'the more Effectual Execution of the several Acts of Parliament for the preservation of Game, and for Defraying the Expence of Prosecutions'. Later in the decade, similar associations were formed in Yorkshire, Nottinghamshire, Herefordshire, Kent and undoubtedly in other counties as well.[58] A national Game Association was founded in 1752, with the support of several hundred landowners from every part of the kingdom. As was noted in the previous chapter, the national Association's principal target was the illicit trade in game which flourished in the poultry markets of London and Westminster, but in the first few years of its existence it also subsidised a number of prosecutions in the provinces. In 1755, for example, it helped prosecute a Wiltshire labourer for killing a hare and a Somerset tailor for using nets to take game. In other years it assisted plaintiffs in Essex, Suffolk, Hampshire, Bedfordshire and Dorset. For reasons which have been discussed already, the national Association was unable to sustain this level of activity after the 1750s, and in the latter half of the century civil prosecution of poachers was once again taken up by local associations of game preservers.[59] These, however, tended to lead a somewhat fitful existence. In Wiltshire, game associations were formed in 1765, 1782 and 1787, but none of them seems to have lasted for more than a year.[60] The Norfolk game association was launched at the summer assizes in 1788 with an initial subscription of almost £1200. Yet, within twenty years, game preservers in that county were once again consulting one another about forming an association 'for the punishment of offenders against the Game Laws'.[61] The reasons for this instability remain obscure. It may be that some associations were never meant to be permanent; others, perhaps, were simply unable to maintain the necessary level of subscriptions after the first prosecutions had removed the immediate threat to the preserves. There may also have been a suspicion among the lesser gentry that the associations tended to benefit large landowners more than gentlemen with only one or two manors to protect. Whatever the reason, the fact remains that, even in major sporting counties like Wiltshire and Norfolk, there was no permanent organisation which could help absorb the costs of civil prosecution. As a result, the number of suits initiated against poachers was probably not very large.[62]

It would be a mistake, however, to conclude from this that the impact of civil prosecution on the enforcement of the game laws was slight. For what mattered to the poacher was that he *could* be prosecuted in this way. At times, the mere threat of a suit was enough to make men literally beg to have their cases brought before a justice of the peace. In 1813, for example, three Bedfordshire poachers petitioned Lord Ongley 'to have the Goodness only to prosecute them before a Magistrate'. 'If you are so good as to let them off without a prosecution in the [Court of] Exch[eque]r,' he was assured, 'they must think themselves very mildly treated.'[63] Five years later, a Yorkshire J.P., Benjamin Newton, noted in his diary: 'Convicted Rainforth of Rainton of killing a hare this morning on his own confession. I expect he caused the information to be laid to avoid being exchequered by Mr. Ramsden.'[64] Perhaps these men were unaware that there was not 'a worse constituted tribunal on the face of the earth, not even that of the Turkish cadi' than a sporting justice in his parlour. More likely, they simply preferred a possible £5 fine to the economic consequences of a civil suit. Just what those consequences could be is illustrated by the case of Hugh Lloyd, a Bedfordshire publican who also acted as Lord St John's gamekeeper.[65] In January 1758 Lloyd had agreed to supply secretly Thomas Whitehead, a local waggoner, with some of his master's game at the rate of 2s. 6d. a head. Several months later, Whitehead was caught 'disposing' of the game in London, and soon after that, Lloyd found himself the defendant in a civil suit brought by the Game Association. As 'Soon as My Misfortune was known,' he told the Association's solicitor,

> my Brewer came upon me for a much larger dep[osi]t than I was able to pay and forc'd me to grant him a Bill of Sale; and other

> Creditors stand open Mouth'd to dev[ou]r me . . . Alas I and
> my poor Children are already Ruined for ever, Six of them
> Crying Round me now with broken Hearts at the thought of
> having their poor Father drag'd from them and Buried a live
> in a Gaol . . . I am so weak allready the Goal will soon kill me;
> for God's sake, for my poor Childrens, Sir, lett me Beg on my
> bare knees for Mercy.[66]

For the man of modest means, the mere fact of a civil suit was a disaster,
regardless of the final verdict. He was likely to agree to anything in order to
escape it, and since game preservers were also anxious to avoid the
expense of litigation, civil suits were often resolved long before they
reached the courtroom.

The principal mode of accommodation in these cases was a bond
requiring the accused not to offend against the plaintiff in the future,
under pain of forfeiting a specified sum of money – usually £10 or £20, but
occasionally as much as £50. Such agreements were, of course, a common
element in many legal proceedings and, indeed, they had been used in
game cases long before passage of the Act of 1722. In 1668, for example,
three nets were found in the house of William Taler in Warwickshire. Taler
was taken before a local J.P., but 'beeing a poore man & haveing a great
Charge of Children a begging hard', he prevailed on his prosecutor 'to
take sureties of him and not send him to the Goayle'. Similarly, in 1698
Richard Hill, a Staffordshire tow-dresser who had been caught shooting in
the woods of Sir Thomas Giffard, 'made his humble Submission' and
bound himself for £10 not to kill game on Giffard's land in the future.[67]
After the introduction of civil prosecution of poachers, bonds of this sort
became more common. By using them, gentlemen could protect their
game and poachers could escape prosecution, all at relatively little cost to
themselves. Admittedly, in return for having the prosecution against him
dropped, a defendant was sometimes obliged to fulfil conditions which
went beyond the mere promise not to poach on the plaintiff's land in the
future. In 1768, for instance, Richard Bagshaw, a Derbyshire squire,
agreed to drop his suit against a barber who had been frequently found
poaching on his land, but only if the latter would pay all of Bagshaw's costs
as well as a compensation fee of one guinea. Other preservers required
poachers to pledge that they would inform on their colleagues in the trade,
and game associations usually insisted on a public acknowledgement by
the accused of his own guilt and their own 'lenity'.[68] How effective these
bonds actually were in deterring poachers it is difficult to say, but some
gentlemen at least seem to have been sceptical: they granted them only on
condition that the poacher not appear in the neighbourhood again.[69]

Such, then, were the alternative ways which game preservers had of
proceeding against poachers. These ranged from the sudden removal of

the poacher from his home to the threat of financial ruin, but they had two characteristics in common. First, they all involved penalties which were much more severe than those prescribed by the game laws (at least up to 1800). Second, due to a variety of factors, gentlemen were unable to impose these penalties very often or on a very large scale. 'Removal', impressment and civil prosecution were, in short, suitable only for special cases – for 'making an example' of a certain poacher, not for punishing large numbers of them. This was clearly recognised at the time. It was necessary 'to discriminate', wrote one defender of the game laws in 1796, 'between the unwary or seduced offender commencing his unprofitable career, and the hardy, continued villain, long and fatally . . . enured to the practice of Idleness and dissipation'. The option of civil prosecution, he continued, gave gentlemen 'a power to make a severe example . . . of the latter, with the hope of deterring the former'.[70] However piously clothed, the power to single poachers out for unusually harsh punishment was obviously open to abuse and injustice, particularly when the urge to make an 'example' began to cloud the distinction between the novice poacher and a 'villain'.[71] Little wonder, then, that some poachers considered themselves lucky when they were summoned before a justice of the peace.

V

Aside from recounting the ordeal of Richard Deller at the hands of the Duke of Buckingham, historians have had very little to say about the summary trial of poachers before J.P.s. This is due, at least in part, to the fact that the surviving evidence makes it very difficult to generalise about these proceedings. Before 1770, J.P.s were not required to record the cases which they heard 'out of sessions', and even after that date their legal obligation to do so extended only to cases involving the Night Poaching and Game Duty Acts – and then only if there had been a conviction. Fortunately, some J.P.s reported convictions under other game acts, both before and after 1770, but for most counties only a small proportion of these returns have survived. Even in Wiltshire, where over a thousand conviction certificates from the eighteenth and early nineteenth centuries have been preserved, the evidence is incomplete. For those known to have been imprisoned for game offences in Wiltshire between 1750 and 1800, for example, slightly less than 30 per cent of the conviction certificates can be found.[72] Thus, it is difficult to state even the number of summary convictions under the game laws during this period, much less how many persons were actually tried. In light of these difficulties, Deller's case has an appealing concreteness to it. Perhaps more influential in moulding historians' judgements, however, has been the assumption that the summary trial of a poacher by a country gentleman *must* have been a

VI. Poachers before the magistrates

mockery of justice, since the court had a natural bias against the defendant, who, in any case, was probably too poor and too frightened to defend himself adequately. To some extent, this is a reasonable assumption and, indeed, there is evidence to suggest that Deller's plight was not unique. In 1769, for instance, Robert Barfoot, another Hampshire farmer, was charged with possessing a brace of hares and tried 'before some gentlemen . . . assembled at the house of Mr. H— (where there is a monthly meeting held for the preservation of the game)'. Not surprisingly, he was convicted and fined £10. In another case, a Staffordshire man and his lawyer were forcibly excluded from the room where his case was being tried.[73] It should be pointed out, however, that not all summary trials moved with the iron efficiency of a kangaroo court. Some defendants were acquitted, while others – Robert Barfoot, for example – successfully appealed their convictions. There is, in fact, good reason to think that poachers were far from helpless when summoned before the local J.P. on a charge of having violated the game laws.

Not the least of the weapons which poachers could, and did, use for their protection was the law itself. While the statutes required little of the J.P. except that he be satisfied as to the truth of the testimony given against the defendant, the courts were more exacting. J.P.s were obliged 'to shew the regularity of their convictions',[74] and the massive summaries of case law which filled each new edition of Burn's *Justice of the Peace* were a tribute to the importance which magistrates attached to this obligation. With their decisions open to challenge on technical as well as on substantive grounds, some J.P.s came to learn the virtues of caution. A stranger found shooting and taken before a justice had little to worry about, one observer complained in 1772: 'the justice inquires what his qualification is, and where it lies; he is told no answer will be given to those questions: that if he convicts, he does it at his own peril. The justice is alarmed, and probably dismisses him.'[75] Those J.P.s who refused to be intimidated ran the risk of being prosecuted themselves. A faulty warrant (or a hostile jury) could be the cause, not only of some embarrassment, but of substantial financial loss as well. In defending themselves against a series of appeals and countersuits, the justices and constables in one case in the North Riding in the 1820s accumulated legal costs in excess of £750.[76] While in most cases the stakes were less grand, it seems likely that 'threats of further proceedings' could have a sobering effect on a J.P.'s enforcement of the game laws.

Just how much sobering was needed depended, of course, on the character of the justice himself. Some J.P.s were passionate game preservers; others were sensitive to the wishes of neighbouring sportsmen. The latter, indeed, may have been particularly harsh judges. 'We have found in Mr Vilett a very useful Magistrate', Lord Ailesbury's steward reported in 1777, following a spate of game convictions. Similarly, in 1824 a Westmorland steward urged his master to send a haunch of venison to Mr Wilson of Abott Hall, since the latter had always been 'very alert and anxious to do you service in his Majesterial capacity against Poachers, trespassers, &c'.[77] Not all J.P.s, however, fitted this description. The Duke of Portland, for example, balked at convicting some Yorkshire poachers twice for the same offence, and the case had to be transferred to another justice 'who was not so scrupulous'.[78] Other J.P.s were notably reluctant to hear cases in which they had a personal interest. The Rev. Benjamin Newton, for instance, refused to try three men accused of poaching because one of them was a parishioner, and other magistrates exhibited a similar concern for the appearance of impartiality. In 1675 the Earl of Bridgwater transferred a game case to another J.P. 'by reason [that] hee is the party injured, and will not be judge in his owne cause'.[79] His scruples were shared by Lord Ailesbury, who remarked to Lord Hardwicke in 1743 that 'it would be improper [for me] . . . to be trying my own causes'.[80] In another case which challenges the stereotype of the justice of the peace in this period, several Essex magistrates adjourned a trial in order to plead that the prosecution be dropped. 'Tho' . . . the evidence . . . would warrant a conviction,' they wrote to the prosecutor, 'still there is such an absence of any aggravating circumstances & such a want of decided Poaching intentions . . . that the Magistrates thought it best to set before you these particular circumstances in [the defendant's] favour.'[81] There were, then, at least some J.P.s who were not solely motivated by self- or class-interest. Considerations of propriety, justice and even mercy also entered into their judgements – if not when determining a man's guilt, then when deciding how he should be punished.

Like the quarter sessions before them, J.P.s had the power to impose penalties which were substantially lower than those prescribed by law; this power was not ignored when they enforced the game laws. It was, for instance, common practice for J.P.s in the eighteenth century to mitigate the fines of first offenders against the Night Poaching and Game Duty Acts. In the case of one Wiltshire J.P., over 60 per cent of those whom he convicted under these Acts had their fines reduced by half.[82] Relief for those convicted under other acts seems to have been less common, perhaps because prosecution under the older, less severe game code was itself considered to be a type of mitigation. Nevertheless, J.P.s were occasionally persuaded to ease the burden of a conviction under the 'old game code'. In 1732 Joseph Quested of Saltwood in Kent was brought before James Brockman, the local J.P., on a charge of setting snares. 'I order'd him to pay 20/–,' recorded Brockman in his diary, 'but he promising not to be guilty of ye like again, I took but 15/–.' Similarly, George Parfrement, a Norfolk carpenter found with six pheasants in his possession, had his fine reduced from £30 to £21, 'out of Compassion to [his] Wife & Family, – she bearing a most excellent Character, having four small Children, & being advanced in Pregnancy'.[83] 'Compassion' in this and other cases may have been spurred by the prospect of having a large and growing family thrown on parish relief, but that does not alter the fact that J.P.s did not always inflict the full penalty prescribed by statute. Leniency, indeed, was considered to be a crucial element in the enforcement of the game laws. Many, perhaps most, country gentlemen would have agreed with the Yorkshire game preserver who thought that the game laws should be 'instruments of frightening, not hurting' poachers and who, therefore, hoped that the justice in his neighbourhood would continue to 'exert his usual humanity'.[84]

By 'frightening' poachers, the gentry hoped to deter them from further destruction of game; by exercising 'humanity', they hoped to obtain the accused's assistance in identifying and convicting other offenders, particularly those who bought and sold game. Individual game preservers regularly offered substantial rewards for information of this kind, but it seems that the prospect of spending several months in prison was a more powerful inducement. J.P.s, by virtue of their commission, had fairly wide discretionary powers with regard to imprisonment, and these were

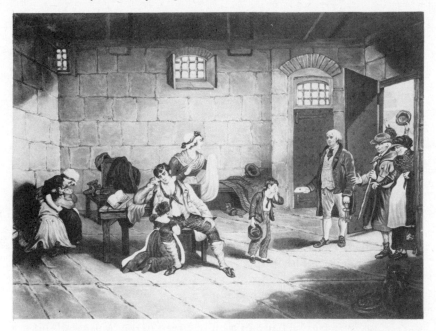

VII. Poachers in prison: arrival of the pardon

increased in 1707, when they were empowered to grant immunity from punishment to any offender against the game laws who informed on a game trader.[85] How effectively these powers could be used was demonstrated by the Rev. F.E. Witts, a Gloucestershire J.P. in the early nineteenth century. On 17 February 1817 an unqualified man named John Turner was brought before Witts and charged by the keeper of Sherborne manor with using a snare to take game. Turner was committed to gaol for 'further examination', but was released three weeks later – after he had testified against John Day, a shepherd from a neighbouring parish who was accused of hunting without a licence. Day, needless to say, was convicted and, since he was unable to pay the £20 fine, was imprisoned in the local bridewell. Within a month, however, Day was also discharged, 'he having informed against the receivers of hares poached on Sherborne manor'.[86] It is not surprising, therefore, that some gentlemen placed great store in the judicious use of 'humanity'. The Wiltshire J.P. who, in 1767, had pardoned a local poacher in return for the latter's testimony against a higgler was not alone in thinking that such deals were 'of great consequence in Striking Terror into the *Receivers* [of game] and weakening, if not destroying, the confidence there is amongst that Nest of Thieves'.[87]

Working against such hopes was the hostility which most Englishmen felt toward those who bore 'the odious name of an informer', a hostility which may have been particularly intense where the game laws were concerned because of the popular conviction that poaching was not a crime. In 1753 it was reported from Marlborough that 'the Effigy of one of the inhabitants of that Town was hung on a Tree and burnt, for informing against several Poachers of Game, etc'. Several years later, the son of a steward in Hertfordshire was shot in the head 'on account of the youth having informed against the criminal for poaching'.[88] Usually, however, popular feeling was expressed in less dramatic ways, as Thomas Bright, a Ramsbury labourer, found out in 1767 when he was caught snaring on Lord Bruce's estate. In order to escape punishment, Bright 'impeached' a higgler, who was subsequently fined £20. According to Bruce's steward, Bright

> says now he is very much abused by everybody for 'peaching. That he has a wife & 3 children & expects another every moment, and that upon applying for relief to Mr Tanner, Mr Jones's Bailiff at Axford Farm, who is [poor law] officer this year, he told him he had done a Roguish thing to impeach and would give him no Relief, tho' the poor Man with tears in his eyes said he had not a bit of bread in the house and did not know where to get any, and he was 50s. in debt to his Master . . . for Rent of his House. He says the people are ready to knock him on the head, not for Poaching but for 'Peaching.

The effect of a community's disapproval can, however, be exaggerated, and Thomas Bright is a case in point. Within less than a year, he was back before a J.P. charged with setting snares, and once again he informed on a higgler 'to whom Bright [had] sold 4 Hares at 2s. apiece'.[89] Faced with imprisonment, other poachers also 'peached' their customers and even their own comrades. Indeed, the prosecution of large poaching gangs in the early nineteenth century was, in many cases, possible only because one of the gang's members had turned King's evidence. 'Without that, they [the gangs] could not have been identified', explained one Bow Street officer; 'the gamekeepers could not or would not identify them'.[90] Popular hostility toward informers, then, was not enough in itself to defeat the gentry's strategy of 'divide and conquer'. Poachers, however, had another, more potent weapon: money.

'It may seem perhaps to be a ridiculous assertion,' conceded Henry Zouch in 1783, 'but the fact is indisputable, that there now actually exists in several places, an *Association* of poachers and abettors of them, who are ready to advance money for the purpose of paying penalties, or otherwise assisting any of their suffering brethren.'[91] Zouch's claim might easily be dismissed were it not for the fact that a surprisingly large number of game offenders in the eighteenth and early nineteenth centuries did, in fact, have enough money to pay the fine imposed by the magistrate and thus escape imprisonment. Of those convicted of game offences in Wiltshire between 1750 and 1820 for whom conviction certificates survive, only 27 per cent ended up in prison.[92] The rest seem to have been able to pay a fine of £5 or more. For a prosperous farmer or tradesman, this was not perhaps an impossible task, but most of the defendants in Wiltshire were labourers, shepherds and cloth-workers, whose average wage rarely rose above eight or ten shillings a week.[93] How were such men able to raise, usually on short notice, the £5 or £10 necessary to secure their freedom? It is unlikely that they would have been able to save so large a sum out of their wages. Few of them, indeed, probably had personal possessions worth £5; thus, the possibility that the fines were paid out of proceeds from the forced sale of the offender's belongings can also be ruled out. The only other available source of 'ready money' was the black market in game. This 'Association', as we have already noted, paid poachers a good price for their game; it may also have advanced them money when they were caught. Zouch, certainly, was not the only one who thought that this was the case. In 1791, for example, it was reported in the press that

> The gentlemen farmers and gentlemen of small fortunes, are
> so much displeased with the additional duty on Game
> licences, that in several counties there are societies which
> employ poachers to secure their game, without qualifying
> themselves; and should the poacher be detected, the whole
> influence of the society is exerted to screen him, or he is
> allowed a snug maintenance if imprisoned.[94]

When frustrated, the gentry were apt to see conspiracies all around them, but, in the light of the success with which poachers were able to evade imprisonment, there seems good reason for believing that this one actually existed.

Whatever the explanation, the ability of poachers to pay the fine obviously blunted the force of the game laws, and the gentry sought to remedy this in a number of ways. First, the fines themselves were drastically increased. Under the Night Poaching and Game Duty Acts passed in the late eighteenth century, poachers became liable to penalties which were two, four and, in some cases, even ten times heavier than those previously imposed. The effect of these Acts was compounded by the ability of game preservers to prosecute a poacher under several different statutes for the same offence. Thus, in 1786 a Sussex man caught laying snares at night was fined £35 after having been convicted on three counts: hunting at night, hunting without being qualified and hunting without a licence. In 1802 Jonathan Green, a Yorkshire labourer, was ordered to pay

Persons committed to prison by J.P.s 'out of sessions' for game offences in
Wiltshire 1760–1830

£45 after a similar prosecution.[95] It is, perhaps, a tribute to the prosperity
of the poaching trade that even these measures were soon deemed
insufficient. After 1800 the option of paying a fine was absent altogether
from the new laws which Parliament passed against night poaching. In its
place was a mandatory prison term.

The gentry's increasing ability to ensure that poachers suffered more than the payment of a fine was, however, only one of the factors behind the extraordinary rise in the number of committals to prison for game offences which began in the second half of the eighteenth century. In Wiltshire, as can be seen from the graph on p. 100, the average number of game committals tripled in each decade between 1760 and 1790. Following a pause during the Napoleonic wars – when the authorities had other places to which they could send poachers – the number of game offenders in prison again began to increase. Where the annual average between 1790 and 1815 had been twelve, in the five years following the battle of Waterloo it was fifty-eight. In the 1820s, it rose even further, to an average of eighty-nine committals per year.[96] Since these figures do *not* include committals under the Night Poaching Acts passed in the early nineteenth century,[97] it seems clear that something more than a change in the law was at work. One factor was undoubtedly that J.P.s were more willing to imprison an offender than they had been earlier in the eighteenth century. The movement for a 'reformation of manners' in society, which became increasingly influential after the 1770s, saw in England's prisons an engine for the transformation of the lower classes – 'a mill for grinding rogues honest and idle men industrious', as Bentham put it.[98] At the urging of men like Sir George Onesiphorus Paul, a number of penitentiaries were constructed in the provinces at the turn of the century designed specifically to turn that vision into a reality. These new prisons were generally cleaner, healthier – and larger – than the buildings which they replaced, and even those justices who doubted that a regime of Bible readings and silent hours on the treadmill would have much effect on the character of the poor were nevertheless unlikely to hesitate about sending a poacher to such a place. Thus, both as a form of punishment and as a method of 'reformation', imprisonment became increasingly attractive to the authorities in the early nineteenth century.

The most important factor behind the massive increase in game committals, however, was probably an increase in poaching itself. There is no way that this can be proven statistically, but there are some indications that committals did, to some degree, reflect the level of poaching activity. On the Longleat estate, for example, the amount spent on prosecuting poachers rose from approximately £23 in the 1770s to £96 in the next decade, but then fell to about £45 in the 1790s. Even more revealing, perhaps, were the payments to watchers on the estate. Of the £260 which was spent on them in the last two decades of the century over 90 per cent was paid out between 1783 and 1792; thereafter, the employment of watchers declined sharply for the rest of the century.[99] Lord Bath apparently felt that his preserves were less endangered in the 1790s than they had been in the preceding decade; this may help to explain why game committals in the county also declined at this time. Certainly some game preservers saw a fairly direct relationship between the threat to their game and the number of poachers in prison. 'We have but few Male Birds left of the Pheasants,' a Bedfordshire steward informed his master in January 1822, 'and those would not be there a single Night if we did not Watch the Woods Night and Day. Poaching is become such a trade in this County that our Gaol is nearly full of Poachers.'[100] It was not, of course, that simple. Poachers, as we have seen, were not entirely helpless in the face of a system dominated by game preservers. Many of them could, and did, avoid imprisonment, even as the gentry became more and more determined to inflict that penalty. But if imprisonment was not automatically the fate of a labourer caught laying a snare or carrying home a brace of pheasants, it is nevertheless the best measure we have of the enforcement of the game laws and perhaps of the incidence of poaching itself. The picture which it drew in the late eighteenth and early nineteenth centuries was an ominous one for game preservers and poachers alike.

VI

The early nineteenth century witnessed a massive increase in poaching activity. The causes of that increase will be discussed in a later chapter, but this seems an appropriate place to examine one of its effects: the passage of a series of very severe Night Poaching Acts. Parliament first began to increase the penalties for hunting game after dark in the 1770s, but it was the passage of the Act of 1800 which signalled the beginning of an era of truly punitive measures. Under this Act, night poachers could be punished as vagrants: at the justice's discretion they could be whipped, imprisoned for up to two years and even impressed into the army or navy. In 1816, this Act was replaced by one which allowed night poachers to be transported for seven years, although only after a jury trial at quarter sessions. When coupled with 'Lord Ellenborough's Law', which made it a capital offence to resist arrest forcibly,[101] the message of these Acts was unmistakeable: the gentry were prepared to deal as harshly with night poachers as they had with deer-stealers a century earlier. Although actually the culmination of previous measures, the Acts of 1816 and 1817 which made night poaching a transportable offence were seen at the time as an innovation. Samuel Romilly warned the House of Commons that the new penalty for night poaching 'changed the whole policy of the game laws',[102] while in Somerset a poaching gang was alarmed enough to threaten that if the law were enforced 'not one gentleman's seat in our county [shall] escape the rage of fire'. The game laws, the poachers declared, 'were too severe [even] before: the Lord of all men sent these animals for peasants as well as for the prince. God will not let his people be oppressed.'[103]

Both their alarm and their faith proved justified. Even before the Act of 1816 had become law, poachers were beginning to feel the full force of the gentry's anger. In Wiltshire, for example, where previously there had been an average of only one conviction a year under the Act of 1800, nine men were convicted as 'rogues and vagabonds' in the winter of 1815–16, and five of these were ordered impressed into the army.[104] Several months later, the new Night Poaching Act came into force, and in the following eleven years more than 1700 persons in England and Wales were convicted under it. Although this constituted only a small proportion of total game law convictions in these years, that was small consolation to those who found themselves caught in the snares of the Night Poaching Act. On the other hand, although all of these 1700 persons were liable to be transported, less than 10 per cent were actually sentenced to suffer this punishment, and as many as a third of these may have never been actually shipped off to Australia.[105] In Wiltshire, 105 night poachers were convicted at quarter sessions between 1816 and 1828, but only 7 per cent were sentenced to be transported. The rest were imprisoned, most of them for terms of a year or less. Occasionally, the Night Poaching Act did show its teeth. In the winter of 1825–6, for example, five of the twenty-three night poachers convicted in Wiltshire were ordered to be transported and another eleven were sentenced to eighteen months in prison.[106] On the whole, however, the Act's enforcement was something less than savage.

It might be suggested that this was because prosecutions under these Night Poaching Acts were heard by a jury at quarter sessions, rather than by individual J.P.s. There were, indeed, complaints at the time that juries tended to be lenient in game cases. One irate Yorkshire game preserver, for example, claimed that 'there is one universal and strong and well-founded impression throughout the whole of the district with which I am connected, that if the poachers are only sent to York, there [sic] are certain of obtaining a complete triumph over country gentlemen'.[107] Modern historians have been rather too eager to accept such statements at face value. That there was a widespread sympathy for poachers among the classes from which these juries were drawn cannot be disputed, but this sympathy was not as readily translated into acquittals as some historians would like to think. Certainly the fact that Wiltshire juries in this period convicted three out of every four defendants charged under the Night Poaching Acts would seem to challenge the conventional wisdom about the attitude of juries when faced with a night poacher.[108] In any event, it was the J.P.s, not the jurors, who sentenced the convicted offenders, and in this, as we have seen, they were not notably harsh. There was, in fact, some agitation by game preservers in the 1820s to have night poaching cases removed to the assizes precisely because J.P.s were thought to be too lenient.[109] In the final analysis, magistrates were no more intent on exacting vengeance than juries were anxious to acquit. Neither wished to see the law fully enforced or fully ignored. By the early nineteenth century, in fact, what both groups wanted was a new law.

VII

The enforcement of the game laws, then, resembled the game laws themselves: it consisted of a series of complex, overlapping elements, whose sole unifying feature was the discretionary power of country gentlemen. As such, it was open to abuse and capable of oppression. We have seen a number of examples of this in the preceding pages: Whigs being hauled before Tory J.P.s and fined for simply keeping a greyhound; farmers condemned by arbitrary and partial magistrates; poachers financially ruined or impressed into the army. The same system of enforcement, however, was open to evasion and capable of mercy. It was possible for a poacher to secure his freedom by paying a fine, signing a bond or betraying a comrade. Alternatively, he could appeal to the compassion of the magistrate and (particularly if he was a first offender) hope for some mitigation of the penalty. The merciful aspects of the game laws' enforcement do not, of course, cancel out the oppressive ones – but they do help to put the latter in perspective. We have seen, for example, that Richard Deller's treatment at the hands of the Duke of Buckingham was not necessarily typical. Indeed, considering the alternatives of impressment and civil prosecution, trial before a 'sporting justice' was apt to be welcomed by an accused poacher, for even if the J.P. was a passionate game preserver his ability to punish was limited in most cases to the imposition of a fine which, as we have also seen, most poachers were capable of paying. Mockery of justice or not, summary trial before a J.P. was often the means by which a poacher was restored to his family and his trade.

It could, in fact, be plausibly argued that the real defect in the enforcement of the game laws was not that it was oppressive, but that it was ineffectual. Certainly, it seems to have done little to inhibit the expansion of the poaching trade in the late eighteenth and early nineteenth centuries. Even after the penalties for night poaching were drastically increased, gangs continued to invade the gentry's preserves and do battle with their gamekeepers with undisguised enthusiasm. The gentry's response to this failure of the game laws to preserve their game is instructive. 'I am at a great Expence in paying a [great] many Men for going out Every Day,' complained one Derbyshire game preserver in 1772, 'yet without [i.e. unless] example is made of Some of them [i.e. the poachers], it will answer no End, as they say they care for nobody.' Similarly, in 1813 Lord Ongley told Samuel Whitbread that poaching 'has got to an alarming height every where & unless . . . every now [and] then a noted offender is transported . . . there will be no stopping it'.[110] It was in the making of 'examples', not in the steady and uniform application of the law, that most country gentlemen placed their trust. Indeed, the whole system of game law enforcement was designed to allow them to make 'examples' without being forced to inflict heavy penalties on all offenders. While this approach to law enforcement saved many a poacher from imprisonment or transportation, it may also have been the reason why the game laws failed to achieve their end. For while the gentry saw an 'example' as a salutary object lesson, poachers may have simply viewed it as an exception to the rule, arbitrarily made and easily ignored. If, however, the gentry's exercise of their discretionary authority seems to have done little to deter poachers, it did have a noticeable impact on other groups in rural society, notably on the farmers and tradesmen who, around the middle of the eighteenth century, came to feel threatened by the operation of the game laws for the first time. When 'examples' began to be made of these men, it was not met with indifference.

5

Early opposition to the game laws

The history of the English game laws between 1671 and 1831 can be divided into two parts. Until the middle of the eighteenth century both the laws and their enforcement were relatively mild. No wholesale confiscation of guns, dogs or other 'engines' took place; nor was there any sustained effort to punish violations of the game laws. Poachers were not, of course, allowed to operate with impunity, but the impact of the Game Act on the rural community as a whole was not as great as its provisions would suggest. Around the middle of the century, however, several changes occurred which profoundly altered the environment in which the game laws operated. In Parliament, a black market in game was unwittingly legislated into existence, while in the countryside improvements in transportation were beginning to make it possible for poachers to supply that market on an almost daily basis. It was also at this time that the transfer of jurisdiction over game cases from the quarter sessions to individual justices of the peace was completed, making it easier to prosecute poachers. By themselves, these developments would have sharpened the perennial conflict between country gentlemen and poachers, but their impact was undoubtedly heightened by the fact that they coincided with the introduction of systematic game preservation into the countryside. The preserves, swarming with half-tame hares, partridges and pheasants, which appeared in many parts of England in the second half of the eighteenth century, were a convenient target for poachers. From such concentrations of game, they could – with a little organisation and some resort to violence – supply the demands of the black market quite easily. The preserves were less popular with other segments of rural society, however. Farmers complained about damage to their crops; fox-hunters feared for the safety of their prey; and most important of all, a large number of tenants, small freeholders and 'reputable tradesmen' deeply resented the restrictions which game preservation placed on their own sporting activities. The customary 'indulgences' were less frequently granted, and a few individuals from these groups even found themselves the object of prosecution. When this happened, they were not pleased to discover that they would be tried, not by a jury of their peers at quarter sessions, but by a local magistrate whose impartiality was, to say the least, suspect. It is not perhaps surprising, then, that the second half of the eighteenth century saw not only an increase in poaching, but also the emergence of a highly vocal opposition to the game laws.

Admittedly, there had not been unanimous support for the game laws even before mid-century. Indeed, the vast majority of the population had never really accepted the gentry's right to a monopoly on game; they continued to believe that hares, partridges and pheasants 'were ordained from the beginning free for anyone who could overtake them'.[1] Consequently, they poached – or winked at those who did – with a free conscience. From time to time they also could be roused to rescue a poacher from the hands of the authorities. When, for instance, Sir Roger Newdigate's gamekeeper and an assistant 'went to Nuneaton with Mr Stratford's warrant to apprehend Ch[arles] Siddal', they 'were attacked by old Sidwell [*sic*] & a mob of people who beat them & rescued him'.[2] Aside from the occasional threatening letter to a game preserver, however, it was not until the very end of the century that the common people began to articulate their opposition.[3] The other early opponents of the game laws, by contrast, were far from silent. The London Company of Poulters lobbied against every major addition to the game code in the first half of the eighteenth century. When, for example, the Act which permitted the civil prosecution of game offenders was going through Parliament in 1722, the Company's clerk was ordered to 'attend Mr Thomas Smith [probably a solicitor] about the Game Bill and to take what Care they Can to prevent the passing thereof'. Similarly, in 1755 the poulterers tried to avert the passage of the Act banning the game trade by ordering that a list of objections 'be Printed and Given to the [House of] Lords'.[4] Since, however, the poulterers' chief objection was simply that these acts threatened 'a very considerable Part of their Trade', their protests were not likely to engage the sympathies of Parliament or the public at large. They were, in fact, ignored.

It was, then, with some justification that Sir Robert Walpole told the House of Commons in 1741 that he had 'heard no general complaints [about the game code], nor [did he] believe that it is look'd upon as a grievance by any, but those whom it restrains from living upon the game, and condemns to maintain themselves by a more honest and useful industry'.[5] It would be wrong, however, to say that the game laws had not been criticised at all in the early eighteenth century. As was noted in the previous chapter, there had been objections from those who feared that 'the disarming of the people' would pave the way for arbitrary government. Some of these attacks, of course, were little more than occasions for opponents of the government to demonstrate their own superior devotion to English liberty: they mingled easily with denunciations of placemen and the excise.[6] But, sincere or not, these early criticisms of the game laws were significant, since they showed that the gentry's monopoly on game was vulnerable, not only in the countryside, but in the forum of public opinion as well.

The character of public debate in the eighteenth century was dominated by a concern for the preservation of 'English liberty', that amalgam of personal and property rights which, in the minds of Englishmen, distinguished them from other nations.[7] Liberty, it was thought, depended on a high degree of civic virtue for its protection. Civic virtue, in turn, was closely linked to the existence of a body of 'independent' men in society – men who lived on their own resources, and thus were able to exercise their judgements freely. Such men could be counted on to discover and resist any threat to the liberties of the people. Thus, there was a close relationship in the public mind between the preservation of 'independence' and the preservation of 'liberty'. Any attempt to limit the former, it was thought, would inevitably threaten the latter. The prime focus of concern, naturally enough, was Parliament, where Walpole and his successors skilfully employed the arts of 'corruption' on those who were supposed to be the guardians of liberty. Once the Court had reduced a majority of these guardians to subservience, it was predicted, the rights of Englishmen would quickly disappear. It was under pretence of averting just such a catastrophe that opposition politicians in the eighteenth century justified their activities. That the rhetoric of 'liberty' was often just a cover for self-interested manoeuvre cannot be denied, but it is significant that opposition charges were sometimes accompanied by demands for changes in the political system – expulsion of placemen, shorter parliaments, more county members – in order to preserve the independence of Parliament and thus prevent the schemes of 'corrupt Ministers' from succeeding. Political debate in the eighteenth century, therefore, did allow for discussion of reform, provided it was carried out within the context of preserving the ability of citizens to resist the dictates of 'Great Men'.

Parliament was not the only place where the spread of 'corruption' was observed and fought. In London and in the provinces, attempts to dictate the choice of the electorate were occasionally, and sometimes successfully, resisted in the name of 'independency'.[8] The threat to liberty in these cases came less often from a 'corrupt Minister' than from a domineering landowner – one who was not content to exercise the 'natural' influence to which his rank and property entitled him, but who instead tried to force his will on his neighbours, often by economic pressure or manipulation of the law. The classic example of this type of landowner was Sir James Lowther, a Whig magnate with extensive holdings in Cumberland and

Westmorland. In 1768 he tried to capture control of both of the county seats for Cumberland – he already controlled one of them – and to that end successfully contested the ownership of property which had long been in the possession of his rival, the Duke of Portland. Lowther's ambition, and the means which he used to further it, were denounced and he ended up losing control of both seats.[9] In the provinces as well as in Parliament, power was suspect and dominance difficult to achieve. Any departure from established practice which threatened to limit rights previously enjoyed was apt to be labelled a threat to the 'independence', and hence to the liberties of Englishmen. And that, in turn, gave those who desired change an opportunity to present their case.

In such a context, the game laws were obviously vulnerable, particularly after the middle of the eighteenth century. In 1671 Parliament had given country gentlemen a monopoly on game, but as long as the laws were not strictly enforced, there was little direct criticism. Once, however, the gentry began to assert their monopoly, howls of protest were almost immediately heard. The 'respectable' but unqualified members of rural society who suddenly found themselves forced to beg for an occasional 'indulgence' – or were deprived of their sport altogether – naturally resented their loss of status and sought some sort of explanation for it. Given the nature of eighteenth-century public debate, it is perhaps not surprising that the gentry were soon confronted with charges that they were trying to reduce respectable farmers and tradesmen to serfdom. What should be done to prevent this, however, was less obvious. Should there be no game laws, or should there simply be new ones – and if the latter, on what principle should they be based? The answers to these questions gradually emerged during the second half of the eighteenth century in a series of debates: first, over the activities of the Game Association in the 1750s; then over the Night Poaching Act of 1770; and finally over John Christian Curwen's bill to repeal the game laws, introduced in 1796. It is on these debates that the following discussion will focus.

II

The first sign that the gentry were beginning to adopt a less indulgent attitude toward the enforcement of the game laws came in the 1740s, when associations 'for the better Preservation of the Game' were formed in several parts of England. To some country gentlemen, even these organisations seemed inadequate for the task. A letter to the *General Evening Post* in 1749 suggested that the time had come for Parliament to enact new measures 'to prevent the present most insolent method of the common people in destroying the game of this kingdom, and [of] carriers and higlers carrying it about without any fear of punishment'.[10] Just what measures the author had in mind was not clear, but there were rumours circulating at this time that poaching would soon be made a felony or that the qualification for sporting would be doubled.[11] There is no direct evidence that changes of that sort were being contemplated, but in the early 1750s the rumours had a certain plausibility. As game preservation first began to be systematically practised in East Anglia and other parts of the country, the suspicion grew in some quarters, notably among farmers and small freeholders, that the large landowners were trying to engross all the game in the countryside for themselves. That innovations in the law should accompany this attempt seemed only natural. Indeed, to a people brought up to suspect the activities of the powerful, it seemed almost inevitable.

Their fears and expectations found confirmation in 1752 when the national Game Association was formed. Not only did the Association include many of the country's major landowners in its ranks, but it also began to enforce the game laws in a highly unusual manner.[12] The Association rarely laid an information before a justice of the peace. Instead, it initiated proceedings in the Court of King's Bench. 'From hence, it happens,' wrote one critic, 'that if a Person be falsely accused of killing a sorry Partridge . . . it shall cost him *Fifty*, *Sixty*, or *Eighty Pounds*, or more, to shew his Innocence . . . Yet, we call ourselves free; we boast of our Laws! we boast of our Liberties!'[13] Equally alarming were the ways in which the Association sought to encourage informations against game law offenders. In addition to the customary half of the fine, the Association now offered informers a £5 bounty on every conviction – and also promised that the informer's identity would be concealed until the time of the trial. Since many civil prosecutions were settled out of court, this meant that the defendant might, 'like the poor *Heretick* in *Spain* or *Portugal*, not so much as know who his Accuser is'.[14] Moreover, the nature of these innovations suggested that they were not directed primarily at poachers. The latter were, by definition, poor men; there could be no point in suing them. Nor was there any reason why a person who informed on poachers should want his identity to be concealed. The Association, its critics concluded, was not really interested in prosecuting poachers at all. It had not been formed 'to suppress a Set of idle and dissolute People' or 'to oblige the Husbandman and Labourer to attend to their proper Avocations'. Rather, its aim was 'to deprive the *Man of Property*, the *industrious Tenant*, or the *fair Sportsman* of a Morning's Recreation, or a Taste of a Hare or Partridge'.[15] The Association denied that it intended to 'Prosecute Farmers without Distinction', but the critics retorted that its actions belied these assurances. 'Threatening Letters' had been sent to 'fair Sportsmen', warning them not to hunt under pain of prosecution. There was, in short, every 'reason to suspect that the subscribing Gentlemen by preserving the Game, do only mean *to preserve it for their own Use*, i.e. *to monopolize and engross it to themselves*'.[16]

Those who felt threatened by the Game Association were not long in making their opposition known. Within a month of the Association's founding, it was reported that

> A great Number of Papers were affix'd . . . in the Avenues [leading] to both Houses of Parliament, drawn up in an impudent ignorant Manner, purporting that the Country Farmers, and their Servants, intended to destroy all the Pheasant and Partridge Eggs, and young Leverets, in case the Gentlemen who enter'd into an Association for the Preservation of Game, did not desist.[17]

At the assizes, the Association's prosecutions attracted a great deal of unfriendly attention. When three Essex men – two of them sons of a substantial farmer, and the third a wheelwright – were prosecuted at the summer assizes in 1754, the trial was attended by 'the greatest Concourse of the midling Landed Interest and reputable Farmers of the County . . . that ever was known on like Occasion'. After the defendants' acquittal, there were 'suitable Rejoicings in divers Parts of Essex'. A year earlier, a Suffolk jury empanelled to try one of the Association's cases simply failed to appear.[18] In Kent and Surrey some farmers threatened to start prosecuting 'Ungentlemen-like Gentlemen that shall trespass wilfully on their lands', in retaliation against the prosecution of a Surrey farmer's son for coursing hares without being qualified. 'And daily still,' their announcement concluded, 'the industrious Farmer is rioted and abused, by arbitrary People, in enjoying the few Diversions from the Plough Nature has allotted to his Calling.'[19]

It was not simply pique at being denied a favourite recreation which led farmers and small freeholders to resist the Association. There was a natural and long-standing tension between the 'midling Landed Interest' and large landowners, a tension which had been heightened in the late seventeenth and early eighteenth centuries by economic difficulties and a shift in the pattern of landownership. During that period, high taxation and low prices had combined to widen the gap between these two levels of rural society. In at least some counties, a significant number of owner-occupiers and lesser gentry were forced to sell much, if not all, of their land. Generally speaking, their farms and woods were bought, not by other small owner-occupiers, but by great landowners, many of them Whig peers whose access to credit and government office enabled them to survive and prosper at a time when smaller men were going under.[20] Thus, by the middle of the eighteenth century there had been a consolidation and expansion of large estates at the expense of small ones. In terms of acreage, the change may have been a relatively modest one. Nevertheless, it was difficult to ignore as whole villages were moved in order to make way for aristocratic 'vistas',[21] and as the great Whig magnates tightened their grip on the social and political lives of their neighbourhoods.

'Are we nothing but Asses, made to bear their Burdens?' demanded one embittered Norfolk farmer in a pamphlet published in 1754.[22] Ostensibly a protest against the rumoured doubling of the sporting qualification, his short tract was actually a *cri de coeur* against aristocratic domination. It breathed a class antagonism which, if not typical, at least helped to articulate the resentments felt by many small freeholders and farmers at that time. While a farmer or a tradesman, said the author, had been 'bred up to Accompts and the Knowledge of his Craft', 'Men of Rank and Fortune [were] bred in High-Life, where they all contract an early contempt for us Plebians'. How could any common man, he wondered, 'imagine that such Men really desire to see him at their Table, or if they do, for what can it be but to laught at? which they often do to our very Faces'.[23] The game laws 'were designed to keep People in Awe', but it was not until the past few years that they had been strictly enforced, 'So that the Use now made of them is a most abusive Perversion' of the law. Worse, in his view, was the prospect that the qualification would be doubled, since such a change would imply that a £100 freeholder was inferior to men with incomes twice as large.

> Now they know if we grant this, we have nothing more to yield, for in that very Breath, the Life, the Soul, of every Englishman is given up, *viz.* his invaluable Privilege of voting in Elections, where the vote of a Man of Forty Shillings a Year, has as much Weight as that of the greatest Subject in the Kingdom: If anyone is so inconsiderate as to think this only a Matter of Form, only a Titular Advantage, let him but consider the wretched Condition of a Bulk of Mankind, who are subject to arbitrary Power.[24]

His logic was far from impeccable, but the point was clear enough: the game laws were only part of a concerted campaign by the aristocracy to strip Englishmen of their liberties.

This fear of aristocratic domination was given a new opportunity for expression in 1756 with the outbreak of the Seven Years War. The military defeats of the first year of the war, particularly the fall of Minorca, were more than just severe blows to English pride. They were widely interpreted as symptoms of a deep and pervasive malady: 'corruption'. England, declared a petition of Yorkshire freeholders following the fall of Minorca, was in the hands of 'self-designing men; who, in proportion as they promise, and dispense, only attempt to enslave, and become the prodigal spendthrifts of our patrimonies'. The nation's salvation obviously required a change of administration, but there also had to be, said the petition, a change in the 'morals' of the country at large. For the former, the public placed its hopes in William Pitt; for the revival of civic virtue, it looked to a re-invigorated militia.[25] The clamour for the Militia Bill inevitably led to renewed criticism of the game laws for 'disarming' the nation. In the wake of the Game Association's activities, however, the target of this criticism was no longer the government: it was the aristocracy. Even before war was officially declared, there were suggestions in the press that 'all gentlemen who enjoy the exclusive privilege of killing game should snatch a few hours from their darling sport, and learn the military exercise of both horse and foot'.[26] After Minorca the tone became much sharper. 'Is this a time,' the Association was asked, 'for some of you to think of little else than scraping up wealth for yourselves, and procuring places, pensions, and preferments for your relations and dependants?'[27] To some, indeed, the Association appeared to pose a greater threat to the liberties of Englishmen than the French. The 'Inhibition of bearing Arms,' warned one critic, 'has ever been deemed, through all Nations of the World, the most flagitous Characteristic of abject Slavery'. Those who conspired to deny the people the right to bear arms were, concluded another, nothing but 'a diabolical Association [set up] to Plunder us of our Provisions, to rob us of our Liberty, and to bring every honest Man to Poverty and Ruin'.[28]

The most strident criticism, it should be noted, was reserved for the Game Association, not the game laws. While they acknowledged that it was the latter which permitted the Association to engage in its objectionable activities, not all of the critics demanded that the game laws be repealed. Some simply urged country gentlemen to revert to their former practice of appointing farmers as gamekeepers and generally giving 'due Regard to their industrious Tenants'.[29] 'Search the kingdom thro',' argued one such opponent of strict enforcement, 'and where you find the greatest plenty of Game, you'll find the greatest indulgence given to considerable renters and substantial yeomen. Tis contrary conduct that destroys Game.'[30] There were others, however, who were clearly sceptical about the gentry's willingness to share the game with those immediately below them in the rural hierarchy, and who, moreover, had other grievances deserving of redress. They were angry about the damage which game did to the crops and about the constant invasion of their farms by qualified sportsmen. They urged, therefore, that the game code be replaced by a new system, one which 'would restrain persons of every rank from invading the property of others, and not gratify the rich at the expence of the poor'. They wanted game to be made the property of the person on whose land it was found.[31]

This was not, of course, a new idea. Both deer and rabbits had long been considered a species of private property. Originally designated as 'the

King's game', they had, by the end of the seventeenth century, become the property of the person on whose land they were found. Except in a few forests and chases where the ancient privileges conferred by the forest laws and royal franchises still applied, no deer or rabbit could be legally hunted except with the permission of the landowner. As we saw in a previous chapter, this change in legal status was not proclaimed by Parliament, but rather came about as a natural consequence of the enclosure of deer into parks and of rabbits into warrens. By their enclosure, they had ceased to be wild animals and, as Lord Chief Justice Willes observed in 1738, 'when the nature of things changes, the rules of the law must change too'.[32] Under the new rules it was legal to hunt deer or rabbits without being qualified, but it was a crime to do so without the permission of the owner of the land. The new rules also made illegal hunting a more serious crime. In 1765, for example, the penalty for killing game without being qualified was a £5 fine or three months in prison, but for killing a deer without the park-owner's consent, it was transportation for seven years. Similarly, the maximum penalty for killing game at night in 1765 was a £5 fine or three months' imprisonment, but for killing rabbits at night it was seven years' transportation.[33] 'Making game property', then, was more than a legal abstraction: its consequences would be felt immediately in the countryside. First of all, it entailed the transfer of sporting rights from a select group of individuals to a much larger and socially diverse body of landowners. It also involved a significant change in the nature of those sporting rights, namely the restriction of sportsmen to the land of those whose permission had been obtained. Finally, it changed the legal status of the animal pursued, which, in turn, altered the seriousness with which the law viewed the unauthorised taking of that animal. When game became property, poaching became an offence against property, and that in the eighteenth century was a very serious matter.

By the 1750s there were signs that what had happened to deer and rabbits was beginning to happen to game as well. Barriers – less in the form of fences than in a new willingness to invoke the law of trespass – were beginning to be erected in the countryside to prevent sportsmen from hunting without the landowner's permission. In addition, through the device of civil prosecution, the penalties for poaching were being increased.[34] Whatever the law might say, game was coming to be treated as a species of private property and this would become increasingly evident in the second half of the eighteenth century. Nevertheless, what the law said mattered a great deal, for, as long as the gentry retained their legal monopoly on the game, lesser landowners were denied the right to hunt game on their own land. Many farmers and freeholders undoubtedly agreed with the writer who found it a 'Strange Absurdity in a free State, [an] unnatural Vassalage, that a free Man should be prohibited by Law from killing the Produce of his own Lands, whatever the Income of them'.[35] By throwing off this 'unnatural Vassalage', farmers and small freeholders would also acquire a weapon with which they could protect themselves from the gentry's passion for sport. If game was recognised as the property of the person on whose land it was found, then farmers would be able to prevent their crops being devoured by the game which sheltered in adjacent preserves. 'Making game property' would also help them to ward off those invasions of their land by 'My Lord —, attended by 20 couples of dogs, a dozen horsemen and some score of footmen . . . in pursuit of a hare'.[36] Only when game was made property in law as well as in fact would the farmer view game preservation as anything but a plot by the gentry to rob him of his sport and even of his crops. It was not until 1831, however, that this was accomplished, and some of the reasons for the long delay can be found in the debate on the Night Poaching Act of 1770.

III

The hours between sunset and sunrise were the poacher's day. It was then that he made his rounds, setting his snares and taking away the squire's expensively reared game. In the eyes of most game preservers, hunting game after dark was synonymous with poaching and it had long been a crime for anyone, qualified or not, to be out after dark in pursuit of game. In 1711 'night poaching' was made punishable by the standard penalty under the game code, a £5 fine or three months in prison.[37] There the penalty remained until 1770, when Sir George Yonge, a wealthy Devonshire baronet, introduced a bill 'for the better Preservation of the Game'. Yonge wanted the penalty for night poaching both increased and extended to the hunting of game on Sundays. While the precise details of his original proposal are not known, it is clear that Yonge would have given offenders the option of paying a fine or being imprisoned.[38] By the time the bill had emerged from committee, however, it had been drastically altered. The fine for night poaching had been completely eliminated; in its place was a mandatory prison term – from three to six months for a first offence, from six to twelve months for a subsequent one – and an equally mandatory public whipping. Those caught sporting on Sundays still had the option of paying a fine, which was set at £20 to £30; if they could not afford that, they were to be imprisoned for a period of three to six months. After a speedy passage through the House of Lords, the bill received royal assent on 12 April 1770.[39]

The lack of controversy which characterised the passage of the Night Poaching Act did not last long. By April 1771 a bill had been introduced in the Commons 'to alter, explain and amend' the Act. It was defeated on second reading,[40] but in the following year the Act's opponents had more success. Their bill for the total repeal of the Night Poaching Act was again denied a second reading,[41] but this time they were able to obtain Sir George Yonge's support for a new measure 'to explain and amend' the Act of 1770. That bill was duly introduced later in the session, and while its exact provisions are unknown, the effect of the bill, as finally approved by the Commons, was undoubtedly to soften the provisions of the Night Poaching Act. At one point, for example, the House approved an amendment which replaced a penalty of twelve months in prison with a £50 fine or six months' imprisonment. When it came to accepting the amendments approved by the House of Lords, however, the Commons balked and, for reasons which are not entirely clear, the bill failed to become law.[42] It was not until the next session that the Act of 1770 was finally removed from the statute books. With the passage of the Night Poaching Act of 1773, night poachers, as well as those caught hunting on Sundays, were once again liable to imprisonment only if they were unable to pay the fine, and no offender was liable to be whipped unless it could be proved that he had been convicted of a like offence twice previously.[43]

Although such changes might seem insignificant, the Act of 1770's opponents obviously did not think so. What was at stake, they said, was nothing less than the survival of English liberty. The Act of 1770 was 'a bastard . . . a foundling . . . the most vindictive, the most oppressive, the most nugatory, the most inexplicable' law ever passed. It was, Richard Whitworth told the Commons, 'an Act which disgraces your statutes, and prescribes a mode of punishment which I am certain is unconstitutional'. He and other critics of the Act pointed particularly to a clause which required that an offender be publicly whipped within three days of his committal, even though he had four days in which to lodge an appeal. This raised the possibility of a man's being punished before he had a chance to appeal his conviction. How could the Commons, Whitworth demanded, 'ever assent to the whipping of probably an innocent man, and allow him liberty afterwards to appeal, and assert his innocence?'[44] More generally, the critics of the Act of 1770 attacked the nature of the proceedings which it sanctioned, particularly the absence of trial by jury. This, they said, was an opening to arbitrary rule: first it would be used against poachers, then against patriots. The question, declared Charles James Fox, was whether 'the game of this country cannot be protected without taking away the rights of English men'.[45]

It did Sir George Yonge and the other defenders of the Act of 1770 little good to object that this threat to liberty was imaginary. They argued that it was highly unlikely that a man would delay appealing for four days when he knew that he would be whipped within three. They also pointed out that summary conviction was the usual procedure in game cases, and that it was the appropriate one, especially in view of the recent increase in gang poaching. Sir Edward Astley, the member for Norfolk, told the House that poachers in his county were operating with a 'high hand: nine or ten Guns go to attack a plantation . . . [and] shoot by Moon light', carrying off great quantities of the game. His colleague, Thomas DeGrey, sought to assure gentlemen that such predators were the real targets of the Act. 'It is to the inferior [person] alone that this Law is addressed', he told them.[46] But it was precisely this point which the Act's opponents said that they doubted. If the Night Poaching Act stood, warned Constantine Phipps, 'it will come home on the backs of some', and he was not convinced that these would only be the backs of idle and dissolute poachers. William Dowdeswell cited the case of 'a Gentleman of four hundred [pounds] a year who escaped whipping' only because an observant J.P. had detected a contradiction in a witness's testimony. While the danger remained that a 'Gentleman upon [the oath of] a single witness might be whipped thro' a town', he declared, opposition to the Act would continue.[47] Since the Night Poaching Act was, in fact, enforced rather infrequently during its short life,[48] the Act's defenders could be forgiven for suspecting that the critics were being less than candid about their real concerns. One gentleman shrewdly observed that he had heard no complaints 'except in the papers' – and there, he might have added, more than just the Night Poaching Act was being attacked.[49]

One of the side effects of the controversy over the Game Association had been to bring the game laws under public scrutiny. Writing to a friend in the country in 1758, a London attorney remarked that 'this affair of the Game' had become 'a topick of discourse' in the metropolis.[50] It did not cease to be one, even after the Association's enthusiasm began to fade in the 1760s. On 26 January 1765, for example, the game laws were discussed at a meeting of Nottinghamshire gentlemen at a tavern in Pall Mall. It was, said one participant, a subject which had 'very often, where I have been, produced agreeable discussion'. That evening, however, a dispute arose between Lord Byron and his cousin, William Chaworth, over how strictly the game laws should be enforced; this eventually led to a duel in which Chaworth was mortally wounded.[51] Horace Walpole, commenting on the affair, dismissed the game laws as a topic fit only for discussion at quarter sessions, but in fact the gentry's monopoly on game was beginning to assume the aspect of an issue – and in some quarters, a grievance. 'It is hard,' wrote the *Monthly Review* in 1764, 'that the first-born booby of a qualified bumpkin should ride over hedge and ditch in pursuit of poor animals perhaps more sagacious than himself, while the honest farmer dares not touch the game which is sheltered and fed on the very ground he rents.' The *Review* hoped that 'such slavish and unequal laws' would soon be consigned to oblivion.[52] Within a very few years it received support from an unexpected source: Sir William Blackstone.

Blackstone's *Commentaries on the laws of England*, first published between 1765 and 1769, was both a description of the common law and a celebration of the existing constitution. Drawing heavily on Coke and the seventeenth-century Whig tradition, Blackstone traced the origin of English liberty back to the Saxons. Although the principal institutions and liberties of the Saxons had been suppressed by the Normans, these had, according to Blackstone, gradually been restored and were now enshrined in Magna Carta, the Bill of Rights and the common law. Into this scheme of history, the game laws fit awkwardly at best. All too clearly they had not been derived from Saxon law or custom; on the contrary, they were part of the 'Norman yoke' which had deprived Englishmen of their rightful liberties for so long. It was, wrote Blackstone, natural and 'most reasonable to fix [property in game] in him on whose land they were found' and that, not surprisingly, had been the practice in Saxon times. After the Conquest, however, the monarch had claimed the '*sole* and *exclusive* right' to take game. As Blackstone pointed out, this 'new doctrine' was still in force. The Game Act in 1671 had not qualified landed gentlemen to kill game: it had only exempted them from punishment for encroaching on the royal prerogative.[53] Thus, among the restored glories of English liberty stood an inexplicably vital remnant of feudal 'slavery'. Blackstone made no attempt to hide his distaste. From the root of the Norman forest laws, he wrote,

> has sprung a bastard slip, known by name of the game law, now arrived to and wantoning in it's [*sic*] highest vigour . . . founded upon the same unreasonable notions . . . and . . . productive of the same tyranny to the commons: but with this difference; that the forest laws established only one mighty hunter throughout the land, [while] the game laws have raised a little Nimrod in every manor.[54]

Equally pernicious was the manner in which the game laws were enforced. To Blackstone, 'our admirable and truly English trial by jury' stood along with Parliament as the protector of the liberties of the citizen; thus, he was suspicious of all summary proceedings. Although 'designed professedly for the greater ease of the subject', the summary powers of J.P.s were, by their very nature, arbitrary; in the wrong hands, they could be used 'to the low ends of selfish ambition, avarice, or personal resentment'. So dangerous, indeed, were these powers that he urged his readers to recognise 'the necessity of not deviating further from our antient constitution, by ordaining new penalties to be inflicted upon summary conviction'.[55]

There is little doubt that Blackstone's strictures had a great impact on the debate over the game laws which was beginning to develop at this time.

He was cited by opponents of the Night Poaching Act of 1770, both in and outside of Parliament.[56] Even where he was not directly cited, the influence of 'the learned Commentator' was readily apparent. It is difficult to believe, for example, that 'Junius' was unfamiliar with the *Commentaries* when he wrote:

> As to the Game Laws, he never scrupled to declare his opinion, that they are a species of the *Forest Laws*; that they are oppressive to the subject; and that the spirit of them is incompatible with legal liberty:– That the penalties imposed by these laws bear no proportion to the nature of the offence:– That the mode of trial, and the degree and kind of evidence necessary to convict, not only deprive the subject of all benefits of a trial by jury, but are in themselves too summary, and to the last degree arbitrary and oppressive.[57]

It was not simply Blackstone's prestige which gave currency to his views. He had, for the first time, set the game laws in a historical context, explaining their development within an easily understandable framework of natural and human law. 'By the law of nature,' he wrote, 'every man from the prince to the peasant, has an equal right' to take game. The exercise of that right, however, could be restricted in the interests of society: to preserve certain species of animals from extinction, to prevent 'popular insurrections and resistance to government, by disarming the bulk of the people' and to prevent 'idleness and dissipation in husbandmen, artificers, and others of lower rank'.[58] The precise nature of these restrictions had changed over the course of history – from Saxon freedom to Norman slavery – and the clear implication of Blackstone's analysis was that the rules could, and indeed should, be changed again. That certainly was the conclusion reached by many of Blackstone's readers, one of whom remarked, 'when I behold laws which are said to be formed for the punishment of laziness, applied as instruments of oppression, I confess I long to have them repealed or put upon a better footing'. He was not alone in that feeling, and to some in the early 1770s it seemed that the hour of redemption was at hand.[59]

Expectations that there would soon be changes in the game laws were not entirely a matter of wishful thinking. Parliament had already shown itself unwilling to expand the legal authority of lords of the manor in matters relating to game. In 1762 an amendment had been proposed which would have permitted lords to file suit for trespass against any person who hunted on their manors without their permission, regardless of the wishes of the actual owner of the land. The amendment was opposed on the grounds that 'inconveniences would follow frequently by great men oppressing little ones', and it was defeated. A similar proposal was rejected again in 1770[60] – even as rumours were circulating in the press that a bill would soon be introduced 'for a repeal of the most oppressive part of the game act'.[61] It never materialised, but in the next year the public was once again assured that a motion would soon be made in Parliament

> to repeal all the game laws now in being, and a new bill proposed, the principle of which is, to make game temporary property of the occupier of the land, with just powers of reservation to the landowner. A law so salutary in itself, and so consistent with the genius and spirit of a free people, that it is hoped no gentleman will be found base enough to give his vote against it.[62]

Small wonder that Sir George Yonge charged the opponents of his Night Poaching Act with 'wish[ing] to have all the Game Laws repealed', or that Thomas DeGrey was convinced that what they really wanted was 'to make [game] property'[63] – especially when it transpired that the author of the bill trumpeted in the press was none other than one of the Night Poaching Act's most outspoken critics, Richard Whitworth.[64]

Whitworth was an eccentric, quarrelsome and slightly pathetic Stafford-shire squire who represented the borough of Stafford between 1768 and 1780. He had a very high opinion of his own abilities and would later describe himself as 'a very ingenious man' who 'was reckon'd to understand the Acts of Parliament as well as if he had been bred to the Law; he spoke well & lov'd Justice to be done to the poor & was always an advocate for Mercy where the Law wou'd allow it'.[65] He also apparently fancied himself as a 'champion of the people, against the aristocratic power of the nobles and the great men'.[66] It was probably this mixture of conceits which prompted him to formulate, and on 9 June 1772 to introduce, a bill to reform the game laws. As advertised, he proposed that most of the major game laws be repealed and that game be made the property of the occupier of the land, unless the landowner reserved the game for himself. That, however, was only the beginning, since this new order of things raised a formidable set of problems. Who, for example, could claim ownership of the game found on commons and wastes? Could landlords insert reservations of sporting rights into existing leases, and what would happen if their tenants refused to agree to such changes? How was the penalty for trespassing in pursuit of game to be applied in neighbourhoods where packs of hounds were accustomed to chase hares without regard for boundary lines? Whitworth provided what answers he could, but these proved to be exceedingly complex, particularly with regard to the vexed question of sporting rights over commons and wastes. Less troublesome, however, was the problem of saving the poor from 'idleness and dissipation'. Whitworth dealt with that by simply re-introducing property qualifications. His bill proposed that anyone lacking four acres of land or forty shillings a year in income who was found with game should be punished, unless he could give a convincing explanation of how he came by it. In addition, anyone who did not have a £5 freehold or a £30 leasehold would be forbidden to possess guns, nets or snares. They, and most offenders under the proposed law, would have been liable to a £5 fine or six months in prison.[67]

Whitworth's bill was introduced too late in the session to be debated, and he did not present it again the following year. Instead, he joined forces with Sir George Yonge to secure passage of the Night Poaching Act of 1773. Once the danger that gentlemen 'might be whipped thro' a town' had passed, the pressure – at least, in Parliament – for fundamental changes in the game laws seems to have quickly subsided. To this extent, the fears of Yonge, DeGrey and others that repeal of the Act of 1770 was but a prelude to the repeal of the entire game code proved to be unfounded. As on other occasions in the eighteenth century – the Excise Crisis, for example, or the uproar over the Jewish Naturalisation Act – the opposition settled for the abandonment of a project which they viewed, rightly or wrongly, as a threat to the liberties of Englishmen. That having been accomplished, they offered no further challenge to the existing order of things. In the case of the game laws, it would be another quarter of a century before a reform bill was again introduced.

But if the opposition to the Act of 1770 accomplished little, it revealed a great deal. The tensions between 'great men' and 'little ones', heightened by the introduction of strict game preservation in the 1750s, had obviously not diminished. Critics in the 1770s, like their predecessors, consistently made the point that, by denying or restricting 'indulgences', game preservers were actually contributing to the destruction of the game. Not only was the farmer's co-operation vital to the rearing of game, but '*he*, and I may say *he only*, has it in his power to destroy the nests of poachers, which abound everywhere, though a gentleman cannot easily detect them'.[68] Contributing to the farmers' alienation was the widespread conviction by the 1770s that the game laws themselves were 'very inequitable and oppressive'. This was a view shared by a broad spectrum of observers: from the conservative William Blackstone to radicals like Sylas Neville, who at a Yarmouth inn in 1771 'Silenced Squire Knights, who endeavoured to defend the Game Laws'.[69] With farmers and freeholders grating under the enforcement of a set of laws, the legitimacy of which was questioned by one of the foremost legal authorities of the day, it is perhaps not surprising that men like Phipps, Dowdeswell, Dunning and Whitworth should try to enhance their reputations by securing the repeal of a poorly worded law which threatened to make the enforcement of the game code even harsher.

It would have been surprising, however, if they had gone further and attempted to return the game laws to Saxon purity. It was one thing to demand the repeal of a new law on the grounds that it threatened the liberties of Englishmen; it was quite another to propose the abolition of an ancient code of laws and replace it with a new system which, as Whitworth's bill tacitly acknowledged, would immediately run into conflict with existing manorial and property rights. Reform of the game laws required a greater enthusiasm for abstract principles than most members of Parliament gave evidence of having. Any measure, indeed, which attempted to alter the relationship between the gentry and their communities was likely to be viewed with suspicion and even hostility. It is true, of course, that the gentry tempered their conservatism with self-interest and that making game property would have strengthened their hand in preserving the game on their estates. At least one gentleman, in fact, advocated reform so that the taking of game could be made a felony. 'A person,' he wrote, 'who deprives us of what we value more than our domestick animals, or perhaps any other part of our property, deserves the punishment of a Thief.'[70] That, however, does not seem to have been the view of most game preservers. At a time when poaching gangs were becoming increasingly active, country gentlemen undoubtedly wanted the penalty for poaching increased, but in the Night Poaching Acts they had the means to effect that without having to forfeit the traditional privileges of their class. Like park- and warren-owners before them, they seem to have been content to leave the qualification on the statute books and, when necessary, enact new legislation in order to protect their property.

Thus, those who made England's laws in the second half of the eighteenth century felt little urgency to make game property in law as well as in fact. The tensions in the countryside and the criticism of the game laws, therefore, continued. During the election of 1780, for example, Coke of Norfolk found himself the target of the following poetic dart:

> How boasts the Prince Pinery [Coke] the game he breeds!
> That game, alas! his ruined tenant feeds:
> Let the poor man but whisper, he's *undone*;
> The keeper's sent to take away his gun,
> Should hares and pheasants spare the corn he grows,
> He must not shoot, not even shoot – at crows.
> And O! ye Gods! shall this *bashaw* be sent
> A senator to Britain's Parliament?
> There to preserve our liberties and laws,
> A peerless guardian in his country's cause?
> Let French invasions never fright your ear,
> 'Tis our domestic tyrants we must fear.[71]

For the moment, Coke and his fellow game preservers could afford to ignore such attacks but, in the final years of the century, complacency gave way to concern. In the wake of the French Revolution, country gentlemen were forced to recognise that their position in society was not as safe and secure as they had thought. The 1790s were, in fact, a very anxious time for them, and it is perhaps this, more than anything else, which explains why, when John Christian Curwen asked leave to bring in a bill to repeal the game laws, he met with a cautiously favourable response. It may also explain why Curwen's bill was eventually defeated.

IV

Curwen made his request in March 1796. In France, according to the revolutionary calendar, it was Year IV of the republican era; in England it was a time of scarcity and unrest. During the previous twelve months the price of wheat had risen from 45s. 4d. to 104s. 2d. a quarter, precipitating a rash of food riots and some desperate countermeasures by the authorities. The government imported large quantities of corn from abroad, while the justices of Berkshire, meeting at Speenhamland, inaugurated a new system of poor relief under which labourers' wages were subsidised by the parish at a rate pegged to the price of bread.[72] The unrest was not, of course, confined to economic grievances. In the latter half of 1795 there had been a resurgence of radical and Jacobin agitation. At the end of October, the London Corresponding Society had held a huge meeting in Copenhagen Fields; three days later, as the King went to open Parliament, thousands of Londoners had swarmed into the streets to shout 'No War!', 'No Pitt!', and even 'No King!' The government responded with the 'Two Acts', the provisions of which were intended to prevent the radicals from propagating their beliefs and from holding mass meetings.[73] Royal assent to the 'Two Acts' on 18 December 1795 marked the effective end of lower-class political agitation for the duration of the war, but this was far from obvious in the early months of 1796. The government, and the propertied classes in general, had had a scare, and this would inevitably affect their response to any proposal to reform the game laws.

That they were necessarily hostile to such a proposal was by no means certain. All through the 1780s and 1790s the attack on the principles of the game laws had continued. Indeed, wrote William Marshall in 1787, 'to say that the game laws are disgraceful to the laws of the country, would only be repeating what has been said a hundred times'. He himself thought that they were 'an absurdity in English jurisprudence', while Edward Willes of the Court of King's Bench felt that 'Nothing can be more oppressive than the present system of the Game Laws'.[74] *The Times* was of the same opinion. 'The Game Act,' it wrote in 1791, 'so ill accords with the free spirit of the British Constitution, that the sooner the whole is repealed, the better.'[75] In many ways the most extraordinary condemnation of the game laws occurred in 1784, when Coke of Norfolk was introducing his night poaching bill. After Coke's motion had been seconded, Charles Turner, a Yorkshire squire, rose from his seat and launched into a passionate denunciation of the game code.

> He said it was a shame that the House should always be enacting laws for the safety of gentlemen; he wished they would make a few for the good of the poor. If gentlemen were not safe in their houses, it was because the poor were oppressed . . . He had been down in Dorsetshire, and he was shocked to see game there more numerous than the human species. For his own part, he was convinced, that if he had been a common man, he would have been a poacher, in spite of all the laws.[76]

Wraxall would later describe Turner as 'one of the most eccentric men who ever sat in Parliament'. Actually, Turner was just old-fashioned: he wore clothes which were forty years out of date, and by the mid-1780s his values were also beginning to seem antique.[77] Protecting property, not relieving the poor, was the concern of most game law critics in the late eighteenth century. They assailed the 'illiberality' of a system which denied the farmer, 'who raises the grain, a share of the birds that feed upon it', and they confidently predicted that if farmers were permitted to sport on their own lands, the breed of game would actually increase. Once farmers had been given an interest in preserving the game, the advocates of reform promised, country gentlemen would gain an ally – and, equally important, poachers would lose one.[78]

Valid or not, the argument had its appeal for game preservers in the late eighteenth century, as they stepped up their efforts to supply sportsmen with more and more game, for it was widely believed that farmers were actively working to frustrate those efforts. 'Their determination,' wrote a correspondent to the *Salisbury Journal* in 1785, 'is to encourage poachers, and in the future, by themselves or their workmen, to destroy the eggs and young game they find on their farms; and I am sure the country gentlemen . . . will acknowledge that they have it in their power.'[79] After 1789, in fact, sabotage of this sort was openly advocated in certain quarters. In 1790, for example, the Canterbury Association for Preserving the Liberty of the Subject called on the farmers of Kent 'to destroy, as soon as hatched, or littered', all game found on their land; several years later, a similar group in Sheffield recommended the same course of action.[80] How much practical effect these pronouncements had may, of course, be questioned, but there can be little doubt that country gentlemen were sensitive to at least some of the farmers' grievances. Even as it was debating Curwen's bill, the Commons gave its approval to an act which delayed the opening of the partridge-shooting season, so that farmers might harvest their crops undisturbed by sportsmen.[81]

There was, then, some reason to think in 1796 that country gentlemen would not be totally adverse to an alteration in the game laws. The well-known hostility of the 'middling landed interest' to the laws, as well as years of battering by legal scholars, agricultural improvers and urban polemicists, had rendered the game laws vulnerable, even in a time of crisis. The year of riots and radical agitation had, however, raised anxieties which would have to be allayed if a reform bill was ever to succeed. Ever since the late 1770s, when poaching gangs first begin to attack the gentry's preserves in full force, some country gentlemen had come to see the game laws as necessary, not so much to preserve the game, as to combat the spread of lawlessness and social disorder. It was, Henry Zouch reminded his readers in 1783, a matter 'of infinite moment that the criminal excesses of the common people should be effectively restrained, by enforcing a due degree of subordination, and a general and uniform obedience to the law of the land'. He saw the nightly affrays which occurred in his district during those years as a 'contest for power'. If the gentry lost that contest, if they failed to keep the lower orders of society 'within the bounds of their duty', chaos would surely follow.[82] His warning, like many others, gained credibility as the English gentry looked across the Channel in 1789.

Although they had been redrawn by Colbert in 1669, the French game laws were essentially feudal in nature. Hunting game was the prerogative of the king, and he in turn extended sporting privileges to the nobility and the lords of the manor. There was no qualification governing who could and could not hunt, only a series of royal franchises attached to the land, the most prestigious of which were the *capitaneries* held by princes of the blood. A *capitanerie* resembled a royal forest under the Plantaganets. Not only did its lord have exclusive sporting rights over a vast tract of land, but the inhabitants of the area were forbidden to do anything which might endanger the game, even if their crops suffered as a consequence. The price of poaching in these areas was particularly high: some offenders ended up in the galleys.[83] Other franchises were more modest in their claims and their punishments, but all were irksome enough that on 11 August 1789 the National Assembly, in one of its first decrees, abolished all exclusive sporting privileges and gave to every landowner the right to hunt game on his property.[84] The public response was enthusiastic. 'One would think that every rusty gun in Provence is at work', remarked Arthur Young in his journal at the end of August. He himself had no objection to making game the property of the landowner, but noted that 'an unruly, ungovernable multitude seize the benefit of the abolition [of the game laws], and laugh at the [thought of] obligations or recompense'. Others noted it also. Horace Walpole, observing 'the present reign of Everybody'

VIII. John Christian Curwen

from the safety of Strawberry Hill, was quick to report the 'massacre' of the game to his friends. 'I never admired game-acts,' he confided to Lady Ossory, 'but I do not wish to see guns in the hands of all the world, for there are other *ferae naturae* besides hares and partridges – and when all Europe is admiring and citing our constitution, I am for preserving it where it is.'[85]

Thus, in the course of a single sentence, were the game laws transformed from a questionable part of the legal code into a revered branch of the English constitution. Not all minds worked as quickly as Walpole's, but during the early 1790s, as it became clear that abolition of the genty's monopoly was part of the radical programme,[86] a new affection for the game laws became evident. John Byng, for instance, found the roots of the game laws to be much more ancient and distinguished than Blackstone had portrayed them to be. 'A love of field sports', he wrote in 1794, had been 'handed down to us from Nimrod; – and confirmed by the Norman Conquest; as a right of [the] gentry'. He prayed that he would not live 'to see the Sans Culottes of this land laying all distinction [to] waste'.[87] Others took attacks on the game laws to be the signal for, rather than just a symptom of, revolution. Lord Mountmorres told Fanny Burney that 'the spirit of the times' would cross the Channel over to England under pretence of reforming the game laws. Lord Milton agreed. 'The Republican party,' he told Lord Kenyon in 1791, 'has made the Game Laws the object of their abuse and detestation; in France, the instant they began to overturn the Constitution and level all distinctions, these were the first they pulled down. It therefore seems to me that they should at all times be most respectfully guarded.'[88]

Unfortunately for the cause of reform, John Christian Curwen did very little to allay these fears. He was a wealthy Cumberland squire with an enthusiasm for agricultural improvement and political reform. Over the course of a long parliamentary career he would espouse Catholic emancipation, abolition of tithes, parliamentary reform and even the establishment of a national health insurance scheme.[89] But in the 1790s his chief cause was opposition to the war with France. When he rose on 4 March 1796 to ask leave to bring in his reform bill, Curwen was unable to hide his sympathy with the ideals of the French Revolution; indeed, he did not try to. After a sober beginning, with allusions to Blackstone and promises that the game would increase in number if his bill became law, Curwen proceeded to the heart of his argument. That argument, it should be noted, was not that the country was presently suffering from any widespread oppression due to the game laws. Those laws, he admitted, 'had not been executed with their utmost vigour'. He went on to argue, however, that 'these . . . were not the times for us to suffer laws to remain upon our statute book which we dare not attempt to execute to their fullest extent'. It was, in short, the nature of 'the times' which required the repeal of the old game code. There had been, he said, an 'astonishing revolution of the public mind' in recent years, a revolution which could not be ignored. 'Sir, so wide, so extended is the diffusion of knowledge through almost every country in Europe, that such Governments, and such Laws, [which] are not calculated honestly and fairly to promote the general ends of all Government, the happiness and prosperity of the people at large, will be submitted to with reluctance, and can only be supported by force.' Even force, he suggested, would be unable to withstand the will of the people forever. The 'remedy must inevitably come', he warned the House, 'and it may perhaps be prudent . . . not to appear so slow and so unwilling to produce it'.[90]

Considering the rather provocative tenor of Curwen's remarks, the initial reaction was remarkably positive. Some support was to have been expected, of course. Charles James Fox, predictably, thought that 'the whole [game law] system was a mass of insufferable tyranny', and William Wilberforce announced his 'utmost abhorence' of the laws in their present form.[91] Others were less enthusiastic, but even as they pointed out the manifold dangers involved in tampering with any part of the constitution, there was a noticeable reluctance to come out openly in defence of the game laws. William Windham confessed that 'he was no friend to the spirit of the game laws', while Lord Liverpool's son, Robert Jenkinson, 'admitted that the principle of the laws was somewhat oppressive'. The Commons seemed to agree: it rejected a motion to adjourn by a vote of fifty to twenty-seven and referred the matter to a committee.[92] By the time the latter met one week later, however, an opposition had begun to form, and its chief argument, not surprisingly, was 'the example of France'. As one member explained, 'he [had] never *liked* France at any period of his life, and at this time he *detested* it. Everything, therefore, which resembled the commencement of the Revolution there, must meet with his opposition.' The Revolution, argued another, had shown that one concession led inevitably to another, 'and the consequence must be a gradual, if not immediate abolition of all privileges, and a dissolution of all property'. With such arguments being voiced, it was only with some difficulty that Curwen finally obtained a first reading for his bill on 17 March.[93]

That bill revealed Curwen to be more conservative and tactful as a legislator than he was as a speaker. He proposed to repeal most of the old game code – but not all of the gentry's traditional sporting privileges. Franchises and manorial rights were to be left undisturbed, as was the legality of clauses reserving for the landowner the exclusive right to hunt game on his tenant's farm. Curwen, indeed, proposed that there be a two-year grace period during which landlords would be permitted to hunt on their tenant's land even without benefit of a game clause. He would have also allowed a sportsman to hunt game from his own land onto another's without being subject to any penalty. Finally, he retained the Game Duty Act, so that if a farmer wished to hunt on his own land, he would first have to pay a duty of three guineas – itself a sizeable property qualification. This, Curwen assured the House, would put hunting 'out of the power of persons who might injure themselves and the Public by mispending [*sic*] their time in pursuit of game'. Curwen, in fact, took a rather tough line on the subject of poaching. Although the standard penalty under his bill would have been a £5 fine or one month's imprisonment, a second offence was punishable by six months in prison. Night poachers, moreover, would have been liable to mandatory terms of imprisonment, and if they resisted arrest, the bill empowered gamekeepers 'to oppose Force with Force' and indemnified the keeper from prosecution if a poacher was

beaten, maimed or even killed in the ensuing struggle.[94] Although some
still thought the bill an invitation to 'French anarchy',[95] it was poachers,
not country gentlemen, who had the most to fear from Curwen's
proposals. Nevertheless, when the bill came up for a second reading on 29
April, it was thrown out by a vote of sixty-five to seventeen.[96]

Why was Curwen's bill defeated? Much of the answer, no doubt, lies in
the deep conservatism of the English upper classes, an attitude which had
been strongly reinforced by the excesses of the French Revolution. The
open hostility toward 'abstract principles' which would pervade political
debate for the next quarter of a century made the task of a reformer a
difficult one at best. In this regard, Curwen's unabashed admiration for
the ideals of the French Revolution did little to improve his chances of
success. It would, however, be wrong to see the defeat of the bill as simply
the reflex reaction of a ruling class intent on preserving its privileges at
whatever cost. Even Curwen's opponents conceded that there was general
support in the Commons for some alteration in the game laws. 'No system
has excited more enemies' than the game laws, remarked one of the bill's
critics; 'no application for redress seems to have obtained greater support.
Many of the respectable characters of all parties have embraced [Curwen's]
proposition with a warmth, generated, I am convinced, by ignorance of its
consequences.'[97] It was not, therefore, widespread affection for the game
laws which led to the bill's defeat. Rather it was anxiety about the effects of
game law reform, not only on the game but on the rural community as
well. Nowhere is this more apparent than in the speech delivered by the
bill's most distinguished opponent, William Pitt, in the debate on second
reading.

Pitt began by sketching a picture of what, in his view, an ideal game code
would be like. 'In viewing the degrees of the right to kill game,' he said,

> . . . he would indulge that privilege in a superior degree to the
> higher orders of society. From their station and habits of life,
> it was an amusement better suited [to them] than to others,
> and their gratification claimed, he thought, the first attention.
> The second class, to whom a participation of this right might
> properly be given, were occupiers of land, but in a limited
> degree, and only on their own grounds.

Lastly, there was a third group, the lower classes, 'who, for their own sake,
and the sake of society, should not be encouraged to engage in such
diversions'. In outline, this resembled Curwen's proposed system, but Pitt
thought the latter was defective in two important respects. The first was the
basis on which farmers were to be permitted to hunt game. Under
Curwen's system, it would be a right, limited only by a landlord's
reservation and the cost of the game licence. Pitt, however, thought it

should not be 'on any general principle of property that the farmer was to enjoy this right [to hunt], but only in a certain limited degree for relaxation and amusement, and as some encouragement to preserve the game'. Sporting, thus, should remain an 'indulgence', to be granted at the discretion of the gentry – and even then only sparingly, lest farmers be 'diverted from more serious and useful occupations'. Pitt's other objection was that, by legalising the sale of game, the bill actually encouraged poaching. He acknowledged that the ban on the game trade was violated daily, but argued that 'if you make [game] free to be brought to market, the more there is sold, the more will be destroyed'. The poacher would be able to undersell the legitimate suppliers of game and would, therefore, be encouraged to continue his depredations. Moreover, unless there were 'forcible restrictions', farmers would be tempted 'to make a lucrative employment of that which was granted only as a limited amusement'. Curwen's bill, therefore, would encourage the poacher in his work and discourage the farmer in his. On these grounds, Pitt urged its rejection.[98]

Pitt's point was essentially that made by Henry Zouch a decade earlier: the true object of the game laws was less the preservation of the game than the preservation of social order. Hunting game was not anyone's right; it was a privilege granted by society in order to obtain certain desirable ends. Thus, the farmer should be 'indulged' in order to obtain his co-operation in preserving the game – but not so much that he would neglect his occupation. The gentry's 'superior' privilege was also granted in order to achieve ends beneficial to society; chief among these was their residence in the countryside. In the early part of the century, the value of resident gentry was thought to be primarily economic – they brought money into an area and promoted industry among the labouring population – but after the French Revolution, they were increasingly presented as a political good, indeed a political necessity. They were to be the bulwark against revolution. So important, indeed, had this idea become by 1796 that Curwen thought it necessary to begin the debate on his bill by assuring the Commons that if he had thought his proposal 'would in the slightest degree interfere with any inducement to gentlemen's [sic] spending their time and fortunes in the country', he would have been prepared 'to sacrifice something of justice' to prevent that from happening.[99] It was not just that the residence of the gentry in the countryside was essential for the orderly administration of justice and the collection of taxes. By his paternal care of the poor, his supervision of local government and his hospitality to his neighbours, the country gentleman vindicated the wisdom and humanity of the existing social and political order. Moreover, without him as a guide, the lower classes would quickly fall prey to Jacobinism, the consequences of which were only too clear to everyone in 1796. The gentry's monopoly on game seemed, indeed, to be a small price to pay for such services. Game was 'the little paraphernalia of a country gentleman', one of the gentry is said to have remarked; it helped 'to keep our place in the State, create a little respect, and bear with good humour the burthens that are laid upon us'.[100] Perhaps they might have gone on bearing those burdens, even without their 'little paraphernalia', but in 1796, Pitt – and Parliament – were unwilling to risk it.

V

With the defeat of Curwen's bill, the debate over the game laws was adjourned until the end of the war. Viewed in terms of practical results, the opponents of the game laws had thus far accomplished very little. The old game code was still in force, denying farmers the legal right to hunt game on their land. The Night Poaching Act of 1770 had, it is true, been repealed, but in 1800 Parliament approved an act much more arbitrary in nature against only token opposition.[101] In terms of the public's perception of the game laws, however, the debate had had an enormous impact. By the end of the eighteenth century, the game laws were no longer an accepted part of the legal code. To conservatives, they were an anomaly, best left undisturbed until the consequences of their repeal had been carefully thought out. To reformers, they were simply an 'insult [to] the first principles of the Constitution'.[102] The person most responsible for this dramatic change was Sir William Blackstone. By linking of the game laws to the 'Norman yoke', he had called their very legitimacy into question. In addition, Blackstone had provided the necessary historical foundation for an alternative system, one based on the property rights of the individual landowner. The 'middling landed interest' had been agitating for the introduction of just such a system since the middle of the eighteenth century. But according to the rules of eighteenth-century public debate, the game laws first had to be discredited before they could be reformed. That is why it was only after the publication of Blackstone's *Commentaries* that the first serious challenge to the game laws was made. By the end of the century, there were few willing to defend publicly the principle of the game laws. As the debate over Curwen's bill indicated, however, this in itself was not enough to bring about a change in the system. There had to be a pressing *need* to reform the game laws. That need was not present either in 1772 or in 1796, but by the time the Napoleonic wars ended, it was beginning to appear.

6

The reform of the game laws

When the debate over the game laws resumed in 1816, it was in a context radically different from that of the late eighteenth century. For even as it was successfully avoiding a political revolution, England was undergoing an economic one, and by the end of the Napoleonic wars the effects of the latter were beginning to become apparent. In addition to an enormous increase in the production of cotton cloth, coal and iron, the Industrial Revolution had also brought about a dramatic change in the physical and social landscape. Canals and turnpikes cut their way through the countryside, speeding the flow of commerce between rural and urban England, while in the Midlands and the north the new engines of production were being installed at an ever-quickening pace. In 1760 there had been only 20 blast furnaces in the country; in 1805 there were 177, and by 1830 there would be twice that number. Factories were also being constructed in large numbers. In 1813 there were 2400 power looms in England; by 1830 there would be 55,000.[1] Around these centres of industry, not surprisingly, grew large concentrations of workers, tradesmen and craftsmen. In the first three decades of the nineteenth century the populations of Birmingham, Liverpool, Manchester and Sheffield all doubled.[2] The sheer size of these new cities made them difficult to ignore, and so did their growing wealth, a good part of which was spent on goods and services which had traditionally been the tokens of gentility: coaches, fine silver, servants – and game. Both the growth and the prosperity of the new industrial cities presented a challenge to the established social order. However much the superiority of land might still be insisted upon, the demands of industrial England for political and social recognition would, sooner or later, have to be accommodated.

That this did not become apparent sooner is perhaps due to the fact that during the war years landed society was undergoing a minor revolution of its own, the most dramatic effect of which was the enclosure of more than three million acres of land.[3] The main impetus behind this transformation was the extraordinarily high price which corn fetched during the war.

Where, in the 1770s and 1780s, the average price of wheat per quarter had been under 50s., in the 1790s it was 63s. and in the first decade of the nineteenth century it rose to 84s. Nor did it stop there: between 1810 and 1813 the average price was 109s. a quarter.[4] Although such prices rested on a rather shaky base of abnormally bad weather and wartime inflation, landowners were encouraged to expand the production of wheat. Enclosure allowed them not only to create larger, more efficient farms from existing arable land, but also to bring large areas of common and waste land under cultivation for the first time. In most cases, the enclosers did not farm the land themselves and thus directly benefit from the high price of corn, but they did lease out the new farms at rents substantially higher than those demanded before the war. Even in areas untouched by the enclosure movement rents rose dramatically during these years. Overall, the average increase during the war was about 90 per cent.[5] With boom prices being paid for their crops, farmers could afford to pay higher rents. They could also afford to pay their labourers more, although often they had little choice in the matter, since the demands of the military and of wartime industry for manpower had created labour shortages in some parts of the country. In Northamptonshire, weekly wages were reported to have risen by a third between 1808 and 1813. In Lincolnshire during the same years, the reported increase was closer to 40 per cent. Chambers and Mingay have estimated that over the entire wartime period agricultural wages rose by 75 per cent.[6] Just how real that increase was, of course, is another matter. With the price of bread – the central element in the labourer's diet – almost doubled, it seems unlikely that there was any genuine improvement in his standard of living. Certainly, the 1790s were a bleak decade for most agricultural labourers, and even after the turn of the century there were several years of great 'distress' in the countryside. Still, as long as the war and enclosure continued to create employment, the erosion of the labourer's standard of living was masked to a large degree. In retrospect, indeed, it seemed to many labourers that the war years had been a golden age.

The sudden injection of wealth into the countryside and the changes in landownership which accompanied it inevitably had their effect on the character of rural society. The relationship between landlords, farmers and labourers changed perceptibly in these years. While each group retained its place in the rural hierarchy, the social distance between them grew, leaving gulfs which were increasingly difficult to bridge. It was, as usual, the upper classes which led the way. Over the course of the eighteenth century, the great landowners had developed a life-style which set them apart from their neighbours. The aristocracy, mourned one observer as early as 1761, 'no longer affect an old-fashioned hospitality, or suffer the locust of the country to eat them up, while they keep open-house, and dispense victuals and horns of beer . . . to all comers'. This had been replaced by 'genteel entertainments', featuring French food and select company.[7] Game preservation, with its withdrawal of sporting privileges from farmers and smaller freeholders, was but another part of this process. The inflated rent-rolls of the war years financed a further retreat from rusticity – and helped lesser landowners to follow the aristocracy's example. Townhouses were built, friends feasted, hounds kennelled, all on an increasingly lavish scale, while the landowner's relationship with his tenants became more distant and exploitative. Even as their rental income rose, some landlords tried to shift the financial burden of repairs onto the farmer; in addition, there was a decline in long leases, thereby ensuring that the farmer would have to share his growing profits with the owner of the land.[8] Meanwhile, the battue was introduced on the great estates, bringing with it even larger concentrations of game and, inevitably, more damage to the farmer's crops. Although compensation in the form of rent reductions or presents of game was normally given, it was not always accompanied by good will. 'I am every day more and more convinced', grumbled one of Lord Walsingham's correspondents, 'that the more Liberally Farmers are treated the more they will exact, and the more unhandsomely they will behave, having not had the Education of Gentlemen'.[9]

Education, indeed, seems to have been the only requisite of a gentleman that many farmers lacked in the early nineteenth century: everything else they had bought. One memorable evening in 1825 William Cobbett visited the farm of a man named Charrington in the Surrey Weald. What had once been 'the scene of *plain manners* and *plentiful living*' had now, to Cobbett's great disgust, acquired 'a *parlour*'.

> Aye, and a *carpet* and *bell-pull*! . . .there was the mahogany table, and the fine chairs, and the fine glass . . . and . . . the decanters, the glasses, the 'dinner set' of crockery-ware, and all just in the true stock-jobber style. And I dare say it has been '*Squire* Charrington and the *Miss* Charrington's, not plain Master Charrington and his son Hodge, and his daughter Betty.[10]

That there were many such dwellings by the end of the war, there can be little doubt, nor that they had inspired in their owners an enhanced sense of social importance. Farmers, complained William Dyott in his diary, had been 'acquiring vast profits, the natural consequence of which . . . gave them habbits and feelings beyond the rank in life to which they belong, and instead of as formerly being respectable yeomen, they have usurped the class of character (now almost extinct) of country esquires'.[11] As with the landowners, the farmers' increased affluence and self-regard had consequences for those beneath them. One of the most important of these was the abandonment of the practice of 'living in', under which farm servants – usually young, unmarried men and women – were fed and housed in the farmer's own house in lieu of regular wages. After the turn of the century, farmers increasingly chose to pay their servants entirely in cash, with which the servants were then expected to procure their own food and shelter. Given the escalating cost of provisions, this saved the farmer some money; it also spared him the indignity of having to share his table with social inferiors. For someone with a parlour, both considerations were important.[12]

As the practice of 'living in' declined, so also did that of hiring farm servants for a year at a time. In some areas, the 'mops' – annual fairs at which milkmaids, ploughmen and the like would hire themselves out to a farmer for a twelve-month period – began to die out as early as the 1790s; in other areas the process took longer, but the general trend in the early nineteenth century was toward ever shorter terms of employment. By the 1820s, most farm servants in the agricultural counties of the south and east had been reduced to the level of casual labourers, hired by the week or even by the day.[13] They joined another group which had fallen victim to the agricultural revolution: the cottagers. These individuals had previously been able to maintain a modest existence by exploiting their access to the village common. Many cottagers actually lived there and all of them depended on the common to support a cow or a pig and to furnish them with fuel in the winter. With the division of common and waste lands into economic farms as a result of the enclosure movement, this last major remnant of subsistence agriculture was destroyed. In some parishes, cottagers were compensated with small plots of land, but these often proved to be too small or too expensive to farm effectively and were soon sold. In any case, this compensation was not extended to squatters on the common, who were simply evicted and forced to depend completely on their wages as labourers to feed, clothe and house themselves and their families.[14] While the immediate economic consequences of the destruction of the common were probably not as dramatic as was once thought,[15] the social result was unmistakeable. Society, wrote Robert Southey in 1816, had lost 'a link in the social chain . . . a numerous, most useful, and most respectable class, who, from the rank of small farmers, have been degraded to that of day labourers'.[16] Cottagers, like the farm servants, had lost more than a small measure of economic security: they had lost their place in rural society. It is difficult to say which loss was the more painful.

As long as the war lasted, the tensions created by these fissures between social classes were slow to surface. High prices helped soothe the resentments of the farmer, high wages those of the labourer. With the end of the war, however, the balm of prosperity was suddenly no longer available. A combination of good weather and monetary deflation caused corn prices to plummet. In 1813 wheat had sold for 109s. 9d. a quarter; in 1815 it fetched only 63s. 7d. There was a slight recovery in the following years, but it did not last; indeed, conditions grew worse. In the early 1820s prices reached a level only slightly above that of the pre-war era; during the entire decade the average price of wheat never rose above 69s.[17] There were, not surprisingly, howls of pain from the farmers, who found themselves saddled with high rents and, in many cases, with large debts as well. The extent of their distress varied from region to region, but most farmers seem to have had difficulty in meeting their commitments, particularly in the first decade after the end of the war. 'I really believe,' ran the typical report of one Norfolk steward in 1816, 'that there are very few Tenants in the County . . . who make any part of their Rents by the Occupation of their Farms, And that by far the greater Number have during the last two Years lost considerably more than their Rents by their Occupations.'[18] As a result, many landlords were forced to lower their tenants' rents, first by temporary abatements and later by permanent reductions on a scale of 10 or 20 per cent. These adjustments, along with the lifting of wartime taxation and the application of more efficient farming techniques, seem to have allowed most landowners and farmers to survive a difficult period with only a minor cut in their standard of living.[19]

Such, unfortunately, was not the case with the agricultural labourer. Whatever relief he might have found in the lower price of bread was more than offset by a decline in the value of his own labour. In addition to the natural increase in the population during these years, demobilisation of the army and the navy unloaded between 250,000 and 400,000 men onto the labour market.[20] Even at the best of times, the economy would have found it difficult to absorb so many men at once; as it was, the years after Waterloo were not the best of times. The fall in corn prices was, not surprisingly, accompanied by a sharp deceleration in the pace of enclosure, and thus in the demand for hedging, fencing and the construction of new farm buildings. In some areas there was actually a contraction in the amount of land under cultivation. As a result, the demand for labour stagnated, even as the supply of it grew. In such circumstances, it is hardly surprising that between 1814 and 1822 the general level of agricultural wages fell by a third.[21] For many labourers, however, the real problem was finding any work at all. The spectre of unemployment was always present in the years after the war, particularly in the late autumn and winter. A normally slack period, it became even more so after 1815 as labourers found themselves competing for work not only with each other, but with machines as well. During the war the scarcity of labour had prompted some farmers to invest in threshing machines; the subsequent economic squeeze may have caused others to follow suit. How widespread the use of these machines was is unclear, but to the agricultural labourer they obviously appeared to be a serious threat. When the labourers rose in revolt in 1830, the destruction of threshing machines was often the first order of business.[22]

The workers needed work, but there was not enough to go around. And without a village common to cushion the impact of hard times, a large part of the labouring population soon descended into pauperism. 'Many of the poor in this Parish,' reported one Gloucestershire gentleman in 1826 to a relation of his living in Surinam, 'are undoubtedly much worse off than the Negroes are with you, for they are provided with food, & other necessary's, whereas our poor just cannot get work, nor a sufficiency of food either for themselves or [their] children.'[23] They had no choice but to seek relief from the parish, which under the poor laws was charged with caring for the sick and the aged and providing work for the unemployed. In addition to these traditional responsibilities, some parishes had, during the war years, begun to subsidise the incomes of the working poor. To help them cope with the high price of bread, a number of parishes sold wheat to the poor at below-market prices; in other places, labourers were given a wage supplement to help bridge the gap between their incomes and the cost of living. These, however, were seen as temporary expedients and were employed only fitfully up until 1814.[24]

After that year the parish began to assume a much larger role in the labourer's life. As unemployment and low wages ate away at his standard of living, the overseers of the poor – particularly in southern and eastern England – were deluged with applications for relief. It is one of the more remarkable facts about this period that the poor law system did not simply collapse under the weight of these demands. Instead, in its own haphazard, highly decentralised fashion, the system rose to the challenge. The unemployed were put to work, either on the roads or, under the 'roundsman' system, on farms in the parish. In addition, many parishes again extended income subsidies to the working poor – subsidies which, by the nature of the crisis, tended to be more-or-less permanent. This undoubtedly prevented widespread famine and disorder, and to that extent the poor law must be accounted a success. It proved, however, to be a costly achievement, one which was paid for by the poor as well as by the ratepayers. The 'roundsman' system, for example, by providing farmers with a pool of cheap labour almost certainly contributed to the depression of wage levels. At the same time, fear of losing their right to relief inhibited labourers from moving to areas like the north where work was more available and wages were relatively higher. Then there was the method of calculating the amount of relief a labourer deserved. The emphasis placed on the size of the applicant's family may have led to the birth of many pauper children. Even without that consideration, the labourer still found that his income was being determined less by his own efforts or ability than by the arbitrary assessment of the overseers of the poor, the attitude of whom was often conditioned by a desire to keep the rates as low as possible. The agricultural labourer had, in effect, purchased his survival by surrendering the last remnants of his independence.[25] He was tied to his parish and locked into a low and deteriorating standard of living. Among the few avenues of escape was poaching.

II

The long and violent struggle between the poacher and the game preserver had begun, as we have seen, in the latter part of the eighteenth century. In the 1770s organised bands of poachers began regularly to invade the game preserves of the gentry, selling their plunder to higglers and coachmen who, in turn, supplied the urban market with game at a handsome profit. Preservers responded by employing bands of keepers and watchers – and, in some areas, by setting spring guns and man traps – to guard their game. They also tried to strengthen the laws against poaching. In the early 1770s night poaching was singled out for particularly heavy penalties, and in 1800 'gangs' of two or more night poachers became liable to imprisonment for as long as two years. Possibly because of such measures – but more likely because the Napoleonic wars drained the countryside of many potential poachers – there was a noticeable levelling off of game offences after the early 1790s. In Wiltshire, for example, the average number of committals under the game laws fell from 16.7 a year in the 1780s to 9.6 in the 1790s; in the first decade of the nineteenth century it was still only 12.4.[26] The deadly affrays between poachers and gamekeepers did not, of course, totally disappear. In 1805, for instances, a gang of thirteen poachers invaded Thorpe Wood in Norfolk to shoot some of Lord Suffield's pheasants; when discovered they fired their guns and wounded several of the watch. Four years later a similar incident took place in Lancashire: on being surprised by gamekeepers, 'the poachers immediately levelled their guns, shot one [of the keepers], and dangerously wounded another'.[27] Nevertheless, both the judicial records and the press accounts indicate that the incidence of poaching did not increase during the war years. Poaching remained a problem, but not a pressing one.

Like so many things in the countryside, this was to change dramatically with the end of the war. In 1816, the first year for which we have any national figures, 868 persons were reported to have been imprisoned for game offences; by 1820 the number had risen to 1467.[28] The real magnitude of the change becomes clearer when we look at individual counties. In the winter of 1812–13, there were eight committals under the game laws in Wiltshire; five winters later there were eighty-five. In Bedfordshire it was the same story: game committals rose from seven in 1813 to seventy-seven six years later. Equally striking is the fact that committals remained at these high levels. In the first half of the 1820s there were, on average, sixty-five game committals a year in Bedfordshire; in Wiltshire there were ninety-two. In the latter county alone over 1300 persons were imprisoned under the game laws in the decade and a half after Waterloo – more than *twice* the number committed in the previous fifty years.[29]

Admittedly, there were several factors working at this time to increase the number of poachers in prison. The greater predisposition of J.P.s to imprison offenders has been noted in a previous chapter, as have the changes in the law which were designed to make it more difficult for poachers to escape incarceration.[30] Both factors, however, had been present for some time without any dramatic effect on the length of the gaol calendar. More important, it seems, was the poacher's declining ability to pay the fine imposed by the justice of the peace. In Wiltshire, 30 per cent of those known to have been summarily convicted of a game offence between 1808 and 1813 had been unable to pay the fine and were sent to prison; in the following six years that figure rose to 42 per cent.[31] 'That is the reason you have so many prisoners', a Surrey J.P. told the Select Committee on the Game Laws in 1823, 'because they cannot pay the penalties'.[32] But why were they not able to? In most cases, a poacher's ability to pay the fine was dependent on the price he received for his game from higglers and coachmen; in the years after Waterloo that price was going down. A brace of pheasants which had once cost a higgler 10s. or 12s. could now be purchased for 5s. or 6s. The poacher's partridges and hares also sold for less. The explanation for this was quite simple: the black market was being flooded with game. One poulterer testified in 1823 that a third of all the game which came into London was never sold. 'I once saw, in a salesman's possession,' he claimed, '2,000 partridges, and . . . I know by my own observation that they were never consumed; they were thrown into the Thames.'[33] Over-supply on such a scale could only have come from an increase in poaching – and, most likely, from an increase in the number of poachers as well. If the gaol calendars are any indication, that increase was a massive one.

This was particularly evident in the activities of poaching gangs in the post-war period. For many, of course, poaching would continue to be a solitary affair, pursued by moonlight with a few snares or a favourite lurcher. But in the neighbourhoods where the game was guarded by battalions of keepers and watchers, the protection of numbers was advisable, indeed essential. It was these areas which, after the war, reported the largest numbers of convictions[34] – and, in addition, some of the most extraordinary scenes of organised resistance to law in the history of rural England. Raids by eight, ten and twelve poachers were commonplace in these years; on occasion, particularly in the 1820s, the numbers could be far larger. In Norfolk an attack by twenty-five poachers was reported; in Gloucestershire a gang of 'about forty men, with white handkerchiefs round their hats, marching in files, drew up upon seeing the keepers and their assistants (about ten in number) and a desperate battle ensued'. In the winter of 1827 Lady Hertford's estate at Temple Newsam in Yorkshire was visited by no less than sixty poachers.[35] 'Here in the North,' reported Lord Tyrconnel from Yorkshire in 1831, 'Men have gone about to the amount of more than 100 defying all Law and all opposition.' 'I myself,' he added, 'saw no less than 55 of these Poachers who came down one hill & across a valley and their right extend[ed] to the opposite hill, forming a line as well as [the] light Infantry.'[36]

The military comparison was apt, as there was an impressive air of discipline surrounding some of these raids. When, for example, Robert Peel's gamekeepers challenged a body of poachers near Lulworth Castle, Dorset, in 1822, the poachers' leader replied, 'We are five and thirty strong, and are for death and glory: but we will not use fire-arms, unless your party fire first.' He then turned to his men – each of whom, like the Gloucestershire poachers mentioned above, had a white handkerchief tied round his head – and threatened to shoot the first man who left the field. After twenty minutes' combat, the poachers executed a strategic withdrawal.[37] Even more remarkable was the raid on preserves of D.S. Dugdale, a Warwickshire M.P., in November 1826. There were, he claimed later, about fifty poachers in the gang which entered his woods at Merevale:

> about 28 of them were armed with guns, about 12 with sticks,
> the remainder with a stone in each hand, by which they kept
> making a noise by knocking them against each other, for the
> purpose of keeping the persons in line in going through the
> woods; and on the outside of the wood were two men on
> horse back, about 50 yards from one another, who had horns,
> and they directed in which way the line should be carried on.
> In that way they thoroughly went through the wood, firing a
> great number of times, and killed a quantity of Pheasants.[38]

Although direct evidence is difficult to come by, it seems likely that a number of poachers had had military training of one sort or another. In 1822, for example the War Office identified William Jackson, a Hertford-shire poacher, as a deserter from the 14th Foot; in 1829 the member of a Warwickshire gang confessed to having been a deserter from the militia.[39]

In other cases, poachers may have been former soldiers, honourably discharged and now putting their experience to use in more profitable endeavours.

But if some poaching gangs had a measure of self-discipline, most exhibited little more than a fierce determination to avoid capture, whatever the cost in human life. The casualty list for this period is a long one, but it is not necessary to recite it in order to document the brutality of the poaching war. That can easily be done by simply recounting the events which occurred in the neighbourhood of Nuneaton on the night of 20 December 1828. At around midnight, D.S. Dugdale's woods, the site of the previously mentioned military operation, were once again invaded, this time by a band of thirteen poachers. Not long afterward, they ran into the gamekeeper and three of his assistants. 'Form the Line', the poachers' leader told his troops; then he shouted to the keeper, 'You d–d bloody —, what brings you here? You d–d scamps be off, or we'll give you something. Cut, be off.' The keeper and his men retreated, but as they did, one of the poachers had second thoughts: 'D–n their eyes, don't let them go off that way, put something into them.' In the chase which followed, several shots were fired but the keepers managed to escape. Even as they did, another confrontation was taking place on Lord Denbigh's estate at Newnham Paddox, fifteen miles to the south-east. It began when a gang of sixteen poachers, in the midst of a foray into Denbigh's preserves, spied the gamekeeper, John Slinn. 'D–n his eyes, here comes that long —, shoot him', cried one of the gang, and when Slinn and his men retreated into the stable yard to get reinforcements, the gang followed, throwing stones at them. Lord Denbigh, who was watching all this from his window, sounded the alarm and soon a force was raised to chase the poachers off. The gang remained defiant, however. Overtaken in a nearby field, the poachers turned on the posse, levelled their guns and shouted, 'come on, we are ready for you'. Within minutes, Slinn and his men were once more in retreat. Before they could take shelter in the sheep-pens, however, two of the gamekeeper's assistants were captured. When Slinn heard one of them cry, 'O Lord, don't murder me!', he went to the man's rescue – and ended up with two gunshot wounds in his stomach. As he was being carried into Lord Denbigh's house, the poachers returned home, having been warned by their leaders that 'if anyone told, they would make him so that he could not tell anyone else'.[40]

That warning was a necessary precaution, for however strong the ties which bound poachers to one another, the threat of transportation could – and did – cause some to betray their comrades. When, for example, Henry Tanner, a Berkshire poacher, was apprehended following a raid on the preserves of a local gentleman, he decided to buy his freedom by testifying for the prosecution against the other eight members of the gang.[41] Similar bargains led to the capture of twelve poachers in Bedfordshire and fourteen more in Norfolk.[42] And in spite of the threat of retaliation, the gangs which attacked Merevale and Newnham Paddox in December 1828 were quickly impeached by three of their colleagues; on the latter's evidence, twenty-seven men were sentenced to transportation, twelve of them for life.[43] Such instances of human perfidy, however, were not common enough to destroy all the poaching gangs in England. The besieged game preservers, therefore, turned for assistance to another quarter. In 1816 the area around Downham in Norfolk was reported to be 'the haunt of an immense body of poachers, whose numbers and daring proceedings so terrified the people around, that the civil authorities were not very forward to act against the desperadoes'. The local gentry decided to send to London for a police officer; soon after his arrival he managed to become a member of the gang. A week or two later, the officer went around one morning and briskly arrested ten of the poachers. The idea was eagerly taken up by other game preservers.[44] By 1823, indeed, William Cobbett was charging that the country was 'filled with *spies*', particularly '*game-spies*', who joined common men in their sport only to betray them later. It was an exaggeration, of course, but there can be no doubt that, whether as undercover agents or simply as investigators free from the pull of local loyalties, police officers from Bow Street and the other stations in the metropolis figured prominently in the capture of many poaching gangs in this period.[45]

Their talents, however, were not enough to slow the seemingly inexorable tide of poaching. The resort to the police, indeed, was a sign of desperation – an admission by the gentry that they were losing control over their own neighbourhoods. With each succeeding year, the gangs appeared to grow more audacious, the assaults more brutal, the gaols more crowded. Equally disturbing, perhaps, was the open, even savage hostility exhibited toward game preservers and their servants in these years. Gamekeepers, of course, were the objects of particular hatred. 'Is that Cross? damn him, blow his brains out', was the cry of one Lancashire gang on meeting a local gamekeeper, whose life they had previously resolved to take. Unlike some other keepers, Cross managed to thwart their design.[46] Gamekeepers, however, were not the only ones singled out for reprisals. In November 1829, D.S. Dugdale – whose Warwickshire estate, as we have seen, was the target of repeated raids – discovered that all the pointers in his kennel had been poisoned. Other gentlemen complained of similar incidents.[47] And at the Cheshire quarter sessions in 1828, Samuel Burgess, a weaver by trade, was convicted of sowing 'quantities of wheat impregnated with arsenic, with intent to destroy the game'. The prosecution claimed that the offence – for which there could be no motive but vengeance – 'was one of frequent occurrence'.[48] Such incidents, perhaps more than the pitched battles which filled the pages of the provincial press in the 1820s, reveal the underlying bitterness of the poaching war. It was a bitterness which the fines and the spring guns, the spies and the transportations did much to deepen and, in some cases, turn into a vengeful hatred. Thus the war fed on itself, and as the battles grew in number and intensity, the gentry were forced to re-examine the rules under which the war was fought.

III

'I think something must be done, or it will be impossible to inhabit the country', Robert Haldane Bradshaw, a Lancashire game preserver, told a parliamentary committee in 1828.[49] Many other country gentlemen agreed with him and began to call for a change in the game laws. At various times in the 1820s, the quarter sessions of Norfolk, Suffolk, Lancashire, Wiltshire and Derbyshire all petitioned Parliament for that purpose. The justices of Norfolk, in fact, petitioned on five separate occasions. They had, they told Parliament, 'found frequent occasion to deplore the injurious moral operation of the existing Game Laws, under which the commitments to the several prisons in that county have of late years increased to an alarming and unprecedented extent'.[50] Their appeal for a drastic change in the game laws was supported by the reports of three different Select Committees, which (in varying degrees) recommended the repeal of the old game code and the enactment of a new system under which game would become the property of the landowner and capable of being legally bought and sold. Bills to implement some or all of these recommendations were introduced in almost every session. In the decade and a half after Waterloo, Parliament considered no less than seventeen bills aimed at reforming the game laws. Yet, in spite of strong support both within and outside Parliament, it was not until 1831 that a Game Reform Act was passed. The responsibility for this delay did not rest solely with 'unblushing' conservatives like Sir John Shelley and Lord Malmesbury, who consistently opposed every proposal to change the existing system. The reformers themselves had much to do with Parliament's failure to respond to the appeals of magistrates and game preservers, for while they all agreed that 'something must be done', they were far from unanimous about what that 'something' should be.

Their disagreement arose, at least in part, because the game laws were no longer being criticised on the same grounds that they had been in the eighteenth century. Before the war, the reformers had railed against the injustice of a set of laws which not only robbed the farmer of the right to kill the game which fed on his crops, but then gave that right to any landed gentleman who happened to be in the neighbourhood. Invoking Blackstone, the critics called for a return to the days of 'Saxon freedom' when game belonged to the landowner, regardless of his income or status. Poaching was rarely mentioned in these debates – except by defenders of the game laws, who argued that change would lead to even greater destruction of the game by the lower classes. With the end of the war, however, there was a significant change in the character of the reformers' case. While the injustice of the game laws was still mentioned, it ceased to be the chief argument in the reformist arsenal. Blackstone all but disappeared from the speeches and pamphlets which called for a fundamental alteration in the existing system.[51] In his place the reformers inserted statistics which showed that committals to prison for game offences were growing at an alarming rate. They dwelt at length on the violence of the nightly affrays, the 'demoralizing' effect of prisons and the likelihood that poachers would soon move on to more serious crime. The prevalence of poaching, in short, was no longer an argument against reform. On the contrary, it had become the central element in the reformers' case. As such, however, it could only be convincing if a causal connection could be established between the game laws and the increase in poaching. It was over the precise nature of that connection that the reformers split.

The most obvious link between the game laws and poaching was, of course, the black market. As early as 1750 the laws' critics had warned that the ban on the game trade ran counter to the natural desire of urban gentlemen for 'Delicacies at their Table'; if these could not be obtained legally, 'great Numbers of Poachers will be encouraged to destroy the Game' to satisfy the demand. Indeed, by prohibiting its sale, wrote another observer in 1777, game 'is made the greater rarity . . . and as such is not to be dispensed with at any genteel table, but must be had at all events; hence the origin of poaching, that vile trade, pregnant with ill'.[52] The gentry's immediate, almost instinctive, response to any mention of the black market was to try to tighten up enforcement of the law. Although the Game Association's efforts in this regard had not been notably successful, many gentlemen continued to believe that if somehow a way could be found to prevent – or at least inhibit – the sale of game, poaching would soon cease to be a problem. It was this expectation which lay behind the passage in 1818 of an act to prohibit the purchase of game. Due (apparently) to an oversight, the Act of 1755 had applied only to the sale of partridges, pheasants and hares; the buyer was not subject to any penalty.[53] The Act of 1818 corrected this anomaly by making every purchaser of game liable to a £5 fine for every head of game bought, and it sought to encourage informations by promising a pardon (and half the fine) to any seller who would give evidence against one of his customers.[54] As with similar attempts in 1707 and 1752, there were some initial signs of success. The London poulterers, once again under pressure, agreed among themselves not to trade in game and to inform against anyone who did. Their resolve, however, did not last long. Fearing 'ill blood in the trade', they shied away from prosecuting those who broke the compact. Moreover, they soon found that their legitimate trade was being taken away from them by 'a parcel of Jews and porters' who felt no compunction about providing the public with what it wanted. 'Good God, what is the use of your running your head against a wall?' a poulterer was asked by one of his regular customers. Within a year the Act was a dead letter; in the market game was being sold 'more than ever'.[55]

The abject failure of Parliament to halt the game trade persuaded a large number of gentlemen that a different approach would have to be taken if the inducement to poaching which the black market provided was ever to be ended. Some argued that English society had undergone a change since the eighteenth century which had rendered any attempt to prohibit the sale of game not only impossible but unjust. Land, they pointed out, was no longer the only source of wealth. The last few decades had seen the rise of 'great and opulent towns filled with merchants, who are bound by their stations and occupations to exercise a liberal hospitality, and especially to support a well appointed table, at which the appearance of game is but a reasonable indulgence'.[56] Others were less tactful. 'Merchants,' said John Bennett, a Wiltshire M.P., 'would have game on their tables, even if it were soiled with the blood of the poachers who procure it for them.'[57] That being the case, the obvious solution was to provide the merchants with a legal source of game and thus rob the poacher of his chief customers. The latter, it was claimed, had a natural preference for legitimate suppliers; even if they did not, the attraction of a lower price would be irresistible. The influx of game from the gentry's estates into the market, predicted Lord Grosvenor, would render game 'so cheap . . . as to make it not worth the poacher's while to follow his nefarious pursuit'.[58] The argument, of course, was not a new one. Similar claims had been made in the eighteenth century, but to a generation which learned its economics from David Ricardo, it had a special appeal. As Joseph Hume assured the House of Commons, 'there was nothing like free trade' to cure the nation's ills. All that was necessary was that country gentlemen enter into commercial competition with the poachers and – according to a resolution signed in 1823 by an impressive list of Yorkshire landowners – poaching 'would speedily cease to exist'.[59]

Others were not so sure. Considerable scepticism was expressed about the ability of country gentlemen – many of whom spent hundreds of pounds a year on game preservation – to compete effectively with poachers in the marketplace. The testimony of poulterers before the Select Committees in the 1820s was at best ambiguous. Some of them said that poachers could be undersold; others, however, predicted that the price of game would actually rise as a result of legalisation, since it was considered unlikely that gentlemen would be able to supply the market as regularly as poachers did.[60] (In any event, the experience of the 1820s, when game flooded onto the market in unprecedented quantities, did not support the reformers' contentions. The resulting fall in price paid to the poacher was not accompanied by a decline in poaching activity; indeed, just the reverse occurred.) The loudest objections to the call for legalisation, however, did not come from sceptics but from other reformers, who vehemently rejected the idea that lifting the ban on the game trade would by itself bring about a decline in poaching. They insisted that legalisation must be accompanied by the abolition of qualifications and the designation of game as the property of the landowner. Unless these changes were also made, they said, the poaching war would continue; indeed, it would grow worse. If Parliament confined itself to legalisation of the sale of game, Lord Wharncliffe warned his fellow peers, 'the country would murmur, and their lordships would find that such a system would not be endured'.[61]

Those who demanded the complete repeal of the old game code were not simply enthusiasts for reform. There was a fundamental difference in outlook between them and the advocates of legalisation. The latter believed that the root cause of poaching was economic. The poor, they thought, were being 'bribed into vice' as the result of a foolish attempt to deprive townsmen of the pleasure of serving game at their tables. The other school of game law reformers, while not denying the ill effects of the black market, tended to view the problem as essentially a moral one, the crux of which was that almost everyone except the gentry thought that the game code was unjust. As a consequence, poachers did not feel the lash of public disapproval; on the contrary, their depredations met with a great deal of sympathy. Thus, the 'principal cause' of the increase in offences against the game laws, Lord Suffield declared in 1828, was 'the just and well-merited detestation in which these laws have been held by the public'.[62] The Night Poaching Acts of 1816 and 1817, for example, were thought to be too severe; faced with sending a poacher to Australia for seven years, juries had shown themselves 'unwilling to do their duty'.[63] Much more damaging, though, was the general belief that poaching was not really theft. It was this 'want of moral feeling' about the taking of game which, these reformers argued, would have to be changed before any decline in poaching could be hoped for. 'The law, as it now stood,' James Stuart-Wortley, the most dedicated of the reformers, told the House of Commons in 1825, 'occasioned most men to look upon a poacher as one who ought not to be condemned, but to be pitied; and he knew of no way of removing that feeling except by altering the legal denomination of game, and making it property.' Once the farmer could legally kill – and sell – the game found on his land, Stuart-Wortley was convinced, 'a different feeling would be introduced into the country'. If it was not, 'human nature was not human nature'.[64]

Needless to say, his confidence was not universally shared. 'Was it to be supposed,' asked an incredulous George Bankes, 'that the feelings of the higher class, and their disgust of crime, would have any operation on the lower ranks of society?'[65] There were undoubtedly some reformers who must have also wondered whether the simple designation of game as property would create scruples where none had been before. The real weakness in the argument, however, did not lie in its assumptions about human nature, but rather in its analysis of the cause of the poaching war. The advocates of property – and, indeed, of legislation as well – claimed that it was the law which was to blame for the ever-lengthening gaol calendars and the battles which raged in the gentry's woods; the law, therefore, would have to be changed before peace could be restored to the countryside. That, however, was not the only explanation which could be offered for the increase in poaching in the post-war years. Lord Eldon, for example, thought that the temptation offered by the large game preserves which had been created to supply sport for the battues was the principal cause of the increase. 'If their lordships did not find some means of destroying these battues,' he said, 'they might as well say that the moon shall not shine, as [that] there shall not be poachers.' Nor was this just the view of unrepentant conservatives. The Commons' Select Committee on Criminal Commitments and Convictions agreed with his analysis, and so did Henry Hunt, the Radical politician. 'Diminish the number of preserves,' the latter told the Commons in 1831, 'and poaching would be stopped in a great degree.'[66] This explanation fit nicely with another: that 'distress' caused by the agricultural depression had forced many normally honest labourers into the poaching trade. It was 'want of employment among the labouring poor [which] was the grand cause of poaching', Lord Carnarvon believed. While it was true that the parish provided work for those who were unable to find it elsewhere, 'that class of persons,' observed another gentleman, '. . . preferred poaching to being employed for a few shillings a week in breaking stones on the highways'. 'There can be no doubt,' agreed a Wiltshire J.P., 'that when men are unemployed they will naturally poach.'[67]

Were, then, the reformers mistaken? Was it, as Lord Malmesbury believed, simply 'the state of the times' – a 'demoralizing' combination of temptation and necessity – which sent men into the woods to do battle for a bag full of pheasants?[68] As we have seen in a previous chapter, the motives behind poaching were many: the prospect of gain, the love of adventure and, of course, the conviction that game was 'the property of those who can take it'.[69] In one sense, therefore, there was no single 'grand cause' of poaching, any more than there was one for smuggling or pickpocketing. If, however, one is seeking to explain the *increase* in poaching in this particular period, it is possible to be more precise. The reformers were undoubtedly correct in thinking that the game laws were, in whole or in part, self-defeating. The black market which Parliament had unwittingly called into existence actively encouraged the destruction of game, while the exclusion of farmers from full sporting rights created resentments which, at the very least, made the detection of poachers more difficult. The game laws, however, had been in effect for many years when the poaching war broke out again in 1815. The changes which were made in the law thereafter – notably the Night Poaching Acts of 1816 and 1817 – may have, as Sir Samuel Romilly contended, excited a new 'spirit of ferocity and inhumanity' among poachers, but it seems unlikely that they could have caused an increase in poaching of the magnitude indicated by the gaol calendars.[70]

On the other hand, there is a good deal of evidence to suggest that the increase in poaching was directly related to the depression which hit the countryside at the end of the Napoleonic wars. Poachers themselves were wont to explain – and excuse – their activities by pointing to their 'distress'. 'Tell me, then, fellow, why do you go out poaching?' one Dorset J.P. asked a defendant in 1828. 'Because I am poor, your worship', he answered; 'I can get no work; and unless I take [up] a gun now and then, I must starve.'[71] However self-serving such statements might be, they were corroborated by the observations of the gentry themselves. Sir Thomas Baring, for example, concluded that most of the men who were committed for offences against the game laws in his county of Hampshire had poached 'in consequence of not being able to obtain employment or such employment as was equal to their support'; one year later, a committee of Hampshire J.P.s echoed their agreement.[72] These and other gentlemen pointed to the comparative youth of the offenders. Poachers, said Lord Malmesbury in 1827, 'were of a different description from those committed formerly. They were young, industrious, healthy men, who were in distress and in want of employment.' Parliamentary returns do, in fact, indicate that a large proportion of poachers were under twenty years of age. In Suffolk, for example, the latter comprised a quarter of all those known to have been convicted between 1827 and 1830; in Hampshire, another county with a high level of poaching activity, the figure was 30 per cent.[73] Youth, indeed, seems to have been their curse, particularly if they lived in the southern and eastern counties where the system of income supplements was pervasive. As men without large families – or without families at all – they were discriminated against in the distribution of both work and relief in favour of those with many mouths to feed. Was it any wonder, asked Lord Malmesbury, that men who 'had been reduced to work on the roads for half a crown a week . . . should have recourse to unlawful measures, to obtain the means of subsistence?'[74]

'Distress', then, seems to have been the major cause of the increase in poaching in the years after Waterloo. This conclusion, however, must be qualified in two important respects. First, 'distress' in this period was chronic, widespread un- and underemployment, not simply an inability 'to obtain the means of subsistence'. The latter could also be caused by a sudden increase in the price of bread, but there is little evidence that levels of poaching activity were closely tied to the cost of living. To judge by the Wiltshire game committals, poaching did indeed increase during the 'famine' years of 1795–6, 1800–1 and 1806–7, but in none of these years did it rise to the level of the 1780s (when the price of wheat was relatively stable), much less approach that of the post-war years.[75] The 'distress' which descended on rural England after 1815 was very different from these previous 'crises of subsistence', as its character was only partially economic. As we have seen, after the war many agricultural labourers were reduced to more-or-less permanent dependence on the parish. Many spent their days doing useless 'work' on the roads; even if they found real employment, it was at a fraction of their previous wages, and thus they were still in need of parish relief. In either case, they often had to endure the contempt and petty tyrannies of the overseers of the poor, whose chief aim was to keep the parish rates down to the barest minimum. The humiliation which such treatment caused was not easily borne; the desire to escape it and regain one's independence and self-respect must have been very powerful. Poaching offered a way out – a way, moreover, which was condoned not only by their peers but by the farmers as well, the latter having their own grievances against the game preserving gentry. It was, in short, pride as well as necessity which turned men into poachers.

The second qualification to the economic explanation of the increase in poaching illustrates this point. Not all poachers carried on their trade in the depressed agricultural regions of the south and east. Some of the most spectacular raids, in fact, occurred north of the Trent, where agricultural wages were higher and alternative employment was available in the new industrial cities. The north did not, of course, enjoy continuous prosperity in the post-war years. There were trade recessions, and poaching committals tended to rise during them.[76] The region did not, however, experience the spiral of despair which so reduced the morale of the labouring classes of the south in these years, in part, perhaps, because the southern system of income supplements was rarely practised. Nevertheless, there was a great deal of poaching in the north. It was, indeed, poaching of a particularly violent kind, conducted by large, well-disciplined bands of men who, as we have seen, did not scruple to back up their threats with force. Many of these poachers were miners, but stocking knitters, ribbon weavers and other industrial workers also regularly went out on raids. Unlike their compatriots in the south, moreover, they tended to have regular employment, often earning between 10*s*. and 15*s*. a week.[77] 'Distress', although not unknown to such men, does not seem to have been the prime motivation behind their raids. A full explanation of their activities must await further research into the history of the industrial working class in the early nineteenth century, but we can perhaps catch a hint of the feelings behind the raids from a ballad sung by some Pennine miners in the 1820s:

> There's the fat men of Oakland, and Durham the same,
> Lay claim to the moors, likewise to the game;
> They sent word to the miners they would have to ken,
> They would stop them from shooting the bonny moor hen.
>
> O these words they were carried to Weardale with speed,
> Which made the poor miners to hang down their heads;
> But sent them an answer they would have to ken,
> They would fight till they died for their bonny moor hen.[78]

An antagonism, long nourished, toward 'fat men' may have had much to do with the battles between keepers and poachers which were fought in the northern counties in these years. Certainly it was a feeling which was not unknown in areas where industrialisation was occurring. The Nottingham Luddites, for example, were apparently accustomed to raiding the preserves of neighbouring estates, and it may be that studies of other industrial communities in this period will yield further evidence of a connection between class antagonism and resistance to the game laws.[79] Until such studies appear, it can only be suggested that necessity was not the sole inspiration for the poaching war.

IV

The long campaign to reform the game laws began in 1816. Earlier in the century there had apparently been a plan to introduce a reform bill, but this came to nothing. During the war, as one reformer later remarked, the gentry were reluctant to make any alteration, 'lest, if a slight opening were made to innovation, all ancient landmarks, and every valuable possession, might be swept away by the force of the torrent'.[80] Even after the defeat of Napoleon, this attitude survived in many quarters, but the sudden increase in the tempo of the poaching war caused enough concern that when Thomas Wood, a Middlesex gentleman, moved for a select committee to inquire into the game laws, the House of Commons agreed.

Wood made no secret of his hopes that the Committee would recommend legalisation of the sale of game. Indeed, he had arranged for several poulterers and game traders to testify before the Committee, but, for reasons yet obscure, they were never permitted to. Some justices of the peace were examined, however, and in little over a month's time, the Committee's report was tabled.[81] In it the Committee recommended that 'all game should be the property of the person on whose lands such game should be found'. This would, it argued, be no more than a recognition of the landowner's right under common law. In addition, the Committee observed that 'the commercial prosperity of the country, and the consequent habits of luxury and indulgence, operate as a constant excitement' to violations of the game laws – an influence 'which no legislative interference that your Committee could recommend appears likely to counteract'.[82] The clear implication was that the ban on the game trade should be lifted. Thus, in effect, the Committee invited Parliament to remodel the game laws along the same lines that Curwen had proposed twenty years earlier.

It was an invitation which not all reformers, much less all country gentlemen, were eager to accept. Thomas Wood, for one, still wished to confine reform to the legalisation of the game trade, and in the following session he introduced a bill limited to that purpose. It soon ran into a cross-fire which was to become all too familiar in the next decade. The conservatives attacked the bill as an inducement to increased poaching, while the advocates of making game property – including John Christian Curwen, still fighting the good fight – complained that it did not go far enough. With both groups against it, Wood was forced to abandon his project at second reading.[83] Possibly as a result of this skirmish, the reformers displayed more unity when, in 1819, a new and more comprehensive measure was brought in by Thomas Brand, a Hertfordshire M.P. Under its provisions, game would become property as well as a saleable commodity. No reformer spoke against it; Wood, indeed, made a speech in its favour. Similar gestures of support did not, however, come from other advocates of legalisation, and some of the latter may have been among those who contributed to the bill's eventual defeat when the House, by a vote of 119 to 59, refused a motion for its committal.[84] Perhaps reflecting their attitude toward Brand's bill, the supporters of legalisation then quickly tried to push through a measure of their own, but that too failed to pass.[85] Thus, by the beginning of the 1820s, the game reformers had achieved nothing, except possibly to demonstrate their own profound disagreement over the proper method of restoring peace to the countryside.

With the defeat of both bills in 1819, the reform movement lost most of the momentum it had gained from the Select Committee's report. The reformers, in fact, were forced to start all over again. In 1821 they moved for the creation of another select committee on the game laws. That motion was rejected, but two years later with the approval of Robert Peel – who, as Home Secretary, had a special interest in finding a solution to the problem of poaching – the House of Commons agreed to another investigation.[86] Reflecting the interests of its chairman, Lord Cranborne, the new Select Committee concentrated on the operation of the black market and its connection with poaching. Poulterers, J.P.s and police officers were brought before it to testify and, on the basis of their evidence, the Committee decided that the ban on the game trade was not only unworkable but pernicious. It recommended, therefore, that the sale of game be legalised, in the hope that this might diminish, if not completely end, poaching.[87] Within days of tabling the report, Cranborne brought in a bill to give it effect but, like Thomas Wood before him, he quickly ran into opposition from reformers as well as conservatives. Henry Brougham, for example, declared that he would not vote for a bill which would only give gentlemen the opportunity of turning their monopoly into a source of profit. Despite Peel's support, the measure was left to die on the order paper.[88] The impact of the 1823 Committee was, however, greater than this episode would suggest. The Committee's report and evidence were printed and, when the contents became public, they caused something of a stir. Of particular interest, it appears, was the revelation that some gentlemen had already taken to sending their game to market. Although the size of this supply was small compared to that provided by poachers, the discovery of this fact tended to discredit the claims of conservative game preservers that they were only interested in preserving the traditional sports of country gentlemen. Some critics suspected that they only wanted to keep the price inflated. 'That Game is at present Sold is very certain,' Sir Thomas Cullum, a non-sporting gentleman, wrote acidly to his son, '& the only question is whether the Baronet & Esquire, or the Peer sell the most to the London Fishmongers & Poulterers.'[89] In addition, the 1823 Committee had another important effect: it sparked the interest of James Stuart-Wortley in the reform of the game laws.

Stuart-Wortley was a Yorkshire game preserver who had had an opportunity to observe the effects of the poaching war on his own estate. In 1819 one of his gamekeepers had been fatally wounded during an affray with a band of poachers. His immediate response had been to install spring guns in his preserves but, after serving on the Select Committee in 1823, he became a champion of game law reform.[90] Although he had seconded Cranborne's legalisation bill, Stuart-Wortley soon placed himself at the head of those who insisted that the designation of game as property was essential if reform was going to be effective. In 1824 he introduced the first of what would prove to be a series of bills designed to make game the

IX. James Stuart-Wortley, Lord Wharncliffe

property of the landowner as well as to legalise its sale. It was, in some respects, a more sophisticated bill than Brand's, anticipating in its provisions many of the practical difficulties which the scheme would create. But that was not enough to ensure success. Peel and the other advocates of legalisation gave, at best, only lukewarm support to the measure, while the conservatives filled the air with dire warnings about everything from the future of fox-hunting to that of the British Constitution.[91] Even more damaging, perhaps, was a flood of petitions urging the Commons to reject the bill – which, in the end, is what the House did by a vote of 123 to 103.[92] The closeness of the division, however, was enough to encourage Stuart-Wortley to try again in the next session. His persistence was rewarded, for this time the Commons approved the bill and sent it to the Upper House.[93] The Lords, unfortunately, were less receptive to the bill's principles, which Lord Westmorland said reminded him of the French Revolution. By a vote of thirty-eight to twenty-three, they refused to give the bill a second reading.[94] From 1825 onward, in fact, the House of Lords formed the major obstacle to the reform of the game laws. The reformers were, therefore, fortunate that in 1826 Stuart-Wortley was created Baron Wharncliffe and thereby allowed to argue his case in person.

Wharncliffe was not without allies when, in 1827, he introduced his reform bill in the House of Lords for the first time. Lord Suffield had long been arguing the case for reform; Thomas Brand now sat in the Upper House (as Lord Dacre), and Lord Lansdowne and the Duke of Richmond were also sympathetic. All of them were willing to follow Wharncliffe's lead.[95] In addition, he could count on the support of magistrates in various parts of the country, petitions from whom for a change in the law were becoming more numerous and insistent at this time.[96] Thus, there was reason to hope that the reform bill might yet meet with the Lords' approval. When, however, the bill reached the report stage, the reformers suddenly found themselves outnumbered and the measure was lost for the want of a single vote.[97] More discouraging than this defeat, perhaps, was the alacrity with which the advocates of legalisation jumped to resurrect their own project. Within days of the defeat of Wharncliffe's measure, legalisation bills were introduced in both Houses. While neither received a third reading,[98] they were an ominous sign that Wharncliffe and his associates had yet to convince a number of their fellow reformers that a comprehensive remodelling of the game code was actually necessary. Meanwhile, the poaching war went on, filling the gaols – and not a few graves – with its casualties. A compromise between the two groups was obviously needed and, in the next session, Wharncliffe set out to arrange one.

In February 1828 the Marquess of Salisbury – who, as Lord Cranborne, had chaired the Commons' Select Committee five years earlier – introduced yet another legalisation bill. Wharncliffe, as usual, opposed it, arguing that to allow the qualified sportsman 'to turn game into money' without, at the same time, permitting the small farmer to hunt on his land would be not only unjust but 'intolerable' to the country at large. He urged instead that a new select committee be appointed, adding that if he and Salisbury could just discuss the matter, an accommodation might be reached. That is precisely what happened. While the third Select Committee on the Game Laws heard evidence from a wide variety of witnesses, Wharncliffe and Salisbury worked out a compromise, the terms of which the Committee then endorsed in its report.[99] The compromise called for Salisbury to accept something more than legalisation and Wharncliffe something less than the designation of game as property of the landowner. Specifically, the qualifications of the original Game Act of 1671 were not to be repealed, but rather extended to include leaseholders having twenty or more acres, as well as to all esquires and persons 'of higher degree', whatever the size – or source – of their income. In addition, lords of manors and all landowners with £100 or more a year could permit any person to sport on their own lands. These provisions were incorporated into Salisbury's legalisation bill, and then the 'alliance' (as Lord Malmesbury disapprovingly called it) proceeded to push the measure through the House. The final vote was close – sixty-nine to sixty-two – but Salisbury and Wharncliffe were successful, and the bill was sent to the House of Commons for its approval.[100] What happened next was almost comic. The Commons interpreted the fines imposed by the Lords' measure as an invasion of their prerogative to initiate 'money bills' and therefore threw it out. They then passed an almost identical bill of their own but, when this was sent to the Lords, it too was rejected. The conservative peers, who had been caught off-balance by the 'alliance' earlier in the session, this time collected enough proxies to deny the Commons' bill a second reading.[101] In 1829 Wharncliffe did not repeat his mistake. The compromise measure was first introduced in the House of Commons (by his son, John Stuart-Wortley) but, when it reached the Upper House, the conservatives once again marshalled their forces. On report, they were able to have the bill thrown out – though only by a majority of two in a remarkably full chamber.[102]

The compromise bill might have yet been passed in the next session, had not events of greater magnitude intervened. A bill sponsored by Lord Chandos – more systematic than Wharncliffe's but, in its retention of some form of property qualification, essentially the same – was ignored by the Commons amidst the political crisis which followed the passage of the Catholic Emancipation Act.[103] The death of George IV in June 1830 necessitated the election of a new Parliament and when, in December of that year, Chandos again tried to secure passage of his bill, he was confronted with a demand from Lord Althorp, Chancellor of the Exchequer in Lord Grey's new ministry, that substantial changes be made in it. Althorp, like most gentlemen, had been alarmed by the labourers' revolt which had swept through southern England in the autumn of 1830. Although poaching did not figure prominently in the disturbances, he clearly felt that there was a connection between the old, unreformed game code and resistance to authority. 'Certainly,' he told the Commons, 'that system which filled our gaols with hardy men, with the most active and intelligent of our population, and educated them in vice, associated them with criminals, and then turned them loose on the country, prepared for all kinds of crimes – certainly, such a system could not be too soon altered.'[104] His principal objection to Chandos' bill was that it retained a property qualification for sporting. Like Wharncliffe before him, Althorp insisted that game be made property but, unlike Wharncliffe, he was not willing to compromise on the point. When Chandos refused to accept his amendments, the government announced that it would bring in a game reform bill of its own.[105] After fifteen years of debate, negotiation and disappointment, the hour of reform was finally at hand.

The reform of the game laws was not, of course, the only change being contemplated in 1831, a fact which tended to complicate the passage of Althorp's bill. His other project, the first Great Reform Bill to remodel the system of parliamentary representation, was introduced at almost the same time, and its defeat in April meant that the game reform bill had to await the outcome of another general election. Even when the new Parliament assembled in June, the bill made only a slow progress through a House of Commons obviously preoccupied with other matters; it was not until the beginning of September that the measure was sent up to the House of Lords.[106] There it ran into trouble from an unexpected quarter: Lord Wharncliffe. The Commons' bill vested the right to kill game in the *occupier* of the land, except where the lease reserved that right for the landlord. Wharncliffe objected that this provision would spell the end of the gentry's accustomed practice of sporting over their tenants' farms. In committee, he secured an amendment which reversed the Commons' formula and made game the property of the landowner, except where the lease gave sporting rights to the tenant.[107] Wharncliffe's anxiety about this matter reveals much about his thinking during the long debate over game law reform in the 1820s. He wanted to create 'a different feeling' in the countryside but, as this episode illustrates, he was not willing to endanger the position of country gentlemen in rural society in order to accomplish this. Under the 1831 amendment as under his own reform bills, sporting by farmers was still to be an 'indulgence', not a right. When the Lords' amendments were presented to the House of Commons, there was a good deal of grumbling over this change. Althorp, however, urged acceptance and, in the end, the Commons complied. With only three dissenting votes, the Game Reform Act was passed, and on 5 October it received royal assent.[108] In law, if not in fact, the gentry's monopoly on game was no more.

V

If the reformers expected dramatic confirmation of their theories, they were disappointed. Far from declining, poaching seems to have either remained at the same level or even increased a little in the years following the passage of the Game Reform Act. Parliamentary returns indicate that

X. The game stall, an 1831 cartoon, depicting Wharncliffe and Richmond trying to sell game to Westmorland and Wellington

in the first twelve months of the Act's existence over 2800 persons were committed to prison in England for game offences. This was well above the figure for either of the previous two years. In the Act's second year of operation, over 3000 persons were imprisoned for game offences.[109] We do not have returns for the remainder of the decade, but it seems unlikely that there was any appreciable decline. Even if there was, it did not last, for in 1844 Parliament was informed that almost 4500 persons had been convicted (although not necessarily committed to prison) in the preceding year.[110] The violence too seems to have continued: in the 1830s and the early 1840s gamekeepers were being murdered at the rate of two a year.[111] The continuation of the poaching war was reported with grim satisfaction by the opponents of reform. 'The Game Act has produced exactly the effect I expected it would', boasted the Duke of Wellington to Lady Shelley. 'Poaching all over the country has increased tenfold, particularly poaching with violence. I never heard before of any serious poaching in my woods; but from the first of November [1831, when the new Act went into force] . . . they were poached by gangs! At last they killed one of my men.' 'There has been a great increase in the poaching tribe since the Act was passed', agreed the Duke of Rutland.[112] Nor was it only unregenerate conservatives who wrote thus. Even supporters of reform acknowledged that the promised transformation of the countryside had not taken place. 'I think it is probable', wrote William Dyott in his diary, that 'the new game act has for the present rather encouraged poachers'.[113]

But if the Game Reform Act was deemed a failure, neither conservatives nor reformers made any serious move to amend it. Outside Parliament, attempts by Radical politicians to enlist farmers in a movement to demand further reform – in particular, repeal of Wharncliffe's amendment – were unsuccessful. The Act, therefore, remained on the statute books relatively intact for the rest of the century. It was not until 1880 that Parliament conceded to farmers the right to kill hares on their land without permission of the landlord.[114] This impressive display of *sang froid* in the face of the Game Reform Act's manifest failure to deliver on its sponsors' promises is, to say the least, curious. It suggests that there was something more involved in the long struggle to reform the game laws than a simple desire to curb poaching. What that was will be discussed in the final chapter.

7

Conclusion

Among historians of eighteenth-century England, the game laws have long been a by-word for tyranny – petty tyranny, to be sure, but real oppression for all that. As the Webbs put it in their classic study of English local government: 'In the hands of the country gentlemen of the eighteenth century, and still more, of the beginning of the nineteenth century, the Game Laws became, it is clear, an instrument of terrible severity, leading, not infrequently, to cruel oppression of individuals of the "lower orders" suspected of poaching.'[1] In the half century since that was written, historians have not had occasion to challenge the Webbs' verdict. Douglas Hay's recent study of the enforcement of the game laws in Staffordshire is, indeed, little more than a restatement – albeit a scholarly and eloquent one – of a view long held by those who write the history of eighteenth-century England.[2] In the light of the preceding chapters, this is perhaps an appropriate occasion to re-examine the conventional wisdom about the game laws. There are really three counts in the indictment: that the game laws were 'savage', or at least unjustifiably harsh; that they were enforced in a manner which made a mockery of justice; and finally, that they were an example of 'blatant class legislation' which took food from the poor in order to give sport to the rich.[3] Let us examine each count in turn.

The game laws, as we have seen, can be divided into two parts. The first, the 'old game code', forbade all but landed gentlemen to hunt game or to possess guns, hunting dogs, snares, nets or game. By 1711, when the code was fully enacted, the maximum fine which could be imposed was £5 for each offence; if the convicted offender was unable to pay this, he could be imprisoned for three months. For the ordinary labourer in eighteenth-century England, £5 was undoubtedly a large sum but, as we have seen, it was not necessarily too large for the industrious poacher. In the second half of the eighteenth century, three out of every four Wiltshire game offenders for whom conviction certificates survive were able to pay fines as large or larger. The advent of civil prosecution of poachers, of course, raised the potential fine well above the level of £5, but such prosecutions, as we have also seen, were exceptional – and, indeed, were meant to be. Until the passage of the Game Reform Act, a majority of game law offenders were fined £5 for their transgressions and, even in the 'distressed' 1820s, a majority of them still seem to have been able to pay it.[4] Judged in the light of this evidence, the 'old game code' does not appear to have been unduly harsh; indeed, compared with other sections of the criminal code, it seems positively tame. Those who stole poultry in the eighteenth century, for instance, could be whipped, imprisoned or even transported, all without the option of paying a fine. Even more instructive is the treatment meted out to those who stole animals which had once been considered 'game' but which, by the eighteenth century, had become private property. Taking a rabbit out of a warren was punishable by three months' imprisonment *plus* payment of treble damages and the costs of prosecution. Those who took deer out of a park could be transported for seven years; even after 1776, when this was reserved for second offenders, deer-stealers still faced a £30 fine or a year in prison.[5] Thus it might be reasonably argued that the 'old game code' actually saved poachers from severe punishment.

The other part of the game laws – those statutes which were applicable to all persons, whether qualified or not – was, of course, less mild, and it is to these laws, particularly to the Night Poaching Acts, that critics point when they speak of severity. The Night Poaching Act of 1773 doubled the standard fine for those who hunted after dark and authorised even more severe punishments for second and third offenders against the Act. The Act of 1800 permitted night poachers to be whipped, imprisoned for up to two years and even impressed into the armed forces. The Act of 1817 made night poaching with 'offensive weapons' punishable by transportation for seven years. These were undoubtedly harsh laws but, once again, they must be viewed in context. By 1816, for instance, rabbit-stealing after dark had been a transportable offence for fifty years; deer-stealing after dark had been a *capital* offence for almost a century.[6] Parliament – a body not noted in the eighteenth century for its reluctance to add capital offences to the statute books – had obviously not rushed into a policy of severity toward night poachers. It had, in fact, been pushed into it by the violence of the poaching war, particularly after the end of the Napoleonic wars. It may not have been wise legislation – certainly it was not very effective – but it was an understandable reaction and, it should also be noted, a short-lived one. The Act of 1800 was repealed within fifteen years, the Act of 1817 within eleven. The Night Poaching Acts of the early nineteenth century were simply not typical of the game laws as a whole and, indeed, most poachers were not tried under them. The vast majority of offenders continued to be charged under the 'old game code' and faced either a modest fine or three months in prison. For those who were imprisoned, the experience was, at the very least, unpleasant and, considering the ever-present threat of 'gaol fever', even dangerous. It was, perhaps, even harder on their families who were thrown on relief. But compared with the punishments inflicted on those who were found guilty of other forms of theft in this period, the sufferings of most convicted poachers were mild.

This, perhaps, might count for little if the administration of the game laws was so biased against the defendant that, regardless of guilt or innocence, he had little chance of escaping punishment. An injustice is not less a one for being mild. Was the gentry's enforcement of the game laws, as the Webbs claimed, 'grossly partial, selfishly biased, and swayed by considerations of their own class interest, even to the verge of corruption'?[7] This charge has been examined at some length in Chapter 4, and from that discussion it should be clear that the evidence is, at best, ambiguous. Examples of 'grossly partial' treatment of suspected poachers can be found, but so can examples of impartial, scrupulous and even merciful judgements. Any conclusion, therefore, must rest less on direct evidence than on an estimation of which type of conduct was more *likely* to occur; that, in turn, must rest on an analysis of the various pressures acting on a J.P. in the performance of his duties. That J.P.s had a 'class interest' in seeing the game laws were enforced is undeniable. Most rural J.P.s in 1671 were probably qualified to sport under the Game Act; after 1732 they definitely were, since a law passed in that year required all justices to possess at least £100 a year from land.[8] Thus, in enforcing the game laws, they were protecting their own sporting privileges. Much the same, however, can be said of their enforcement of the laws against larceny: in punishing thieves they were protecting their own property. However true, this observation fails to establish a *prima facie* case for 'corruption' on the part of the J.P.s. The critics of the game laws have, in fact, something more precise in mind: that most J.P.s were passing judgement on men accused of poaching either on their own estates or on the estates of those to whom the J.P.s were beholden. Does what we know about justices of the peace and their activities in the eighteenth and early nineteenth centuries tend to support these accusations?

There were, of course, justices who heard cases in which they had a personal interest. Samuel Whitbread, for example, regularly tried game offenders brought before him by his own gamekeeper, William Woodcraft.[9] On the other hand, an examination of 465 Wiltshire conviction certificates for the period 1740–1800 fails to yield a single instance of a J.P. hearing a case in which his gamekeeper was either the informer or a witness.[10] In trying to decide whether Whitbread's conduct was actually typical, it is important to remember that active game preservers – whose estates were the most tempting targets for poachers – were often aristocrats who held only titular places on the rural bench. They were usually content to leave the actual performance of magisterial duties to country gentlemen with more modest estates, the income from which was in many cases insufficient to pay for a programme of intensive game preservation. James Richmond Webb, for example, was one of the most conscientious of the Wiltshire J.P.s in enforcing the game laws, but he does not appear to have employed a single gamekeeper himself.[11] The aristocratic element on the bench seems to have increased slightly in the nineteenth century, but it was far out-weighed by the influx of clerical J.P.s who, while notoriously fond of sporting, usually did not have preserves of their own to defend.[12] Many game preservers, then, even if they felt no scruples about judging men accused of poaching on their own estates, lacked the opportunity to do so. Until more evidence to the contrary is produced, therefore, it seems likely that openly biased tribunals were less common than the game laws' critics have assumed.

There still remains, however, the matter of indirect bias. A justice, while not personally interested in a case, might nevertheless be under the influence of a game preserver who was, and, as a consequence, fail to give the defendant a fair hearing. Many of the gentry and clergymen who stocked the commission of the peace in this period were undoubtedly anxious to oblige their more exalted neighbours, to whom indeed they may have owed their own position on the bench. Evidence of collusion between J.P.s and prosecutors can be produced and, even where it cannot, the possibility remains that there was a tacit understanding between them which operated to the prejudice of the accused.[13] With that said, however, it must be noted that the wishes of neighbouring game preservers were not the only factor which might influence a J.P.'s conduct. Even if one dismisses the possibility that conscience might have entered into his deliberations, there was still the law to be taken into account. Appeals and civil suits against J.P.s were not so rare that a justice could afford to flout openly the requirements of the law.[14] Even more influential, perhaps, was the opinion of a justice's non-game-preserving neighbours.

However much a J.P. might be under the thumb of a local magnate, he nevertheless lived in a community and was expected to observe certain standards of conduct in office. Some of these standards, as E.P. Thompson has recently shown, grew out of a long tradition of paternalistic care for the poor and were, on occasion, asserted quite forcefully by the latter.[15] Other standards of conduct were of more recent origin. Use of a J.P.'s powers for purposes of political harassment, for example, was increasingly frowned upon after the middle of the eighteenth century.[16] Even before then the justice's role as a mediator of local disputes was becoming established, and this too imposed certain limits on the manner in which he exercised his powers. Whatever a J.P.'s party or rank, there was growing pressure on him, from 1750 onward, at least to appear impartial in the performance of his duties, and there is evidence that by the early nineteenth century, if not before, J.P.s were becoming sensitive to this pressure. Benjamin Newton, a Yorkshire J.P., remarked in 1816 that a petty sessions was 'not near so respectable if only one Magistrate attends and [it] does not carry the same weight in the eyes of the country'. A decade later, William Dyott noted 'an eagerness in some magistrates' in this county of Staffordshire to bind over for trial at quarter sessions cases 'of a trifling nature . . . undeserving [of] the inquiry of a jury'.[17] This caution on the part of 'the country' and of the J.P.s themselves grew only gradually and was by no means universal, even in 1830. But where it existed, a brake was applied to the abuse of summary powers. Thus, while J.P.s cannot be totally acquitted of the charge of biased judgements, the latter were becoming less likely by the early nineteenth century, the very period in which the largest number of persons were being tried for offences against the game laws. In short, the trial of Richard Deller may have been less of a sign of the times than historians have made it out to be.

Of the truth of the final count in the indictment – that the game laws were an example of 'blatant class legislation' – there can be little doubt. The Game Act of 1671 awarded the landed gentry an exclusive and valuable privilege, and that, as we have seen, was its intent. To modern historians, raised in a culture which espouses egalitarian principles, such legislation naturally seems repugnant and indefensible. It is worth asking, however, what alternative they would have found more palatable. In 1671, for example, Parliament could have declared game to be the property of the person on whose land it was found. That, however, would have made the taking of game without the landowner's permission a form of theft, and the latter was a very serious crime in the eighteenth-century criminal code. Rabbit-stealers and deer-stealers, as we have seen, were liable to be transported for seven years. It seems unlikely that modern historians would have been enthusiastic about a system which would have imposed similar penalties on game poachers. Parliament, on the other hand, could have enacted a licensing system like that created in 1784, but this would have required would-be sportsmen to pay an annual fee of £2 or £3. Licensing, in reality, is just another form of property qualification; as such, it would have excluded large numbers of Englishmen from the legal right to hunt. Would not this have also been 'blatant class legislation'?

A third alternative would have been to have no game laws at all. That is what poachers – and, it would seem, a large portion of the rural population – wanted and, considering the defects of the other systems, perhaps this would have been the best choice. In a country with an expanding population, however, it remains questionable whether the game would have long survived a general permission to sport. Informal agreements to preserve the game – like those used in the nineteenth century to ensure an adequate supply of foxes for the hunt – might have been arranged, but it is equally possible that the breed of game would have been exterminated, as indeed the wild boar had been by the time the eighteenth-century game laws were enacted. Such a consideration might well seem petty to a modern reader faced with the violence and bitterness of the poaching war. Hunting, after all, was just a sport. Surely the preservation of the game could not be worth the alienation of the rural community, much less the deaths of so many gamekeepers and poachers. Yet the fact remains that the gentry considered the enjoyment of their traditional sports to be a matter of great importance, not just to themselves, but to the nation. Before handing down a verdict, it is perhaps worthwhile considering their defence.

II

The game laws were born out of a desire to enhance the status of country gentlemen in the bitter aftermath of the Civil War. Their message was that land was superior to money, a blunt assertion of privilege which for a long time was accepted, or at least was not openly contradicted. By the early nineteenth century, however, the gentry's claim to special status was coming under increasingly sharp criticism. The protectionist corn laws, the distinctly unrepresentative electoral system and, of course, the game laws themselves were all attacked in the press, reflecting a pervasive, though far from universal, dissatisfaction with the landed oligarchy which had dominated England for well over a century. 'A war now rages against the Aristocracy,' announced *Blackwood's Magazine* in 1827, 'the object of which is to degrade it from its place in society, and to accomplish its virtual annihilation as a separate Estate of the Realm.'[18] 'There was a regular system to run down country gentlemen,' agreed Lord Malmesbury, 'and it pervades all classes. You could not go into the city but you heard the lord mayor pronounce a condemnation of the Game Laws.'[19] Smarting under this criticism, country gentlemen rose again and again during the long debate over the game laws to defend their class and assert its claim to a special position in English society.

Understandably, their speeches tended to concentrate on a theme which had special meaning for men who had lived through the French Revolution: the blessings which flowed from having gentlemen reside in the countryside. 'The residence of gentlemen on their estates,' George Bankes told the House of Commons in 1819, 'had, more than anything else, contributed to the prosperity of the nation, and had enabled her to hold her head higher among the kingdoms of Europe.' England, he declared, was indebted to the gentry 'for the good name they sustained, the hospitality they practiced, the liberality they evinced, and the thousand virtues that emanated from them among their own circles'. If anything was done to discourage gentlemen from living in their communities, he warned, 'the most dreadful results might ensue'. Memories of the Revolution were fresh enough in the minds of his hearers that further elaboration was unnecessary.[20] This, however, was not the heart of the conservative's argument, since reformers also declared their utmost devotion to the maintenance of a resident gentry. Curwen, Brand and Wharncliffe all denied that they had any wish to prevent the gentry 'from pursuing that course of humanisation and civilisation for which they were so remarkable'.[21] Even the decidedly unconservative Sydney Smith waxed eloquent on the virtues of a resident gentry. 'A great man returning from London to spend his summer in the Country,' Smith wrote, 'diffuses intelligence, improves manners, communicates pleasure, restrains the extreme violence of subordinate politicians, and makes the middling and lower classes better acquainted with, and more attached to their natural leaders.'[22] If the reformers were sincere in their desire to see gentlemen continue to bring these blessings to the countryside – and there is no reason to suppose that they were not – why, then, were conservatives so distrustful of the measure which the reformers advocated?

One of the principal reasons, of course, was that reform would strip them of a privilege to which they had become attached and force them to share the game with their social inferiors. Bankes grumbled that reform would 'make the country people ten times more vicious and indolent' than they already were, but one of his colleagues probably expressed the conservatives' concern more candidly when he predicted that reform would 'give to the yeomanry of this country the habits and character of sportsmen; and take from them that respectful submission and manly dependence . . . which at present characterized them'.[23] It would be easy enough to leave it at that, and let the conservatives stand condemned as callous defenders of the *ancien régime*, determined to preserve their privileged position, even at the cost of much suffering and loss of life. To do so, however, would mean ignoring a good deal of evidence that the opponents of reform were acutely aware of the 'distress' experienced by the labouring population at this time and anxious to see it ameliorated. It was, after all, conservatives like Sir John Shelley and Lord Malmesbury, not the reformers, who persistently pointed to the pitiful state of the agricultural labourer whenever the game laws were being debated. Their motives may have been, at least in part, tactical, but the speeches which they delivered on the subject exhibit very little complacency about the state of rural England in the 1820s. What their speeches do reveal is, first of all, a sense of frustration that the real causes of the poaching war were being ignored and, secondly, a sense of outrage that, because of the reformers' faulty analysis, gentlemen were being asked to embrace the habits and outlook of the very people they most despised, the urban bourgeoisie.

The gentry's monopoly on game, explained one opponent of reform, was 'a sort of feather in their cap, one of those counter balancing gratifications which make amends for the difference in income which arises from capital vested in land, and that which arises from funded property, or commerce'.[24] This was more than just a flattering mark of distinction. It symbolised what the gentry considered to be a profound difference in attitude between landed and moneyed men. The former exercised 'hospitality', expending their income for the benefit of their neighbours and dependants; the latter were preoccupied with grubbing for more money, which they then would spend only on themselves. The picture, of course, was self-congratulatory and none too accurate, but it was central to the creed of the country gentleman and helps to explain much of the opposition to the reform of the game laws. 'We preserve our Game often at considerable sacrifice of income,' this same opponent of reform went on to say, '[in order] that we may gratify one set of friends by giving them the amusement of pursuing and killing it, and another set by paying them the compliment of sending them little presents, as tokens of recollection and esteem.'[25] If game became a saleable item, the conservatives feared, it would lose its significance and assume 'a mercenary sordid character'. Worse still, reform would undermine that difference in outlook which distinguished the landed from the moneyed classes. It would 'degrade the country gentlemen into hucksters', men who were not mindful of 'gentlemanlike and liberal feelings' but interested only in 'paultry profit'.[26]

It is, of course, easy enough to demolish the conservatives' argument. Since the seventeenth century, deer had been the property of the landowner and could be purchased on the open market. Yet venison was still highly prized as a gift, and the owners of parks continued to be capable of 'gentlemanlike and liberal feelings'. To argue in this manner, however, would be to miss the conservatives' real point, which was that acceptance of reform would undermine the relative position of the landed gentry in English society. While reform would not necessarily degrade country gentlemen into 'hucksters', the fact remained that under the new system they would be no *better* than 'hucksters'. The game which they preserved would no longer be a symbol – 'a sort of feather in their cap' – of their special position in society. Instead, it would become a commodity, available to anyone with money enough to purchase it. Thus money, not land, became the prerequisite for acquiring game, and in this reversal of the Game Act's formula the conservatives saw the eclipse of their class. When the gentry lost their monopoly on game, Sir John Shelley told the

Commons in 1819, it would not be long before the nation would 'dwindle into that which it had been contemptuously asserted by Buonaparte to be – a nation of shopkeepers'.[27] This, in turn, would be followed by the eclipse of Britain itself, as its army came to be officered by urban men 'who spent their time lounging in the streets or sauntering . . . from one clubhouse to another, and passing their nights where they ought not to be passed'.[28] For some country gentlemen in the 1820s, the equation between cities and ruin was just as obvious and inevitable as it had been for their ancestors in 1671.

The reformers, obviously, did not share these fears. They too wished to preserve the gentry's position in English society. It was for precisely that reason that they were determined to jettison a set of laws which were not only unpopular but actually dangerous to the continued power and influence of the landed classes. 'The whole [game law] system, my dear sir, is one of *exclusion*', wrote Lord Suffield to a friend in 1823, 'it is founded upon exclusive rights, it is supported upon selfish principles, and its chief enjoyment consists in the possession of that which your neighbour has *not*, and perhaps *cannot* have'.[29] It was hardly surprising, thought the reformers, that such a system inspired resentment against society's 'natural leaders' among men who should have been their principal supporters: the farmers, small freeholders and 'reputable' tradesmen of rural England. That alone was sufficient reason to alter the game laws, but the system, in fact, was productive of even greater evils. 'The greatest practical mischiefs flowed from the present [game law] system,' Thomas Brand declared in 1819, 'one of the most prominent of which was, that the great body of the lower classes were opposed to the higher classes on this point, and [as a result] the morals of the country were deteriorated to an alarming degree.'[30] It was the present threat of social disorder, not the potential one of domination by moneyed men, which alarmed the reformers and inspired their tireless agitation for a change in the game laws. The essential element in that change had to be the elimination of the aura of exclusive privilege which had surrounded the old game laws. Some reformers hoped to accomplish this simply by allowing the urban bourgeoisie to purchase game legally, but they were blocked by their own colleagues who insisted that the property qualification would also have to be sacrificed. 'To make game saleable, and retain it in the hands of a privileged class,' Sir John Sebright bluntly told the Commons, 'was what the country would not endure.'[31] In short, the reformers argued that if the gentry wished to preserve their position, they could not act in defiance of the feelings of the society they claimed to lead.

In the end the reformers triumphed and, although the Game Reform Act failed to end the poaching war, they nevertheless had reason to feel relief and satisfaction at its passage. The old game code, as one petitioner to Parliament remarked in 1830, was 'not congenial with the nineteenth century'.[32] There were a number of reasons for this, but one of the most important was simply that England was no longer a society in which any activity or possession could be the monopoly of a single social class. To refuse to answer the market's demand for game was unacceptable – and, as the prosperity of the black market indicated, impossible as well. In a capitalist economy, everything had to have its price. By conceding the point, the Game Reform Act put the sports of the gentry back on a defensible basis. All claim to class privilege was given up, and both game and sport were made available to anyone who could afford them. Since country gentlemen, by means of Lord Wharncliffe's amendment, retained effective control over who could and could not legally hunt in their neighbourhoods, these concessions might seem trivial, but in fact they were not. As the conservatives had warned, the price of reform was the acceptance of a system of values which was essentially alien to the type of society which the gentry wished to preserve. In a world where everything had its price, there was little room for tradition, loyalty or deference. Even before the Reform Act was passed, it was obvious to some which way the wind was blowing. 'For some time a *Revolution* has been commenced & is regularly *progressing* in our *feelings*, our *measures*, & our *principles political* & religious', wrote one perceptive Yorkshire gentleman to Sir Robert Buxton in the spring of 1829:

> We are no longer the same people that we were seventy years ago: there is no longer the same hospitality amongst acquaintance[s], nor the same warm attachment amongst connections, even the nearest; there are no *gradations* of rank in society, either in regard to *birth*, to *dress*, to *manners*, nor even to *acquirements*. A general appearance of equality pervades all classes without leaving any distinction between them. Even between the *rich* & the *poor* there is little apparent difference; all persons live a like however different may be their income; indeed the fluctuations of property is so rapid, that he who is poor today may be by some fortunate speculation be rich tomorrow, & the great capitalist may be at once plunged into poverty.

He lamented the change, but conceded that 'Posterity . . . will be brought up with different principles & sentiments, & may regard things in a different light.'[33] To judge by posterity's treatment of the English game laws, he was more correct than he could have possibly imagined.

APPENDIX

A guide to the laws relating to deer, rabbits and game 1660–1831

Principal statutes, 1275–1831

1275	3 Edward I, c. 20
1293	21 Edward I, st. 2
1389	13 Richard II, st. 1, c. 13
1485	1 Henry VII, c. 7
1495	11 Henry VII, c. 17
1503	19 Henry VII, c. 11
1523	14 & 15 Henry VIII, c. 10
1533	25 Henry VIII, c. 11
1539	31 Henry VIII, c. 12
1540a	32 Henry VIII, c. 8
1540b	32 Henry VIII, c. 11
1541	33 Henry VIII, c. 6
1548	2 & 3 Edward VI, c. 14
1549	3 & 4 Edward VI, c. 7
1562	5 Elizabeth I, c. 21
1580	23 Elizabeth I, c. 10
1601	43 Elizabeth I, c. 6
1603	1 James I, c. 27
1605	3 James I, c. 13
1609a	7 James I, c. 11
1609b	7 James I, c. 13
1661	13 Charles II, st. 1, c. 10
1671a	22 & 23 Charles II, c. 9
1671b	22 & 23 Charles II, c. 25
1692	3 & 4 William & Mary, c. 10
1693a	4 & 5 William & Mary, c. 13

1693b	4 & 5 William & Mary, c. 23
1695	6 & 7 William III, c. 13
1697	8 & 9 William III, c. 11
1703	2 & 3 Anne, c. 20
1707	5 Anne, c. 14
1711	9 Anne, c. 25
1717	3 George I, c. 11
1718	5 George I, c. 15
1719	5 George I, c. 28
1722	8 George I, c. 19
1723	9 George I, c. 22
1737	10 George II, c. 32
1753	26 George II, c. 2
1755a	28 George II, c. 12
1755b	28 George II, c. 19
1756	29 George II, c. 6
1762	2 George III, c. 19
1765	5 George III, c. 14
1770	10 George III, c. 19
1773a	13 George III, c. 55
1773b	13 George III, c. 80
1776	16 George III, c. 30
1784	24 George III, sess. 2, c. 43
1785	25 George III, c. 50
1786	26 George III, c. 82
1791	31 George III, c. 21
1796a	36 George III, c. 39
1796b	36 George III, c. 124
1799	39 George III, c. 34
1800	39 & 40 George III, c. 50
1802	42 George III, c. 107
1803	43 George III, c. 112
1804	44 George III, c. 98
1808a	48 George III, c. 55
1808b	48 George III, c. 93
1810	50 George III, c. 67
1811	51 George III, c. 120
1812	52 George III, c. 93
1816	56 George III, c. 130
1817	57 George III, c. 90
1818	58 George III, c. 75
1825	6 George IV, c. 7
1826a	7 George IV, c. 10
1826b	7 George IV, c. 11
1827a	7 & 8 George IV, c. 18
1827b	7 & 8 George IV, c. 29
1827c	7 & 8 George IV, c. 27
1828	9 George IV, c. 69
1831	1 & 2 William IV, c. 32

I. Offences committed by any person

A. *Unlawful hunting*

1. without permission

a. deer

As of 1660: In enclosed ground. Penalty: imprisonment for 3 months and fine of £10 or treble damages plus costs; to remain in prison without bail until sureties for 7 years found (1605 as amended by 1609b).

1661   In any ground. Penalty: £20 fine, or 6 months in house of correction at hard labour, or 1 year in gaol without bail; not to be released until sureties for 1 year are found.

1692   In enclosed ground. Penalty: fine of £20, or if deer are taken or killed, fine of £30 per deer; in default of fine, to be imprisoned for 1 year without bail and to be set in pillory for 1 hour on market day.

1718   If convicted under 1692, to be imprisoned until recognisance of £50 for good behaviour given.

1719   In enclosed ground and deer wounded or killed. Penalty: to be transported for 7 years.

1737   2nd offence in unenclosed ground. Penalty: to be transported to America for 7 years.

1776   1605, 1609b, 1661, 1692, 1718, 1737 repealed.
In any ground. Penalty: for 1st offence, £30 fine, or imprisonment for 1 year without bail; for subsequent offence, to be transported to America for 7 years.

1802   In enclosed ground. Penalty: to be transported for 7 years.
In unenclosed ground. Penalty: £50 fine, or imprisonment for 6 months without bail; for subsequent offence, to be transported for 7 years.

1811   If convicted under 1802, fines may be mitigated to no less than £20.

1827c   1719, 1776, 1802, 1811 repealed.

1827b   In enclosed ground. Penalty: to be transported for 7 years, or to be imprisoned for up to 2 years and (if offender is male) to be whipped up to 3 times if court directs.
In unenclosed ground. Penalty: fine of up to £50 or imprisonment up to 6 months at hard labour; for subsequent offence: same as for hunting in enclosed ground.

b. conies

As of 1660: see Hunting conies at night (I.C.3.a.)

1671b   In enclosed or unenclosed warrens. Penalty: fine of treble damages plus costs and imprisonment of 3 months; not to be discharged until sureties for good behaviour found.

1765   Made lawful: hunting conies in daytime on sea-banks and river-banks, or within 1 furlong of them, in Lincolnshire.

1827b   1765 confirmed.
In enclosed or unenclosed warrens. Penalty: fine up to £5 or imprisonment up to 2 months at hard labour.

1827c   1671b repealed.

1831   Trespass in pursuit of conies in daytime. Penalty: fine up to £2 or (if in group of 5 or more persons) up to £5, plus costs; in default of fine, to be imprisoned up to 2 months.

c. game
1831   Trespass in pursuit of game in daytime. Penalty: fine of up to £2, or (if in group of 5 or more persons) up to £5, plus costs; in default of fine, to be imprisoned up to 2 months.
        See also: II.B.1831.

d. by soldiers
1693a   Taking game or conies. Penalty: if by officer, £5 fine; if by soldier, his commanding officer to be fined 10/–; in default of fine, officer to forfeit his commission. Except for period 1698–1701, clause repeated in each Mutiny Act until 1703.
1703   Clause altered: for offence by soldier, his commanding officer to be fined 20/–. Repeated in every Mutiny Act until 1826.
1756   1693a as amended by 1703 included in every Mutiny Act for marine forces until 1826.
1826ab Taking game. Penalty: if by officer, £5 fine. Repeated in every Mutiny Act for army and for marine forces through 1831.

2. with prohibited 'engines'
As of 1660: Using setting-dogs, nets, snares, or other 'engines' to take partridges or pheasants. Penalty: to be imprisoned for 3 months without bail, unless fine of 20/– per bird is paid and £20 recognisance is given. (1609a)
1671b   Setting or using snares, hare-pipes, or other 'engines' to take hares or conies. Penalty: fine of up to 10/– or imprisonment in house of correction for up to 1 month.
1776   Setting or using any net, wire, slip noose, toil, or other 'engine' to take deer. Penalty: for 1st offence, to be fined from £5 to £10; for subsequent offence, to be fined from £10 to £20; in default of fine, to be imprisoned for 1 year without bail.
1827b   Setting or using snares or other 'engines' to take deer. Penalty: to be fined up to £20; in default of fine, to be imprisoned at hard labour for up to 6 months.
1827c   1776 repealed.
1831   1609a and 1671b repealed.

B. *Hunting on prohibited days*

1. on Sunday or Christmas
1770   Hunting game on Sundays. Penalty: to be fined from £20 to £30; in default of fine, to be imprisoned for 3 to 6 months without bail.
1773b   1770 repealed.
        Hunting game on Sunday or Christmas in daytime. Penalty: to be fined from £10 to £20 (for 1st offence) or from £20 to £30 (for 2nd offence); in default of fine, to be imprisoned for 3 months. For subsequent offence, to be fined £50; in default of fine, to be imprisoned from 6 to 12 months and, if court directs, to be whipped once.
1831   1773b repealed.

Hunting game on Sunday or Christmas Day. Penalty: to be fined up to £5 plus costs; in default of fine, to be imprisoned for up to 2 months.

2. out of season

a. partridge
As of 1660: Between 1 July and 31 August. Penalty: to be imprisoned for 1 month without bail, unless fine of 40/– plus 20/– per bird is paid (1609a).
1762   Between 12 February and 1 September. Penalty: fine of £5 per bird.
1796a   Between 12 February and 14 September. Penalty: same as 1762.
1799   1796a repealed.
        Between 1 February and 1 September. Penalty: same as 1762.
1831   1609a, 1762, 1799 repealed.
        Between 1 February and 1 September. Penalty: fine of up to £1 per bird plus costs; in default of fine, to be imprisoned up to 2 months (if fine is less than £5) or up to 3 months (in any other case).

b. pheasant
As of 1660: Between 1 July and 31 August. Penalty: to be imprisoned for 1 month without bail, unless fine of 40/– plus 20/– per bird is paid (1609a).
1762   Between 1 February and 1 October. Penalty: fine of £5 per bird.
1831   1609a, 1762 repealed.
        Between 1 February and 1 October. Penalty: fine of up to £1 per bird plus costs; in default of fine, to be imprisoned up to 2 months (if fine is less than £5) or up to 3 months (in any other case).

c. black game
1762   Between 1 January and 20 August. Penalty: fine of £5 per bird.
1773a   Between 10 December and 20 August. Penalty: for 1st offence, to be fined from £10 to £20; for subsequent offence, to be fined from £20 to £30; in default of fine, to be imprisoned for 3 to 6 months at hard labour.
1803   In the New Forest, between 10 December and 1 September. Penalty: same as 1773a.
1810   In Somerset and Devon, between 10 December and 1 September. Penalty: same as 1773a.
1831   1762, 1773a, 1803, 1810 repealed.
        Between 10 December and 20 August or, if in the New Forest, Somerset, or Devon, between 10 December and 1 September. Penalty: fine of up to £1 per bird plus costs; in default of fine, to be imprisoned up to 2 months (if fine less than £5) or up to 3 months (in any other case).

d. grouse
1762   Between 1 December and 25 July. Penalty: fine of £5 per bird.
1773a   Between 10 December and 12 August. Penalty: for 1st offence, to be fined from £10 to £20; for subsequent offence, to be fined from £20 to £30; in default of fine, to be imprisoned for 3 to 6 months at hard labour.
1831   1762, 1773a repealed.
        Between 10 December and 12 August. Penalty: fine of up to £1 per bird plus costs; in default of fine, to be imprisoned up to 2 months (if fine less than £5) or up to 3 months (in any other case).

e. bustard

1773a   Between 1 March and 1 September. Penalty: for 1st offence, to be fined
         from £10 to £20; for subsequent offence, to be fined from £20 to £30; in
         default of fine, to be imprisoned for 3 to 6 months at hard labour.
1831   1773a repealed.
         Between 1 March and 1 September. Penalty: fine of up to £1 per bird plus
         costs; in default of fine, to be imprisoned up to 2 months (if fine less than
         £5) or up to 3 months (in any other case).

f. hare

As of 1660: Tracing hares in the snow. Penalty: to be imprisoned for 3 months
without bail, unless fine of 20/– per hare paid, or unless after 1 month in prison 2
sufficient sureties are found for £20 recognisance (1603).
1831   1603 repealed.

g. wild ducks

1711   Between 1 July and 1 September. Penalty: to be fined 5/– per bird; in
         default of fine, to be committed to house of correction from 14 days to 1
         month, there to be whipped and kept at hard labour.
1737   Between 1 June and 1 October. Penalty: same as 1711.
1831   1711 and 1737 repealed.

C. Hunting at night or in disguise

1. deer

As of 1660: At night or in disguise. Made a felony (1485).
1723   In disguise and armed with swords, firearms, or other offensive weapons,
         in any enclosed ground. Penalty: death, as a felony without benefit of
         clergy.
1827c   1485 and 1723 repealed.

2. game

a. at night

As of 1660: Partridge or pheasant. Penalty: fine of 10/– per partridge and 20/–
per pheasant; in default of fine, to be imprisoned for 1 month without bail. And to
be bound not to repeat the offence for 2 years (1580).
1711   Any game. Penalty: to be fined £5 per bird or hare; in default of fine, to be
         imprisoned in house of correction without bail for 3 months (if 1st offence)
         or 4 months (for subsequent offence).
1770   Any game. Penalty: to be imprisoned without bail for 3 to 6 months (for 1st
         offence), or for 6 to 12 months (for subsequent offence), and within 3 days
         of commitment to be publicly whipped once.
1773b   1770 repealed.
         Any game. Penalty: to be fined from £10 to £20 (for 1st offence), or from
         £20 to £30 (for 2nd offence); in default of fine, to be imprisoned for 3
         months. For subsequent offence, to be fined £50; in default of fine, to be
         imprisoned for 6 to 12 months and, if court directs, to be publicly
         whipped once.

1816   Any game or rabbit. Penalty: to be transported for 7 years, or receive such other punishment as may by law be inflicted for a misdemeanour.
1817   1816 repealed (see I.C.2.b.1817).
1828   1817 repealed.
        Any game or rabbit. Penalty: to be imprisoned at hard labour for up to 3 months (if 1st offence) or up to 6 months (if 2nd offence); to be imprisoned at hard labour a further 6 months or 1 year (respectively) if sureties are not found for recognisance of £10 for 1 year or of £20 for 2 years (respectively). For subsequent offence, to be transported for 7 years, or to be imprisoned at hard labour for up to 2 years.
1831   1580, 1711, 1773b repealed.
        See also: for hares, I.C.3.a.1827b.

b. armed at night
1800   To protect, aid, or assist night poachers. Penalty: for 1st offence, to be committed to house of correction for up to 6 months at hard labour; for subsequent offence, to be committed to house of correction at hard labour from 6 months to 2 years, during which time, the offender may be whipped and, if male over 12 years of age, may be sent to be employed in H.M. service, land or sea, if court directs.
1816   1800 repealed.
        To protect, aid, or assist night poachers. Penalty: to be transported for 7 years, or to receive such other punishment as may by law be inflicted for a misdemeanour.
1817   1800 and 1816 repealed.
        To poach or aid poachers. Penalty: to be transported for 7 years, or to receive such other punishment as may by law be inflicted for a misdemeanour.
1828   1817 repealed (see I.C.2.c.1828)
        See also: for hares, I.C.3.b.

c. in groups at night
1800   Two or more persons. Penalty: for 1st offence, to be committed to house of correction for up to 6 months at hard labour; for subsequent offence, to be committed to house of correction at hard labour from 6 months to 2 years, during which time, the offender may be whipped and, if male over 12 years of age, may be sent to be employed in H.M. service, land or sea, if court directs.
1816   1800 repealed.
1828   Three or more persons, any of whom are armed. Penalty: every person in group to be transported for 7 to 14 years, or imprisoned at hard labour for up to 3 years.

3. conies

a. at night
As of 1660: In enclosed ground. Penalty: to be imprisoned for 3 months and fined £10 or treble damages plus costs; to remain in prison without bail until sureties for 7 years are found (1605 as amended by 1609b).
1671b   On borders of warrens or other enclosed grounds. Penalty: to be fined up to 10/- plus damages; in default of fine, to be imprisoned for up to 1 month.

1765   In any ground. Penalty: to be transported for 7 years, or suffer lesser punishment by whipping, fine, or imprisonment, if court directs.
1827b   Conies or hares, in any ground. Penalty: to be transported for 7 to 14 years, or to be fined, imprisoned, or both, if court directs.
1827c   1605, 1609b, 1671b, 1765 repealed.

b. armed in disguise
1723   Conies or hares, in enclosed ground. Penalty: death, as a felony without benefit of clergy.
1827c   1723 repealed.

D. Unlawful buying, selling, or possession

1. deer

a. buying or selling
As of *1660*: Penalty: to be fined 40/– per deer (1603).
1827c   1603 repealed.

b. possession of deer or 'engine' for taking deer
1692   Deer or 'toyls'. Penalty: £30 fine; in default of fine, to be imprisoned for 1 year without bail and to be set in pillory for one hour on market day.
1723   1692 confirmed.
1776   1692 repealed.
        Deer or 'engine' for taking deer. Penalty: to be fined from £10 to £30; in default of fine, to be imprisoned for 1 year without bail.
1827b   1723, 1776 repealed.
        Deer or 'engine' for taking deer. Penalty: £20 fine; in default of fine, to be imprisoned for up to 6 months at hard labour.

2. game

a. selling
As of *1660*: Except partridges or pheasants reared in houses or brought from abroad. Penalty: fine of 10/– per partridge, 20/– per pheasant, 10/– per hare (1603).
1707   By any higgler, chapman, carrier, innkeeper, victualler, or alehouse keeper. Penalty: to be fined £5 per bird or hare; in default of fine, to be imprisoned without bail for 3 months (if 1st offence) or 4 months (if subsequent offence).
1755a   By any person. Penalty: same as 1707.
1762   Except hares, by any person, out of season. Penalty: fine of £5 per bird.
1773a   Black game, grouse, or bustard, out of season. Penalty: for 1st offence, to be fined from £10 to £20; for subsequent offence, to be fined from £20 to £30; in default of fine, to be imprisoned from 3 to 6 months at hard labour.
1831   1603, 1707, 1755a, 1762, 1773a repealed.
        J.P.s may annually license persons (if they are not innkeepers, victuallers, carriers, higglers, licensed to sell beer by retail, or drivers of any mail coach or other public conveyance) to deal in game, which licence is not valid without certificate that £2 stamp duty has been paid. Innkeepers may sell game for consumption in their inns. Qualified persons (i.e., with game certificates) may sell game to licensed dealers. But:
        1. No unlicensed person may deal in game. Penalty: to be fined £2 plus costs.

2. No qualified person may sell game to anyone not licensed to deal in game. Penalty: to be fined £2 plus costs.
3. No qualified person or licensed dealer may sell game 10 days or more after the end of the season. Penalty: to be fined up to £1 per bird or hare plus costs.

In default of fine, to be imprisoned up to 2 months (if fine less than £5) or up to 3 months (in any other case).

b. buying
As of 1660: Except partridges or pheasants reared in houses or brought from abroad. Penalty: fine of 10/– per partridge, 20/– per pheasant, 10/– per hare (1603).

1707   By any higgler, chapman, carrier, innkeeper, victualler, or alehouse keeper. Penalty: to be fined £5 per bird or hare; in default of fine, to be imprisoned without bail for 3 months (if 1st offence) or 4 months (if subsequent offence).

1762   Except hares, by any person, out of season. Penalty: fine of £5 per bird.

1773a   Black game, grouse, or bustard, by any person, out of season. Penalty: for 1st offence, to be fined from £10 to £20; for subsequent offence, to be fined from £20 to £30; in default of fine, to be imprisoned from 3 to 6 months at hard labour.

1818   By any person. Penalty: fine of £5 per bird or hare.

1831   1603, 1707, 1762, 1773a, 1818 repealed.
        See I.D.2.a.1831.
        1. No person or licensed dealer may buy game 10 days or more after the end of the season. Penalty: to be fined up to £1 per bird or hare plus costs.
        2. No person (other than a licensed dealer) may buy game except from a licensed dealer. Penalty: to be fined up to £5 per bird or hare plus costs.
        3. No licensed dealer may buy game except from a qualified person or another licensed dealer. Penalty: to be fined up to £10 plus costs.
        In default of fine, to be imprisoned up to 2 months (if fine less than £5) or up to 3 months (in any other case).

c. possession
1693b   Without a good explanation. Penalty: to be fined from 5/– to 20/– per bird or hare; in default of fine, to be imprisoned from 10 days to 1 month in house of correction, there to be whipped and kept at hard labour.

1707   By any higgler, chapman, carrier (except when game carried is sent by qualified person), innkeeper, victualler, or alehouse keeper. Penalty: to be fined £5 per bird or hare; in default of fine, to be imprisoned without bail for 3 months (if 1st offence) or 4 months (if subsequent offence).

1711   See II.C.4.1711.

1755a   By any poulterer, salesman, fishmonger, cook or pastry cook. Penalty: same as 1707.

1762   By any person, out of season, except hares. Penalty: fine of £5 per bird.

1773a   Any black game, grouse, or bustard, out of season, by any person. Penalty: for 1st offence, to be fined from £10 to £20; for subsequent offence, to be fined from £20 to £30; in default of fine, to be imprisoned for 3 to 6 months at hard labour.

1831   1693b, 1707, 1711, 1755a, 1762, 1773a repealed.
        See I.D.2.a.1831.
        1. No licensed dealer may possess game 10 days or more after the end of

the season. Penalty: to be fined up to £1 per bird or hare plus costs.
2. No person may possess game 40 days or more after the end of the season. Penalty: to be fined up to £1 per bird or hare plus costs.
In default of fine, to be imprisoned up to 2 months (if fine less than £5) or up to 3 months (in any other case).

E. Offences against game preservation

1. destroying pales or walls around parks
1692   At night. Penalty: to be imprisoned for 3 months without bail.
1718   At any time. Penalty: £30 fine; in default of fine, to be imprisoned without bail for 1 year and shall be set on the pillory for 1 hour on market day.
1776   1692, 1718 repealed.
        At any time. Penalty: £30 fine; in default of fine, to be imprisoned for 1 year without bail.
1827b   At any time. Penalty: to be fined up to £20; in default of fine, to be imprisoned at hard labour for up to 2 months (if fine £5 or less), or up to 4 months (if fine £10 or less), or up to 6 months (if fine more than £10).
1827c   1776 repealed.

2. burning heath
1693b   Burning grig, ling, heath, furze, goss, or fern, between 2 February and 24 June. Penalty: to be committed to house of correction from 10 days to 1 month, there to be whipped and kept at hard labour.
1707   Burning ling, heath, or brakes in Nottinghamshire. Penalty: to forfeit 10/– and all the ashes.
        Buying ashes from such unlawful burning. Penalty: to be fined 10/– per peck of ashes.
        In default of fine, to be committed to house of correction for 1 month, there to be kept at hard labour.
1755b   Burning goss, furze, or fern. Penalty: to be fined from 40/– to £5; in default of fine, to be imprisoned for 3 months.
1827c   1693b and 1755b repealed.
1831   1707 repealed.

3. stealing eggs or destroying eggs in nests
As of 1660: Eggs of wild fowl. Penalty: imprisonment for 1 year and fine of 20*d*. per egg of crane or bustard, 8*d*. per egg of bittern, heron or shoveller, and 1*d*. per egg of mallard, teal, or other wild fowl (1533 as confirmed by 1549).
Eggs of partridge or pheasant. Penalty: to be imprisoned without bail for 3 months, unless fine of 20/– per egg paid or unless after 1 month in prison sureties found for £20 recognisance (1603).
1831   1603 repealed.
        Eggs of any game bird or of wild duck, teal, or widgeon. Penalty: to be fined up to 5/– per egg plus costs: in default of fine, to be imprisoned for up to 2 months (if fine less than £5) or up to 3 months (in any other case).

4. poisoning ground
1831   Where game is kept or in highway. Penalty: to be fined up to £10 plus costs; in default of fine, to be imprisoned for up to 2 months (if fine less than £5) or up to 3 months (in any other case).

F. Setting spring guns and man traps

1827a   Except in dwelling houses between sunset and sunrise. Penalty: to be punished as a misdemeanour.

II. Offences committed by an 'unqualified' person

A. Qualification

1. property and rank

1389   To keep dogs or to use ferrets, nets, or other 'engines' to take deer, hares, conies, or 'other gentleman's game':
   1. layman: lands or tenements of value of 40/– p.a.
   2. clergy: income of £10 p.a.

1541   To keep or shoot a crossbow, hand gun, hagbut or demi-hake:
   1. lands, fees, annuities, or offices of value of £100 p.a.
   2. gentlemen, yeomen, and servants of peers.
   3. knights, esquires, gentlemen, and inhabitants of cities, boroughs, and market towns.
   4. those who dwell more than 2 furlongs from any city, borough, or market town.

1603   To keep greyhounds, setting dogs, or nets to take game:
   1. lands, tenements, or hereditaments of value of £10 p.a.
   2. copyhold of same of value of £30 p.a.
   3. goods or chattels of £200.
   4. sons of 'any knight, or of any baron of parliament, or of some person of higher degree, or son and heir apparent of any esquire'.
   To take partridge or pheasant (in daytime between Michaelmas and Christmas, with nets, on own land):
   1. lords of manor, or those with right of free warren.
   2. lands, tenements, or hereditaments of value of £10 p.a.
   3. copyhold of same of value of £30 p.a.
   4. goods or chattels of value of £200.

1605   To use gun, bow, or crossbow, or to keep dogs, ferrets, or engines, to take deer or conies:
   1. manors, lands, tenements, or hereditaments of value of £40 p.a.
   2. goods or chattels of value of £200.
   3. ground enclosed for keeping deer or conies (if conies increase by value of £40 p.a.).
   4. keepers or warreners in grounds belonging to their charge.

1609a   To take partridge and pheasant (in daytime, between Michaelmas and Christmas, on own land):
   1. lords of manors, or those with right of free warren.
   2. lands, tenements, or hereditaments of value of £40 p.a.
   3. copyhold of same of value of £80 p.a.
   4. goods or chattels of value of £400.

1671b   To keep or use guns, bows, greyhounds, setting-dogs, ferrets, coney-dogs, lurchers, hays, lowbels, hare-pipes, gins, snares, or other 'engines' to take game or conies:
   1. lands, tenements, or other estate of inheritance of value of £100 p.a.

    2. copyhold or leasehold (for 99 years or longer) of same of value of £150 p.a.

    3. the son and heir apparent of an esquire, or other person of higher degree.

    4. owners and keepers of forests, parks, chases, or warrens, stocked with deer or conies for their own use.

1827c 1605 repealed.

1831   1389, 1541, 1603, 1609a, and 1671b repealed.

    Any person with game certificate (see II.A.2) is qualified to kill game, subject to the law of trespass. Landlord may reserve the right to hunt on his tenant's land for himself and any other certificate-holder he may designate. Lord of manor has right to take game on any waste or common within his manor.

    See also: Gamekeepers' qualifications (III.A).

2. certificate

1784   Before they kill game, persons qualified by property and rank must take out a game certificate and pay a stamp duty of £2.2.0.

1785   1784 repealed.

    Every person (except a gamekeeper) who shall use dog, gun, net, or other 'engine' to take game must take out certificate and pay stamp duty of £2.2.0.

1791   Stamp duty raised to £3.3.0.

1812   Stamp duty raised to £3.13.6.

1831   All previous laws regarding game certificates confirmed (see II.A.1).

    See also: Gamekeepers' qualifications (III.A).

B. Hunting game without qualification

As of 1660: Hunting game or wild fowl without 1609a qualification. Penalty: to be imprisoned for 3 months without bail, unless fine of 20/- per bird or hare paid, or unless after 1 month in prison sureties are found for £20 recognisance (1603 as amended by 1609a).

1671b Hunting game without 1671b qualification. Prohibited, but no penalty given.

1707   Hunting game without 1671b qualification. Penalty: to be fined £5; in default of fine, to be imprisoned for 3 months (if 1st offence) or 4 months (if subsequent offence) without bail.

1784   Hunting game without 1784 qualification. Penalty: £50 fine.

1785   1784 repealed.

    Hunting game without 1785 qualification. Penalty: £20 fine; in default of fine, to be imprisoned for 6 months or for 3 months.

1786   1785 clarified: in default of fine, to be imprisoned for 3 months.

1808b 1603 as relates to hares, repealed.

1812   Hunting game without 1785 qualification. Penalty: to be fined £20 plus duty on certificate; in default of fine, to be imprisoned for up to 6 months.

1831   1603, 1609a, 1671b, 1707 repealed.

    Hunting game without 1785 qualification. Penalty: to be fined up to £5 plus costs; in default of fine, to be imprisoned up to 2 months. This penalty may be imposed in *addition* to that given under 1812.

    Hunting by tenant without permission of landlord. Penalty: to be fined up to £2 and up to £1 per bird or hare taken or killed, plus costs; in default of fine, to be imprisoned for up to 2 months (if fine less than £5) or up to 3 months (in any other case).

C. Possessing without qualification

1. nets, snares, or other 'engines'

As of 1660: Nets for taking partridge or pheasant. Penalty: to be imprisoned for 3 months without bail, unless fine of 40/– is paid, or unless after 1 month in prison sureties are found for a £20 recognisance (1603).

1671b   Nets, lowbells, hare-pipes, gins, snares, or other 'engines' for taking game or conies, without 1671b qualification. Prohibited, but no penalty given.

1693b   Nets, tunnels, lowbells, hare-pipes, snares, or other 'engines' for taking game, without 1671b qualification. Penalty: to be fined from 5/– to 20/– per 'engine'; in default of fine, to be committed to house of correction from 10 days to 1 month, there to be whipped and kept at hard labour.

1707   Tunnels, or other 'engines' for taking game, without 1671b qualification. Penalty: to be fined £5; in default of fine, to be imprisoned without bail for 3 months (if 1st offence) or 4 months (if subsequent offence).

1831   1603, 1671b, 1693b, and 1707 repealed.

See also: 'engines' for taking deer (I.D.1.b).

2. dogs

As of 1660: Greyhound or setting-dog, without 1603 qualification. Penalty: to be imprisoned for 3 months without bail, unless fine of 40/– is paid, or unless after 1 month in prison sureties are found for £20 recognisance (1603).

1671b   Greyhounds, setting-dogs, ferrets, coney-dogs, or lurchers, without 1671b qualification. Prohibited, but no penalty given.

1693b   Greyhounds, setting-dogs, ferrets, coney-dogs, or lurchers, without 1671b qualification. Penalty: to be fined from 5/– to 20/– per dog; in default of fine, to be committed to house of correction from 10 days to 1 month, there to be whipped and kept at hard labour.

1707   Greyhounds, setting-dogs, lurchers, without 1671b qualification. Penalty: to be fined £5; in default of fine, to be imprisoned without bail for 3 months (if 1st offence) or 4 months (if subsequent offence).

1796b   Tax on dogs:
   1. every greyhound, pointer, setting-dog, spaniel, lurcher, terrier, or dog of other breed if 2 or more are kept: duty of 5/– per dog per year.
   2. every other dog, where 1 is kept by person assessed for duty on dwelling house, windows, or lights: duty of 3/– per dog per year.
   3. packs of hounds may be compounded for £15 per pack per year.

1808a   Tax on dogs:
   1. every greyhound, hound, pointer, setting-dog, spaniel, lurcher, terrier, or dog of other breed if 2 or more are kept: duty of 11/6 per dog per year.
   2. every other dog, where 1 is kept: duty of 7/– per dog per year.
   3. packs of hounds may be compounded for £34 per pack per year.
   Persons not assessed for tax on dwelling house exempt from duty.

1812   Tax on dogs:
   1. every greyhound: duty of £1 per dog per year.

2. every hound, pointer, setting-dog, spaniel, terrier, lurcher, or dog of other breed if 2 or more are kept: duty of 14/- per dog per year.
3. every other dog, where 1 is kept: duty of 8/- per dog per year.
4. packs of hounds may be compounded for £36 per pack per year.
Persons not assessed for tax on dwelling house exempt from duty.

1825   Exemption from dog tax for persons not assessed for tax on dwelling house continued, notwithstanding repeal of tax on dwelling houses.

1831   1603, 1671b, 1693b, and 1707 repealed.

3. guns

As of 1660: Without 1541 qualification. Penalty: £10 fine (1541). Not registering qualification with J.P. Penalty: 20/- fine (1548).

1671b   Without 1671b qualification. Prohibited, but no penalty given.

1695   1548 repealed.

1831   1541 and 1671b repealed.

4. game

1693b   See I.D.2.c.1693b.

1707   Without 1671b qualification. It shall be lawful for J.P. or lord of the manor to seize game from unqualified persons, and to keep it for his own use.

1711   Without 1671b qualification. Penalty: to be fined £5 per bird or hare; in default of fine, to be imprisoned without bail for 3 months (if 1st offence) or 4 months (if subsequent offence).

1831   1693b, 1707, and 1711 repealed.

III. Gamekeepers

A. Qualifications

1671b   All lords of manors, or other royalties, not under the degree of esquire may authorise one or more gamekeepers to preserve the game within their manors or royalties.

1711   No lord of manor may appoint more than one gamekeeper per manor. Each gamekeeper must have his name registered with, and receive a certificate from, the clerk of the peace.

1717   No person may be appointed a gamekeeper unless he is:
1. qualified to kill game by 1671b; or
2. a servant of the lord of the manor; or
3. a person specifically appointed to take and kill game for the use of the lord of the manor.

1784   Every gamekeeper must annually register with the clerk of the peace and take out a certificate on which a stamp duty of 10/6 shall be paid.

1785   1784 confirmed.

1791   Stamp duty raised to £1.1.0.

1804   If gamekeeper is not subject to the duty on servants, the duty on his certificate is raised to £3.3.0.

1808b   1717 repealed.

1812   Stamp duty raised to £1.5.0. (if keeper assessed as a servant) or to £3.13.6 (if keeper not assessed as a servant).

1831   1671b and 1711 repealed. Statutes related to stamp duty confirmed.

Person with game certificate on which the duty is £3.13.6 may appoint one or more gamekeepers to preserve game within the limits of his own land. Deputation is not valid unless registered with the clerk of the peace and a gamekeeper's certificate taken out.

B. Powers

As of 1660: Servants of those with 1609a qualification may be authorised to take and kill partridges and pheasants within master's free warren, manor, or freehold in the daytime between Michaelmas and Christmas (1609a).

1671b   May seize any game, dogs, or 'engines' used by those without 1671b qualification within the manor of his deputation. In the daytime, may search (even without warrant from J.P.) the houses of unqualified persons, and may seize any guns, dogs, or 'engines' to take game or conies, which may be destroyed or kept by the lord of the manor.

1692   Keeper of ground enclosed for keeping deer may oppose and resist those who unlawfully hunt there and shall be indemnified from prosecution if offenders are killed.

1693b   Gamekeepers may oppose and resist night poachers and shall be indemnified from prosecution if offenders are killed.

1707   Gamekeepers may be empowered to kill game within the manor of deputation.

1776   1692 repealed.
Keepers of any ground where deer are kept may seize dogs or 'engines' from those who unlawfully hunt on such ground, to be kept for the use of the owner of the ground.

1784   Gamekeepers' certificates valid only within the manor of deputation.

1785   1784 confirmed.

1808b   Gamekeeper may kill game for his own use or that of any other person specified in deputation.

1827b   1776 confirmed; may also seize guns or other firearms.

1831   1609a, 1671b, 1693b, 1707, and 1808b repealed.
Gamekeeper may kill game on lands of his deputation; may seize dogs, nets, or other 'engines' used there by those without game certificate; may also seize game from those hunting on master's land without permission. Gamekeeper with written permission from his master may sell game to licensed dealer.

C. Offences committed by gamekeepers

1. keepers of ground where deer are kept.

1718   Taking or killing deer without permission. Penalty: to be fined £50 per deer; in default of fine, to be imprisoned for 3 years without bail and to be set in the pillory for 2 hours on market day.

1776   1718 repealed.
Hunting deer on ground in his charge without permission. Penalty: to be fined £60; in default of fine, to be imprisoned for 1 year without bail; for subsequent offence, to be transported to America for 7 years.

1802   Hunting deer on unenclosed ground in his charge without permission. Penalty: to be fined £100; in default of fine, to be imprisoned for 6 months without bail; for subsequent offence, to be transported for 7 years.

1811   J.P. may mitigate fine imposed by 1802 to no less than £20.

1827c 1776, 1802, and 1811 repealed.

2. gamekeepers
1707 Selling or disposing of game without consent of his master. Penalty: to be imprisoned for 3 months at hard labour.
1831 1707 repealed.

D. *Assault on a gamekeeper*
1737 By an armed person in any ground where deer are kept. Penalty: to be transported to America for 7 years.
1776 1737 confirmed.
1827b By any person in any ground where deer are kept. Penalty: to be transported for 7 years, or imprisoned for up to 2 years and (if offender is male) to be whipped up to 3 times if court directs.
1827c 1737, 1776 repealed.
By any 5 persons (or more), any of whom are armed, in any ground, in daytime, who assault, intimidate, or menace. Penalty: every person in group to be fined up to £5 plus costs, in addition to any other penalty to which he may be liable; in default of fine, to be imprisoned for up to 2 months.

IV. Appendix: procedure

A. *Trespass*
As of 1660: If any action (not concerning title or inheritance of lands) is brought in any court of Westminster, and it shall appear to the court that the damages do not amount to 40/– or above, the plaintiff shall not be awarded costs greater than the sum of the damages (1601).
1671a 1601 confirmed.
1693b If an 'inferior' tradesman or apprentice shall hunt on another's land (without being in the company of a master, qualified by 1671b), he may be prosecuted for wilful trespass and the plaintiff may recover not only damages but the full costs of the suit.
1697 If trespass is 'wilfull and malicious', the plaintiff may recover not only damages but the full costs of the suit.
1831 1693b repealed. Right to sue for trespass confirmed.

B. *Criminal procedure*

1. deer stealing cases
As of 1660: Cases may be determined by justices of oyer and terminer; of assizes in circuit; or of peace and gaol delivery in sessions. No essoin, wager of law, or protection shall be allowed (1605).
1661 Offenders may be convicted on oath of one credible witness before one J.P.
1692 In cases of unlawful possession of deer or 'engines' to take deer, defendant to be convicted unless he can 'give a good account' of how he came to possess. Prosecutions for unlawful hunting must commence within 12 months of the offence.

Certiorari not to be allowed unless offender becomes bound to prosecutor for £50.

1718   Certiorari not to be allowed unless offender becomes bound to prosecutor for £60.

1723   Prosecutions under 1692 must commence within 3 years of the offence.

1776   1692 and 1718 repealed. 1661 confirmed.

Certiorari not to be allowed unless offender becomes bound to prosecutor for £100, and to J.P. for £60. Prosecutions under 1776 must commence within 12 months of the offence.

Appeals to quarter sessions to be decided 'on the merits of the case' and not on want of proper form. No appeal may be quashed or removed by any writ.

1827c   1776 repealed.

1827b   1661 confirmed.

Appeals to quarter sessions may not be quashed or removed by any writ.

2. game poaching cases

As of 1660: Offenders may be convicted on oath of 2 credible witnesses before 2 J.P.s (1609a).

1671b   Offenders may be convicted on oath of 1 credible witness before 1 J.P.

1693b   Certiorari not to be allowed unless offender becomes bound to prosecutor for £50.

In cases of unlawful possession of game or 'engines', defendant to be convicted unless he can 'give a good account' how he came to possess.

1707   Offender who informs on higgler, chapman, etc. for possessing, buying, or selling game, to be relieved from punishment for his own crime.

1711   1707 extended to include informing on any unqualified person.

1722   For any offence against the game laws liable to fine, the prosecutor has the option of laying an information against offender before a J.P. or suing by action of debt (for the half-fine due the informer) in any court of record; if the latter, the plaintiff may recover double costs, and no essoin, protection, wager of law, or more than one imparlance shall be allowed. Suit must be brought before end of the next term after offence is committed.

1753   1722 altered: suits may be brought before the end of the 2nd term after offence is committed.

1762   1722 altered: plaintiff may recover full fine, plus double costs; suits must be brought within 6 months after offence is committed.

1770   Appeals against summary conviction (for Sunday or night poaching) may be made to quarter sessions within 4 days of conviction, provided the offender becomes bound by recognisance.

1773b   1770 altered: appeals may be made within 3 months of conviction.

3rd or subsequent offences of night poaching to be tried by quarter sessions.

1816   Night poaching cases to be tried by quarter sessions.

1817   1816 confirmed.

1828   1817 repealed.

Night poaching cases to be tried before 2 J.P.s; 3rd offences to be tried before quarter sessions.

1831   All other game law offences to be tried before 2 J.P.s. Appeals to quarter sessions must be made within 3 days of conviction. Neither summary conviction nor appeal may be removed or quashed by any writ.

Notes

List of abbreviations

A.O.	Archives Office
B.L.	British Library
C.J.	*Journals of the house of commons*
C.S.P.D.	*Calendar of state papers, domestic*
C.U.L.	Cambridge University Library
D.N.B.	*Dictionary of national biography*
Econ. Hist. Rev.	*Economic History Review*
1823 Game Report	*Report from the select committee on the laws relating to game (Parl. Papers, 1823, IV, 107-53)**
1827 Crime Report	*Report from the select committee on criminal commitments and convictions (Parl. Papers, 1826-7, VI, 5-74)**
1828 Crime Report	*Report from the select committee on criminal commitments and convictions (Parl. Papers, 1828, VI, 419-523)**
1828 Game Report	*Report from the select committee of the house of lords appointed to take into consideration the laws relating to game (Parl. Papers, 1828, VIII, 333-438)**
H.M.C.	Historical Manuscript Commission (followed by the short title of the Report)
L.J.	*Journals of the house of lords*
Parl. Deb.	T. C. Hansard, ed., *The parliamentary debates from the year 1803 to the present time*
Parl. Hist.	William Cobbett and John Wright, eds., *The parliamentary history of England, from the earliest period to the year 1803*
Parl. Papers	House of Commons, *Sessional papers, 1801-1900*
Parl. Papers, 1731-1800	House of Commons, *Sessional papers, 1731-1800*
P.R.O.	Public Record Office
Parl. Reg.	*The parliamentary register; or, history of the proceedings and debates of the house of commons*
R.O.	Record Office
S.C.L.	Sheffield Central Library

*Citations in notes refer to the internal pagination of the Report.

Introduction

1   In the following pages, the terms 'hunt' and 'sport' will be used inter-changeably to denote coursing, netting, hawking and shooting, as well as hunting in the strict sense of the word.

2   Sidney and Beatrice Webb, *English local government* (new edn, London, 1963), I: *The parish and the county*, p. 598; J.L. and Barbara Hammond, *The village labourer* (new edn, London, 1948), p. 184; B.A. Holderness, *Pre-industrial England: economy and society, 1500–1750* (London, 1976), pp. 43-4.

3   J.D. Chambers, *Nottinghamshire in the eighteenth century: a study of life and labour under the squirearchy* (2nd edn, London, 1966), pp. 74-5. See also G.E. Mingay, *The gentry: the rise and fall of a ruling class* (London & New York, 1976), pp. 131-3.

4   The Scottish qualification, enacted in 1621, required a sportsman to possess 'a plough of land in heritage'; under another act passed in 1685, the keeping of setting dogs was restricted to those with at least £1000 Scots (approximately £70 in English currency) in rents. The latter requirement was declared obsolete by the courts in 1780 and, in fact, was probably never strictly enforced after the fall of James VII and II. That left only the qualification of a 'plough' of land which, because of its indeterminate nature, was never a serious barrier to the pursuit of game. In practice, most landowners had the right to hunt – and to empower others to hunt – on their own land. For a good summary of the Scottish game laws, see *1828 Game Report*, pp. 57-65.

In Ireland, a sporting qualification was first enacted in 1698. Under its provisions, a sportsman had to possess land worth £40 a year or £1000 in 'personal estate' to keep setting dogs. In 1763, however, landowners were given 'sole and absolute property in all kinds and species of game found on their respective estates'. The Qualification Act still remained in force but, as in Scotland, it seems to have had little practical significance after the middle of the eighteenth century. For the major Irish game laws, see *The statutes at large, passed in the parliaments held in Ireland* (Dublin, 1786–1801), *sub* 10 Wm III, c.8; 11 Geo. II, c. 12; 19 Geo. II, c. 14; 3 Geo. III, c. 23; 13 & 14 Geo. III, c. 42, ss. 6-8; 27 Geo. III, c. 35.

In Scotland, the sale of game in season was legal throughout the eighteenth century; in Ireland it was not outlawed until 1787.

5   There have been no studies of the game laws in either Scotland or Ireland. It is, therefore, difficult to judge their impact; further research may show that it was greater than is now supposed. Certainly there was criticism of them in Scotland in the early 1770s: see, for example, *A candid inquiry into the present state of the laws relative to the game in Scotland* (Edinburgh, 1772) or *The present state of the game laws, and the question of property, considered* (Edinburgh, 1772).

6   9 Anne, c. 25, s. 4; 10 Geo. II, c. 32, s. 10.

7   E.g., J.J. Bagley, ed., *The great diurnal of Nicholas Blundell of Little Crosby, Lancashire* (Record Society of Lancashire and Cheshire, 1968–72), II, 21, 23, 56, 57.

8   The physical differences between rabbits and hares are slight, but they do suggest some reasons why country gentlemen would be inclined to enclose the former before the latter. Due to their larger hind legs, hares were faster than rabbits. This, plus their ability to turn quickly, made hares a much more challenging prey for sportsmen. Hare meat, moreover, was deemed to be tougher than rabbit meat (unless tenderised by several hours' chase through the countryside); thus there was less incentive to breed hares for the market.

9 Joseph Chitty, *A treatise on the game laws and on fisheries* (London, 1812), II, 1067.

10 Quoted in Robert Fulford, *Samuel Whitbread, 1764–1815: a study in opposition* (London, 1967), pp. 224-5.

Chapter 1

1 Sir William Blackstone, *Commentaries on the laws of England* (9th edn, London, 1783), IV, 174.

2 Not including the annual Mutiny Acts, each of which contained a clause prescribing the punishment for unlawful hunting by soldiers: see Appendix I.A.1.d.

3 Joseph Addison, Sir Richard Steele, *et al.*, *The Spectator* (Everyman edn, 1970), I, 7 (No. 2); Chitty, *Treatise*, II, 1183-92.

4 Hammond, *Village labourer*, p. 185.

5 Eric J. Evans, 'Some reasons for the growth of English rural anti-clericalism, c. 1750–c. 1830', *Past & Present*, no. 66 (1975), p. 103n.

6 Jacob Viner, 'Man's economic status', *Man versus society in eighteenth-century Britain*, ed. James L. Clifford (Cambridge, 1968), pp. 39-40. Professor Viner may have been thinking of 'illegal shooting' of deer, but his reference to 'exclusive privileges artificially established by law for the very rich' would suggest that he was not – or at least that he was unaware that the property qualification for hunting deer was obsolete by the eighteenth century.

7 John Manwood, *A treatise of the laws of the forest*, (3rd edn, London, 1665), preface. On the laws and administration of the forests, see also J.C. Cox, *The royal forests of England* (London, 1905), pp. 10-24, and P.A.J. Pettit, *The royal forests of Northamptonshire: a study in their economy, 1558–1714* (Northants. Record Society, XXIII [1968]), pp. 18-44.

8 George Hammersley, 'The revival of the forest laws under Charles I', *History*, XLV (1960), 85-102; Pettit, *Royal forests of Northants*, pp. 83-95.

9 Cox, *Royal forests*, pp. 2, 26.

10 Sir William Holdsworth, *A history of English law* (7th edn, London, 1956), I, 101. No person with a right of free warren, however, was permitted to hunt on the freehold of another person within that free warren without the latter's permission (11 Hen. VII, c. 17).

11 See Chester and Ethyn Kirby, 'The Stuart game prerogative', *English Historical Review*, XLVI (1931), 239-46.

12 The granting of franchises also increased the number of animals to which the king laid claim. Strictly speaking, the forest laws reserved deer and boar for the king's sport, but not game (except in Somerset, where one forest preserved hares as well): see Cox, *Royal forests*, p. 26. The range of animal life protected in a free warren was much more extensive.

13 Kirby, 'Stuart game prerogative', pp. 243-54.

14 Paul L. Hughes and James F. Larkin, eds., *Tudor royal proclamations* (New Haven & London, 1964–9), III, 219. See also Sir James F. Stephen, *A history of the criminal laws of England* (London, 1883), III, 276-7; and H.M.C., *14th Report*, IV, 42.

15 13 Rich. II, st. 1, c. 13. Priests and clerks were required to have incomes of at least £10 a year.

16 1 Jas I, c. 27; 3 Jas I, c. 13; 7 Jas I, c. 11. For details, see Appendix II.A.1. 1603, 1605, 1609.

17 *C.S.P.D. 1676–7.* p. 298.

18   Kirby, 'Stuart game prerogative', p. 251.
19   *C.S.P.D. 1676–7*, p. 266.
20   22 & 23 Chas II, c. 25. The wording of the Act was occasionally obscure. It was, for example, unclear whether a copyholder had to have £100 or £150 a year to qualify, whether members of corporations or fellows of colleges were qualified and whether a gamekeeper had to have a J.P.'s warrant in order to search an unqualified person's house. On these and other technicalities, see Chitty's *Treatise* and also Edward Christian, *A treatise on the game laws* (London, 1817). In only a few instances did judicial decisions alter the game laws; those cases will be noted in the following chapters.
21   22 & 23 Chas II, c. 9, s. 136 (which confirmed 43 Eliz. I, c. 6, s. 2). In 1697 the restriction was dropped (by 8 & 9 Wm III, c. 11, s. 4), but it was still necessary to prove that prior notice not to trespass had been given to the defendant. This requirement also inhibited suits against sportsmen.
22   This is a controversial point. Legal commentators at the beginning of the eighteenth century, basing their opinion on an ambiguous decision in the 1690s (Sutton v. Moody, for which see Chitty, *Treatise*, II, 984-6), claimed that landowners had a 'qualified' property in game found on their land. According to this view, game belonged to the landowner so long as it remained on his land; when it left (unless it was being hunted by the landowner at the time), it ceased to be his property. (E.g., Giles Jacob, *The game laws* [London, 1705], pp. 45-6; William Nelson, *The laws of England concerning the game* [3rd edn, London, 1736], pp. 206-7.) The idea was taken up by opponents of the game laws in the early nineteenth century, notably by Edward Christian, to support their claim that under the common law game was the property of the person on whose land it was found (Christian, *Treatise*, pp. 39-56).

   Whatever the merits of Christian's case, it seems clear that the courts in the eighteenth century did not view game as a type of private property. The taking of game was not treated as larceny unless the animal was either dead, tame or confined in a mews (e.g., Chitty, *Treatise*, II, 1176). And while Christian argued that a jury in a trespass case 'ought' to consider loss of game when assessing damages, there is no evidence that this was actually done, except in cases involving invasion of a free warren – that is, where sporting privilege was itself a species of property (ibid., pp. 1166-7). In fact, Christian's very anxiety to prove that game was the property of the landowner suggests that his was not the orthodox view. Much more representative were Blackstone, *Commentaries*, II, 418; Richard Burn, *The justice of the peace and parish officer* (15th edn, London, 1785), II, 249-53; George Clark, *The game laws from King Henry III to the present period* (London, 1786), pp. 12-14.

   For a modern defence of Christian's view, however, see P.J. Cook, 'Property and prerogative in game: the legal background to the English game and forest laws' (Ph.D. thesis, University of Birmingham, 1975).
23   E.g., H.M.C., *Buccleuch*, III, 15; *13th Report*, IV, 336-7; *Various collections*, II, 371.
24   No estimate has been made of the number of manors in England in the eighteenth century, but there may have been as many as 20,000 of them. The actual number of lords was substantially less than this, however, since many noblemen and gentlemen owned more than one manor. Gregory King estimated in 1688 that there were 4500 persons who were esquires or 'of higher degree'. It seems safe to assume that most of these men were lords of

manors. Another estimate, made in 1784, put the number of lords of the manor at 5000 (*Facts, fully established, and submitted to the consideration of every member of both houses of parliament* . . . [Bath, 1784], p. 61).

25 5 Anne, c. 14, s. 4.
26 H.M.C., *9th Report*, II, 17; House of Lords R.O., Committee Book, H.L., 10 April 1671.
27 22 & 23 Chas II, c. 25, s. 10.
28 For a vivid picture of the organisation of New Forest in the late seventeenth century, see Christopher Morris, ed., *The journeys of Celia Fiennes* (2nd edn, London, 1949), pp. 50-1. For the activities of a minor forest court in the eighteenth and nineteenth centuries, see Epping Forest Commission, *The rolls of the court of attachments of the royal forest of Waltham in . . . Essex, from . . . 1713 to . . . 1848* (London, 1873). For the treatment of deer-stealers in forests in the eighteenth and early nineteenth centuries, see the Gloucestershire gaol calendars in Glos. R.O., Q/SG and the Essex summary convictions in Essex R.O., Q/RSC 1/1-3. There were some exceptions to this picture of decay, notably in Windsor Forest, for which see E.P. Thompson, *Whigs and hunters: the origin of the Black Act* (New York, 1975), ch. 1.
29 E.g., in 1812, Richard Howard sought to have his rights of chase and free warren recognised in the act which enclosed Congham Common in Norfolk (Norfolk R.O., How 750/44-5).
30 4 & 5 Wm & Mary, c. 23, s. 4. See also 21 Edw. I, st. 2 and 3 & 4 Wm & Mary, c. 10, s. 5.
31 Kirby, 'Stuart game prerogative', p. 253. A vestige of the old royal gamekeeperships remained in the area around Newmarket, where a keeper of 'his Majesty's game' was appointed, somewhat fitfully, throughout the eighteenth century: see O.F. Morehead, 'H.M. gamekeeper', *Notes & Queries*, CLXIV (1933), 373. The king, of course, also continued to appoint gamekeepers for his own manors.
32 Blackstone, *Commentaries*, IV, 416.
33 B.L., Add. MS 39616, ff. 215, 217-18, 220.
34 *C.J.,* IX, 219, 225-6, 229, 236-7. When introduced, the title was 'A Bill to Prevent the Destruction of Coneys, and other Game'; on report, it had become 'A Bill to Preserve the Game, and For Securing Warrens Not Inclosed, and the Several Fishings of the Realm'.
35 W. Suffolk R.O., E18/905/1. The document is undated, but internal evidence suggests that it was written in 1660 or 1661. See also J.C. Cox, *Three centuries of Derbyshire annals* (London, 1890), II, 81.
36 13 Chas II, st. 1, c. 10.
37 *C.J.*, VIII, 616, 618.
38 *C.S.P.D. 1667–8*, p. 20.
39 See Alan Everitt, *The community of Kent and the great rebellion, 1640–1660* (Leicester, 1966), pp. 143-55 and his *Change in the provinces: the seventeenth century* (Leicester, 1969), p. 45.
40 Quoted in Perez Zagorin, *The court and the country* (New York, 1969), p. 119.
41 See D.C. Coleman, 'London scriviners and the estate market in the late seventeenth century', *Econ. Hist. Rev.*, 2nd ser., IV (1951), 221-30.
42 H.J. Habakkuk, 'Landowners and the civil war', *Econ. Hist. Rev.*, 2nd ser., XVIII (1965), 149.
43 Anchitel Grey, *Debates of the house of commons from the year 1667 to the year 1694* (London, 1769), I, 350-2; D.T. Witcombe, *Charles II and the cavalier house of commons, 1663–1674* (Manchester, 1966), pp. 108, 110-11, 113-14.

44   Richard Grassby, 'English merchant capitalism in the late seventeenth century. The composition of business fortunes', *Past & Present*, no. 46 (1970), pp. 93-4; D.W. Jones, 'London merchants and the crisis of the 1690s', *Crisis and order in English towns, 1500–1700*, ed. Peter Clark and Paul Slack (Toronto, 1972), p. 336.

45   Lawrence Stone, 'Social mobility in England, 1500–1700', *Past & Present*, no. 33 (1966), pp. 30-1.

46   See Charles Wilson, *England's apprenticeship, 1603–1763* (London, 1965), chs. 8, 10.

47   See F.J. Fisher, 'The development of the London food market, 1540–1640', *Econ. Hist. Rev.*, V (1935), 47-86; E.A. Wrigley, 'A simple model of London's importance in changing English society and economy, 1650–1750', *Past & Present*, no. 37 (1967), pp. 44-86.

48   Grey, *Debates*, I, 301. See also Caroline A. Edie, 'New buildings, new taxes and old interests: an urban problem in the 1670s', *Journal of British Studies*, VI (1966–7), 35-63.

49   Grassby, 'English merchant capitalism', pp. 103-7. See also Peter Borsay, 'The English urban renaissance: the development of provincial urban culture, c. 1680–c. 1760', *Social History*, no. 5 (1977), pp. 581-603.

50   See John Loftis, *Comedy and society from Congreve to Fielding* (Stanford, Calif., 1959), pp. 23-4.

51   Kent. A.O., U1015, C13/4-6. See also W.A. Speck, 'Conflict in society', *Britain after the glorious revolution, 1689–1714*, ed. Geoffrey Holmes (London, 1969), pp. 145-6. The same prejudice may have also affected the lives of younger sons. Addison wrote of great families 'who had rather see their Children starve like Gentlemen, than thrive in a Trade or Profession that is beneath their Quality' (*The Spectator*, I, 331 [No. 108]).

52   William Congreve, *The way of the world* (1700), III. xv.

53   Christopher Hill, *Reformation to industrial revolution: a social and economic history of Britain, 1530–1780* (London, 1967), p. 157. See also G.E. and K.R. Fussell, *The English countryman: his life and work, A.D. 1500–1900* (London, 1955), p. 71.

54   Nicholas Cox, *The gentleman's recreation* (2nd edn, London, 1677), pp. 1-2.

55   Quoted in Roger Longrigg, *The history of foxhunting* (London, 1975), pp. 40-1.

56   See A. Harris, 'The rabbit warrens of East Yorkshire in the eighteenth and nineteenth centuries', *Yorkshire Archaeological Journal*, XLII (1967–70), 429-43; Fisher, 'Development of the London food market', pp. 61, 63.

57   1 Jas I, c. 27, s. 2; see also Christian, *Treatise*, p. 155. An exception was the setting of snares, hare-pipes or other 'engines' to take hares as well as conies. The Game Act *did* impose a new penalty for this offence (22 & 23 Chas II, c. 25, s. 6), but it applied to all persons, whether qualified or not, and the preamble indicates that it was enacted to prevent poaching near warrens – that is, the taking of enclosed game. On the tendency to equate enclosed hares with rabbits, see below, n. 91.

58   5 Anne, c. 14, s. 4. Imprisonment could be extended to four months if there had been a previous conviction.

59   22 & 23 Chas II, c. 25, s. 2; 4 & 5 Wm & Mary, c. 23, s. 3; 5 Anne, c. 14, s. 4. Guns might also be seized, but the unqualified possessor of them was not liable to any penalty. For a discussion of whether the game laws 'disarmed' the population, see below, pp. 79-82.

60   4 & 5 Wm & Mary, c. 23, s. 3; 5 Anne, c. 14, 2. 4; 9 Anne, c. 25, s. 2.

61   3 & 4 Wm & Mary, c. 10. If the offence occurred outside a park, the penalty was marginally less: see 13 Chas II, st. 1, c. 10. Hunting rabbits without the

landowner's permission also carried a more severe punishment: payment of treble damages plus costs *and* at least three months in prison (22 & 23 Chas II, c. 25, s. 4).

62   This was also true of hares, whose enclosure in many areas predated that of partridges and pheasants. For a discussion of eighteenth-century game preservation, see Chapter 2.

63   The property qualification for hunting deer (3 Jas I, c. 13, amended by 7 Jas I, c. 13) remained on the statute books throughout the eighteenth century; it was finally repealed in 1827 (by 7 & 8 Geo. IV, c. 27) but had been ignored, both in law and in fact, from the time of the Restoration, if not earlier. The qualification act for hunting rabbits was actually the Game Act of 1671, which forbade the unqualified to hunt rabbits as well as game. Subsequent game laws, however, did not include rabbits in the group of animals under their protection, and surviving records of quarter sessions and summary conviction yield no instances of persons being prosecuted for hunting rabbits without legal qualification. 'Deer-stealers' and 'cony-catchers' *were* prosecuted, however, for breaking and entering enclosed grounds and for hunting without the permission of the owner of those grounds. Thus, enclosure of 'game' brought with it distinct changes in the law, even though this might not be directly acknowedged in the statute books.

64   *Monthly Review*, LXXXV (1818), 83; see also below, pp. 144-5.

65   George Crabbe, *Tales of the hall* (London, 1819), II, 309.

66   32 Hen. VIII, c. 8; 1 Jas I, c. 27, s. 4. The latter statute made the sale of venison or game punishable by a fine. It was, however, rarely enforced, and poulterers continued to supply game to the public: see below, p. 55.

67   5 Anne, c. 14, s. 2.

68   28 Geo. II, c. 12. For the origins of this Act, see below, p. 57.

69   C.U.L., Buxton MSS, Box 6, John Buxton to Robert Buxton, 24-5 Dec. 1780; see also *Norwich Mercury*, 23 Jan. 1779.

70   *Gentleman's Magazine*, XIX (1749), 62.

71   On the surface this might seem to be a solecism: one prosecutes in a criminal court, but sues in a civil one. But the line between criminal and civil proceedings was less clearly defined in the eighteenth century than in the twentieth. Trespass, for example, was a tort but that did not prevent it from being dealt with by quarter sessions. Similarly, offences against the game laws came under the criminal code, but prosecutors were given the option of proceeding against offenders in courts of record. Under such circumstances, 'civil prosecution' seems the most accurate label.

72   8 Geo. I, c. 19. See alterations in 26 Geo. II, c. 2 and in 2 Geo. III, c. 19, s. 5, the latter of which assigned the entire fine to the plaintiff. For an earlier attempt to inject civil prosecution into the game laws, see 4 & 5 Wm & Mary, c. 23, s. 10 and Chitty, *Treatise*, II, 1125-30.

73   For a full discussion of the uses of civil prosecution, see below, pp. 89-93.

74   In 1791 the duty was raised to three guineas for sportsmen and one guinea for gamekeepers; in 1812 it was further increased to £3 13s. 6d. and £1 5s. respectively (31 Geo. III, c. 21; 52 Geo. III, c. 93, sch. L). The hunting tax was not an entirely original idea. Many aspects of Pitt's game duty had been suggested at the beginning of the century in *A letter to a member of parliament, with proposals for a game-act* (n.p., 1709), the only known copy of which is in the Bodleian Library.

75   This was more a matter of necessity than choice. When the game duty bill was first introduced in 1784, it proposed to tax all hunters, whether they

were qualified or not, but under attack from Sheridan, Pitt agreed to tax only qualified sportsmen and their gamekeepers (*Parl. Reg.*, XVI, 401-5; 24 Geo. III, sess. 2, c. 43). In the following year, however, the Act was repealed and replaced by one which required every person, regardless of qualification, to have a valid licence before hunting game (25 Geo. III, c. 50, amended by 26 Geo. III, c. 82, ss. 7-8). The Attorney General, Pepper Arden, expressed his own reluctance to extend the tax to unqualified persons, but, he said, 'it appeared impossible to avoid it' (William Stockdale, ed., *Debates of the third session of the 16th parliament* [London, 1785], III, 477). The problem was that under the Act of 1784 the prosecutor had to prove both that the defendant had hunted without a valid licence and that he was not qualified under the Game Act. After the law was changed, only the lack of a valid licence had to be established, thus greatly expediting the enforcement of the law.

76   For the case of four Yorkshire poachers who did take out licences, see *Salisbury Journal*, 28 Nov. 1785. See also H.M.C., *Fortesque*, VIII, 489.

77   Civil prosecution was not totally divorced from the operation of the Game Duty Act, since it was possible to sue for recovery of fines imposed under this Act as well as under the 'old game code': see 25 Geo. III, c. 50, s. 21.

78   23 Eliz. I, c. 10. Hares, however, were not protected by this statute.

79   9 Anne, c. 25, s. 3.

80   10 Geo. III, c. 19. For the first offence, the prison term ranged from three to six months; for subsequent offences, the night poacher could be imprisoned for six to twelve months. For hunting on Sundays, there was a fine of £20 to £30 or three to six months in prison.

81   13 Geo. III, c. 80. For a discussion of the opposition to the Act of 1770, see below, pp. 115-22.

82   The penalties also applied to those who hunted on Sundays and on Christmas Day.

83   See Blackstone, *Commentaries*, IV, 224. For a similar development in the laws relating to rabbits, see Appendix I.C.3.a. Laws protecting deer, however, made no distinction between offences committed at night and during the day. A move in that direction (3 Jas I, c. 13, s. 8) was cut short in 1609 (by 7 Jas I, c. 13, s. 2); thereafter, the principal distinction was whether the offence took place in enclosed or unenclosed ground. Why the deer laws differed in this respect is unclear.

84   Henry Zouch, *An account of the present daring practices of night-hunters and poachers* (London, 1783), p. 1.

85   *Norwich Mercury*, 29 Nov. 1781. At the Lent assizes in 1782, three men were charged with murder in connection with this incident, but the grand jury rejected the presentment. One of the accused, however, was subsequently charged with possessing stolen goods; he was fined 1s. 'and delivered to sea service' (ibid., 23 Mar. 1782).

86   For examples, see *Salisbury Journal*, 8 Nov. 1773, 2 Dec. 1776, 1 Mar. 1784, 19 Feb. 1787; *Norwich Mercury*, 31 Jan., 14 Nov. 1778; 8 Dec. 1781; 20 Jan., 1 Sept. 1787; William B. Daniel, *Supplement to rural sports* (London, 1813), p. 413.

87   *Parl. Reg.*, VI, 282; *Parl. Papers, 1731–1800*, Bills, XII, No. 397. Two years later, the West Riding quarter sessions made a similar appeal for strong measures to deal with 'the Practices of Night Poachers . . . [which] are become very serious and alarming' (S.C.L., OD 1385: resolution, 19 Apr. 1784).

88   Under curious circumstances. The *Parl. Reg.* (VII, 210) records that in the debate on a motion for a second reading of the bill (actually, third reading: see *C.J.*, XXXVIII, 1037), the Attorney General described 'several [of the] restraints which the bill imposed as absolutely intolerable in a free government'. At this, Coke, 'almost without hesitation', proposed that the bill be withdrawn. Coke prided himself on his concern for the 'liberties of the people', but that does not satisfactorily explain his conduct, since he apparently had not scrupled to introduce the bill and support it for two readings. Thirty-five years later, Coke claimed that the bill had been withdrawn after three noted lawyers (Lord Kenyon, John Dunning and John Lee) 'gave it as their opinion that game was, legally, private property' (*Parl. Deb.*, 1st ser., XXXIX, col. 1082). Why this should have compelled Coke to drop the bill remains unclear. All that is known is that during the election of 1784, he faced some criticism for his sponsorship of the measure (A.M.W. Stirling, *Coke of Norfolk and his friends* [new edn, London & New York, 1912], I, 138).

89   39 & 40 Geo. III, c. 50. The Vagrant Act was 17 Geo. II, c. 5.

90   57 Geo. III, c. 90. The Act was actually the second replacement for the Night Poaching Act of 1800. The first, passed in 1816 (56 Geo. III, c. 130), had made simple – that is, unarmed – night poaching punishable by seven years' transportation, but the outcry against this was loud enough to encourage Parliament to repeal the Act and replace it with one which limited the penalty to those found with 'offensive weapons': see *Parl. Deb.*, 1st ser., XXXV, cols. 338-47, 1220-2; XXXVI, cols. 126-8.

91   9 Geo. IV, c. 69. This Act, like those of 1816 and 1817, also applied to night poaching of rabbits. Similarly, the Black Act (9 Geo. I, c. 27) made the taking of hares, as well as rabbits and deer, by persons 'disguised' and armed with 'offensive weapons' a non-clergiable felony, and the Larceny Reform Act (7 & 8 Geo. IV, c. 29, s. 30) made the taking of hares as well as rabbits at night punishable by transportation for seven to fourteen years. There was, then, a tendency to couple hares and rabbits when Parliament was enacting laws against armed or nocturnal poaching. It should be noted, however, that the Black Act and the Larceny Reform Act refer only to the taking of hares from warrens, and that the Night Poaching Acts of 1816, 1817 and 1828 were enacted at a time when the enclosure of hares was much more widespread than it had been in the eighteenth century. It was, in short, enclosure which turned hares from a species of game into a type of private property, and thus turned the taking of hares into a particularly heinous type of crime.

92   A similar argument has recently been made for the eighteenth-century criminal code as a whole: see Douglas Hay, 'Property, authority and the criminal law', *Albion's fatal tree: crime and society in eighteenth-century England*, ed. Douglas Hay, Peter Linebaugh and E.P. Thompson (New York, 1975), pp. 17-63.

Chapter 2

1   A rough indication of the number of qualified sportsmen can be found in the returns of game licences taken out after 1785. A study of these for Wiltshire in the late eighteenth century indicates that qualified sportsmen constituted less than 0.5 per cent of the population: see P.B. Munsche, 'The game laws in Wiltshire, 1750–1800', *Crime in England, 1550–1800*, ed. J.S.

Cockburn (London, 1977), p. 218. In the 1820s the number of game licences for the entire country fluctuated between 35,000 and 40,000 a year, which tends to confirm the Wiltshire estimate: see *Parl. Papers*, 1821, XVI, 327; ibid., 1826–7, XX, 527.

2   'Diary of Thomas Smith, Esq', *Wiltshire Archaeological and Natural History Magazine*, XI (1869), 205; see also Clementina Black, ed., *The Cumberland Letters* (London, 1912), p. 92.

3   A.F.J. Brown, ed., *Essex people, 1750–1900* (Chelmsford, 1972), pp. 91-100.

4   Chitty, *Treatise*, II, 1128.

5   Bagley, *Great diurnal,* II, 84, 150, 244; John Beresford, ed., *The diary of a country parson: the Reverend James Woodforde* (Oxford, 1924–31), I, 303; F.G. Stokes, ed., *The Blechley diary of the Rev. William Cole, 1765–67* (London, 1931), pp. 109, 121-2, 138, 143, 287. See also Beds. R.O., HW 69 and *Gentleman's Magazine*, XXXVIII (1768), 504.

6   Kent A.O., Q/SB 29, f. 128; *Salisbury Journal*, 25 Aug. 1777.

7   Staffs. R.O., D593/L/4/10: 9 Oct. 1818; D593/K/1/3/11: 23 Mar. 1823. In some areas, there were also customs which suspended the operation of the game laws for a day: see Robert W. Malcolmson, *Popular recreations in English society, 1700–1850* (Cambridge, 1973), p. 81.

8   S.C.L., OD 1385: printed resolution, 2 Nov. 1751. For more on game associations, see below, pp. 56-9, 90-1.

9   Hugh Gladstone, 'Oldest game book', *Notes & Queries*, CXCIII (1948), 79. On the importance of providing game for one's table, see *Salisbury Journal*, 5 Sept. 1774.

10   Wilts. R.O., 383/114: game lists, 1807. Some local residents came to expect such presents as their due. Parson Woodforde, for example, was irate when sportsmen shot over his land 'but never sent me a single Bird' (Beresford, *Diary of a parson*, IV, 131; V, 273).

11   The complexities of manorial ownership were many. Lordships of the manor could be bought and sold like any other type of property. Thus it was possible for a lord of a manor to be someone who did not actually own land within the boundaries of the manor. It was also possible for several persons to share a single lordship among themselves. An additional complication was the overlapping of manors, with each lord claiming to be 'lord paramount'. For some examples, see Kent A.O., U55, E57; Wilts. R.O., 490/968, 490/1019/1; *Salisbury Journal*, 7 Aug., 21 Aug. 1780. For a general introduction to manors in the eighteenth century, see Sidney and Beatrice Webb, *English local government* (new edn, London, 1963), II-III: *The manor and the borough*.

12   5 Anne, c. 14, s. 4. This permission to kill game was actually a restoration of the gamekeeper's power, rather than an extension to it. The Jacobean game laws had permitted servants of qualified persons to kill game for their masters' use (see 1 Jas I, c. 27, s. 6; 7 Jas I, c. 11, s. 7), and it is, in fact, possible that lords of manors did not pay much attention to the omission of this provision from the Game Act of 1671. John Wentworth, a Yorkshire squire at the time the Act was passed, is known to have authorised his gamekeeper to kill game (see Sir Thomas Lawson-Tancred, ed., *Records of a Yorkshire manor* [London, 1937], pp. 93-4), and it may be that the Act of 1707 did no more than legalise existing practice. The gamekeeper's powers in this regard were further clarified in 1808, when he was specifically authorised to take game

for his own use and that of any other person specified in his deputation (48 Geo. III, c. 93, ss. 2-3).

13 This assumption, in turn, led lords of manors to claim equally wide sporting rights for themselves, arguing that any authority the gamekeeper had must have been derived from their own as lord of the manor. The matter became the subject of some controversy at the beginning of the nineteenth century, when Edward Christian asserted that the sporting rights of both lord and gamekeeper were limited to the manorial waste lands and the lord's own property (see Christian, *Treatise*, pp. 136-53). A rebuttal to the argument can be found in *A treatise on the rights of manors* (London, 1817). The question was never clearly settled before 1831, and on most manors the situation seems to have been that described by a writer in 1800: 'men do shoot over those estates of which they are lords, even though it be admitted they cannot strictly justify doing so' (*Concise thoughts on the game laws* [Leicester, 1800], p. 13). See also Chitty, *Treatise*, I, 23-5.

14 *Salisbury Journal*, 11 Nov. 1771.

15 C.P. Fendall and E.A. Crutchley, eds., *The diary for Benjamin Newton, rector of Wath, 1816–1818* (Cambridge, 1933), p. 158. For the background to this agreement, see ibid., pp. 100-1, 108, 109-10.

16 Wilts, R.O., QS/Roll of Gamekeepers Deputations, 1782; Essex R.O., D/DAr C1/114. See also H.M.C., *14th Report*, I, 141.

17 3 Geo. I, c. 11. The Act was repealed in 1808 (by 48 Geo. III, c. 93).

18 Beds. R.O., HW 76 (I have modernised the spelling). For other examples, see Kent A.O., U270, C1: 29 Aug., 1 Sept., 5 Sept. 1719; Berks. R.O., D/EBy C3: Ireland to Benyon, 23 Aug. 1781; Sidney, Lord Herbert, ed., *Pembroke papers, 1780–94* (London, 1950), pp. 328, 331; and L. F. Salzman, ed., *Record of deputations of gamekeepers* (Sussex Record Society, LI [1950]).

19 9 Anne, c. 25, s. 1. The restriction did not reduce the value of the lord of the manor's privilege. On the contrary, the right to appoint a gamekeeper was so much in demand by the end of the century that there was an attempt to detach it from the lordship of the manor and treat it as a separate species of property. In 1797, for example, Lord Cornwallis paid a 'consideration' of £350 for the right to appoint a gamekeeper for Cavenham manor in Suffolk for the following thirty-one years (W. Suffolk R.O., Listing of Townshend Family Documents, auctioned in 1967, Lot 329). In 1803 agreements of this kind were declared illegal by the courts: see Richard Burn, *The justice of the peace and parish officer* (22nd edn, London, 1814), II, 558.

20 Wilts. R.O., Savernake MSS, Bill to Bruce, 22 July, 24 July 1762. Since he had already given the corporation permission to hunt over his own manors, Lord Bruce was advised to counter Marlborough's advances with an occasional venison feast for the gentlemen (ibid., 2 Aug. 1762).

21 Kent A.O., U269, C149/10, 11, 13-16, 20. See also Wilts. R.O., Savernake MSS, Bill to Bruce, 12 Jan. 1762.

22 Fendall & Crutchley, *Diary of Benjamin Newton*, p. 227.

23 *Facts, fully established*, p. 52.

24 Gervase Markham, *Country contentments* (London, 1615), I, 3; Dennis Brailsford, *Sport and society: Elizabeth to Anne* (London & Toronto, 1969), pp. 19, 21, 27-8, 110-11.

25 Richard Blome, *The gentleman's recreation* (2nd edn, London, 1710), pt. ii, p. 141.

26 François, duc de la Rochefoucauld-Liancourt, *A Frenchman in England, 1784*, trans. S. C. Roberts (Cambridge, 1933), pp. 52-3. For a vivid account of a hare hunt in the early eighteenth century, see Addison, *The Spectator*, I, 352-5 (No. 116); see also John Smallman Gardiner, *The art and pleasures of hare-hunting* (London, 1750).

27 A. S. Turberville, ed., *Johnson's England* (Oxford, 1933), I, 366-7; Markham, *Country contentments*, I, 31. See also G. Eland, ed., *Purefoy letters, 1735–53* (London, 1931), II, 216.

28 Sir Gyles Isham, ed., *The journal of Thomas Isham, of Lamport . . . 1671 to 1673*, trans. Norman Marlow (Farnborough, Hants., 1971), p. 173, and also pp. 147, 153, 163, 165, 171. See also Morris, *Journeys of Celia Fiennes*, p. 197, and Giles Jacob, *The compleat sportsman* (London, 1718), pp. 50-5.

29 Bagley, *Great diurnal*, I, 272-3.

30 Beresford, *Diary of a parson*, I, 33.

31 E.g., Bagley, *Great diurnal*, I, 72, 192, 238; Beresford, *Diary of a parson*, I, 33, 330; II, 52, 119, 272; III, 377. See also Holkham MSS, Country Accounts, 1722, 1725, 1727; Essex R.O., D/DBy A196, A204; Berks. R.O., D/EZ 30 F1: 12 Oct. 1742.

32 H.M.C., *13th Report*, VI, 247-8; Markham, *Country contentments*, pp. 97-106; Bagley, *Great diurnal*, I, 78.

33 Christina Hole, *English sports and pastimes* (London, 1949), p. 19; Turberville, *Johnson's England*, I, 368; Herbert, *Pembroke papers*, p. 67; *Salisbury Journal*, 4 Dec., 11 Dec. 1780; 10 Dec. 1781; 8 Dec., 15 Dec. 1783. After the mid-1780s, matches between Wiltshire and Norfolk no longer seem to have been held, but annual coursing meets on Salisbury Plain continued: e.g., ibid., 22 Oct. 1792.

34 C. B. Andrews, ed., *The Torrington diaries* (London, 1934), II, 385.

35 Henry Alken, *The national sports of Great Britain* (London, 1825), *sub* 'Coursing: Picking up'; Fendall & Crutchley, *Diary of Benjamin Newton*, p. 54.

36 Alken, *National sports*, *sub* 'Coursing: Hiloo! Hiloo!' On improvements in the breeding of hounds, see Longrigg, *History of foxhunting*, p. 84.

37 H.M.C., *13th Report*, VI, 247-8; see also F. P. and M. M. Verney, eds., *Memoirs of the Verney family during the seventeenth century* (London, 1904), II, 317.

38 *Salisbury Journal*, 4 Dec. 1780, 14 Apr. 1788. See also Herbert, *Pembroke papers*, p. 67.

39 Charles Chenevix Trench, *A history of marksmanship* (London, 1972), pp. 103-26; Michael Brander, *The hunting instinct: the development of field sports over the ages* (Edinburgh & London, 1964), pp. 87-101; Turberville, *Johnson's England*, I, 369.

40 Gladys Scott Thomson, *Life in a noble household, 1641–1700* (London, 1937), pp. 227-32; Chenevix Trench, *History of marksmanship*, p. 126; Jacob, *Compleat sportsman*, p. 29. Hawking, of course, did not completely die out, but its practice seems to have been confined in the eighteenth and nineteenth centuries to eccentric and rich sporting enthusiasts like Colonel Thomas Thornton (ca. 1755–1823). Probably the best-known sportsman of his day, Thornton was the co-founder (along with Lord Orford) of the Falconry Club of Great Britain in 1771, and he actively pursued the sport in Yorkshire and in Wiltshire for most of his life: see *British sporting painting, 1650–1850* (Arts Council of Great Britain, 1974), p. 65. See also A. M. W. Stirling, ed., *The diaries of Dummer* (London, 1934), pp. 102-3.

41 Addison, *The Spectator*, I, 371 (No. 122).

42 Bagley, *Great diurnal*, I, 316, 159, 199; II, 33, 77, 83-4, 87, 270, 239. See also *Sussex Archaeological Collections*, III (1850), 157-8; Elizabeth Hamilton, *The Mordaunts: an eighteenth-century family* (London, 1965), pp. 116-17.

43 Turberville, *Johnson's England*, I, 369; Bagley, *Great diurnal*, I, 201; *Gentleman's Magazine*, XLIII (1773), 579. Not all accidents, of course, were the fault of the weapon, as the shooting career of the Duke of Wellington illustrates. One morning, 'after wounding a retriever ... and, later on peppering the keeper's gaiters, he inadvertently sprinkled the bare arms of an old woman who chanced to be washing clothes at her cottage window'. 'I'm wounded, Milady!' cried the woman to Lady Shelley – who then proceeded to admonish her that 'this ought to be the proudest moment of your life. You have had the distinction of being shot by the great Duke of Wellington!' (Richard Edgcumbe, ed., *The diary of Frances Lady Shelley, 1787–1873* [London, 1913], II, 73-4). There was, in fact, more distinction in not having been shot by the Duke.

44 *Thoughts on the present laws for preserving the game* (London, 1750), p. 12. See also George Edie, *A treatise on English shooting* (Dublin, 1774), p. 27.

45 E.g., Kent A.O., U31, E2 (game book of Leonard Bartholomew, 1739–57). On improvements in the flintlock, see Chenevix Trench, *History of marksmanship*, pp. 129-34.

46 Glos. R.O., D1833/F3/7; Andrews, *Torrington diaries*, II, 289. See also Wilts. R.O., Savernake MSS, Bill to Bruce, 20 Jan. 1770 and C.U.L., Buxton MSS, Box 34, John Buxton to Robert Buxton, 21 Sept. 1781.

47 Sir Ralph Payne-Gallwey, ed., *The diary of Colonel Peter Hawker* (London, 1893), II, 358-66. Hawker was the author of a popular guide for shooters, *Instructions to a young sportsman in all that relates to guns and shooting*, which was first published in 1814 and went through numerous editions in the nineteenth century.

48 James Edward Harris, 2nd Earl of Malmesbury, *Half a century of sport in Hampshire*, ed. F. G. Aflalo (London, 1905), passim.

49 W. Suffolk R.O., E2/21/2, Sir Thomas Cullum to his son, 7 Dec. 1823. After some initial hostility to these 'high flying Noblemen or Gentlemen', Sir Thomas seems to have warmed to them. 'Our sporting Gentlemen entertain the Woolastons, Sir Wm Parker, General Conran, & many others; they spend a good deal of money, & I believe tho a little lively have given no offence' (ibid., 4 Jan., 13 Jan. 1824).

50 W. Suffolk R.O., E2/25/1, ff. 276-276v. See also *The Times*, 17 Aug. 1791.

51 S.C.L., EM 821, Rules of the Association for Protecting Game in the Manor of Midhope. The subscription was £10 and probably a good investment, since a report in 1815 noted that 'on all the free moors ... there are as many sportsmen as birds; but on the preserved ones ... the destruction of game has been very large' (*Warwick Advertiser*, 9 Sept. 1815).

52 Andrews, *Torrington diaries*, III, 88. See also ibid., II, 294; III, 69, 100; Surrey R.O., 203/30/14; *Facts, fully established*, pp. 27-8; and n. 49 above.

53 See Alken, *National sports*, sub 'Pheasant-Shooting' and 'Partridge-Shooting'; Edie, *Treatise on English shooting*, pp. 21-2, 27; and Basil Taylor, *Stubbs* (London, 1971), plates 47-52.

54 Chenevix Trench, *History of marksmanship*, pp. 141-3. Hares and rabbits were also driven into the line of fire by beaters. On the origin and introduction of the battue, see Norman H. Pollock, 'The English game laws in the nineteenth century' (Ph. D. thesis, Johns Hopkins University, 1968), pp. 47-9.

55   See Stirling, *Coke of Norfolk*, I, 209-10; H.M.C., *Fintry*, pp. 59-60; Kent A.O., U1050, C175.

56   John Mayer, *The sportsman's directory; or, park and gamekeeper's companion* (Colchester, 1815), p. 122. The presence of all these servants did not always make the task of the sportsman easier. Lord St Asaph complained in his diary that 'I was often prevented from shooting by a fear of hurting a beater' (E. Sussex R.O., Ashburnham MS 2507, p. 84 [2 Dec. 1828]).

57   Addison, *The Spectator*, I, 352 (No. 116).

58   William B. Daniel, *Rural sports* (London, 1801-2), II, 406; Daniel, *Supplement*, p. 401. The precision of these figures gives a rather false impression of the sport. At one of Lord Talbot's battues, eight guns killed ninety-five pheasants, forty-five hares and five rabbits (in four hours), but the next day, when the keepers went over the 'scene of action, and brought in the killed and wounded, which during the rapid firing, had not been found', the total was increased by twenty head (*Warwick Advertiser*, 10 Feb. 1816).

59   Reginald W. Jeffery, ed., *Dyott's diary, 1781–1845* (London, 1907), II, 17. In addition, they shot 432 rabbits, 74 woodcocks and 27 partridges.

60   Norfolk R.O., Walsingham MSS, XVIII/35.

61   Col. John Cook, *Observations on fox-hunting and the management of hounds in the kennel and the field* (London, 1826), p. 43. See also Payne-Gallwey, *Diary of Peter Hawker*, I, 159, and Daniel, *Supplement*, p. 399.

62   This was true even of the battue, where it was customary for the ladies to join the shooters in the afternoon to watch the conclusion of the day's sport: see Pollock, 'Game laws', pp. 37-8.

63   Lady Margaret Verney, ed., *Verney letters of the eighteenth century from the MSS at Claydon House* (London, 1930), I, 236; Wilts. R.O., Longleat MSS, Account Books, 1784, 1786, 1787, 1792, 1793. John Byng disapproved of the cutting of these paths, adding 'but I suppose it is *right*, being the high fashion' (Andrews, *Torrington diaries*, III, 18).

64   One effect of this may have been to limit the participation of women in field sports. In the late seventeenth and early eighteenth centuries, it was not unusual for the wives and daughters of the gentry to hunt, hawk and net game. Lady Aylesford, for example, reported to her husband that 'ye girls was a Hunting to day, & ye Hare took [us] through ye Town of Coleshill, & fatch'd out all ye women to See ye little Dogs they had hear'd so much of, Mr. Dilks came allso . . . his wife looks big, her riding is spoil'd . . .' (Aylesford MSS, Letter-book in study, No. 33: Lady to Lord Aylesford, 10 Feb. n.y. [1720?]). For other examples, see H.M.C., *12th Report*, V, 25, 36; Hamilton, *The Mordaunts*, p. 82; *British sporting painting*, pp. 34, 37. Later in the eighteenth century some women still rode to the hounds, but at coursing matches and battues they seem to have been spectators only. I have found very few instances of women shooting game in this period. A number of explanations could be advanced for this. Perhaps one of them is that contests between women and game were acceptable in the eighteenth century, but contests between women and men were not.

65   Wilts. R.O., 383/115.

66   Isham, *Journal of Thomas Isham*, p. 61; Bagley, *Great diurnal*, II, 83.

67   H.M.C., *13th Report*, II, 274; John Aubrey, *The natural history of Wiltshire,* ed. John Britton (London, 1847), p. 59.

68   Burn, *Justice of the peace* (15th edn), II, 253; H. E. R. Widnell, *The Beaulieu record* (n.p., 1973), pp. 46-7, 52, 57, 62, 64, 70, 74.

69   See Earl of Cardigan, *The wardens of Savernake Forest* (London, 1949), p. 146.

70 E.g., Isham, *Journal of Thomas Isham*, p. 143n; H.M.C., *12th Report*, V, 78. On breeding game in mews, see Sir John Marsham's notes on husbandry, in Kent A.O., U1121, E6/2: 'One Cock [Pheasant] is enough for 2 Henns, in March or April they lay 20 Eggs which are better brought up under an Henn, for 15 daies you must feed them with Barley flower tenderley sodd & cooled, on which you must sprinkle a little wine: afterward you shall give ym Wheat, Grasshoppers & Ants Eggs.' To stock a mews, game birds could be bought on the open market: see J. W. F. Hill, ed., *The letters and papers of the Bankes family of Revesby Abbey, 1704–60* (Lincoln Record Society, XLV [1952], p. 26.
71 Daniel Defoe, *A tour through England and Wales* (Everyman edn, 1927), I, 196.
72 Isham, *Journal of Thomas Isham*, p. 143n; R. W. Ketton-Cremer, *Country neighbourhood* (London, 1951), p. 69.
73 Katherine Frances Doughty, *The Betts of Wortham in Suffolk, 1480–1905* (London, 1912), p. 177, quoting a MS treatise (ca. 1721) which has apparently been lost. See also Blome, *Gentleman's recreation*, pt. ii, pp. 180-1.
74 E.g., Wilts. R.O., Longleat MSS, Account Books, 1765–1800, *sub* 'Pheasantry'; W. Sussex R.O., Goodwood MSS 244-7, *sub* 'Pheasantry' and 'Game'; Essex R.O., D/DBy A198-A229. As early as 1743 the Earl of Leicester had built a 'menagerie' at Holkham and stocked it with fifty brace of pheasants (Holkham MSS, Country Accounts, 1743).
75 E.g., Essex R.O., D/DBy A210, A212-13, A216-21, A316; see also H. G. Mundy, ed., *The journal of Mary Frampton* (London, 1885), p. 27. Fields of buckwheat were sown for the same purpose: see W. Sussex R.O., Goodwood MSS 244-7, *sub* 1785–7; Norfolk R.O., Walsingham MSS, XLVIII/9 (particularly Lord Walsingham's note in 1807 that 'want of Buck wheat is an old Complaint about Merton'). Partridges were given less attention by game preservers, but on some estates in East Anglia fields of turnips were planted as coverts for them.
76 Andrews, *Torrington diaries*, I, 325. See also W. Sussex R.O., Goodwood MSS 244-7, *sub* 1788–1805 (payments for 'thatching buckwheat' and decline in pheasantry expenditure); Holkham MSS, Domestic Accounts, 1795–1800 (payments for 'buckstacks'); Wilts. R.O., Longleat MSS, Account Books, 1786–1801 (payments for 'thatching Buck wheat ricks' and decline in pheasantry expenditure); Daniel, *Rural sports*, II, 388.
77 On new warrens, see, for example, Wilts. R.O., Longleat MSS, Account Books, 1772, 1781–2, 1787, 1791. On hedgerows, see E. W. Bovill, *English country life, 1780–1830* (Oxford, 1962), pp. 176-7. On payments for hares, see, for example, Essex R.O., D/DBy A208, A215.
78 William Cobbett, *Rural rides* (Everyman edn, 1912), I, 119; Edgcumbe, *Diary of Lady Shelley*, I, 39. See also W. Suffolk R.O., E2/21/2, Sir Thomas Cullum to his son, 13 Jan. 1824.
79 Wilts. R.O., Longleat MSS, Account Books, 1760–1801 (particularly after 1770). For a professional vermin-catcher who, like Bishop, also caught rabbits, see *Salisbury Journal*, 23 Sept. 1771.
80 2 Geo. III, c. 19; 13 Geo. III, c. 55; for details of which see Appendix I.B.2.a–g. These statutes compelled sportsmen to delay their shooting much longer than had been the custom in the first half of the eighteenth century, when it was common to begin shooting or netting in July or early August. (E.g., Bagley, *Great diurnal*, II, 235-6; Hamilton, *The Mordaunts*, p. 116; Berks. R.O., D/EZ 30 F1: 29 July 1742, 29 July 1743.) Hares were not accorded similar protection by Parliament, however. At the beginning of the seventeenth century, the tracing of hares in the snow had been outlawed (by 1 Jas I, c. 27,

s. 2), but this was practically obsolete by the eighteenth century. Tracing, indeed, seems to have been a popular winter pastime for some sportsmen (e.g., Bagley, *Great diurnal*, I, 202, 243, 278-9; Beresford, *Diary of a parson*, II, 115, 119, 226, 291; *Warwick Advertiser*, 1 Mar. 1823). An attempt was made in 1773 to establish a season for hunting hares, but it failed: see *C.J.*, XXXIV, 236, 333, 359, 366, 379; *L.J.*, XXXIII, 678.

81   E.g., Norfolk R.O., How 750/27.

82   E.g., *Salisbury Journal*, 31 Dec. 1770, 2 Sept. 1771, 22 Aug. 1774, 3 Aug. 1778. The Swaffham Coursing Club issued a warning of this kind (*Norwich Mercury*, 23 Sept. 1780), as did the Duke of Marlborough, owner of a hare warren at West Lavington, Wilts. (*Salisbury Journal*, 4 Aug. 1788).

83   *Salisbury Journal*, 4 Sept. 1786. See also Kent A.O., U749, E34: 'Instruction for the Game Keeper' (n.d.): 'If He meets Gentlemen a Shooting, He is to tell them He has His Masters Orders to forbid every body shooting on the manor, But as they appear to be Gentlemen, He is sure they might have His Masters leave [if they ask for it] . . . and hopes they wont think [it] amiss of Him, for acting according to His Orders.'

84   *Warwick Advertiser*, 19 Feb. 1814; the figure is probably an exaggeration. After 1755 or so, the August, September and October numbers of provincial and national newspapers carried reports on the state of the game. Although often unreliable, these reports were significant as a reflection of the transformation of the game from a prey into a crop.

85   22 & 23 Chas II, c. 25, s. 2; 5 Anne, c. 14, s. 4. See n. 12 above.

86   E.g., Verney, *Letters*, I, 79; Wilts. R.O., 383/114: memo, 16 Sept. 1721. For use of tenants as gamekeepers, see above, pp. 30-1. The lack of importance attached to gamekeepers in the early eighteenth century is reflected in the records of their deputations. Not until 1711 were lords of manors required (by 9 Anne, c. 25, s. 1) to register the names of their gamekeepers with the clerk of the peace and, even then, the record was far from complete. A comparison of the Longleat and Savernake MSS with the Wiltshire Roll of Gamekeepers' Deputations, for example, indicates that it was not until 1784, when the Game Duty Act required that gamekeepers take out an annual licence, that a considerable number of keepers were enrolled, although they had been employed in that office for years.

87   E.g., Holkham MSS, Country Accounts, 1724–31. (The huntsman on the same estate at this time was paid £20 a year and the whipper-in £6 a year.) See also H.M.C., *Various collections*, VIII, 223, 233; Aylesford MSS, Shelf 48/6: 14 May 1733.

88   *Gentleman's Magazine*, XIX (1749), 252. The Duke of Dorset seems to have paid his gamekeeper in this manner as late as 1760 (see Kent A.O., U269, E29, and E. Sussex R.O., Glynde MS 858), and some other lords of the manor continued the practice up to the beginning of the nineteenth century (see Daniel, *Rural sports*, II, 428). These, however, were exceptions to the rule after 1750.

89   Beds. R.O., W1/6149. See also John Mordant, *The complete steward* (London, 1761), I, 351-2.

90   Beds. R.O., W1/6157. See also ibid., W1/251 and W1/6165; Wilts, R.O., Savernake MSS, Bill to Ailesbury, 22 Jan. 1780.

91   For advertisements, see *Salisbury Journal*, 19 Sept. 1763, 3 Sept. 1770, 30 Jan. 1775, 9 Aug. 1779, 15 Oct. 1781, 9 Feb. 1784, 8 Nov. 1784, 23 Apr. 1787, 23 Aug. 1790. For letters of recommendation and solicitation, see E. Riding

R.O., DDGR/43/31, 40; Essex R.O., D/DAr C7/15; Staffs. R.O., D260/M/E/159: 13 Feb. 1826.

92 William Taplin, *Observations on the present state of the game in England* (London, 1772), pp. 26-8.

93 Essex R.O., D/DByA11 (agreement at back); Wilts. R.O., Longleat MSS, Account Books, 1775–1801; Holkham MSS, Domestic Accounts, 1793–1800.

94 Norfolk R.O., How 758/5; see also How 757/19, 32, 35, 48, and How 750/61, 64, 87; Wilts. R.O., Longleat MSS, Account Books, 1770, 1774, 1778, 1787, 1788.

95 Wilts. R.O., Longleat MSS, Account Books, 1786–96, 1801; see also 1778.

96 S.C.L., Arundel Castle MSS, S 542.

97 Wilts. R.O., Savernake MSS, Bill to Ailesbury, 31 Oct. 1779; see also ibid., Bill to Bruce, 16 Nov. 1765, and Taplin, *Observations*, p. 28. For a graphic picture of one gamekeeper's finances, see the account book of Henry Ayling, in W. Sussex R.O., Mitford MS 884: for 1830–1 his personal deficit was £23 16s. 9d.; the previous season it had been £7 9s. 9d. and the following season it would be £3 7s. 3d.

98 E.g., Beds. R.O., W1/6159; see also Cook, *Observations on fox-hunting*, p. 45. This perquisite made gamekeepers just as anxious to preserve rabbits on the manor as their masters were to preserve game. They were particularly hostile to anyone who endangered their supply of skins (see Norfolk R.O., How 750/69-70, How 757/60, 68-9, How 758/23). Farmers, for their part, were equally hostile to any attempt to keep large numbers of rabbits near their crops (see Wilts. R.O., Savernake MSS, Bill to Ailesbury, 21 Dec. 1779). This conflict of interest may have had a lot to do with the gamekeeper's bad image in this period.

99 Mordant, *Complete steward*, I, 352-3; Taplin, *Observations*, p. 24. See also *Gentleman's Magazine*, V (1735), 195; Christian, *Treatise*, p. 297; *Parl. Deb.*, 2nd ser., XI, col. 390.

100 E.g., Wilts. R.O., 383/114: G. L. Michell to R. C. Hoare, 3 Dec. n.y. [early 1800s?]; Norfolk R.O., How 758/27.

101 Essex R.O., D/DBy A211-A220; Wilts. R.O., Longleat MSS, Account Books, 1780–9; W. Sussex R.O., Goodwood MSS 244-5. Expenditure continued to rise in the nineteenth century. At Audley End, for example, the game establishment cost £687 a year by the 1820s (Essex R.O., D/DBy A230); see also F. M. L. Thompson, *English landed society in the nineteenth century* (London & Toronto, 1963), p. 138.

102 Ibid., p. 137.

103 Quoted in Hole, *English sports*, p. 11.

104 E.g., *Norwich Mercury*, 1 Sept. 1753, 1 Jan. 1780; *Salisbury Journal*, 30 Aug. 1756, 13 Oct. 1777, 3 Nov. 1788; Aylesford MSS, Letterbook in study, Lady to Lord Aylesford, 15 Jan. n.y.; *London Magazine*, XXV (1756), 228-9; Norfolk R.O., NRS 22696 Z64: Smyth to Suffield, 1 Aug. 1816.

105 Holkham MSS, Country Accounts, 1748, 1750; see also W. Sussex R.O., Goodwood MS 244: Ladyday 1778.

106 *Salisbury Journal*, 9 Feb., 27 July, 30 Nov. 1778 and 25 Oct. 1779; see also *Norwich Mercury*, 7 Sept. 1771.

107 *The Senator*, XV, 1200; see also Kent A.O., U951, C95/3-4. There was a law against hunting game in standing corn (23 Eliz. I, c. 10, s. 4), but it was a dead letter by the eighteenth century.

108   *The Senator*, XXII, 994; 36 Geo. III, c. 39. The Act may not have been scrupulously observed in every place: see *The Senator*, XXII, 987.

109   Ibid.; 39 Geo. III, c. 34. For a good account of these debates, see *The Senator*, XVIII, 1637; XXII, 986-9, 991-4, 1072, 1109-10; XXIII, 1353-7, 1362-4. See also C.U.L., Buxton MSS, Box 11, C. Wallrington to R. J. Buxton, 6 Aug. 1799.

110   Payne-Gallwey, *Diary of Peter Hawker*, I, 104, 145, 240; Malmesbury, *Half a century of sport*, p. 63; Beds. R.O., W1/6175, H/WS 1588; *Warwick Advertiser*, 24 Aug. 1816.

111   *London Magazine*, XXVI (1757), 87; William Marshall, *The rural economy of Norfolk* (London, 1787), I, 172. See also *Some considerations on the game laws and the present practice of executing them* (London, 1753), p. 36, and Norfolk R.O., NRS 22696 Z64: Smyth to Suffield, 1 Aug. 1816. It may have been for this reason that, earlier in the century, Defoe found that the hare warren at Wilton made 'all the countrymen turn poachers and destroy the hares, by what means they can' (*Tour*, I, 196).

112   *Some considerations* (1753), p. 37; see also Marshall, *Norfolk*, I, 174-5.

113   Norfolk R.O., NRS 22696 Z64: John Dugmore to Lord Suffield, 16 Sept. 1814; Richard Mackenzie Bacon, *A memoir of the life of Edward, 3rd Baron Suffield* (Norwich, 1838), p. 144. The person referred to in this passage is the 2nd Lord Suffield, brother of the game law reformer. See also Staffs. R.O., D593/K/1/3/11: James Loch to Mr Ford, 23 Mar. 1823.

114   Staffs. R.O., D260/M/E/159: Edward Littleton to his major tenants, 6 Sept. 1828. See also *Parl. Deb.*, 2nd ser., XI, col. 392; 2nd ser., XVII, col. 742; 3rd ser., V, col. 938.

115   Herbert, *Pembroke papers*, p. 331; see also Malmesbury, *Half a century of sport*, p. 49.

116   E.g., Joan Wake and Deborah Champion Webster, eds., *The letters of Daniel Eaton, 1725–32* (Northants. Record Society, XXIV [1971], p. 118; Beds. R.O., W1/6166; Wilts. R.O., Longleat MSS, Account Books, 1753, 1755; Essex R.O., D/DBy A207, A214, A216.

117   See David C. Itzkowitz, *Peculiar privilege: a social history of English foxhunting, 1753–1885* (London, 1977).

118   Herbert, *Pembroke papers*, pp. 327-8; Wilts. R.O., 383/114: W. Philips to R. C. Hoare, n.d. [early nineteenth century].

119   Ibid. See also Cook, *Observations on fox-hunting*, p. 191, and M. W. Farr, ed., 'Sir Edward Littleton's fox-hunting diary, 1774–89', *Essays in Staffordshire history presented to S. A. H. Burne,* ed. M. W. Greenslade (*Collections for a history of Staffordshire*, 4th ser., VI [1970]), pp. 154-70.

120   Cook, *Observations on fox-hunting*, p. 42. On packs given up, see Wilts. R.O., 383/114: William Wyndham to R. C. Hoare, 20 Nov. 1806; C.U.L., Buxton MSS, Box 9: A. H. Eyre to R. J. Buxton, 14 Nov. n.y.; *1827 Crime Report*, p. 41.

121   Wilts. R.O., Savernake MSS, Bill to Bruce, 24 Dec. 1770.

122   E.g., Kent A.O., U269, E29; U471, E24; and Norfolk R.O., How 750/3.

123   On the matter of qualified farmers, see Wilts. R.O., Savernake MSS, Bill to Bruce, 20 Jan. 1770, 10 Nov. 1779. On suits for trespass on a tenant's land, see the attempts, in 1762 and 1770, to change the law: H.M.C., *14th Report*, IX, 315, and *CJ.*, XXXII, 971.

124   Wilts. R.O., Savernake MSS, Bill to Neate, 10 Jan. 1770 (copy).

125   See Norfolk R.O., Walsingham MSS, XLVIII/32: E. Stracey to Lord Walsingham, 9 Oct. 1816, and extract from Suffolk leases, 1816; Edward, Baron Suffield, *Considerations on the game laws* (London, 1825), p. 69n; W.

Sussex R.O., Cowdray MSS 38, 43. For earlier use of game clauses, see C. W. Chalkin, *Seventeenth-century Kent: a social and economic history* (London, 1965), p. 67.

126   *Gentleman's Magazine,* V (1735), 195.
127   Vincesimus Knox, 'On the animosities occasioned in the country by the game laws', in *Essays Moral and Literary* (17th edn, London, 1815), III, 10. The essay was written in 1779. For other examples of farmers' reactions to the enclosure of the game, see below, pp. 109-15.
128   Taplin, *Observations*, p. 17.
129   Mordant, *Complete steward*, I, 351; see also John Lawrence, *The modern land steward* (London, 1801), p. 65.
130   Quoted in Esmé Wingfield-Stratford, *The lords of Cobham Hall* (London, 1959), p. 359.
131   *1828 Game Report*, p. 37; Staffs. R.O., D593/1/4/10: 'Instructions to the Gamekeeper', 9 Oct. 1818; *The Times*, 1 Oct. 1828.
132   Marshall, *Norfolk*, I, 179-80.
133   *Parl. Deb.*, 1st ser., XXXVI, cols. 927-8.
134   *The Senator*, XV, 1612-13.

Chapter 3

1   C. E. Long, *Considerations on the game laws* (London, 1824), p. 38. For examples of 'patrician poachers', see Payne-Gallwey, *Diary of Peter Hawker*, I, 12-13; E. D. Cuming, ed., *Squire Osbaldeston: his autobiography* (London, 1927), p. 11; E. Suffolk R.O., HA 11/B1/1/2. For the raids on Windsor, see Stirling, *Coke of Norfolk*, I, 392, and Stirling, *Diaries of Dummer*, pp. 57-8.
2   S.C.L., OD 1385: Gilbert Slater to William Bagshaw, 19 Dec. 1780.
3   Thomas Otway, *The orphan* (1680), III.i.
4   *1823 Game Report*, pp. 38-9; *Parl Deb.,* 2nd ser., X, col. 905.
5   Hamilton, *The Mordaunts*, p. 130.
6   *Thoughts on the present laws for preserving the game* (London, 1750), pp. 9, 11; *Gentleman's Magazine*, XXVII (1757), 159. See also ibid., XXI (1751), 111-12; Taplin, *Observations*, p. 12.
7   *Gentleman's Magazine*, XXXVIII (1768), 504.
8   1 Jas I, c. 27, s. 1. See also 7 Jas I, c. 11, s. 8, and 22 & 23 Chas II, c. 25, s. 1.
9   Giles Jacob, *The game law* (London, 1705), pp. viii-ix. See also Edward Laurence, *The duty of a steward to his lord* (London, 1727), p. 57, and Mordant, *Complete steward*, I, 351.
10   *Concise thoughts*, p. 21; *A letter on the game laws* (London, 1815), pp. 20-1. See also Daniel, *Rural sports*, I, 218-19, and Suffield, *Considerations*, p. 19.
11   *1823 Game Report*, p. 43.
12   *Essays on the game laws, now existing in Great Britain* (London, 1770), pp. 4-5.
13   1 Jas I, c. 27, s. 4; P.E. Jones, *The worshipful company of poulters of the city of London: a short history* (2nd edn, London, 1965), p. 88; F. J. Fisher, 'The development of London as a centre of conspicuous consumption in the sixteenth and seventeenth centuries', *Transactions of the Royal Historical Society*, 4th ser., XXX (1948), 50.
14   James E. Thorold Rogers, *A history of agriculture and prices in England* (Oxford, 1866–1902), V, 368, 371; see also Jones, *Company of poulters*, pp. 142-3.
15   S. C. Ratcliff and H. C. Johnson, eds., *Warwick county records* (Warwick, 1935–64), VII, 199; *C.S.P.D. 1687-9*, p. 214.

16   5 Anne, c. 14. Higglers and chapmen were itinerant traders, the former specialising in poultry.

17   Guildhall Library, MS 2148/1: 25 Apr. 1707. The Company had lobbied against passage of the Act of 1707: see ibid., 18 Feb., 26 Feb. 1706/7; H.M.C., *House of Lords*, n.s., VII, 68.

18   *Reasons humbly offered to the right honourable the lords spiritual and temporal, in parliament assembled, against passing a bill ... for better preservation of the game, in the manner 'tis now fram'd* (London, 1707); Guildhall Library, MS 2148/1: 5 Feb. 1719/20.

19   *Wiltshire Archaeological and Natural History Magazine*, XXI (1884), 200n; Charles Deering, *Nottinghamia vetus et nova, or an historical account of Nottingham* (Nottingham, 1751), p. 72. For the latter reference I am indebted to Robert Malcolmson. See also J. W. Walker, ed., *Hackness manuscripts and accounts* (Yorks. Archaeological Society, Record Series, XCV [1937]), pp. 29, 42, 50, 63.

20   B.L., Add. MS 32713, f. 227; see also S.C.L., OD 1385: resolution of the Derbys. game association, 1751.

21   *Daily Advertiser*, 20 Feb., 21 Feb. 1752; S.C.L., OD 1385: broadsheet of the Game Association, 22 Apr. 1752. In the latter, the number of subscribers listed was 276; on 11 Dec. 1752, the *Daily Advertiser* reported that the Association had 570 subscribers.

22   Eland, *Purefoy letters*, II, 219; *Daily Advertiser*, 21 Feb., 28 Mar., 16 Apr. 1752; S.C.L., OD 1385: broadsheet of the Game Association, 22 Apr. 1752. Initially, the Association had offered a double reward for information leading to the conviction of game traders.

23   *Norwich Mercury*, 29 Feb., 21 Mar., 1 Aug. 1752.

24   For a discussion of the opposition to the Game Association, see below, pp. 109-15.

25   *Norwich Mercury*, 4 Nov. 1752; see also *Salisbury Journal*, 27 Nov. 1752.

26   *Norwich Mercury*, 4 Aug. 1753; Chitty, *Treatise*, II, 1105-8.

27   28 Geo. II, c. 12. The bill was introduced by Lord Strange (heir to the Earl of Derby), who was listed in 1752 as a subscriber to the Game Association (*CJ.*, XXVII, 155, 164, et passim).

28   Guildhall Library, MS 2148/2: 6 Jan., 8 Feb., 2 May 1758; 'Ash Wednesday' [16 Feb.], 19 Feb. 1763; *Daily Advertiser*, 1 Feb. 1762.

29   Ibid., 2 Feb. 1761, and repeated, with some variations, for the next five years.

30   Wilts. R.O., 383/114: Orders of the Game Association, 10 Feb. 1761. MS notes on this document indicate that the fee went up to six guineas later in the century.

31   Regular announcements of meetings in the *Daily Advertiser* end 27 Jan. 1766. The last reports of prosecutions I have found are in *Annual Register*, VI (1763), 56, and *Gentleman's Magazine*, XXXIII (1763), 358. For the establishment of provincial game associations, see *Annual Register*, XII (1769), 153; *Salisbury Journal*, 11 Oct. 1773, 19 Nov. 1787; *Norwich Mercury*, 10 Jan. 1789; *Salisbury Journal*, 12 Sept. 1791.

32   Taplin, *Observations*, pp. 5-6. For evidence of the Association's continued existence, see Essex R.O., D/DBy, A205-A217 (annual payment of subscription fees, 1774–86); William Taplin, *An appeal to the representatives on the part of the people respecting the present destructive state of the game* (London, 1792), p. 102; Daniel, *Rural sports*, II, 428.

33   Warws. R.O., CR 136, diary of Sir Roger Newdigate, 12 Sept., 28 Sept., 30

Sept., 7 Oct., 14 Oct. 1754; 7 May 1755.

34 *Salisbury Journal*, 19 Nov. 1787; Norfolk R.O., Walsingham MSS, XLVIII/3: Townshend to Walsingham, 23 July 1788.

35 See Bovill, *English country life,* pp. 139-57; A. F. J. Brown, 'Colchester in the eighteenth century', *East Anglian studies*, ed. L. M. Munby (Cambridge, 1968), p. 159-60; J. W. Walker, *Wakefield: its history and people* (3rd edn, Wakefield, 1967), II, 502-6.

36 For this and what follows, see *1823 Game Report*, pp. 6-29, 33-6; *1828 Game Report*, pp. 9-32, 42-8, 68-74, 88-94.

37 On gamekeepers, see particularly *1823 Game Report*, pp. 14, 23, 33; and Daniel, *Rural sports,* II, 427.

38 Significantly, both the Wiltshire and the Dorset game associations offered to 'give every *encouragement* to inn-holders, [and] proprietors of stagecoaches and waggons who *discourage* their coachmen, waggoners, ostlers, horse-keepers, and other servants, from buying or receiving game' (*Salisbury Journal*, 19 Nov. 1787, 12 Sept. 1791).

39 *1823 Game Report*, pp. 7, 12, 23, 28, 31; *1828 Game Report*, pp. 11, 18, 23, 25, 38, 46, 71, 89; see also Bovill, *English country life*, p. 195. The profit margin may have been larger in the 1820s than in the preceding decades. As we shall see in a later chapter (below, p. 139), the price which a poacher received for his game dropped sharply after the end of the Napoleonic wars; in the poultry shops, however, prices remained steady.

40 Zouch, *An account*, p. 21; Daniel, *Rural sports*, II, 427-8. See also Taplin, *Observations*, p. 25; *Facts, fully established*, p. 31. It should be noted that coachmen, unlike higglers, did not have to pay carriage charges on the game they brought to market: see *1828 Game Report*, pp. 16, 70.

41 Daniel, *Supplement*, p. 97n. See also *Bell's Weekly Messenger*, 17 Nov. 1816; Pollock, 'Game laws', p. 84.

42 *1823 Game Report,* pp. 34-5; *C.J.*, LXXII, 266. See also *1823 Game Report*, p. 19, and *1828 Game Report*, p. 25.

43 *C.J.,* LXXII, 266.

44 *1823 Game Report*, pp. 6, 20, 21.

45 Norfolk R.O., Walsingham MSS, LII/30: ? to Swan Talrum, 31 Jan. 1824. I have modified the punctuation.

46 E.g., J. C. Drummond and Anne Wilbraham, *The Englishman's food: a history of five centuries of English diet* (London, 1939), pp. 249-50.

47 See below, p. 149.

48 See J. W. F. Hill, *Georgian Lincoln* (Cambridge, 1966), pp. 152-3.

49 *1823 Game Report*, p. 32; see also Daniel, *Rural sports,* II, 434.

50 *1827 Crime Report*, p. 41. Compare his remarks with those of Samuel Whitbread's gamekeeper above, p. 42.

51 *1827 Crime Report*, pp. 34, 42; *1828 Game Report*, p. 50. See also *1823 Game Report*, pp. 41-2.

52 B.L., Add. MS 42598, f. 180.

53 *Hertfordshire county records* (Hertford, 1905–57), I, 288.

54 Ibid., p. 365, VI, 392; Aylesford MSS, Letterbook in study, No. 30: Lady to Lord Aylesford, 15 Jan. n.y. [ca. 1730]. A 'tunnel' was a type of snare: see *The Times*, 12 Sept. 1791.

55 S.C.L., OD 1385: resolution of the Derbys. game association, 1751; Cumberland R.O., Grand Jury Book, 1771–95, pp. 5-6. See also *Facts, fully established*, pp. 33-4.

56 Marshall, *Norfolk*, I, 178-9; see also Zouch, *An account*, p. 15.

57   Wilts. R.O., Savernake MSS, Bill to Bruce, n.d. [1770s?].
58   For a description of poachers' methods in the eighteenth century, see Taplin, *Observations*, pp. 19-22, and Charles Chenevix Trench, *The poacher and the squire* (London, 1967), pp. 142-5. On the training of young poachers, see *1827 Crime Report*, p. 21, and *1828 Game Report*, p. 38.
59   *The case of the distressed warreners of England, humbly presented to this honourable parliament* (n.p., n.d. [ca. 1710]). 'It begins,' they added, 'by Jugging of Partridge, Killing of Hares, Pheasants, and other Game, and so, thro' Habits of Idelness . . . into Gangs to Rob Parks, Warrens, and Chases.' See also E. P. Thompson, *Whigs and hunters: the origin of the black act* (New York, 1975). Thompson warns that the term 'gang' should be used with care in connection with eighteenth-century crime, since it implies a greater degree of organisation and continuity than was often the case (ibid., pp. 194-5). In what follows, 'gang' is used only to denote groups of men co-operating, even temporarily, to take game.
60   *Gentleman's Magazine*, XIX (1749), 62; Wilts. R.O., Savernake MSS, Bill to Bruce, 9 Feb. 1765. See also *Salisbury Journal*, 4 May 1752.
61   The monopoly, it should be noted, was never complete. The Select Committees on the game laws in the 1820s heard testimony that game traders also received considerable quantities of game from gentlemen (see *1823 Game Report*, pp. 14, 16-17, 19-20, 23, 33, 35; *1828 Game Report*, pp. 10-11). This was probably true, but claims that up to a third of the market was supplied by qualified sportsmen are suspect. The poulterers who testified before these committees wanted the game trade legalised; establishing that gentlemen could and would compete with poachers in the marketplace was important to their case. It is likely, therefore, that they exaggerated the extent to which gentlemen already supplied the market. Only one poulterer presented statistical evidence of the amount of game sent to him by country gentlemen, and this showed that he received less than 10 per cent of his supply from qualified sources (see *1828 Game Report*, pp. 42-3).
62   *Norwich Mercury*, 6 Sept. 1788. For other examples of persons being hired to poach, see Norfolk R.O., How 758/7, and Kent A.O., U442, O40/3: deposition of George Eliott, 14 Oct. 1815.
63   *Norwich Mercury*, 23 Jan. 1779; S.C.L., Arundel Castle MSS, S 607: 28 Feb. 1820; *1828 Game Report*, p. 31. See also ibid., p. 67, and *Norwich Mercury*, 8 Dec. 1781.
64   Edward Hughes, ed., *The diaries and correspondence of James Losh, 1811–1833* (Publication of the Surtees Society, CLXXI, CLXXIV [1962–3]), II, 59.
65   Northumberland R.O., ZM1/S76/48/43; see also ZM1/S76/48/32, 35, 41. Somewhat surprisingly, gypsies do not figure prominently in the poaching trade. There is almost no evidence that they were – or were thought to be – active poachers in our period. The only instance I have come across involved the illegal taking of rabbits: see C.U.L., Buxton MS, Box 8, R. J. Buxton to John Buxton, 21 Oct. 1803. However, see also Taplin, *Observations*, p. 29.
66   Zouch, *An account*, pp. 2-3; H.M.C., *Lothian*, p. 320. See also *1823 Game Report*, p. 31.
67   Zouch, *An account*, p. 20. See also *Salisbury Journal*, 9 Oct. 1780, and Peter Hawker, *Instructions to a young sportsman* (11th edn, London, 1859), pp. 308-9.
68   *Salisbury Journal*, 23 Mar. 1778. See also Daniel, *Rural sports*, II, 428, and Radcliff & Johnson, *Warwickshire records*, VI, 157. On alehouses in general, see R. F. Bretherton, 'Country inns and alehouses', *Englishmen at rest and play:*

some phases of English leisure, 1558–1714, ed. Reginald Lennard (Oxford, 1931), pp. 145-201.

69 E. Riding R.O., DDGR/42/30: Pennington to John Grimston, 25 Jan. 1780. When Pennington offered a reward for informing on the culprits, the poachers 'Tore down the papers I put up . . . and declar'd if any person inform'd "They wou'd give Them hire and do for them", and such like Expressions, which detered every Body'. See also ibid., 26 Jan., 6 Feb. 1780.

70 *1823 Game Report*, p. 33. See also Beds. R.O., W1/341.

71 See below, p. 140. On the other hand, some followed the time-honoured tradition of deer-stealers and blackened their faces in order to avoid detection: e.g., *The Times,* 16 Nov. 1829.

72 E.g., *Warwick Advertiser*, 23 Nov. 1816; Edward Peacock, 'Trial under the game laws', *Notes & Queries*, 7th ser., III (1887), 221-2.

73 *1823 Game Report*, pp. 31, 38. On the Berkeley Castle incident, see also Peacock, 'Trial under the game laws', pp. 221-2, and A. J. Peacock, *Bread or blood: a study of the agrarian riots in East Anglia in 1816* (London, 1965), p. 53.

74 See *1823 Game Report*, pp. 29, 31; *1828 Game Report*, p. 40. See also Suffield, *Considerations*, pp. 26-7.

75 *Norwich Mercury,* 14 Nov. 1778; 23 Jan., 20 Mar., 10 Apr., 31 July 1779.

76 A. L. Lloyd, *Folk song in England* (New York, 1967), p. 237. The 'buck' in this case was a buck hare.

77 Beresford, *Diary of a parson*, II, 218-19; see also *Norwich Mercury*, 31 Dec. 1785. Three years later a man was executed for Twaites' murder, having been convicted on the testimony of another member of the gang: see Beresford, *Diary of a parson*, III, 3; *Norwich Mercury*, 2 Feb., 8 Mar., 22 Mar. 1788.

78 Goodwood: *Salisbury Journal,* 27 Dec. 1779; *Annual Register*, XXII (1779), 238-9; XXIII (1780), 210. Blickling: see above, p. 25.

79 Aylesford MSS, Shelf 28/19: memo book, 16 Jan. 1670/1. I have modernised the spelling and the punctuation. See also *Herts. Records*, I, 387.

80 *Salisbury Journal*, 22 Jan. 1787; see also ibid., 19 Feb. 1787.

81 Ibid., 17 Nov. 1783; *Norwich Mercury*, 20 Jan. 1787; *The Times*, 16 Dec. 1790; *Salisbury Journal*, 3 Mar. 1788.

82 Wilts. R.O., Savernake MSS, Bill to Bruce, 9 Feb. 1765.

83 No accurate count of the number of gamekeepers in England can be made before 1785, when the Game Duty Act forced lords of manors to register their gamekeepers annually (see Chapter 2, n. 86). On some estates, an increase can be seen in the second half of the eighteenth century. The number of keepers at Longleat, for instance, rose from two in 1750, to five in 1769, to seven in 1787. But this probably reflects the expansion of the estate and the demands of game preservation, more than the need to protect the game from poachers.

84 Aylesford MSS, Shelf 47/1: account book, 1777–9; Wilts. R.O., Longleat MSS, Account Books, 1783–9; W. Sussex R.O., Goodwood MSS 244-5: Midsummer 1786–Ladyday 1790. See also Essex R.O., D/DBy A216, A221.
    Watchers were commonly given liquid refreshment by their employers, presumably to help keep them warm (and awake) during their vigils. During the 1787-8 season, for example, the watchers at Longleat consumed £4 17s. 10d. worth of beer. Other game preservers supplied the watch with spirits. Lord Stafford, for instance, provided his watchers with a ration of gin (see Staffs. R.O., D590/620: 24 Dec. 1787; D593/L/4/10). It seems likely, therefore, that poachers fresh from an evening in the village alehouse were not the only ones steamed up and ready for a fight when they encountered the keeper

and his men during a raid on a local game preserve.

85   *1828 Game Report*, p. 78; *Parl. Deb.*, 2nd ser., XII, col. 954; Jeffery, *Dyott's diary*, I, 319. (Jeffery was unable to decipher 'awe', but see the original MS in Staffs. R.O., D661/11/2/3/1/11: Jan. 1818).

86   Miller Christy, 'Man-traps and spring-guns', *Outing*, XLI (1902–3), 729-34. Most man traps and spring guns were probably made by local blacksmiths, but it seems that spring guns were also sold commercially (see Glos. R.O., D2067: J. C. Hayward to M. P. Wiltens, 14 Feb. 1816). I have been unable to find out how much they cost.

87   Mayer, *Sportsman's directory*, p. 91; see also Daniel, *Rural sports*, II, 428.

88   E.g., *1828 Game Report*, p. 34. For a (perhaps genuine) notice, see Wilts. R.O., 383/114.

89   *Norwich Mercury*, 14 Nov., 5 Dec. 1778; 9 Jan., 25 Sept. 1779; 23 Sept., 4 Nov. 1780; 5 Jan., 16 Nov. 1782; 24 Nov. 1787; 27 Dec. 1788. For evidence that they had been installed in Essex by 1789, see Essex R.O., D/DU 181/24.

90   *Salisbury Journal*, 16 Sept 1793; for his previous troubles, see ibid., 13 Sept. 1779, 8 Oct. 1792. Some traps were set before the 1790s, but none of them specifically for poachers (e.g., ibid., 26 Sept. 1763).

91   Ibid., 28 Nov. 1785. On the question of liability, see Bacon, *Memoir of Suffield*, pp. 211-18.

92   Suffield, *Considerations*, pp. 76-7; Bacon, *Memoir of Suffield*, p. 256. See also *Annual Register*, LV (1813), 16.

93   W. Suffolk R.O., E2/21/2: Sir Thomas Cullum to his son, 1 Apr. 1825. Wilson recovered, but Archer died of his wounds (ibid., 10 May 1825). For other accidental deaths and injuries caused by these devices, see Bacon, *Memoir of Suffield*, p. 241; *The Times*, 3 Jan. 1826; and *Parl. Papers*, 1826–7, XX, 695.

94   *1828 Game Report*, p. 76; see also ibid., pp. 54, 74; *Observations on Lord Suffield's considerations on the game laws* (London, 1825), pp. 21-2. Spring guns and man traps were outlawed by 7 & 8 Geo. IV, c. 18. This, however, did not bring about their complete abolition. They could still be set in private dwellings at night; in the game preserves, some gentlemen evaded the law by installing 'humane' man traps – that is, traps without teeth – and also by digging deep pits into which poachers might fall: see Christy, 'Man-traps and spring guns', p. 732; *The Times*, 15 Nov., 19 Nov. 1828.

95   *Parl Deb.*, 2nd ser., XII, col. 529. See also ibid., 2nd ser., XIII, col. 1268; 2nd ser., XVII, cols. 24-5.

96   Edward Lloyd Williams, *Observations on the game laws* (London, 1828), pp. 8-9.

97   Jeffery, *Dyott's diary*, II, 47-8.

Chapter 4

1   *Parl. Deb.*, 2nd ser., VIII, cols. 1292-8; see also Cobbett, *Rural rides*, I, 191-3.

2   Henry, Lord Brougham, *Speeches of Henry Lord Brougham* (Philadelphia, 1841), I, 545 (speech on law reform, 7 Feb. 1828).

3   Chambers, *Nottinghamshire*, p. 74. G. E. Mingay has been more cautious: see his *English landed society in the eighteenth century* (London & Toronto, 1963), p. 120.

4   Esther Moir, *The justice of the peace* (Harmondsworth, 1969), pp. 126-7.

5   Webb, *English local government*, I, 597-9; see also p. 378. Both Chambers and Moir drew their conclusions directly from the Webbs, who in turn seem to

have been heavily influenced by Fielding's portrait of Squire Western as a J.P. (see *Tom Jones*, bk. vii, ch. 9). It is perhaps worth noting that, however critically Fielding might have portrayed the enforcement of the game laws in the eighteenth century, he was not above convicting the occasional offender himself: e.g., *Norwich Mercury*, 3 Feb. 1753.

6   22 & 23 Chas II, c. 25, s. 7. Game Acts earlier in the seventeenth century had required the presence of two J.P.s and the testimony of two witnesses for a conviction.

7   Other authorities claimed a residual interest. Well into the eighteenth century, stewards formally asked at every meeting of the manorial court whether the jurors wished to present any person for violation of the game laws (see Kent A.O., U438, M7/2; Essex R.O., D/DHh, M88; and for an actual presentment, see Kent A.O., U908, M19). Game cases were also occasionally heard at some borough quarter sessions: e.g., Edward Hughes, *North country life in the eighteenth century* (Oxford, 1952–65), I, 40n.

8   E. Sussex R.O., QO/EW 10: Jan. 1691/2. The surviving diaries of J.P.s for this period confirm that they did little to enforce the game laws beyond issuing warrants and attending quarter sessions: see, for example, Warws. R.O., CR 103 (diary of Sir William Bromley, 1685–1728); Kent A.O., U23, 01 (diary of Ralph Buffkin, 1689–1705); Essex R.O., D/DCv 1 (diary of Sir William Holcroft, 1661–88); B.L., Add. MS 42598 (diary of William Brockman, 1689–1721).

9   Ratcliff & Johnson, *Warwick records*, XI, p. liii; 'The Marchant diary', *Sussex Archaeological Collections*, XXV (1873), 194. See also ibid., p. 175: 'I laid a bottle of wine with Mr Scutt some time ago, that Dick Buckwell would not be indicted at the next Assizes for poaching. So to-night we paid each 1s. cash, and had the wine. Whoever loses is to repay the other shilling' (12 Dec. 1715).

10 Kent A.O., U310, O14, pt. 2, pp. 66, 106; Berks. R.O., D/EZ 30, F1: 27 Apr. 1743. The development can also be seen in the Kent petty sessions' records (see Bibliography). The minute book of the Sevenoaks division shows justices hearing and deciding cases as early as 1710; J.P.s were also active in Wingham in the early eighteenth century. By the middle of the century, however, evidence of enforcement by the petty sessions becomes more difficult to find, even though more minute books survive for this period. After the 1760s, game cases almost completely disappear from the minute books. Petty sessions, then, seem to have been a transitional stage in the transfer of jurisdiction over game cases from the quarter sessions to the individual J.P. They performed the same function in the early nineteenth century, only this time jurisdiction was moving in the opposite direction. As criticism of summary trials by J.P.s grew, game cases again began to be tried at petty sessions; by the 1820s, their number was substantial in divisions like Wingham and Upper Scray.

11 Trial at quarter sessions was required by law for third or subsequent offences against the Night Poaching Acts of 1773 and of 1828, or for any offence against the Night Poaching Acts of 1816 or 1817.

12 J. M. Beattie, 'The pattern of crime in England, 1660–1800', *Past & Present*, no. 62 (Feb. 1974), pp. 78–83. The transfer of jurisdiction was encouraged by court decisions which held that poaching was not an 'indictable' offence: see Chitty, *Treatise*, II, 1047, 1078.

13 Kent A.O., Q/SB 1739: Thomas [?Bleckonden] to David Fuller, 11 July 1739, and summons list, 12 July 1739; *Herts. records*, I, 301, 305-6.

14   Aside from the Night Poaching Act of 1770 (which was repealed after only three years), the chief exception to this rule was the Night Poaching Act of 1800 which allowed J.P.s to imprison night poachers for up to two years and to impress them into the King's service. This was repealed in 1816.

15   For the pre-1707 period, the penalties were rather more complicated than this summary suggests; for details, see Appendix II.B. and II.C.

16   See J. G. A. Pocock, *The Machiavellian moment* (Princeton, N.J., 1975), pp. 409-14, and J. R. Western, *The English militia in the eighteenth century* (London & Toronto, 1965), pp. 3-29. See also Lois G. Schwoerer, *'No standing armies!' the anti-army ideology in seventeenth-century England* (Baltimore & London, 1974), chs. 6-9.

17   Henry Horwitz, ed., *The parliamentary diary of Narcissus Luttrell, 1691-1693* (Oxford, 1972), p. 444. The Bill of Rights in 1689 had given only a cautious endorsement of the right to bear arms ('Subjects, which are Protestants, may have arms for their Defence suitable to their Conditions, and as allowed by law'); hence the need to amend the Game Act. For a similar amendment, which was defeated in 1730, see *C.J.*, XXI, 566-7.

18   *The Craftsman*, No. 657 (10 Feb. 1739), quoted in *Gentleman's Magazine*, IX (1739), 82. For other examples, see G. M. Trevelyan, *England under Queen Anne* (London, 1930–4), III, 34; Western, *English militia*, p. 72. The argument was being made as late as 1762: see *London Magazine,* XXXI (1762), 68-9.

19   A. H. A. Hamilton, *Quarter sessions from Queen Elizabeth to Queen Anne* (London, 1878), p. 269. Their reluctance was, perhaps, strengthened by the knowledge that in 1686 James II had attempted to use these provisions of the game laws to disarm several counties: see J. R. Western, *Monarchy and revolution: the English state in the 1680s* (London, 1972), p. 145.

20   *Quarter sessions records for the county of Somerset* (Somerset Record Society, XXXIV [1919]), p. 178. For other examples, see J. C. Atkinson, ed., *Quarter sessions records* (North Riding Record Society: London, 1884–92), VI, 258; Kent A.O., U310, 14, pt. 1, p. 22; B.L., Add. MS 42599, p. 55.

21   S.C.L., Arundel Castle MSS, S 541.

22   Atkinson, *Q.S. records*, VII, 47, 133, 175, 208; VIII, 171, 173, 176, 180, 186; see also S.C.L., Arundel Castle MSS, S 541. On the courts' attitude, see Chitty, *Treatise*, II, 972.

23   Atkinson, *Q.S. records*, VII, 86; VIII, 160, 166.

24   Mary Sturge Gretton, [ed.], *Oxfordshire justices of the peace in the seventeenth century* (Oxon. Record Society, XVI [1934]), pp. 40-1. On the popularity of shooting matches, see *C.S.P.D., 1686–7*, p. 314; Bagley, *Great diurnal*, II, 17; III, 95. See also Francis W. Steer, ed., *Farm and cottage inventories of mid-Essex, 1635–1749* (2nd edn, London & Chichester, 1969), pp. 150, 167, 175, 200, 227, 271.

25   Chitty, *Treatise*, II, 1068-74, 1103-4. See also below, n. 45.

26   Berks. R.O., D/EZ 30, F1: 9 Nov. 1743; see also *Salisbury Journal*, 12 Feb. 1753.

27   *Parl. Reg.*, XLIV, 511 (25 Apr. 1796). The same sentiments can be found earlier in the century. In 1714, for example, a man was rejected as a steward by Lord Arlington because 'he was a man of Pleasure, keeping a pack of dogs' (Norfolk R.O., MC1/29). See also Malcolmson, *Popular Recreations*, p. 93; Zouch, *An account*, pp. 17-18. The irony was that some farmers were obliged by the lord of the manor to keep dogs, albeit for the latter's use: see Laurence, *Duty of a steward*, p. 59; S.C.L., OD 1385: Brian Hodgson to William Bagshaw, 9 Mar. 1755.

28   Isham, *Journal of Thomas Isham*, p. 67. See also Hay, *Albion's fatal tree*, pp. 196, 238.

29   Aylesford MSS, Letterbook in study, No. 30: Lady to Lord Aylesford, 15 Jan. n.y. [ca. 1730]. I have modernised the spelling.

30   Joan Wake, *The Brudenells of Deene* (London, 1953), pp. 218-19; E. Riding R.O., DDGR/42/28: James Collins to John Grimston, 15 Oct. 1778. By the latter date, shooting had become the most common method of destroying dogs. Earlier in the century, however, dogs were usually hanged. Douglas Hay has described this practice as 'a parody of the rites of Tyburn' (*Albion's fatal tree*, p. 196), but in fact, gentlemen used the noose to destroy their own dogs as well: see Bagley, *Great diurnal*, I, 193; Wake and Webster, *Letters of Daniel Eaton*, p. 30; Ketton-Cremer, *Country neighbourhood*, p. 89.

31   E.g., *Herts. records*, I, 261-3; Cumberland R.O., D/Pen: Joseph Herbert to Sir Joseph Pennington, 7 Apr. 1738.

32   *C.J.*, XLVI, 145; see also William Marshall, *The rural economy of Yorkshire* (London, 1788), pp. 382-6.

33   *Gentleman's Magazine*, V (1735), 195; *Salisbury Journal*, 5 Feb., 19 Feb. 1753; *Norwich Mercury*, 24 Feb., 8 Dec. 1753; *C.J.*, XXVII, 165, 174, 186, 197, 199, 202, 246, 267, 274; XXXV, 677, 681. See also *Gentleman's Magazine*, XXVII (1757), 159; XXXII (1762), 21-2; and Norfolk R.O., Walsingham MSS, LV/66: Heads for an Act of Parliament, ca. 1763.

34   Andrews, *Torrington diaries*, II, 371; see also III, 292; IV, 48.

35   36 Geo. III, c. 124; 48 Geo. III, c. 55; 52 Geo. III, c. 93; for details, see Appendix II.C.2. For the petitions, see *C.J.*, XL, XLVI, XLVII, LI, passim: most of them were written in response to a severe outbreak of rabies in 1791.

36   All who owned sporting dogs (greyhounds, pointers, setters, spaniels, lurchers, etc.) were subject to the tax, but only those assessed to pay duty on their dwelling houses, windows and lights were subject to the tax on *non-sporting* dogs. Thus, the 'babbling currs' of most labourers were exempt. For Pitt's views, see *Parl. Reg.*, XLIV, 364-9, 430-1, 506-19; *Parl. History*, XXXII, cols. 994-1006. See also Stephen Dowell, *A history of taxation and taxes in England* (3rd edn, New York, 1965), III, 261-4; Stirling, *Coke of Norfolk*, I, 116.

37   *C.J.*, XLVI, 145. The Warwickshire freeholders who wrote this petition were aware that they were proposing a new approach: 'the Petitioners would see with double Pleasure this Effect of the preventive Means which they suggest, if the Severer Part of the Game Laws should become thereby unnecessary, as their Want of Efficacy, and the notorious Diminution of Game, seem to show that other Measures are necessary to be adopted'.

38   *Parl. Reg.*, XLIV, 510. For Pitt's argument in 1785, see Stockdale, *Debates*, III, 478.

39   E.g., Beds. R.O., W1/309. Examples of any use of the search-and-seize provisions of the game laws are hard to find after 1800.

40   See J. H. Plumb, *Sir Robert Walpole* (London, 1956–60), I, 41-2, 69, 111, 213; Moir, *Justice of the peace*, pp. 81-2, 88-9; Norma Landau, 'Gentry and gentlemen: the justices of the peace, 1680–1760' (Ph.D. thesis, University of California, Berkeley, 1974), pp. 103-38.

41   There are, for example, numerous prosecutions in the late seventeenth century for the crime of 'night walking' – i.e., for being out at night without a legitimate explanation. These may or may not have been poachers. Even for specific offences against the game laws, there is sometimes an element of ambiguity. At the Easter sessions in Lincolnshire in 1683, for example, eight

people (including, very unusually, three women) were indicted for various offences against the game laws. An examination of other indictments against these defendants in previous and subsequent sessions, however, suggests that in the cases of as many as five of them (including two of the women), their real crime was non-attendance at church on Sundays. Thus, the indictments may have been a form of harassment against Catholics or dissenters, rather than retaliation against poachers: see S.A. Peyton, ed., *Minutes of proceedings in quarter sessions held for the parts of Kesteven in the country of Lincoln, 1674–1695* (Lincoln Record Society, XXV–XXVI [1931]), p. 154, and pp. 141, 156, 163, 168, 169, 178, etc.

42   Hertfordshire, Buckinghamshire, Warwickshire and the North Riding, supplemented by evidence from Oxfordshire, Lincolnshire and Kent. Printed sources for the first six counties are listed in the bibliography; the source for Kent is its quarter sessions' process books, 1649–1792, in Kent A.O., Q/SPi 1-3; Q/SPi E1-E3; Q/SPi W1-W5.

43   Ratcliff & Johnson, *Warwick records*, VII, 213, 227, 236-7, 243; VIII, 8, 10, 19.

44   Gretton, *Oxfordshire justices*, pp. 49-52, 68. For an earlier example of this, see Cox, *Three centuries*, II, 81.

45   N. 43 above; Atkinson, *Q.S. records*, VII, 36, 51, 55-6, 60, 67, 71. There is a reason why prosecutions for unlawful 'possession' focused on dogs rather than guns. The Game Act of 1671 had authorised the seizure of guns from the unqualified, but neither it nor its successors prescribed a penalty for illegally possessing a gun. In order to prosecute someone for possessing a gun, therefore, it was necessary to charge him with violating the Tudor gun-control laws, which required a person to have both £100 a year and a licence before he could legally possess a gun (33 Henry VIII, c. 6; 2 & 3 Edw. VI, c. 14) and which still remained on the statute books in the late seventeenth century. For examples of such prosecutions, see Atkinson, *Q.S. records*, VI, 161; Ratcliff & Johnson, *Warwick records*, VI, 195; William LeHardy and Geoffrey Ll. Reckitt, eds., *County of Buckingham: calendar to the sessions records* (Aylesbury, 1933–9), I, 137. In the late seventeenth century, however, both the courts and Parliament moved to block further prosecutions under these statutes. The courts quashed several convictions because of minor technical flaws (Chitty, *Treatise*, II, 940-2, 946-7, 973, 977) and, in 1695, Parliament repealed one of the Tudor Acts (2 & 3 Edw. VI, c. 14) on the grounds that it had become a vehicle for 'malicious' prosecution of qualified sportsmen (6 & 7 Wm III, c. 13). After that date, prosecutors were reduced to arguing that guns were 'engines' to take game; as we have already noted (above, p. 81), this argument was dismissed by the courts in 1739.

46   LeHardy & Reckitt, *Bucks. Records*, I, 211, 306, 315. This is the only instance I have found in the late seventeenth and early eighteenth centuries of a poacher's being imprisoned.

47   Radcliff & Johnson, *Warwick records*, VIII, 19, 72, 227; see also IX, 33.

48   On Matthewes, see ibid., VII, 237, 240, 252, 261; VIII, xxxvi. His name was dropped from the commission in 1692. On Birmingham as a centre of dissent in this period, see Conrad Gill and Asa Briggs, *History of Birmingham* (Oxford, 1952), I, 59. See also above, n. 41.

49   Warws. R.O., CR 136, diary of Sir Roger Newdigate, 6 Nov. 1766; Ketton-Cremer, *Country neighbourhood*, p. 204. For another example, see Glos. R.O., D 1283/2, p. 3 (6 Mar. 1817).

50   On naval impressment, see Christopher Lloyd, *The British seaman, 1200–1860* (London, 1968), chs. 7, 10, 12; Daniel Baugh, *British naval administration*

in the age of Walpole (Princeton, N.J., 1965), pp. 148-62. On the operation of the Recruiting Acts, see R. E. Scouller, *The armies of Queen Anne* (Oxford, 1966), pp. 106-17; Trevelyan, *England under Queen Anne*, I, 219; and Arthur N. Gilbert, 'Army impressment during the war of the Spanish succession', *The Historian*, XXXVIII (1976), 689-708.

51 *Salisbury Journal*, 6 Sept. 1779.

52 Wilts. R.O., Longleat MSS, Account Book, 1756-7; E. Riding R.O., DDGR/42/27: Philip Langdale to John Grimston, 9 Jan. 1777. William Burton 'was some time aprentice to a tallow chandler, but quitted that and went to Sea, which he quitted about half a year ago, now lives with his mother, has no visible way of getting a livelyhood, but is suppos'd to live by killing Game'. Thomas Burton 'was some time aprentice with a Cooper, some time with a Cabinet maker, but quitted both, has no visible way of getting a livelyhood and esteem'd also a Poacher'. Their uncle was the parish constable 'and from this tis suppos'd they escap'd being press'd'.

53 Quoted in Daniel, *Supplement*, p. 70; 'Anglers' were fish poachers. On the Quota Acts, see Michael A. Lewis, *A social history of the navy, 1793–1815* (London, 1960), pp. 116-27. Impressment became a formal punishment under the game laws in 1800, when Parliament empowered J.P.s to press night poachers. The power does not appear to have been used very much, however. In Wiltshire, only seven men were pressed under this Act, and, of these, five were convicted in the final year of the Act's existence, 1816 (see Wilts. R.O., QS/Great Rolls, 1800–16: Gaol Calendars). Poachers themselves were not above impressing their comrades in order to keep them from testifying: see *The Times*, 25 Jan. 1814.

54 George Bankes, *Reconsiderations on certain proposed alterations of the game laws* (London, 1825), p. 34. 'Bankes,' wrote Lady Shelley in 1819, 'is all for *economy*, and yet for severity in the Game Laws, and for arbitrary power in every way. Canning said the other day that Bankes' ideal Government would be *cheap* tyranny' (Edgcumbe, *Diary of Lady Shelley*, II, 89-90).

55 See above, pp. 23-4. 'Double costs' actually meant one-and-a-half times the costs of prosecution. See Chitty, *Treatise*, I, 184-9 for details of the procedures involved in prosecutions of this kind.

56 *Some considerations on the game laws and the present practice of executing them* (London, 1753), p. 14; Chitty, *Treatise*, II, 1056-9.

57 *Norwich Mercury*, 3 Aug. 1751; *Salisbury Journal*, 20 Mar. 1786; see also *Daily Advertiser*, 23 Mar. 1754. 'Treble costs' meant one-and-three-quarters times the costs of prosecution.

58 There was a sporting agreement 'Amongst the Gentlemen, and other Qualified Persons of East Kent' in 1736 which, in addition to establishing a season for coursing and hare hunting, bound its signers to punish every unqualified person found killing game. There was no subscription raised, however; so this was not, strictly speaking, a game association. The first known subscription society for the preservation of the game was the one established in the Peak district in 1742. For East Kent, Peak district and Yorkshire associations, see S.C.L., OD 1385; for Nottinghamshire, see B.L., Add. MS 32713, ff. 225, 227; for Herefordshire, see *Gloucester Journal*, 10 Oct. 1749; for Kent, see *Kentish Post*, Nov. 1748. For the last two references I am indebted to, respectively, Robert Malcolmson and Norma Landau.

59 See above, pp. 56-62. On prosecutions: for Essex, see *London Magazine*, XXII (1753), 147, and *Norwich Mercury*, 24 Aug. 1754; for Suffolk, see ibid., 18 Aug. 1753; for Hampshire, see ibid., 11 Aug. 1753; for Dorset, see *Daily Advertiser*,

21 Mar. 1755; for Wiltshire, see *Salisbury Journal*, 18 Aug. 1755; for Somerset, see *Norwich Mercury*, 30 Aug. 1755; for Bedfordshire, see below, n.66.

60 Munsche, 'Game laws in Wiltshire', p. 224.

61 Norfolk R.O., Walsingham MSS, XLVIII/3: Lord Townshend to Lord Walsingham, 19 July, 23 July, 3 Oct. 1788, and subscription list, n.d. [1788]; *Norwich Mercury*, 10 Jan. 1789. A copy of the association's prospectus is in the Rye and Coleman Local History Libraries, Norwich. For discussions twenty years later, see C.U.L., Buxton MSS, Box 8: draft notice of the Thetford game association, n.d. [1808]; and Box 9: Lord Albemarle to Robert Buxton, 13 Feb. 1808; see also Norfolk R.O., MS 20640: diary of Robert Buxton, 5 Mar. 1808.

   Bedfordshire provides another example. The St Neots game association, founded in 1808, gave way in 1816 to the Bedfordshire game association: see Beds. R.O., H/WS 1583-7; LL 17/314.

62 Once again, lack of evidence makes it difficult to be more precise. Under the *nisi prius* system, most civil prosecutions were tried at the local assizes. The minute books for at least some of the circuits have survived, but the notations in thèm are usually too general to be very helpful. Occasionally it is possible to identify a game case (e.g., P.R.O., Assi 22/4; Dorset assizes, 10 July 1788, Lord Milton v. Barnes), but others may have been described as 'Debt', since that was the technical category of the suit. There are, however, some occasional reports in the press: e.g., *Norwich Mercury*, 4 Aug. 1781.

63 Beds. R.O., W1/355; see also W1/354, 356, 369, all partially printed in Alan E. Cirket, ed., *Samuel Whitbread's notebooks, 1810–11, 1813–14* (Beds. Historical Record Society, L [1971]), pp. 105-6. Ongley was a member of the St Neots game association, for which see ibid., p. 20.

64 Fendall & Crutchley, *Diary of Benjamin Newton*, pp. 126-7. To be 'exchequered' (or just 'chequered') was to be sued in the Court of Exchequer. Since suits were invalid if the defendant had already been convicted of the offence by a magistrate, a poacher could pre-empt a civil suit by having a friend lay an identical information before a J.P. and then confessing to it. That is what appears to have been done in this case.

65 Not surprisingly, conventional wisdom held that a publican was 'the last person to whom [a gamekeeper's deputation] should be given'. Nevertheless, such appointments were not unheard of. Lord Pembroke, for example, deputed two publicans in a row as gamekeeper of one of his manors, while in 1812 Peter Hawker 'visited Mr. Coltatt of Wraxall [Wilts.], who is keeper over all these manors, and landlord of the "Plough" inn'. The lord of the manor may have hoped to buy the publican's co-operation in this way, but Lord Buckinghamshire was probably correct in looking on it as 'a dangerous experiment' (Norfolk R.O., Walsingham MSS, XLVIII/3: T. Chamberleyne to Lord Walsingham, 13 Oct. [1788]; Wilts. R.O., QS/Roll of Gamekeepers' Deputations, 1767, 1778; Payne-Gallwey, *Diary of Peter Hawker*, I, 40; Norfolk R.O., How 747/3).

66 Beds. R.O., D.D.J. 1257-60. I have made minor alterations in the punctuation.

67 Aylesford MSS, Shelf 28/19: memo book, 7 Sept. 1668; Staffs. R.O., D590/555. For other examples, see Wilts. R.O., 490/1055; W. Suffolk R.O., 458/6/15.

68 On Bagshaw, see the collection of bonds in S.C.L., OD 1385; for the associations' use of bonds, see *Daily Advertiser*, 30 Jan. 1754; *Norwich Mercury*, 27 Jan. 1787. For other examples, see Wilts. R.O., 283/248, 383/957;

Salisbury Journal, 25 Dec. 1786. See also *Some considerations* (1753), p. 15.

69 *Considerations on the game laws, together with some strictures on Dr Blackstone's Commentaries relative to this subject* (London, 1777), p. 59n.

70 *Some considerations on the game laws, suggested by the late motion of Mr Curwen for the repeal of the present system* (London, 1796), p. 69.

71 See, for example, C.U.L., Buxton MSS, Box 8, R. J. Buxton to Mr Palmer, 3 Apr. 1802: 'I am much obliged to you for your attention in catching the Hare poaching fellows . . . Mr Brown [an attorney] of Diss is now in town [and] I have given him my directions to proceed against them . . . You may depend on it: they shall not escape, for I am determined to make an example, and I am glad it has fallen upon them who I believe have been long in the habit of poaching upon my property.'

72 Munsche, 'Game laws in Wiltshire', pp. 224-5.

73 *Annual Register*, XII (1769), 153; *Parl. Deb.*, 3rd ser., VI, cols. 767-8.

74 Chitty, *Treatise,* II, 1047-8.

75 *A letter to Richard Whitworth, Esq.* (London, 1772), p. 26. See also Staffs. R.O., D661/11/2/3/1/11: 8 Oct. 1829.

76 N. Riding R.O., ZK 12201-9, particularly 12207. For other examples of suits and threats of suits, see Jeffery, *Dyott's diary*, II, 21; *Gentleman's Magazine*, XLVI (1776), 142; *Herts. records*, VIII, 398; Norfolk R.O., How 750/68 and How 758/2; Glos. R.O., D1283/2, pp. 68, 88, (21 Sept. 1820, 27 Dec. 1821). Prosecutors could also find themselves the objects of prosecution. In 1790, for example, William Bishop, a clerk in the estate office at Longleat, stopped George Ayres, 'a notorious poacher', on the road and searched him for game. None was found, and Ayres sued for assault. The case was settled out of court when Lord Bath promised to pay the costs, which amounted to £15 15s. (Wilts. R.O., Longleat MSS, Account Book, 1790).

77 Wilts. R.O., Savernake MSS, Bill to Ailesbury, 9 Nov. 1777; Surrey R.O., 203/30/140. For a fuller discussion of J.P.s' biases, see below, pp. 161-3.

78 S.C.L., Arundel Castle MSS, S 607: 20 Jan., 23 Jan. 1817. The prosecution wanted the defendants to be convicted under the Game Duty Act as well as under the old game code. The practice was legal, but considered severe: see *Warwick Advertiser*, 2 Mar. 1816.

79 Fendall & Crutchley, *Diary of Benjamin Newton*, p. 107; *Herts. records*, I, 261-3. The virtue of Bridgwater's action is perhaps diminished by the fact that the J.P. to whom he transferred the case was his own son. Still, the scruple is significant. Cf. Dorothy Ross, 'Class privilege in seventeenth-century England', *History*, XXVIII (1943), 152-3.

80 Quoted in Landau, 'Gentry and gentlemen', pp. 297-8.

81 Essex R.O., D/DAr C8. For another incident of this type – incongruously titled 'Severity of the game laws' – see *The Times*, 1 Feb. 1826.

82 Based on the conviction certificates of James Richmond Webb, about which see Munsche, 'Game laws in Wiltshire', p. 225. See also Surrey R.O., 203/33/6, and Beds. R.O., W1/335.

83 B.L., Add. MS 42599, p. 46v; Norfolk R.O., How 750/75. See also ibid., How 750/63. Some justices also granted poachers considerable time to raise the necessary amount of money: e.g., W. Suffolk R.O., P/T1: 15 July 1818, 20 Jan. 1819.

84 E. Riding R.O., DDGR/42/28: William Strickland to John Grimston, 25 Sept. 1778. See also Staffs. R.O., D661/11/2/3/1/11: 8 Nov. 1825, and Beds. R.O., W1/1242.

85 5 Anne, c. 14, s. 3.

86   Glos. R.O., D1283/2, pp. 2-3, 5 (17 Feb., 6 Mar., 1 Apr. 1817); see also ibid., p. 40 (25 Mar. 1819).
87   Wilts. R.O., Savernake MSS, Bill to Bruce, 23 Jan. 1767; see also ibid., 18 Jan. 1768.
88   *Northampton Mercury,* 19 Nov. 1753; *Norwich Mercury,* 12 Jan. 1771. I am indebted to Robert Malcolmson for the reference to the Marlborough demonstration, which may have been a protest against the Game Association's use of informers.
89   Wilts. R.O., Savernake MSS, Bill to Bruce, 23 Jan. 1767, 18 Jan. 1768. Ten years later, Bright was again caught setting snares and fined £20 under the Night Poaching Act. Since he did not have the money and the Act contained no provision by which he could obtain a pardon in exchange for 'peaching' a higgler, Bright was committed to the bridewell – for the first time, apparently, in a long career (ibid., Bill to Ailesbury, 9 Nov. 1777).
90   *1823 Game Report,* p. 32; for some examples, see Chapter 3, n. 77, and below, pp. 141-2. For instances of poachers informing on game traders, see Wilts. R.O., Savernake MSS, Bill to Ailesbury, 25 Oct. [1776?], 21 Oct. 1778; *Salisbury Journal,* 14 Nov. 1791; Beds. R.O., W1/328; Staffs. R.O., D661/11/2/3/1/11: 8 Nov., 14 Dec. 1825.
91   Zouch, *An account,* pp. 4-5. Thirty years later, William Daniel repeated – or rather, plagiarised – Zouch's claim: see Daniel, *Supplement,* pp. 412-13.
92   Wilts. R.O., QS/Summary Convictions: Game; A2/4/73-342; QS/Great Rolls, 1782–1820.
93   See Elizabeth W. Gilboy, *Wages in eighteenth-century England* (Cambridge, Mass., 1934), pp. 80-1, 148, 173-4.
94   *Salisbury Journal,* 28 Feb. 1791. In 1791 the game duty had been raised from two to three guineas. See also *Some considerations* (1796), p. 70.
95   *Gentleman's Magazine,* LVI (1786), 902; *The Times,* 6 Jan. 1802. For other examples, see *Warwick Advertiser,* 21 Sept. 1816; Cirket, *Samuel Whitbread's notebooks,* p. 104; and above, n. 78.
96   Based on the gaol calendars, in Wilts. R.O., A2/4/99ff.; QS/Great Rolls, 1782–1831. The calendars are 96 per cent complete for 1760–1831, and 99 per cent complete for 1770–1831. Poaching was, of course, a seasonal crime, and committals for it tended to be concentrated in the months between August and March. In order to reflect more accurately the movement of committals, I have arranged the data on the graphs according to 'season', rather than calendar year. The 'season' is defined as running from Michaelmas session of the year noted on the graph to the Trinity session of the year following.
97   The graph does not include committals under the Night Poaching Acts of 1816, 1817 and 1828, since these were ordered by quarter sessions, rather than by justices 'out of sessions'. For committals under these Acts, see below, p. 103.
98   Quoted in Esther Moir, 'Sir George Onesiphorus Paul', *Gloucestershire studies,* ed. H. P. R. Finberg (Leicester, 1957), p. 215; see also U. R. Q. Henriques, 'The rise and decline of the separate system of prison discipline', *Past & Present,* no. 54 (1972), pp. 61-93.
99   Wilts. R.O., Longleat MSS, Account Books, 1780–1800.
100   Beds. R.O., KK 869.
101   43 Geo. III, c. 58.
102   *Parl. Deb.,* 1st ser., XXXV, col. 339. It is worth noting that at least one

defender of the Act thought its purpose was 'to treat game like property' (ibid., col. 341).

103 *The Times*, 21 Oct. 1816, quoting the *Bath Herald*.
104 Wilts. R.O., QS/Great Rolls, 1800–16: Gaol Calendars. See above, n. 53.
105 A. G. L. Shaw, *Convicts and colonies: a study of penal transportation from Great Britain and Ireland to Australia and other parts of the British empire* (London, 1966), pp. 150, 157-8. See also *Parl. Papers*, 1819, XVII, 65.
106 Wilts. R.O., QS/Great Rolls, 1816–28: Gaol Calendars. There does not appear to have been any prosecution under 'Lord Ellenborough's Law' in Wiltshire during this period. There were prosecutions in other counties, however: eg., Cobbett, *Rural rides*, II, 151-6.
107 *1828 Game Report*, p. 75.
108 Wilts. R.O., QS/Great Rolls, 1816–28: Gaol Calendars. Cf. Hay, *Albion's fatal tree*, p. 211.
109 See *Parl. Deb.*, 3rd ser., II, cols. 599-600.
110 S.C.L., OD 1385: Brian Hodgson to [?Richard Bagshaw], 3 Feb. 1772; Beds. R.O., W1/354.

Chapter 5

1 A farmer, quoted in Robert Fulford, *Samuel Whitbread, 1764–1815: a study in opposition* (London, 1967), pp. 224-5.
2 Warws. R.O., CR 136, diary of Sir Roger Newdigate, 28 Oct. 1758. In the next two days, two men and two women 'concerned in ye Riot at Nuneaton' were bound over to appear at the assizes (ibid., 29 Oct., 30 Oct. 1758).

   Tumultuous rescues of poachers seem to have been more common in the years after 1815, or at least more evidence from this period has survived. In February 1829, for example, 'an immense multitude from the county [of Cheshire] assembled and rescued [twenty poachers], as they were being conveyed in irons to the magistrates office. They were recaptured, however, and brought back to the [Nantwich] Bridewell. As fresh multitude[s] poured into town, a second rescue was feared, and an express was sent to Chester for military aid. Two hundred soldiers were immediately dispatched, who conveyed the prisoners to Chester Castle' (*Bell's Weekly Messenger*, 15 Feb. 1829). For other examples, see *The Times*, 16 Dec. 1818, 23 Jan. 1826; and Peacock, *Bread or blood*, p. 43.
3 See E. P. Thompson, 'The crime of anonymity', in *Albion's fatal tree*, ed. Hay, pp. 260, 269.
4 Guildhall Library, MS 2148/1: 7 Feb. 1721/2; MS 2148/2: 21 Feb., 3 Apr. 1755. See also ibid., MS 2148/1: 22 Apr. 1720; MS 2148/2: 3 Feb. 1764.
5 *A collection of the parliamentary debates in England, from the year M,DC,LXVIII to the present time* (n.p., 1742), XXI, 380. Walpole was referring specifically to the powers granted by the game laws to search for guns, dogs, nets and 'engines'. Note that he assumes that the law was enforced only against those who were 'living upon the game'.
6 See above, p. 80. Not everyone thought that attacking the game laws was politically smart. In 1707 Sir Thomas Cave, a Whig, wrote to his brother-in-law, 'I must thank your Lordship for the Domestick News and the indeavours to repeal the Game Act; I wish you could inform me who first mentioned it in the House, and whether Churchman or Fanatick, if the first the information may be of service to us' (Verney, *Verney letters*, I, 235).

7   See Pocock, *The Machiavellian moment*, chs. 12-14; John Brewer, *Party ideology and popular politics at the accession of George III* (Cambridge, 1976), ch. 12.

8   E.g., Nicholas Rogers, 'Aristocratic clientage, trade and independency: popular politics in pre-radical Westminster', *Past & Present*, No. 61 (Nov. 1973), pp. 70-106; Sir Lewis Namier and John Brooke, eds., *The house of commons, 1754–1790* (London, 1964), I, 2-7.

9   Ibid., pp. 242-5; Edward Hughes, *North country life in the eighteenth century* (Oxford, 1952–65), II, 239-43. This incident led to the celebrated 'Nullum Tempus' Act.

10   Quoted in *Gentleman's Magazine*, XIX (1749), 62.

11   Ibid., pp. 62-3; *London Magazine*, XXII (1753), 31; *The N—f—k farmer's sentiments upon the report of a bill being brought into parliament for doubling the qualification of sportsmen* (London, 1754), pp. 27-8.

12   See above, pp. 56-7.

13   *Some considerations* (1753), pp. 14-15; see also ibid., p. 24, and *The N—f—k farmer's sentiments*, pp. 24-5.

14   *Some considerations* (1753), p. 12; see also ibid., p. 16, and *Remarks on the laws relating to the game and the association set on foot for the preservation of it* (London, 1753), p. 17.

15   Ibid., p. 2.

16   *Gentleman's Magazine*, XXII (1752), 598; *Some considerations* (1753), pp. 18-19.

17   *Daily Advertiser*, 13 Mar. 1752.

18   *Norwich Mercury*, 24 Aug. 1754, 18 Aug. 1753.

19   *Daily Advertiser*, 3 Oct. 1755.

20   H. J. Habakkuk, 'English landownership, 1680–1740', *Econ. Hist. Rev.*, X (1940), 2-17; Mingay, *The gentry*, pp. 69-73; J. V. Beckett, 'English landownership in the later seventeenth and eighteenth centuries: the debate and the problems', *Econ. Hist. Rev.*, 2nd ser., XXX (1977), 567-81.

21   E.g., Plumb, *Walpole*, II, 81; Edward Hyams, *Capability Brown and Humphrey Repton* (London, 1971), pp. 15, 20; Alan Harris, *The rural landscape of the East Riding of Yorkshire, 1700–1850* (Oxford, 1961), pp. 75-7.

22   *The N—f—k farmer's sentiments*, p. 10. Although he was anonymous, the author's self-identification as a farmer seems genuine enough. In a preface, he apologises for his lack of learning, and the language in the rest of the pamphlet suggests that this was not a literary pretence.

23   Ibid., pp. 12-13.

24   Ibid., p. 9. Aristocratic restraints on elections, rather than those on sporting, may have been the author's real target. He roundly condemned 'that infamous Practice of Compromising' by which Whigs and Tories avoided expensive election contests by splitting county seats between themselves. This was the practice in Norfolk at the time, and at least some readers took the pamphlet to be an attempt to upset the arrangement: see ibid., pp. 14-19, 22, 26; Namier & Brooke, *House of commons*, I, 339; *Monthly Review*, X (1754), 320, 395.

25   *Gentleman's Magazine*, XXVI (1756), 496-7; Western, *The English militia*, pp. 127-40. See also Nicholas Rogers, 'London politics from Walpole to Pitt: patriotism and independency in an era of commercial imperialism' (Ph.D. thesis, University of Toronto, 1975), pp. 167-210.

26   *Gentleman's Magazine*, XXV (1755), 488; *Salisbury Journal*, 23 Feb. 1756, and also 14 Feb. 1757.

27   *Gentleman's Magazine*, XXVI (1756), 384-5.

28   John Shebbeare, *A third letter to the people of England on liberty, taxes and the*

application of public money (London, 1756), p. 13; *An alarm to the people of England shewing their rights, liberties, and properties, to be in the utmost danger from the present destructive and unconstitutional association, for the preservation of the game all over England* (London, 1757), p. 10.

29 *Remarks on the laws*, p. 12; see also *Some considerations* (1753), p. 38; *Norwich Mercury*, 3 Feb. 1753; and *Thoughts on the present laws for preserving the game* (London, 1750), pp. 24-5.

30 *Gentleman's Magazine*, XIX (1749), 63; see also ibid., pp. 251-2.

31 Ibid., XXIV (1754), 3-4; see also ibid., XVII (1747), 79, and XXIII (1753), 517-18.

32 Chitty, *Treatise*, II, 1067.

33 See Appendix I.A.1.a and I.C.3.a.

34 See above, pp. 41, 89.

35 John Shebbeare, *A fifth letter to the people of England on the subversion of the constitution and the necessity of its being restored* (London, 1757), p. 35.

36 *Gentleman's Magazine*, XXIII (1753), 517; see also *London Magazine*, XXII (1753), 31.

37 See above, p. 53.

38 *C.J.*, XXXII, 755 et passim; *Parl. Papers, 1731–1800*, Bills, V, no. 171. Most game laws up to that time had divided the fine equally between the informer and the overseers of the poor of the parish where the offence had been committed. But in one version of Yonge's bill, the fine was to be divided between the informer and the owner of the land on which the offence was committed (see ibid., no. 172). The latter was the normal procedure in deer-stealing cases, and this is an indication that gentlemen were beginning to think of their game as property. In its final form, however, the bill called for the traditional division of the fine.

39 Ibid., no. 172; *LJ.*, XXXII, 511 et passim; 10 Geo. III, c. 19. The Sabbatarian provisions may have been an early reflection of Evangelical sentiment (see W.B. Whitaker, *The eighteenth-century English Sunday: a study of Sunday observance from 1677 to 1837* [London, 1940], chs. 5-6). Yonge, however, was no Evangelical himself (see entries in *D.N.B.* and Namier & Brooke, *House of commons*); it seems more likely that the ban on Sunday hunting was simply an acknowledgement that, aside from night-time, the Lord's Day was the part of the week when labourers had the most opportunity to take game. In Wiltshire in the last quarter of the eighteenth century, half of all known convictions under the Night Poaching Act of 1773 were for hunting on Sunday.

40 *C.J.*, XXXIII, 343, 351, 356. The vote on second reading was 34-24.

41 Ibid., pp. 490, 499, 548, 553, 646. The fatal division on this bill was 71-51. See also *Salisbury Journal*, 16 Mar. 1772.

42 *C.J.*, XXXIII, 553, 633, 646, 656, 677, 735, 765, 770, 953-4; *Parl. Papers, 1731–1800*, Bills, VI, no. 202; *LJ.*, XXXIII, 416 et passim. The Lords' amendments themselves seem to have been fairly innocuous. Possibly they encroached 'upon one of the Commons' prerogatives, or maybe the supporters of the Act of 1770 had marshalled their forces for the occasion.

43 *C.J.*, XXXIV, 107 et passim; *LJ.*, XXXIII, 664 et passim; 13 Geo. III, c. 80. For details, see Appendix, I.C.2.a.1773b.

44 B.L., Egerton MS 234, p. 252; *Parl. Hist.*, VI, 700. Whitworth was, strictly speaking, referring to 'the Dog Act' in this passage. This was a companion measure to the Night Poaching Act of 1770, designed to deter the theft of dogs (10 Geo. III, c. 18). Since both Acts shared the same defects, most

attempts to repeal one also tried to repeal the other. But, significantly, once the Night Poaching Act was gone, demand for the repeal of the 'Dog Act' quickly faded away. The 'Dog Act' remained on the statute books until 1827, when it was repealed by 7 & 8 Geo. IV, c. 27.

45   B.L., Egerton MS 234, pp. 255-6.
46   Ibid., pp. 253, 260; see also ibid., p. 258, and *Parl. Hist.*, VI, 702.
47   B.L., Egerton MS 234, pp. 251, 257-8.
48   See *A letter to Richard Whitworth, Esq.* (London, 1772), p. 2. In Wiltshire, only three men were convicted under the Act of 1770, all of them in 1771 (see Wilts. R.O., A2/4/203, 206, 212). For examples in other counties, see *Norwich Mercury*, 9 Feb. 1771; *Salisbury Journal*, 27 Jan. 1772; *Annual Register*, XVI (1773), 73.
49   B.L., Egerton MS 229, p. 233.
50   *Sussex Archaeological Collections*, X (1858), 47-8. See also *Felix Farley's Bristol Journal*, 3 Mar. 1753, where the game laws are described as being 'the Subject of Conversation in most Companies'. (I am indebted to Robert Malcolmson for this latter reference).
51   Thomas Bayley Howell and Thomas Jones Howell, eds., *A complete collection of state trials and proceedings for high treason and other crimes and misdemeanours from the earliest period* (London, 1809–26), XIX, cols. 1176-1236. See also B.L., Add. MS 35887, ff. 78-85, and Kent A.O., U471, C12, for related documents. Byron was found guilty of manslaughter by the House of Lords and, although exempted from punishment, became a recluse for the remainder of his life. His grandnephew, the poet, succeeded him to the title in 1798: see *D.N.B.*, sub 'Byron, George Gordon, 6th Baron'.
52   W. S. Lewis, ed., *The Yale edition of Horace Walpole's correspondence* (New Haven, Conn., 1937–74), XXII, 284 (Walpole to Horace Mann, 11 Feb. 1765); *Monthly Review*, XXXII (1764), 391. See also ibid., XLII (1770), 493.
53   Blackstone, *Commentaries*, II, 410-19. See also Christopher Hill, 'The Norman yoke', in *Puritanism and revolution* (London, 1958), pp. 50-122.
54   Blackstone, *Commentaries*, IV, 416.
55   Ibid., pp. 280-2.
56   E.g., B.L., Egerton MS 234, p. 251; Samuel Purlewent, *A dialogue between a lawyer and a country gentleman, upon the subject of the game laws, relative to hares, partridges and pheasants* (2nd edn, London, 1771), p. 47. Blackstone, in turn, supported the opponents of the Act of 1770. In the fifth edition of the *Commentaries* (Oxford, 1773), he inserted a footnote summarising the Act and then added: 'This statute hath now continued three sessions of parliament unrepealed!' (IV, 175, n. 1).
57   'Junius', *The letters of Junius* (new edn, London, 1791), pp. 308-9 (Letter LXIV: 2 Nov. 1771).
58   Blackstone, *Commentaries*, II, 411-12; see also IV, 174.
59   Purlewent, *Dialogue*, p. 54; see also *Gentleman's Magazine*, XL (1770), 7-8, 122; XLII (1772), 120-1.
60   H.M.C., *14th Report*, IX, 315; *C.J.*, XXXII, 971, 974, 977. In 1762 the division was 46-32; in the 1770 division the vote was 52-28.
61   *Salisbury Journal*, 8 Jan., 15 Jan. 1770.
62   *Norwich Mercury*, 23 Feb. 1771.
63   B.L., Egerton MS 234, pp. 256, 254; see also p. 261.
64   *Salisbury Journal*, 26 Aug. 1771; *Norwich Mercury*, 31 Aug. 1771, 1 Feb. 1772.
65   William Salt Library, Whitworth MSS, 26/22/45 (Whitworth's 'Panegyric on himself', [ca. 1800?]). See also Namier & Brooke, *House of commons*, III, 634-5,

and S. A. H. Burne, 'Presidential address. Parochial documents. With special reference to the Whitworth MSS', *Transactions of the North Staffordshire Field Club*, LXII (1928), 15-58. Stafford was one of the most venal boroughs in England, and the cost of winning and keeping it apparently taxed Whitworth's modest estate greatly. Although associated with the opposition early in his parliamentary career, he made his peace with the Administration in 1772 in return for a secret service pension worth £600 a year. The Administration also subsidised his re-election campaign in 1780, but he lost to Richard Sheridan (who, ironically, also became a vocal critic of the game laws). Whitworth lived until 1811, and his final years were plagued by debts and loneliness (see his letters to his nephew, in Kent A.O., U269, C341).

66 *Letter to Whitworth*, p. 14. See also Kent A.O., U269, C342: 'Description of a well known Public Character in the counties of Stafford & Salop.', a poem written (ca. 1806) by Whitworth, presumably about himself, which includes the following lines:

> Always ready at his Country's Call,
> Sacrifices Ease, his Comforts and his All.
> He Shuns the Great Man's Lofty Doors,
> As well the Cringing Quest of Sinecures Abjures. . .

67 *C.J.*, XXXIII, 956-7; *Parl. Papers, 1731–1800*, Bills, VI, no. 203. Most of the blanks in the bill can be filled in by consulting *Letter to Whitworth*, passim.
68 *Letter to Whitworth*, p. 25; see also Taplin, *Observations*, p. 4; *Essays on the game laws*, pp. 5-6.
69 Ibid., p. 1; Basil Cozens-Hardy, ed., *The diary of Sylas Neville, 1767–1788* (Oxford, 1950), p. 93. For other examples of radical opinion, see Joseph Priestley, *An essay on the first principles of government* (2nd edn, London, 1771), pp. 22, 65, 75, and Caroline Robbins, *The eighteenth-century commonwealthman* (new edn, New York, 1968), p. 364.
70 *Essays on the game laws*, p. 8.
71 Quoted in Stirling, *Coke of Norfolk*, I, 122-3. See also *Facts, fully stated*, p. vi.
72 Walter M. Stern, 'The bread crisis in Britain, 1795–96', *Economica*, n.s., XXXI (1964), 168-87; John Stevenson, 'Food riots in England, 1792–1818', *Popular protest and public order: six studies in British history, 1790–1920*, ed. J. Stevenson and R. Quinault (London, 1974), pp. 33-74; E. P. Thompson, *The making of the English working class* (London, 1963), pp. 67-8, 142-3.
73 Ibid., pp. 140-9.
74 Marshall, *Norfolk*, I, 181; Chitty, *Treatise*, II, 1209.
75 *The Times*, 27 Sept. 1791; see also *Gentleman's Magazine*, LVIII (1788), 817-18.
76 *Parl. Reg.*, VI, 283 (I have made some minor alterations in the punctuation). On Coke's bill, see above, p. 26.
77 Henry B. Wheatley, ed., *Memoirs of Sir Nathaniel William Wraxall, 1772–1784* (London, 1884), II, 267-8.
78 *The Times*, 24 Sept. 1791; *Poetical remarks on the game laws* (London, 1797), pp. 12-23.
79 *Salisbury Journal*, 29 Aug. 1785; for a similar report from the north, see ibid., 19 Sept. 1785.
80 *Salisbury Journal*, 15 Nov., 6 Dec. 1790; Chester Kirby, 'English game law reform', in *Essays in modern English history in honor of Wilbur Cortez Abbott* (Cambridge, Mass., 1941), p. 358.
81 See above, p. 46.
82 Zouch, *An account*, pp. 9, 22-3.

83   Arthur Young, *Travels in France during the years 1787, 1788 and 1789,* ed. Jeffrey
      Kaplow (Garden City, N.Y., 1969), pp. 9, 441-2. Cf. Oliver Goldsmith, *A
      history of the earth and animated nature* (Glasgow, 1837–40), III, 143.
84   J. M. Roberts and John Hardman, eds., *French revolution documents* (Oxford,
      1966–73), II, 152.
85   Young, *Travels in France*, p. 195; Lewis, *Yale Edn of Walpole's Correspondence*,
      XXXIV, 64, 69 (Walpole to Lady Ossory, 13 Sept., 26 Sept. 1789).
86   See Thomas Paine, *The rights of man* (Everyman edn, 1915), pp. 52, 232; G. D.
      H. Cole and A. W. Filson, eds., *British working class movements: select documents,
      1789–1875* (London, 1951), pp. 49, 57. See also Kirby, 'English game law
      reform', p. 359.
87   Andrews, *Torrington diaries*, IV, 10.
88   Charlotte Barrett, ed., *Diary and letters of Madame D'Arblay* (London, 1904), IV,
      340; George T. Kenyon, *The life of Lloyd, first Lord Kenyon, lord chief justice of
      England* (London, 1873), p. 266. (For the latter reference, I am grateful to
      Daniel Duman.)
89   See Hughes, *North country life*, II, 115-32, 209-92. At this time Curwen was
      still a strict game preserver. When, for example, several young men were
      found coursing on one of his manors in 1790, he wrote to his agent, 'I should
      be glad to prosecute Mr Ellwoods son . . . I am fully determined to make
      some examples' (Cumberland R.O., D/Cu/3/59: J. Christian [Curwen] to
      Charles Udale, [?Mar., 1790]). In 1816, however, he ceased all game
      preservation on his estates (see ibid., D/Cu/3/43, p. 314), presumably on
      principle.
90   *Parl. Reg.*, XLIV, 231-9; *Senator*, XV, 1186-98.
91   *Parl. Reg.,* XLIV, 242-3, 245.
92   Ibid., pp. 241-2, 246; *C.J.*, LI, 475.
93   *Senator*, XV, 1253-5; *Parl. Reg.*, XLIV, 332-3; *C.J.*, LI, 499, 504, 524, 526.
94   *Parl Papers, 1731–1800*, Bills, XXVI, no. 771; *Parl. Reg.*, XLIV, 236.
95   E.g., *Some considerations* (1796), pp. 87-9; H.M.C., *Verulam*, p. 165.
96   *C.J.*, LI, 644. Several days later, Curwen tried to bring in a bill to take away
      the option of civil prosecution for game offences, but that too was defeated:
      see *Senator*, XV, 1612-13.
97   *Some considerations* (1796), p. 3; see also *Senator*, XV, 1254.
98   *Parl. Reg.*, XLIV, 564-5.
99   Ibid., p. 232; see also pp. 240-1. For earlier praise of resident gentry, see
      Laurence, *Duty of a steward*, p. 57.
100   Quoted in Kenyon, *Life of Kenyon*, p. 267.
101   The Act permitted J.P.s summarily to imprison, whip and impress members
      of poaching 'gangs'. See Appendix, I.C.2.c.1800 for details, and *Senator*,
      XXV, 965, 1114-15, 1342-3 for the debate.
102   *Parl. Reg.,* XLIV, 238.

Chapter 6

1   R. M. Hartwell, *The industrial revolution and economic growth* (London, 1971), p.
     121; E. J. Hobsbawm, *Industry and empire: an economic history of Britain since
     1750* (London, 1968), p. 47.
2   Brian R. Mitchell and Phyllis Deane, *Abstract of British historical statistics*
     (Cambridge, 1962), pp. 24, 26.
3   A. H. John, 'Farming in wartime, 1793–1815', *Land, labour and population in*

the industrial revolution: essays presented to J. D. Chambers, ed. E. L. Jones and G. E. Mingay (London, 1967), pp. 30-2.

4 Mitchell & Deane, *Abstract*, p. 488.

5 Thompson, *English landed society*, pp. 217-22; J. D. Chambers and G. E. Mingay, *The agricultural revolution, 1750–1880* (London, 1966), pp. 111-18.

6 John, 'Farming in wartime', pp. 32-3; Chambers & Mingay, *Agricultural revolution*, pp. 118-19.

7 *Annual Register*, IV (1761), pt. 2, pp. 207-8. I am indebted to Robert Malcolmson for this reference. See also E. P. Thompson, 'Patrician society, plebian culture', *Journal of Social History*, VII (1973–4), 388-9, and James Obelkevich, *Religion and rural society: South Lindsey, 1825–75* (Oxford, 1976), ch. 2.

8 Thompson, *English landed society*, pp. 227-30.

9 Norfolk R.O., Walsingham MSS, XLVIII/32: E. Stracey to Lord Walsingham, 30 Sept. 1816.

10 Cobbett, *Rural rides*, I, 265-6.

11 Jeffery, *Dyott's diary*, I, 343; see also Robert Southey, 'The poor', *Quarterly Review*, XV (1816), 196.

12 E. J. Hobsbawm and George Rudé, *Captain Swing* (New York, 1968), pp. 38-46; see also Cobbett, *Rural rides*, I, 266-7.

13 Hobsbawm & Rudé, *Captain Swing*, pp. 42-4.

14 Chambers & Mingay, *Agricultural revolution*, pp. 96-8; Thompson, *Making of the English working class*, pp. 217-18.

15 See J.D. Chambers, 'Enclosure and the labour supply in the industrial revolution', *Econ. Hist. Rev.*, 2nd ser., V (1953), 319-43.

16 Southey, 'The poor', p. 197. See also J. R. Poynter, *Society and pauperism: English ideas on poor relief, 1795–1834* (London & Toronto, 1969), pp. 98-105.

17 Mitchell & Deane, *Abstract*, p. 488.

18 Norfolk R.O., How 750/76.

19 Thompson, *English landed society*, pp. 233-5; Chambers & Mingay, *Agricultural revolution*, pp. 126-8. See also David Grigg, *The agricultural revolution in South Lincolnshire* (Cambridge, 1966), pp. 117-36.

20 Hobsbawm & Rudé, *Captain Swing*, p. 72; E. L. Jones, 'The agricultural labour market in England, 1793–1872', *Econ. Hist. Rev.*, 2nd ser., XVII (1964–5), 325.

21 Chambers & Mingay, *Agricultural revolution*, p. 129.

22 Hobsbawm & Rudé, *Captain Swing*, pp. 357-65.

23 Glos. R.O., D2067: J. C. Hayward to Isaac Hayward, 11 Sept. 1826.

24 Poynter, *Society and pauperism*, pp. 76-85; Daniel A. Baugh, 'The cost of poor relief in south-east England, 1790–1834', *Econ. Hist. Rev.*, 2nd ser., XXVIII (1975), 57-9.

25 Hobsbawm & Rudé, *Captain Swing*, pp. 49-53, 76-7; Baugh, 'Cost of poor relief', pp. 62-7. See also Mark Neuman, 'Speenhamland in Berkshire', *Comparative development of social welfare*, ed. E. W. Martin (London, 1972), pp. 85-127.

26 Wilts. R.O., QS/Great Rolls, 1780–1810: Gaol Calendars; see also Munsche, 'Game laws in Wiltshire', pp. 226-7.

27 *The Times*, 23 Jan. 1805, 11 Jan. 1809; for other examples, see ibid., 21 July 1795, 16 Feb. 1801, 2 Jan. 1804, and *Annual Register*, XLVII (1805), 435; LIII (1811), 8.

28 *C.J.*, LXXVII, 1190. Although much more accurate than the returns of game

convictions, these totals of committals should be treated cautiously, since they were based on the somewhat shaky statistical skills of the clerks of the peace. They are significant, however, since it was on these figures that proponents of the game law reform based their case: see p. 144 below.

29   Wilts. R.O., QS/Great Rolls, Gaol Calendars, 1812–17; *Parl. Papers*, 1826, VI, 35. These figures include both summary committals and those ordered by quarter sessions and assizes. See also *1827 Crime Report*, pp. 39, 41, for Suffolk committals.

30   See above, pp. 99-101.

31   Based on the 361 surviving conviction certificates for these years, on deposit in the Wilts. R.O.

32   *1823 Game Report*, p. 46.

33   Ibid., p. 13; see also p. 31; *1827 Crime Report*, p. 42; *1828 Game Report*, pp. 38, 46, 71-2, 89; and *Warwick Advertiser*, 4 Nov., 25 Nov. 1815.

34   See Pollock, 'Game Laws', pp. 27-9.

35   *The Times*, 7 Jan. 1820, 11 Jan. 1825, 24 Dec. 1827; see also ibid., 28 Dec. 1827, 20 Dec. 1828, 29 Dec. 1828.

36   W. Sussex R.O., Goodwood MS 636: Earl of Tyrconnel to Duke of Richmond, 3 Oct. 1831. See also Goodwood MS 628: R. B. Laudenor to [Lord Eldon], 24 Sept. 1831, which gives a similar description for the area around Newcastle.

37   *The Times*, 25 Dec. 1822.

38   *1828 Game Report*, p. 32.

39   Beds. R.O., H/WS 1502; *Warwick Advertiser*, 18 Apr. 1829.

40   Ibid., 3 Jan., 11 Apr., 18 Apr. 1829. For similar incidents, see *The Times*, 30 Jan. 1816, 5 Jan. 1824, 23 Dec. 1826, 2 Jan. 1827, 24 Dec. 1827, 4 Feb. 1828; *Bell's Weekly Messenger*, 9 Dec. 1827, 16 Dec. 1827; *1828 Game Report*, p. 101.

41   *The Times*, 4 Feb. 1828. 'Curse thee,' the defendants were reported to have said to Tanner, 'if we had got a rope round thy neck, with the end round a beam, we would pull it tight enough to do thy business.' Since the jury found only three of the defendants guilty, some of his former associates may have had an opportunity to act on this threat (see ibid., 5 Mar. 1828).

42   Ibid., 1 Mar. 1820, 2 Jan. 1829; see also *Warwick Advertiser*, 22 Feb. 1823, and above, p. 98.

43   *Warwick Advertiser*, 2 May 1829. The sentences were this severe because the defendants were indicted for felonious assault; had they been charged under the game laws, the punishments would have been lighter. Cf. Hammond, *Village labourer*, pp. 191-2.

44   *The Times*, 30 Jan. 1816. See also *Herts. records*, II, 257-8; *1823 Game Report*, pp. 29-33.

45   Cobbett, *Rural rides,* I, 228-9. For examples of their success, see *Warwick Advertiser*, 27 Jan. 1816, 10 Jan. 1829; *The Times*, 25 Nov. 1823, 16 Jan. 1828, 4 Feb. 1828, 22 Dec. 1828; *Bell's Weekly Messenger,* 24 Jan. 1830.

46   *1828 Game Report*, p. 101; see also Edward Peacock, 'Trial under the game laws', pp. 221-2.

47   Jeffery, *Dyott's diary*, II, 65; W. Sussex R.O., Goodwood MS 628: Reginald Bray to the Duke of Richmond, 20 Sept. 1831.

48   *Annual Register*, LXX (1828), 142-3; see also *Warwick Advertiser*, 27 Dec. 1823, and C. E. Long, *Considerations on the game laws* (London, 1824), p. 33.

49   *1828 Game Report*, p. 79.

50   *C.J.*, LXXXI, 235. See also ibid., LXXVIII, 250; LXXIX, 325; LXXX, 103; LXXXI, 337-8; LXXXII, 433; LXXXV, 26; *L.J.*, LVI, 238; LVII, 35-6; LVIII,

112, 315; LIX, 179; LXII, 20; and Sydney Smith, *The works of the Rev. Sydney Smith* (4th edn, London, 1848), II, 328.

51   Indeed, when he was not ignored by the reformers, he was criticised by them, especially for his assertion that from the time of the Conquest game had been the property of the monarch. With great show of erudition – but not much evidence – the reformers insisted that under common law game was, and always had been, the property of the landowner (see Chitty, *Treatise*, I, 3-10; Christian, *Treatise*, pp. 22-56; *Parl. Deb.*, 2nd ser., XVI, col. 682). Such a view undoubtedly helped the reformers' case. If game already was the property of the landowner, then reform of the game laws became a conservative measure: a confirmation of the status quo. Small wonder, then, that Blackstone was summarily dismissed in favour of lesser lights like Edward Christian, whose condescending treatment of 'the learned Commentator' would have, in any other circumstances, been recognised as ludicrous presumption.

52   *Thoughts on the present laws for preserving the game* (London, 1750), pp. 8-9; *Considerations on the game laws* (London, 1777), p. 5. See also *Essays on the game laws*, pp. 22-3, and Taplin, *An appeal*, pp. 40-1.

53   Unless the buyer was a higgler, chapman, carrier, innkeeper, victualler, or alehouse keeper, the purchase of game by whom had already been prohibited by the Act of 1707 (5 Anne, c. 14, s. 2).

54   58 Geo. III, c. 75. This Act – which did not completely end the anomaly, since buyers of game were not subject to imprisonment in default of paying the fine – was opposed by most reformers. There were, however, exceptions, the most notable being Sir Samuel Romilly. 'It is the buyers of game who encourage and make poachers', he wrote in his diary, justifying his support of the bill: *Memoirs of the life of Sir Samuel Romilly* (2nd edn, London, 1840), III, 345. For the debate on the bill, see *Parl. Deb.*, 1st ser., XXXVII, cols. 508-10; XXXVIII, cols. 540-8, 757-60, 1071-6, 1185-6.

55   *1823 Game Report*, pp. 11, 18; *1828 Game Report*, pp. 20-1. For the reaction of the Act's sponsor to its failure, see Bankes, *Reconsiderations*, pp. 43-4.

56   *A letter on the game laws. By a country gentleman* (London, 1815), pp. 13-14. See also *Parl. Deb.*, 1st ser., XXXVIII, cols. 543-4, and *1828 Game Report*, p. 80.

57   *Parl. Deb.*, 2nd ser., X, col. 920; see also ibid., 2nd ser., XII, col. 953, and Jeffery, *Dyott's diary*, I, 373.

58   *Parl. Deb.*, 2nd ser., XI, col. 1200; see also ibid., 2nd ser., XIX, col. 283; 3rd ser., II, col. 600.

59   Ibid., 3rd ser., V, col. 939. *The Times*, 19 Mar. 1823. See also *Parl. Deb.*, 3rd ser., II, col. 599. For similar arguments in the eighteenth century, see *Considerations of the game laws* (1777), pp. 60-1, and *Salisbury Journal*, 8 Dec. 1788.

60   Compare, for example, *1823 Game Report*, pp. 21, 35, with ibid., p. 26, and *1828 Game Report*, pp. 13, 45. For examples of conservative scepticism on this point, see *Parl. Deb.*, 1st ser., XXXVI, col. 923; 2nd ser., X, col. 905; 2nd ser., XXI, col. 465.

61   Ibid., 2nd ser., XIX, col. 285; see also ibid., 2nd ser., X, col. 1420; 2nd ser., XVIII, col. 353.

62   Ibid., 2nd ser., XIX, cols. 279-80; see also ibid., 1st ser., XXXVI, col. 924, and *Letter on the game laws*, p. 8.

63   *Parl. Deb.*, 2nd ser., XVI, col. 686; see also *1828 Game Report*, pp. 74-7, and Smith, *Works*, II, 327.

64   Ibid., 2nd ser., XI, col. 1201; 2nd ser., XIII, col. 307; 2nd ser., X, col. 925.

See also ibid., 2nd ser., XVII, cols. 740-1, and Lord Suffield, *Considerations on the game laws* (London, 1825), pp. 68-70.

65   *Parl. Deb.*, 1st ser., XXXIX, col. 945; see also ibid., 2nd ser., X, cols. 904-5, and *A letter to Sir John Shelley on the game laws* (London, 1819), p. 6.

66   *Parl. Deb.*, 2nd ser., XVII, col. 270; *1828 Crime Report*, p. 7; *Parl. Deb.*, 3rd ser., V, col. 950. See also ibid., 2nd ser., XXI, col. 466, and Bankes, *Reconsiderations*, p. 41.

67   *Parl. Deb.*, 2nd ser., XVIII, col. 357; 2nd ser., IX, col. 645; *1828 Game Report*, p. 38. See also *Parl. Deb.*, 2nd ser., XIII, col. 300; 2nd ser., XVI, cols. 687-8.

68   Ibid., 2nd ser., XIX, col. 286; see also ibid., 2nd ser., XVII, col. 735, and Jeffery, *Dyott's diary*, II, 70.

69   See above, pp. 62-4.

70   *Memoirs of Romilly*, III, 283.

71   *The Times*, 10 Nov. 1828; see also *Warwick Advertiser*, 22 Feb. 1823, and Hammond, *Village Labourer*, pp. 188-9.

72   *1828 Crime Report*, p. 24; *The Times*, 29 Jan. 1829. See also *1828 Crime Report*, p. 34, and *1823 Game Report*, p. 32.

73   *Parl. Papers*, 1830-1, XII, 573-89. In Wiltshire, the average age of those committed for game offences in the three years before Waterloo was thirty-two; in the following three years, the average age was twenty-five. The percentage of those committed who were twenty years of age or under in these two periods was thirty and thirty-six respectively.

74   *Parl. Deb.*, 2nd ser., XVII, col. 735; see also *1827 Crime Report*, pp. 16, 28, 33, 41.

   An 'experiment' conducted by Lord Carnarvon on his Hampshire estates in this period is instructive. In the mid-1820s he abolished income supplements for his labourers and instead raised their wages to more than a subsistence level. In addition, he instituted a programme of winter employment for his labourers. The result, he claimed, was the complete reformation of the labouring population in these parishes. Those who had been 'loose and idle' became 'tidy and genteel'; poaching almost disappeared, while in neighbouring parishes it continued unabated: see *1828 Game Report*, pp. 84-8. See also Jones, 'Agricultural labour market', p. 327.

75   See graph, p. 100.

76   See, for example, the committals to New Bailey, Salford, in these years: *1828 Crime Report*, p. 104.

77   *1828 Game Report*, pp. 34, 67, 75, 78.

78   Quoted in C. J. Hunt, *The lead miners of the northern Pennines in the eighteenth and nineteenth centuries* (Manchester, 1970), p. 223. A preceding verse states that the times were hard and 'the miners were starving almost' when this incident occurred, and that may have been so. This should not, however, overshadow the evident class feeling against 'fat men' who attempted to interfere with a pastime in which the miners regularly indulged, whatever the economic climate.

79   On the Luddites, see Thompson, *Making of the English working class*, p. 411, and J. L. and Barbara Hammond, *The skilled labourer, 1760–1832* (London, 1919), pp. 225, 241.

80   *Beauties of the game laws exhibited* (London, 1823), p. 1; see also Rev. William Herbert, *A letter to the chairman of the committee of the House of Commons on the game laws* (London, 1823), pp. 3-4.

81   *C.J.*, LXXI, 381, 393, 400, 516; *Parl. Deb.*, 1st ser., XXXIV, cols. 586-7; *A second letter on the game laws. By a country gentleman, a proprietor of game* (London, 1817), pp. 8-30.

82 *Parl. Papers*, 1816, IV, 507-9. Edward Christian (see n. 51 above) claimed, characteristically, that the Committee's report was based completely on his own criticisms of Blackstone (see his *Treatise*, preface and p. 68). There may be some truth to the claim.

83 *Parl. Deb.*, lst ser., XXXV, cols. 876-9; 1st ser., XXXVI, cols. 921-8. For the bill, see *Parl. Papers*, 1817, I, 179-82.

84 *Parl. Deb.*, 1st ser., XXXIX, cols. 937-50, 1078-90; 1st ser., XL, cols. 374-84. For the bill, see *Parl. Papers*, 1819, I, 723-38.

85 *C.J.*, LXXIV, 496, 503, 549, 565, 572; *Parl. Papers*, 1819, I, 741-5.

86 *Parl. Deb.*, 2nd ser., V, cols. 38-42; 2nd ser., VIII, cols. 541-3.

87 *1823 Game Report*, pp. 3-4.

88 *C.J.*, LXXVIII, 251, 253, 358, 368, 439; *Parl. Deb.*, 2nd ser., IX, cols. 644-8; *Parl. Papers*, 1823, I, 541-62.

89 W. Suffolk R.O., E2/21/2: Sir Thomas Cullum to his son, [Mar.] 1824, 'No. 7'. See also Chapter 3, n. 61.

90 *The Times*, 15 Oct. 1819; *Parl. Deb.*, 2nd ser., XIII, cols. 1266-7. On his career in general, see entry in the *D.N.B.*, and Caroline Grosvenor and Charles Beilby Stuart Wortley, *The first Lady Wharncliffe and her family, 1779–1856* (London, 1927).

91 For a discussion of the conservatives' case against reform, see below, pp. 164-8.

92 *Parl. Deb.*, 2nd ser., X, cols. 187-90, 902-26, 1415-23; 2nd ser., XI, cols. 389-92, 956-9; *Parl. Papers*, 1824, I, 579-659. For the petitions, including one from William Cobbett, against the bill, see *C.J.*, LXXIX, 203-4, 212, 234, 313, 320, 332, 354, 366, 441. Following the bill's defeat, the supporters of legalisation once again brought in a measure of their own, this time in the House of Lords. It, however, was withdrawn before second reading: see *Parl. Deb.*, 2nd ser., XI, cols. 1097, 1199-1201.

93 Ibid., 2nd ser., XII, cols. 528-9, 950-7; 2nd ser., XIII, cols. 300-7; *Parl. Papers*, 1825, II, 401-66.

94 *Parl. Deb.*, 2nd ser., XIII, cols. 449-53.

95 Not that they all agreed with Wharncliffe on everything. Lord Suffield, for instance, favoured (and eventually secured) the abolition of spring guns and man traps, while Wharncliffe defended their use. Suffield also disagreed with the form of Wharncliffe's bill, preferring a simple repeal of the game code and dependence thereafter on the law of trespass: see Bacon, *Memoir of Suffield*, p. 258.

96 In addition to those cited in n. 50 above, see also *LJ.*, LIX, 115 (from Bury St Edmunds), and *C.J.*, LXXXII, 371 (from Devizes, Devon). The Bury St Edmunds petition was engineered by Lord Calthorpe, another reforming peer, and was used as the occasion for the introduction of Wharncliffe's bill in 1827: see W. Suffolk R.O., E2/21/2: Sir Thomas Cullum to his son, 25 Jan. 1827.

97 *Parl. Deb.*, 2nd ser., XVI, cols. 680-92; 2nd ser., XVII, cols. 268-70, 733-43.

98 *C.J.*, LXXXII, 465, 469, 508-9, 531, 586; *LJ.*, LIX, 333, 377, 381, 391, 403-4, 412, 416.

99 *Parl. Deb.*, 2nd ser., XVIII, cols. 350-9; *1828 Game Report*, pp. 3-4.

100 *Parl. Papers,* 1828, I, 39-47; *Parl. Deb.,* 2nd ser., XIX, cols. 279-89, 360-5, 595-6. The original compromise would have qualified leaseholders with ten acres, but Wharncliffe agreed to double this.

101 *C.J.*, LXXXIII, 348, 349, 385, 410, 411, 420, 429, 432, et passim; *Parl. Deb.*, 2nd ser., XIX, cols. 1364-6, 1690-3; *Parl. Papers*, 1828, I, 49-79.

102 *Parl. Deb.*, 2nd ser., XX, cols. 369-71; 2nd ser., XXI, cols. 465-7, 1241-52,

1592-5; *Parl. Papers*, 1829, I, 555-96. The fatal division was ninety-one to eighty-nine.

103   *Parl. Deb.*, 2nd ser., XXII, col. 845; *C.J.*, LXXXV, 92, 157, et passim; *Parl. Papers*, 1830, II, 373-95.

104   *Parl. Deb.*, 3rd ser., I, cols. 812-13; see also Hobsbawm & Rudé, *Captain Swing*, pp. 99, 128. Reported committals for game offences in the winter (Nov.–Feb.) of 1830–1 actually declined by a third from the level of the previous winter: see *Parl. Papers*, 1831–2, XXXIII, 171-95.

105   *Parl. Deb.*, 3rd ser., II, cols. 393, 555-6, 594-6.

106   Ibid., 3rd ser., V, cols. 387, 939-66; 3rd ser., VI, cols. 954-5, 1061-3; *Parl. Papers*, 1830–1, II, 9-49.

107   *Parl. Deb.*, 3rd ser., VII, cols. 129-34, 493-94; *L.J.*, LXIII, 1015-17. This was the bill's major hurdle in the House of Lords. The conservatives, perhaps anticipating the struggle over the second Great Reform Bill, decided 'that we had better take this bill' (2nd Duke of Wellington, ed., *Despatches, correspondence and memoranda of Field Marshall Arthur, Duke of Wellington* [London, 1867–80], VII, 540-1).

108   *Parl. Deb.*, 3rd ser., VII, cols. 891-3; *C.J.*, LXXXVI, 880-1, 890; 1 & 2 Wm IV, c. 32. For details of the Act, see Appendix.

109   *Parl. Papers*, 1831-2, XXXIII, 171-95; ibid., 1833, XXIX, 221-54.

110   Ibid., 1844, XXXIX, 313-53. See also D. J. V. Jones, 'The poacher: a study in Victorian crime and protest', *Historical Journal*, XXII (1979), 829-32.

111   *Parl. Papers*, 1844, XXXIX, 311-13; see also Hobsbawm & Rudé, *Captain Swing*, pp. 285-87.

112   Edgcumbe, *Diary of Lady Shelley*, II, 209, 214. See also Malmesbury, *Half a century of sport*, p. 93, and Thompson, *English landed society*, p. 139.

113   Jeffery, *Dyott's diary*, II, 120. For other negative comments, see Glos. R.O., D2067: J. F. Hayward to Isaac Hayward, 4 Feb. 1832; Surrey R.O., 203/30/82.

114   43 & 44 Vic., c. 47. See also Chester Kirby, 'The attack on the game laws in the forties', *Journal of Modern History*, IV (1932), 18-37.

Chapter 7

1   Webb, *English local government*, I, 598.

2   Douglas Hay, 'Poaching and the game laws on Cannock Chase', *Albion's fatal tree*, ed. Hay *et al.*, pp. 189-253. While the virtues of Dr Hay's study are many, it should be pointed out that the grievances which he describes cannot all be attributed to the operation of the game laws. The centrepiece of the study, the battle over the rabbit warrens, was a conflict over common rights and would have occurred even if a property qualification for sporting had never been enacted. Similarly, the trouble over deer grew out of the Pagets' claim to a royal franchise of chase, not out of the game laws (the purpose of which was to confer sporting rights on a class, rather than on individuals). It might also be pointed out that there were very few areas in eighteenth-century England where rights of chase were still exercised. Most deer had long since been enclosed in parks, and thus were unable to cause the damage to crops that the Pagets' deer were responsible for. The game laws actually played only a minor part in the episodes which Dr Hay so admirably recounts. The real conflict on the Chase was over customary rights – both the Pagets' right of chase and the villagers' right of access to the common. Since the Pagets

used gamekeepers to enforce their rights – and to deny the villagers theirs – the game laws inevitably got drawn into the dispute, but it was not the gentry's collective monopoly on the game (as opposed to Lord Uxbridge's individual one) which was really at issue. While the gentry's monopoly was undoubtedly rejected by most of the villagers, it was the attempt to deny them their customary rights of common which led them openly and collectively to defy the lord of Beaudesert.

3   The phrase is J. P. Kenyon's in *The Stuart constitution, 1603–1688* (Cambridge, 1966), p. 494.

4   See, for example, *Parl. Papers,* 1820, XII, 253, a return of all game convictions in England between 1 Jan. 1819 and approximately 1 June 1820. Of the 1267 reported convicted, 662 were fined £5. See also above, p. 139.

5   See Appendix: I.A.1.a–b.

6   See ibid.: I.C.1–3.

7   Webb, *English local government,* I, 597, and above, p. 76.

8   5 Geo. II, c. 18. See also Landau, 'Gentry and gentlemen', pp. 238-9.

9   Circket, *Samuel Whitbread's notebooks*, pp. 30-1, 99, 102-3, 132-3. In two of these cases, a conviction resulted; in one, prosecution was waived in return for a 'promise of amendment'. The resolution of the fourth case is unclear.

10 This is open to some challenge. Most certificates of conviction under the Night Poaching and Game Duty Acts (22 per cent of the total surviving certificates for this period) omit the names of the informer and the witness. In addition, reasonably complete lists of gamekeepers are not available before 1785 (see Munsche, 'Game laws in Wiltshire', n. 31); thus the true identity of some informers and witnesses may be different from that given on the certificate.

11 On Webb, see Munsche, 'Game laws in Wiltshire', p. 225. For an analysis of the changing social composition of the commission of the peace, see Landau, 'Gentry and Gentlemen', chs. 6-7.

12 Evans, 'English rural anti-clericalism', pp. 101, 104.

13 See Hay, *Albion's fatal tree,* pp. 242-4, 246-7; see also above, p. 95.

14 See above, pp. 94-5.

15 E. P. Thompson, 'The moral economy of the English crowd in the eighteenth century', *Past & Present*, no. 50 (1971), pp. 76-136.

16 See Landau, 'Gentry and gentlemen', ch. 8.

17 Fendall & Crutchley, *Diary of Benjamin Newton,* p. 80; Jeffery, *Dyott's diary*, I, 385; see also ibid., II, 71. The early nineteenth century saw the re-entry of game cases into petty sessions jurisdiction: see Chapter 4, n. 10.

18 David Robinson, 'The game laws', *Blackwood's Magazine*, XXII (1827), 644.

19 *Parl. Deb.*, 2nd ser., XVII, cols. 737-8. Similar sentiments were expressed by William Heygate in a letter to 2nd Marquess of Salisbury at this time: see Hatfield, Salisbury MSS, Heygate to Salisbury, [misdated 1826: it was probably written in March or April 1827]. I am grateful to Mr R. H. Harcourt Williams, Librarian to Lord Salisbury, for pointing out this letter to me.

20 *Parl. Deb.*, 1st ser., XXXIX, cols. 945, 947; see also *Letter to Sir John Shelley*, p. 21.

21 The quotation is from Brand's speech in *Parl. Deb.*, 1st ser., XXXIX, col. 941. For Curwen see above, p. 130; for Wharncliffe see *Parl. Deb.,* 2nd ser., X, cols. 187-8.

22 Smith, *Works*, II, 35. See also Joseph Chitty, 'Observations on the game

laws', *The Pamphleteer*, IX, no. 17 (Jan. 1817), 181-2.

23   *Parl. Deb.*, 2nd ser., V, col. 39; ibid., 1st ser., XL, col. 377. See also *Letter to Sir John Shelley*, p. 14.
24   Ibid., p. 17.
25   Ibid., pp. 16-17; see also *Parl. Deb.*, 2nd ser., XVII, cols. 269, 737.
26   Ibid., 2nd ser., V, col. 41; 2nd ser., XI, col. 957; *Letter to Sir John Shelley*, p. 17; *Parl. Deb.*, 2nd ser., X, col. 905.
27   *Parl. Deb.*, 1st ser., XL, col. 374.
28   Ibid., 2nd ser., XVII, col. 737.
29   Bacon, *Memoir of Suffield*, pp. 184-5; see also Suffield, *Considerations*, p. 104.
30   *Parl. Deb.*, 1st ser., XXXIX, col. 1090.
31   Ibid., 2nd ser., X, col. 1420; see also above, p. 146.
32   *C.J.*, LXXXVI, 50.
33   C.U.L., Buxton MSS, Box 9: A. H. Eyre to Sir Robert Buxton, 31 May 1829.

Bibliography

Note: the Bibliography has been divided into the following sections:
  I. Manuscript sources
    1. Public record repositories
    2. Private collections
  II. Printed sources
    1. Documents and debates
    2. Correspondence and diaries
    3. Pamphlets, treatises and literature
    4. Newspapers and periodicals
    5. Secondary sources
  III. Unpublished theses

I. Manuscript sources

1. Public record repositories

Bedfordshire Record Office, Bedford.
W1   Whitbread MSS: estate correspondence.
H/WS   Wilshere MSS: documents.
HW   How of Apsley Guise MSS: letters.
D.D.J.   St John of Bletsoe MSS: letters.
              Miscellaneous documents from other collections.

Berkshire Record Office, Reading.
D/EZ 30 F1 Diary of Robert Lee of Binfield, J.P., 1742–4.
D/EBy   Benyon MSS: estate correspondence.

British Library, Dept. of MSS, London.
Add. MSS, 32715   Newcastle MSS: letters.
              35887   Hardwicke MSS: documents.
              36916   John Starkey's newsletters, 1667–72.
              42598-9 Brockman MSS: diary of William Brockman, J.P., 1689–1721; diary of William Brockman, James Brockman and Ralph Drake, J.P.s, 1721–81.
Egerton MSS 215-63 Diary of Henry Cavendish, M.P., 1768–74.

Cambridge University Library, Dept. of MSS, Cambridge.
Buxton MSS: personal correspondence.

Cumberland Record Office, Carlisle.
D/Cu   Curwen MSS: estate correspondence and accounts.
D/Pen   Pennington MSS: estate correspondence.
          Grand Jury Book, 1771–96
Q/4/1-3   Summary Conviction Books, 1769–72, 1799–1829.

East Riding Record Office, Beverley.
DDGR   Grimston MSS: personal correspondence.

East Suffolk Record Office, Ipswich.
HA11   Rous Family Archives: letters.
HA12   Flixton Hall MSS: game books.
HA247   Edgar Family Archives: diary of Devereux Edgar, J.P., 1703–16.

East Sussex Record Office, Lewes.
Ashburnham Archives: diary of Visct St Asaph, 1827–9.
Frewen Archives: personal correspondence.
Glynde Place Archives: estate correspondence.
Quarter Sessions Order Books, 1685–1700.

Essex Record Office, Chelmsford.
D/DAr   Mark Hall Estate Papers: estate and personal correspondence.
D/DBy   Braybrooke Papers: estate accounts (Audley End).
D/DCv   Cavendish Collection: diary of William Holcroft, J.P., 1661–88.
Q/RSc   Summary Conviction Books, 1791–1832.
          Miscellaneous documents from other collections.

Gloucestershire Record Office, Gloucester.
D1283   Witts Collection: diaries of the Rev. F. E. Witts, J.P., 1815–25.
D1833   Rooke Family MSS: letters.
D2067   Hayward of Beverstone MSS: personal correspondence.
Q/SG   Gaol Calendars, 1728–1823.

Guildhall Library, London.
MS 2148   Order Books of the Company of Poulters, 1690–1790.

Hampshire Record Office, Winchester.
5M50   Daly MSS: letters.

House of Lords Record Office, London.
Committee Minute Books, House of Lords, 1671, 1693.

Kent Archives Office, Maidstone.
U23   Wykeham Martin MSS: diary of Ralph Buffkin, J.P., 1689–1713.
U31   Geary MSS: game book.
U269   Sackville of Knole MSS: estate correspondence and papers, personal
          correspondence.
U310   Norman MSS: diary of William Emmett, J.P., 1711–37.
U442   Ward Collection: diary of Paul D'Aranda, J.P., 1707–9.

U565   Darnley of Cobham Hall MSS: game book.
U771   Osborne Family Papers: diary of John Aucher, J.P., 1690–1702.
U951   Knatchbull MSS: personal correspondence; diary of Sir Wyndham Knatchbull, J.P., 1734–45; diary of Sir Edward Knatchbull, J.P., 1819–22.
U1015   Papillon MSS: personal correspondence.
U1121   Marsham MSS: estate papers.
U1359   Townsend (Sydney) MSS: estate papers.
PS/   Petty Sessions Minute Books for divisions of Wingham, Bearstead, Bromley, Malling, Tonbridge, Upper Scray, North Aylesford, Sevenoaks and Ashford.
Q/SB   Quarter Sessions Papers, including summary convictions and gaol calendars, 1670–1820.
Q/SPi   Quarter Sessions Process Books, 1649–1792.
          Miscellaneous documents from other collections.

Norfolk Record Office, Norwich.
How   Howard (Castle Rising) Collection: estate correspondence.
MS 20640 Diary of Robert Buxton of Shadewell, 1794, 1808.
NRS 22696 Suffield MSS: estate correspondence.
          Walsingham MSS: estate and personal correspondence.
          Miscellaneous documents from other collections.

North Riding Record Office, Northallerton.
ZK   Kirkleatham Hall Archives: letters.

Northumberland Record Office, Newcastle upon Tyne.
ZM1/S   Belsay MSS: letters.

Sheffield Central Library, Sheffield.
          Arundel Castle MSS: estate correspondence and papers.
EM 821   Elmhirst MSS: documents.
OD 1385   Bagshawe of Oakes (Derbys.) MSS: letters and documents.
Wh.M.   Wharncliffe Muniments: estate and personal papers.

Staffordshire Record Office, Stafford.
D260   Hatherton Collection: estate correspondence.
D554   Bill Family Papers: letters.
D590   Giffard MSS: estate papers and accounts.
D593   Sutherland MSS: estate correspondence, papers and accounts.
D661   Dyott MSS: game books; diary of Gen. William Dyott, J.P., 1781–1845.

Surrey Record Office, Kingston.
203   Howard (Ashstead) Papers: estate correspondence.

Warwickshire Record Office, Warwick.
CR 103   Diary of Sir William Bromley, J.P., 1685–1728.
CR 136   Newdigate MSS: diary of Sir Roger Newdigate, 1751–1806.

West Suffolk Record Office, Bury St Edmunds.
E2   Cullum MSS: personal correspondence.
          Miscellaneous documents from other collections.

West Sussex Record Office, Chichester.
Cowdray Archives: estate papers.
Goodwood MSS: estate accounts and papers; personal correspondence.
Mitford Archives: account book of Henry Ayling, gamekeeper, 1830–1.

William Salt Library, Stafford.
26/22   Whitworth MSS: personal papers.

Wiltshire Record Office, Trowbridge.
229   Diary of Sir Richard Colt Hoare, J.P., 1815–34.
           Longleat MSS: estate accounts.
332   Penruddocke MSS: letters and documents.
           Savernake MSS: estate correspondence.
383   Stourhead MSS: game books; papers and diary of Sir Richard Colt
           Hoare, J.P., 1785–1815.
           Gamekeepers' Deputation Roll, 1760–1830.
           Gaol Calendars, 1728–1830.
           Summary Convictions, 1740–1822.
           Miscellaneous documents from other collections.

2. Private collections

Aylesford MSS, Packington Hall, Warwickshire.
   Letters, estate accounts, personal papers.
Holkham MSS, Holkham Hall, Norfolk.
   Estate accounts.
Salisbury MSS, Hatfield House, Hertfordshire.
   Letters of the 2nd Marquess of Salisbury.

II. Printed sources

1. Documents and debates

Atkinson, J. C., ed. *Quarter sessions records*. 9 vols. London: Publication of the North Riding Record Society, 1884–92.
Calendar of state papers, domestic series, James II, preserved in the Public Record Office. 3 vols. London, 1960–72.
Calendar of state papers, domestic series, of the reign of Anne, preserved in the Public Record Office. 2 vols. London, 1916–24.
Calendar of state papers, domestic series, of the reign of Charles II, preserved in the state paper department of Her Majesty's Public Record Office. 28 vols. London, 1860–1939.
Calendar of state papers, domestic series, of the reign of William and Mary, preserved in the Public Record Office. 11 vols. London, 1895–1937.
Cobbett, William, and Wright, John, eds. *The parliamentary history of England, from the earliest period to the year 1803*. 36 vols. London, 1806–20.
Cole, G. D. H., and Filson, A. W., eds. *British working class movements: select documents, 1789–1875*. London, 1951.
A collection of parliamentary debates in England, from the year M,DC,LXVIII to the present time. 22 vols. N.p., 1742.
Epping Forest Commission. *The rolls of the court of attachments of the Royal Forest of Waltham in the county of Essex, from the 31st October A.D. 1713 to the 6th December A.D. 1848*. 5 vols. London, 1873.

Fowle, J. P. M., ed. *Wiltshire quarter sessions and assizes, 1736.* Publication of the Wiltshire Archaeological and Natural History Society, XI (1955).

Gretton, Mary Sturge. *Oxfordshire justices of the peace in the seventeenth century.* Publication of the Oxfordshire Record Society, XVI (1934).

Grey, Anchitell. *Debates of the house of commons from the year 1667 to the year 1694.* 10 vols. London, 1769.

Hansard, T. C., ed. *The parliamentary debates from the year 1803 to the present time.* Series 1-3. 222 vols. London, 1803–91.

Hertfordshire county records. 10 vols. Hertford, 1905–57.

Historical Manuscript Commission. *Fourteenth report of the royal commission on historical manuscripts.* London, 1896.

The manuscripts of the house of lords. New series. 11 vols. London, 1900–62.

The manuscripts of J. B. Fortesque, Esq., preserved at Dropmore. 8 vols. London, 1899–1927.

Ninth report of the royal commission on historical manuscripts. 3 vols. London, 1883–4.

Report on manuscripts in various collections. 8 vols. London, 1901–14.

Report on the manuscripts of the Earl of Verulam. Preserved at Gorhambury. London, 1906.

Report on the manuscripts of His Grace the Duke of Buccleuch and Queensbury, K.G., K.T. Preserved at Montagu House, Whitehall. 3 vols. London, 1899–1926.

Report on the manuscripts of the Marquess of Lothian. Preserved at Blickling Hall, Norfolk. London, 1905.

Supplementary report on the manuscripts of Robert Graham, Esq., of Fintry. London, 1942.

Thirteenth report of the royal commission on historical manuscripts. London, 1892.

Twelfth report of the royal commission on historical manuscripts. London, 1890.

House of Commons. *Sessional papers, 1731–1800.*

Sessional papers, 1801–1900.

Howell, Thomas Bayley, and Howell, Thomas Jones, eds. *A complete collection of state trials and proceedings for high treason and other crimes and misdemeanours from the earliest period.* 33 vols. London, 1809–26.

Hughes, Paul L., and Larkin, James F., eds. *Tudor royal proclamations.* 3 vols. New Haven & London, 1964–9.

Journals of the house of commons.

Journals of the house of lords.

Lawson-Tancred, Sir Thomas, ed. *Records of a Yorkshire manor.* London, 1937.

Le Hardy, William, and Reckitt, Geoffrey Ll., eds. *County of Buckingham. Calendar to the sessions records.* 3 vols. Aylesbury, 1933–9.

The parliamentary register; or, history of the proceedings and debates of the house of commons. 112 vols. London, 1775–1813.

Peyton, S.A., ed. *Minutes of proceedings in quarter sessions held for the parts of Kesteven in the county of Lincoln, 1674–1695.* 2 vols. Publication of the Lincoln Record Society, XXV-VI (1931).

Pickering, Danby, ed. *The statutes at large.* 46 vols. Cambridge, 1762–1807.

Quarter sessions records for the county of Somerset. Vol. IV: *Charles II (1666–1677).* Publication of the Somerset Record Society, XXXIV (1919).

Ratcliff, S.C., and Johnson, H.C., eds. *Warwick county records.* 9 vols. Warwick, 1935–64.

Roberts, J. M., and Hardman, John, eds. *French revolution documents.* 2 vols. Oxford, 1966–73.

Salzman, L. F., ed. *Record of deputations of gamekeepers.* Publication of the Sussex Record Society, LI (1950).

The Senator; or, Clarendon's parliamentary chronicle. Series 1-2. 32 vols. London, 1790–
    1802.
The statutes at large, passed in the parliaments held in Ireland. 20 vols. Dublin, 1786–1801.
Steel, Robert, ed. *Tudor and Stuart proclamations, 1485–1714.* 2 vols. Oxford, 1910.
Steer, Francis W., ed. *Farm and cottage inventories of mid-Essex, 1635–1749.* 2nd end.
    London & Chichester, 1969.
Stockdale, William, ed. *Debates of the third session of the sixteenth parliament.* 3 vols.
    London, 1785.
Tomlins, T. E., Raithby, J., *et al.*, eds. *The statutes of the United Kingdom.* 29 vols.
    London, 1804–69.
Walker, J. W., ed. *Hackness manuscripts and accounts.* The Yorkshire Archaeological
    Society, Record Series, XCV (1937).

2. Correspondence and diaries

Andrews, C. B., ed. *The Torrington diaries.* 4 vols. London, 1934.
Bagley, J. J., ed. *The great diurnal of Nicholas Blundell of Little Crosby, Lancashire.* 3 vols.
    Publication of the Record Society of Lancashire and Cheshire, 1968–72.
Barrett, Charlotte, ed. *Diary and letters of Madame D'Arblay.* 6 vols. London, 1904.
Beresford, John, ed. *The diary of a country parson: the Reverend James Woodforde.* 5 vols.
    Oxford, 1924–31.
*A Berkshire bachelor's diary: being the diary and letters of Francis Prior, recusant and gentleman
    farmer of Ufton, Berks., in the latter half of the 18th century.* Newbury, 1936.
Black, Clementina, ed. *The Cumberland letters: being the correspondence of Richard
    Dennison Cumberland and George Cumberland between the years, 1771 and 1784.*
    London, 1912.
Branch-Johnson, William, ed. *The Carrington diary.* London, 1956.
Brockbank, W., and Kenworthy, F., eds. *The diary of Richard Kay, 1716–1751, of
    Baldingstone, near Bury: a Lancashire doctor.* Publication of the Chetham Society,
    3rd series, XVI (1968).
Brown, A. F. J., ed. *Essex people, 1750–1900.* Chelmsford, 1972.
Buxton, Charles, ed. *Memoirs of Sir Thomas Fowell Buxton, Baronet.* London, 1848.
Christian, Garth, ed. *A Victorian poacher: James Hawker's journal.* London, 1961.
Circket, Alan E., ed. *Samuel Whitbread's notebooks, 1810–11, 1813–14.* Publication of
    Bedfordshire Historical Record Society, L. (1971).
Colchester, Charles, 2nd Baron, ed. *The diary and correspondence of Charles Abbott, Lord
    Colchester.* 3 vols. London, 1861.
Cox, Rev. Ernest W., ed. 'An old Sussex household diary', *Sussex Archaeological
    Collections*, LXVII (1926), 196-202.
Cozens-Hardy, Basil, ed. *The diary of Sylas Neville, 1767–1788.* Oxford, 1950.
    Mary Hardy's diary. Publication of the Norfolk Record Society, XXXVII (1968).
Cuming, E. D., ed. *Squire Osbaldeston: his autobiography.* London, 1927.
'Diary of Thomas Smith, Esq.', *Wiltshire Archaeological and Natural History Magazine*,
    XI (1869), 82-105, 204-17, 308-14.
Dickinson, H. T., ed. *The correspondence of Sir James Clavering.* Publication of the
    Surtees Society, CLXXVIII (1967).
Edgcumbe, Richard, ed. *The diary of Frances Lady Shelley, 1787–1873.* 2 vols. London,
    1913.
Eland, G., ed. *Purefoy letters, 1735–1753.* 2 vols. London, 1931.
Farr, M. W., ed. 'Sir Edward Littleton's fox-hunting diary, 1774–89', *Essays in
    Staffordshire history presented to S. A. H. Burne:* Ed. M. W. Greenslade. *Collections for
    a History of Staffordshire*, 4th series, VI (1970).

Fendall, C. P., and Crutchley, E. A., eds. *The diary of Benjamin Newton, rector of Wath, 1816–1818*. Cambridge, 1933.

Gillow, J., and Hewitson, A., eds. *The Tyldesley diary*. Preston, 1873.

Henning, Basil Duke, ed. *The parliamentary diary of Sir Edward Dering, 1670–1673*. New Haven, 1940.

Herbert, Sidney, Lord, ed. *Pembroke papers, 1780–94*. London, 1950.

Hill, J. W. F., ed. *The letters and papers of the Bankes family of Revesby Abbey, 1704–1760*. Publication of the Lincoln Record Society, XLV (1952).

Horwitz, Henry, ed. *The parliamentary diary of Narcissus Luttrell, 1691–1693*. Oxford, 1972.

Hughes, Edward, ed. *The diaries and correspondence of James Losh, 1811–1833*. 2 vols. Publication of the Surtees Society, CLXXI, CLXXIV (1962–3).

Isham, Sir Gyles, ed. *The journal of Thomas Isham, of Lamport (1658–81), kept by him in Latin from 1671 to 1673 at his father's command*. Trans. Norman Marlow. Farnborough, Hants., 1971.

Jeffery, Reginald W., ed. *Dyott's diary, 1781–1845*. 2 vols. London, 1907.

Ketton-Cremer, R. W., ed. *Country neighbourhood*. London, 1951.

Lewis, W. S., ed. *The Yale edition of Horace Walpole's correspondence*. 38 vols. New Haven, 1937–74.

Malmesbury, James, 2nd Earl of. *Half a century of sport in Hampshire*. Ed. F. G. Aflalo. London, 1905.

'The Marchant diary', *Sussex Archaeological Collections*, XXV (1873), 163-203.

Memoirs of the life of Sir Samuel Romilly, written by himself; with a selection from his correspondence. Ed. by his sons. 2nd edn. 3 vols. London, 1840.

'Memorandum book of Sir Walter Calverley, Bart.', in *Yorkshire diaries and autobiographies in the seventeenth and eighteenth centuries*. Publication of the Surtees Society, LXXVII (1886).

Morris, Christopher, ed. *The journeys of Celia Fiennes*. 2nd edn. London, 1949.

Mundy, H. G., ed. *Journal of Mary Frampton*. London, 1885.

Newman, A. N., ed. *The parliamentary diary of Sir Edward Knatchbull, 1722–1730*. Publication of the Camden Society, 3rd series, XCIV (1963).

Payne-Gallwey, Sir Ralph, ed. *The diary of Colonel Peter Hawker*. 2 vols. London, 1893.

La Rochefoucauld-Liancourt, François, duc de. *A Frenchman in England, 1784, being the Mélanges sur l'Angleterre of François de la Rochefoucauld*. Trans. S. C. Roberts. Cambridge, 1933.

Sachse, W. L., ed. *The diary of Roger Lowe*. London, 1938.

Shenstone, J. C., ed. 'A yeoman's common-place book at the commencement of the nineteenth century', *Essex Review*, XVI (1907), 78-89.

Stirling, A. M. W., ed. *The diaries of Dummer*. London, 1934.

Stokes, F. G., ed. *The Blechley diary of the Rev. William Cole, 1765–1767*. London, 1931.

Verney, Frances Parthenope, and Verney, Margaret M., eds. *Memoirs of the Verney family during the seventeenth century*. 2 vols. London, 1904.

Verney, Margaret, Lady, ed. *Verney letters of the eighteenth century from the MSS. at Claydon House*. 2 vols. London, 1930.

Wake, Joan, and Webster, Deborah Champion, eds. *The letters of Daniel Eaton, 1725–32*. Publication of the Northamptonshire Record Society, XXIV (1971).

Wellington, Arthur, 2nd Duke of, ed. *Despatches, correspondence and memoranda of Field Marshall Arthur, Duke of Wellington*. 8 vols. London, 1867–80.

Wheatley, Henry B., ed. *Memoirs of Sir Nathaniel Wraxall, 1772–1784*. 5 vols. London, 1884.

Whiting, C. E., ed. *Two Yorkshire diaries*. Yorkshire Archaeological Society, Record Series, CXVII (1951).

3. Pamphlets, treatises and literature

Addison, Joseph; Steele, Sir Richard; *et al. The Spectator.* Everyman edn, 1945.

An alarm to the people of England shewing their rights, liberties and properties, to be in the utmost danger from the present destructive, and unconstitutional association, for the preservation of the game all over England. London, 1757.

Alken, Henry. *The national sports of Great Britain.* London, 1825.

Aubrey, John. *The natural history of Wiltshire.* Ed. John Britton. London, 1847.

Bankes, George. *Reconsiderations on certain proposed alterations of the game laws.* London, 1825.

Beauties of the game laws exhibited, in a short view of their enactment as to the right of property in game, the qualification for sporting, and the penalties on unqualified persons. London, 1823.

Beckford, Peter. *Thoughts on hunting. In a series of familiar letters to a friend.* N.p., 1781.

Blackstone, Sir William. *Commentaries on the laws of England.* 5th edn. 4 vols. Oxford, 1773.

Commentaries on the laws of England. 9th edn. 4 vols. London, 1783.

Blome, Richard. *The gentleman's recreation.* 2nd edn. London, 1710.

Brougham, Henry, Lord. *Speeches of Henry Lord Brougham.* 2 vols. Philadelphia, 1841.

Burn, Richard. *The justice of the peace and parish officer.* 15th edn. 4 vols. London, 1785.
The justice of the peace and parish officer. 22nd edn. 5 vols. London, 1814.

A candid inquiry into the present state of the laws relative to the game in Scotland. By an admirer of the truth. Edinburgh, 1772.

The case of the distressed warreners of England, humbly presented to this honourable parliament. N.p., [ca. 1710].

Chitty, Joseph. *A continuation of a treatise on the law respecting game and fish.* London, 1816.

'Observations on the game laws', *The Pamphleteer*, IX, No. 17 (Jan. 1817), 172-204.

A treatise on the game laws and on fisheries. 2 vols. London, 1812.

Christian, Edward. *A treatise on the game laws.* London, 1817.
Observations on the sale of game. London, 1821.

Clark, George. *The game laws from King Henry III to the present period.* London, 1786.

Cobbett, William. *Rural rides.* 2 vols. Everyman edn, 1912.

Concise thoughts on the game laws, in which an attempt is made to shew what part of them ought to be retained, and what repealed. By a Leicestershire free-holder. Leicester, 1800.

Congreve, William. *The way of the world.* London, 1700.

Considerations on the game law in answer to a pamphlet intitled, The present state of the game law, and the question of property considered. Edinburgh, 1772.

Considerations on the game laws, together with some strictures on Dr Blackstone's Commentaries relative to this subject. London, 1777.

Cook, Col. John. *Observations on fox-hunting and the management of hounds in the kennel and the field.* London, 1826.

The country gentleman's companion. 2 vols. London, 1753.

The country in full cry, after poachers and hunters of various denominations. [Edinburgh?], 1766.

Cox, Nicholas. *The gentleman's recreation.* 2nd edn. London, 1677.

Coxwell, Rev. Charles. *The partridge's lamentation on the approach of September.* Privately printed. Abington, Glos., 1773.

Crabbe, George. *Tales of the hall.* 2 vols. London, 1819.

Cunningham, Timothy. *A new treatise on the laws for the preservation of the game.* London, 1764.

Daniel, William B. *Rural sports*. 2 vols. London, 1801–2.

 Supplement to the rural sports. London, 1813.

Day, Thomas. *A dialogue between a justice of the peace and a farmer*. London, 1785.

Defoe, Daniel. *A tour through England and Wales*. 2 vols. Everyman edn, 1927.

Edie, George. *A treatise on English shooting*. Dublin, 1774.

Elford, Sir William. 'A few cursory remarks on the obnoxious parts of the game laws', *The Pamphleteer*, X, No. 19 (June 1817), 19-31.

Essays on the game laws, now existing in Great Britain; and remarks on their principal defects. London, 1770.

Facts, fully established, and submitted to the consideration of every member of both houses of parliament, to the lords of manors, and to the attention of the people at large, who consider themselves aggrieved by the abuse of power, displayed in the cruelty and oppression of the game laws. Bath, 1784.

Fairfax, J. *The complete sportsman; or, country gentleman's recreation*. 2nd edn. London, 1795.

Fielding, Henry. *The history of the adventures of Joseph Andrews, and of his friend, Mr Abraham Adams*. London, 1742.

 The history of Tom Jones, a foundling. London, 1749.

Gardiner, John Smallman. *The art and the pleasures of hare-hunting. In six letters to a person of quality*. London, 1750.

Gay, John. *The poetical works of John Gay*. 3 vols. Edinburgh, 1777.

Goldsmith, Oliver. *A history of the earth and animated nature*. 4 vols. Glasgow, 1837–40.

The hare; or, hunting incompatible with humanity. Dublin, 1800.

Hawker, Peter. *Instructions to young sportsmen in all that relates to guns and shooting*. 11th edn. Ed. Maj. P. W. L. Hawker. London, 1859.

Herbert, Rev. William. *A letter to the chairman of the committee of the House of Commons on the game laws*. London, 1823.

Hegel, Georg Wilhelm Friedrich. 'The English reform bill', *Hegel's political writings*. Trans. T. M. Knox. Oxford, 1964.

The hunting of the hare's garland. [Newcastle, 1770?].

Jacob, Giles. *The compleat sportsman*. London, 1718.

 The game law; or, a collection of the laws and statutes made for the preservation of the game in this kingdom. London, 1705.

 The game law. Part II, being an explanation of the acts of parliament, recited in the first part, for the preservation of the game of this kingdom. 2nd edn. London, 1718.

Johnson, Samuel. *Dictionary of the English language*. 2 vols. London, 1831.

'Junius'. *The letters of Junius*. London, 1791.

Knox, Vicesimus. 'On the animosities occasioned in the country by the game laws', *Essays moral and literary*. 17th edn. 3 vols. London, 1815.

Laurence, Edward. *The duty of a steward to his lord*. London, 1727.

Lawrence, John. *The modern land steward*. London, 1801.

A letter on the game laws. By a country gentleman, a proprietor of game. London, 1815.

A letter to a member of parliament, with proposals for a game act. [London?], 1709.

A letter to Richard Whitworth, Esq. member of parliament for the town of Stafford; on his publishing a bill, proposed to be brought into parliament, for amending the laws relating to the game, and pretended to be for the ease and liberty of the people. London, 1772.

A letter to Sir John Shelley on the game laws. By a country gentleman. London, 1819.

Long, C. E. *Considerations on the game laws*. London, 1824.

Manwood, John. *A treatise of the laws of the forest*. 3rd edn. London, 1665.

Markham, Gervase. *Country contentments*. London, 1615.

Marshall, William. *The rural economy of Norfolk*. 2 vols. London, 1787.

 The rural economy of the southern counties. 2 vols. London, 1798.

The rural economy of the west of England. 2 vols. London, 1796.

The rural economy of Yorkshire. 2 vols. London, 1788.

Mayer, John. *The sportsman's directory; or, park and gamekeeper's companion.* Colchester, 1815.

Mordant, John. *The complete steward.* 2 vols. London, 1761.

Nelson, W. *The laws of England concerning the game.* 3rd edn. London, 1736.

The N—f—k farmer's sentiments upon the report of a bill being to be brought into p—m—t for doubling the qualification of sportsmen. London, 1754.

Observations on Lord Suffield's considerations on the game laws. London, 1825.

Otway, Thomas. *The orphan; or, the unhappy-marriage: a tragedy.* London, 1680.

Page, Thomas. *The art of shooting flying.* 5th edn. London, 1784.

Paine, Thomas. *The rights of man.* Everyman edn. 1915.

Poetical remarks on the game laws: shewing how far they are badges of slavery, and inconsistent with real liberty. London, 1797.

The present state of the game law, and the question of property, considered. Edinburgh, 1772.

Priestley, Joseph. *An essay on the first principles of government, and on the nature of political, civil, and religious liberty.* 2nd edn. London, 1771.

Purlewent, Samuel. *A dialogue between a lawyer and a country gentleman, upon the subject of the game laws, relative to hares, partridges, and pheasants.* 2nd edn. London, 1771.

Reasons humbly offered to the right honourable the lords spiritual and temporal, in parliament assembled, against passing a bill, now before their lordships, for better preservation of the game, in the manner 'tis now fram'd. London, 1707.

Remarks on the laws relating to the game and the association set on foot for the preservation of it. In a letter from a country gentleman to his friend in town. London, 1753.

Rivers, George, Baron. *An authentic account of a late negotiation for the purpose of obtaining the disenfranchisement of Cranborne Chase.* London, 1791.

Robinson, David. 'The game laws', *Blackwood's Magazine*, XXII (1827), 643-58.

A second letter on the game laws. By a country gentleman, a proprietor of game. London, 1817.

Shebbeare, John. *A fifth letter to the people of England, on the subversion of the constitution and the necessity of its being restored.* London, 1757.

A third letter to the people of England on liberty, taxes and the application of public money. London, 1756.

Smith, Rev. Sydney. *The works of the Rev. Sydney Smith.* 4th edn. 3 vols. London, 1848.

Some considerations on the game laws and the present practice of executing them; with a hint to the non-subscribers. London, 1753.

Some considerations on the game laws, suggested by the late motion of Mr Curwen for the repeal of the present system. London, 1796.

Southey, Robert. 'The poor', *Quarterly Review*, XV (1816), 187-235.

The sportsman's and gamekeeper's pocket book. London, 1794.

The sportsman's directory; or, the country gentleman's companion in all rural recreations. 2 vols. London, 1735.

Suffield, Edward, 3rd Baron. *Considerations on the game laws.* London, 1825.

Taplin, William. *An appeal to the representatives on the part of the people respecting the present destructive state of the game and the operative spirit of laws erroneously said to be framed for its increase and preservation.* London, 1792.

Observations on the present state of the game in England. London, 1772.

Thornton, Col. Thomas. *A sporting tour through the northern parts of England, and a great part of the Highlands of Scotland.* London, 1804.

Thoughts of the expediency of legalising the sale of game. By a country gentleman. London, 1823.

Thoughts on the present laws for preserving the game. And some methods proposed for making a game law both useful and effectual. London, 1750.
'Three letters on the game laws. By a country gentleman, a proprietor of game', *The Pamphleteer*, XI, No. 22 (Mar. 1818), 325-71.
A treatise on the rights of manors, as deduced from the most ancient and best authorities; with a report on the game laws, and comment. London, 1817.
Williams, Edward Lloyd. *Observations on the game laws, containing suggestions as to the temptations for infringing them, and a proposed remedy.* London, 1828.
Wycherley, William. *Love in a wood; or, St. James's Park.* London, 1672.
Young, Arthur. *Travels in France during the years 1787, 1788 and 1789.* Ed. Jeffrey Kaplow. Garden City, N.Y., 1969.
Zouch, Henry. *An account of the present daring practices of night-hunters and poachers.* London, 1783.

4. Newspapers and periodicals

Annual Register, 1758–1831.
Bell's Weekly Messenger, 1807–30.
Daily Advertiser, 1750–70.
Gentleman's Magazine, 1730–1831.
London Magazine, 1732–80.
Monthly Review, 1749–1820.
Norwich Mercury, 1750–90.
Salisbury Journal, 1750–1800.
The Times, 1790–1830.
Warwick Advertiser, 1815–30.

5. Secondary sources

Bacon, Richard Mackenzie. *A memoir of the life of Edward, 3rd Baron Suffield.* Norwich, 1838.
Bahlman, Dudley, W. R. *The moral revolution of 1688.* New Haven, 1957.
Baker, J. H. 'Criminal courts and procedure at common law, 1550–1800', *Crime in England, 1550–1800.* Ed. J. S. Cockburn. London, 1977.
Baugh, Daniel A. *British naval administration in the age of Walpole.* Princeton, N.J., 1965.
   'The cost of poor relief in south-east England, 1790–1834', *Economic History Review*, 2nd ser., XXVIII (1975), 50-68.
Beattie, J. M. 'The pattern of crime in England, 1660–1800', *Past & Present*, no. 62 (1974), 47-95.
Beckett, J. V. 'English landownership in the later seventeenth and eighteenth centuries: the debate and the problems', *Economic History Review*, 2nd ser., XXX (1977), 567-81.
Beloff, Max. *Public order and popular disturbances, 1660–1714.* London, 1938.
Bergstrom, E. Alexander. 'English game laws and colonial food shortage', *New England Quarterly*, XII (1939), 681-90.
Bloom, Edward A., and Bloom, Lillian D. *Joseph Addison's sociable animal.* Providence, R.I., 1971.
Borsay, Peter. 'The English urban renaissance: the development of provincial urban culture, c. 1680–c. 1760', *Social History*, no. 5 (1977), 581-603.
Bovill, E.W. *English country life, 1780–1830.* Oxford, 1962.

Brailsford, Dennis. *Sport and society: Elizabeth to Anne*. London & Toronto, 1969.

Brander, Michael. *The hunting instinct: the development of field sports over the ages*. Edinburgh & London, 1964.

Brewer, John. *Party ideology and popular politics at the accession of George III*. Cambridge, 1976.

British sporting painting, 1650–1850. The Arts Council of Great Britain, 1974.

Brock, Michael. *The great reform act*. London, 1973.

Brown, A. F. J. 'Colchester in the eighteenth century', *East Anglian studies*. Ed. Lionel M. Munby. Cambridge, 1968.

Burne, S. A. H. 'Presidential address. Parochial documents. With special reference to the Whitworth MSS.', *Transactions of the North Staffordshire Field Club*, LXII (1928), 15-58.

Burnett, John. *Plenty and want: a social history of diet in England from 1815 to the present day*. London, 1966.

Cardigan, Earl of. *The wardens of Savernake Forest*. London, 1949.

Chalkin, C. W. *Seventeenth-century Kent: a social and economic history*. London, 1965.

Chambers, J. D. 'Enclosure and labour supply in the industrial revolution', *Economic History Review*, 2nd ser., V (1953), 319-43.

  Nottinghamshire in the eighteenth century: a study of life and labour under the squirearchy. 2nd edn. London, 1966.

Chambers J. D. and Mingay, G. E. *The agricultural revolution, 1750–1880*. London, 1966.

Chenevix Trench, Charles P. *A history of marksmanship*. London, 1972.

  The poacher and the squire: a history of poaching and game preservation in England. London, 1967.

Christy, Miller. 'Man-traps and spring-guns', *Outing*, XLI (1902-3), 729-34.

Clay, Christopher. 'Marriage, inheritance and the rise of large estates in England, 1660–1815', *Economic History Review*, 2nd ser., XXI (1968), 503-18.

Cockburn, J. S. *A history of English assizes, 1558–1714*. Cambridge, 1972.

Coleman, D. C. 'London scriveners and the estate market in the late seventeenth century', *Economic History Review*, 2nd ser., IV (1951), 221-30.

Cox, John Charles. *The royal forests of England*. London, 1905.

  Three centuries of Derbyshire annals. 2 vols. London, 1890.

Davis, Dorothy. *Fairs, shops and supermarkets: a history of English shopping*. Toronto, 1966.

Dent, Anthony. 'Game and the poacher in Shakespeare's England', *History Today*, XXV (1975), 782-6.

Doughty, Katherine Frances. *The Betts of Wortham in Suffolk, 1480–1905*. London, 1912.

Dowell, Stephen. *A history of taxation and taxes in England, from the earliest times to the present day*. 3rd edn. 4 vols. New York, 1965.

Drummond, J. C., and Wilbraham, Anne. *The Englishman's food: a history of five centuries of English diet*. London, 1939.

Edie, Caroline A. 'New buildings, new taxes and old interests: an urban problem in the 1670s', *Journal of British Studies*, VI (1966-7), 35-63.

Evans, Eric J. 'Some reasons for the growth of English rural anti-clericalism, c. 1750–c. 1830', *Past & Present*, no. 66 (1975), 84-109.

Everitt, Alan. *Change in the provinces: the seventeenth century*. Leicester, 1969.

  The community of Kent and the great rebellion, 1640–1660. Leicester, 1966.

  'Social mobility in early modern England', *Past & Present*, no. 33 (1966), 56-73.

Fisher, F. J. 'The development of London as a centre for conspicuous consumption in the sixteenth and seventeenth centuries', *Transactions of the Royal Historical*

Society, 4th ser., XXX (1948), 37-50.

'The development of the London food market, 1540–1640', *Economic History Review*, V (1935), 47-86.

Fulford, Roger. *Samuel Whitbread, 1764–1815: a study in opposition*. London, 1967.

Fussell, G. E. *The English rural labourer*. London, 1949.

Fussell, G. E., and Fussell, Kathleen R. *The English countryman: his life and work, A.D. 1500–1900*. London, 1955.

Gash, N. 'Rural unemployment, 1815–34', *Economic History Review*, VI (1935–6), 90-3.

Gilbert, Arthur N. 'Army impressment during the war of the Spanish succession', *The Historian*, XXXVIII (1976), 689-708.

Gilboy, Elizabeth. *Wages in eighteenth-century England*. Cambridge, Mass., 1934.

Gill, Conrad, and Briggs, Asa. *History of Birmingham*. 2 vols. Oxford, 1952.

Gladstone, Hugh S. 'Oldest game book', *Notes & Queries*, CXCIII (1948), 77-9.

Godber, Joyce. *History of Bedfordshire, 1066–1888*. Luton, 1969.

Gonner, E. C. K. *Common land and inclosure*. 2nd edn. London, 1966.

Grassby, Richard. 'English merchant capitalism in the late seventeenth century. The composition of business fortunes', *Past & Present*, no. 46 (1970), 87-107.

Grigg, David. *The agricultural revolution in south Lincolnshire*. Cambridge, 1966.

Grosvenor, Caroline, and Wortley, Charles Beilby Stuart. *The first Lady Wharncliffe and her family, 1779–1856*. 2 vols. London, 1927.

Habakkuk, H. J. 'English landownership, 1680–1740', *Economic History Review*, X (1940), 2-17.

'Landowners and the civil war', *Economic History Review*, 2nd ser., XVIII (1965), 130-51.

Hamilton, A. H. A. *Quarter sessions from Queen Elizabeth to Queen Anne*. London, 1878.

Hamilton, Elizabeth. *The Mordaunts: an eighteenth-century family*. London, 1965.

Hammersley, George. 'The revival of the forest laws under Charles I', *History*, XLV (1960), 85-102.

Hammond, J.L., and Hammond, Barbara. *The village labourer, 1760–1832*. New edn. London, 1948.

The skilled labourer, 1760–1832. London, 1919.

Harris, Alan. 'The rabbit warrens of east Yorkshire in the eighteenth and nineteenth centuries', *Yorkshire Archaeological Journal*, XLII (1967–70), 429-43.

The rural landscape of the East Riding of Yorkshire, 1700–1850: a study in historical geography. Oxford, 1961.

Hartwell, R. M. *The industrial revolution and economic growth*. London, 1971.

Hay, Douglas; Linebaugh, Peter; and Thompson, E. P., eds. *Albion's fatal tree: crime and society in eighteenth-century England*. New York, 1975.

Henriques, U. R. Q. 'The rise and decline of the separate system of prison discipline', *Past & Present*, no. 54 (1972), 61-93.

Hill, Christopher. 'The Norman yoke', *Puritanism and revolution*. London, 1958.

Reformation to industrial revolution: a social and economic history of Britain, 1530–1780. London, 1967.

Hill, J. W. F. *Georgian Lincoln*. Cambridge, 1966.

Hobsbawm, E. J. *Industry and empire: an economic history of Britain since 1750*. London, 1968.

Hobsbawm E. J. and Rudé, George. *Captain Swing*. New York, 1968.

Holderness, B. A. *Pre-industrial England: economy and society, 1500–1750*. London, 1976.

Holdsworth, Sir William. *A history of English law*. 7th edn. 14 vols. London, 1956.

Hole, Christina. *English sports and pastimes*. London, 1949.

Hughes, Edward. *North country life in the eighteenth century*. 2 vols. Oxford, 1952–65.

Hunt, C. J. *The lead miners of the northern Pennines in the eighteenth and nineteenth centuries.* Manchester, 1970.

Hussey, Christopher. *English gardens and landscapes, 1700–1750.* London, 1967.

Huxley, Gervas. *Lady Elizabeth and the Grosvenors: life in a Whig family, 1822–1839.* London, 1965.

Hyams, Edward. *Capability Brown and Humphrey Repton.* London, 1971.

Inglis, Brian. *Poverty and the industrial revolution.* London, 1971.

Itzkowitz. David C. *Peculiar privilege: a social history of English foxhunting, 1753–1885.* London, 1977.

John, A. H. 'Farming in wartime, 1793–1815', *Land, labour and population in the industrial revolution: essays presented to J. D. Chambers.* Ed. E. L. Jones and G. E. Mingay. London, 1967.

Jones, D. J. V. 'The poacher: a study in Victorian crime and protest', *Historical Journal,* XXII (1979), 825-60.

Jones, D.W. 'London merchants and the crisis of the 1690s', *Crisis and Order in English towns, 1500–1700.* Ed. Peter Clark and Paul Slack. Toronto, 1972.

Jones, E. L. 'The agricultural labour market in England, 1793–1872', *Economic History Review,* 2nd ser., XVII (1964–5), 322-38.

Jones, P. E. *The worshipful company of poulters of the city of London: a short history.* 2nd edn. London, 1965.

Kenyon, George T. *The life of Lloyd, first Lord Kenyon, lord chief justice of England.* London, 1873.

Kenyon, J. P. *The Stuart constitution, 1603–1688.* Cambridge, 1966.

Kerr, Barbara. 'The Dorset agricultural labourer, 1750–1850', *Proceedings of the Dorset Natural History and Archaeological Society,* LXXXIV (1962), 158-77.

Kirby, Chester. 'The attack on the game laws in the forties', *Journal of Modern History,* IV (1932), 18-37.

   'English game law reform', *Essays in modern English history in honor of Wilbur Cortez Abbott.* Cambridge, Mass., 1941.

   'The English game law system', *American Historical Review,* XXXVIII (1933), 240-62.

   'The literary history of English field sports, 1671–1850', *Studies in British History.* Ed. Cornelius de Kiewiet. *University of Iowa Studies in the Social Sciences,* XI (1941).

Kirby, Chester, and Kirby, Ethyn. 'The Stuart game prerogative', *English Historical Review,* XLVI (1931), 239-54.

Lennard, Reginald, ed. *Englishmen at rest and play: some phases of English leisure, 1558–1714.* Oxford, 1931.

Lewis, Michael. *A social history of the navy, 1793–1815.* London, 1960.

Lloyd, A. L. *Folk song in England.* New York, 1967.

Lloyd, Christopher. *The British seaman, 1200–1860: a social survey.* London, 1968.

Loftis, John. *Comedy and society from Congreve to Fielding.* Stanford, Calif., 1959.

Longrigg, Roger. *The history of foxhunting.* London, 1975.

Malcolmson, Robert W. *Popular recreations in English society, 1700–1850.* Cambridge, 1973.

Marshall, Dorothy. 'The role of the justice of the peace in social administration', *British government and administration: studies presented to S. B. Chrimes.* Ed. H. Hearder and H. R. Loyn. Cardiff, 1974.

Martin, E. W. *The shearers and the shorn: a study of life in a Devon community.* London, 1965.

Mathias, Peter. 'The social structure of the eighteenth century: a calculation by Joseph Massie', *Economic History Review,* 2nd ser., X (1957–8), 30-45.

Mingay, G. E. *English landed society in the eighteenth century.* London & Toronto, 1963.
   The gentry: the rise and fall of a ruling class. London & New York, 1976.
Mitchell, Brian R., and Deane, Phyllis. *Abstract of British historical statistics.* Cambridge, 1962.
Moir, Esther. *The justice of the peace.* Harmondsworth, 1969.
   Local government in Gloucestershire, 1775–1800. Publication of the Bristol and Gloucestershire Archaeological Society, VIII (1969).
   'Sir George Onesiphorous Paul', *Gloucestershire studies.* Ed. H. P. R. Finberg. Leicester, 1957.
Moreshead, O. F. 'H. M. gamekeeper', *Notes & Queries*, CLXIV (1933), 373.
Munsche, P. B. 'The game laws in Wiltshire, 1750–1800', *Crime in England, 1550–1800.* Ed. J. S. Cockburn. London, 1977.
Namier, Sir Lewis, and Brooke, John, eds. *The house of commons, 1754–1790.* 3 vols. London, 1964.
Neuman, Mark. 'Speenhamland in Berkshire', *Comparative development in social welfare.* Ed. E. W. Martin. London, 1972.
Norman, Philip. 'Notes on Bromley and the neighbourhood', *Archaeologia Cantiana*, XXIV (1900), 139-59.
Obelkevich, James. *Religion and rural society: South Lindsey, 1825–75.* Oxford, 1976.
Ogg, David. *England in the reign of Charles II.* 2nd edn. Oxford, 1956.
Peacock, A. J. *Bread or blood: a study of the agrarian riots in East Anglia in 1816.* London, 1965.
Peacock, Edward. 'Trial under the game laws', *Notes & Queries*, 7th ser., III (1887), 221-2.
Pettit, P. A. J. *The royal forests of Northamptonshire: a study in their economy, 1558–1714.* Publication of the Northamptonshire Record Society, XXIII (1968).
Plumb, J. H. *Sir Robert Walpole.* 2 vols. London, 1956–60.
Pocock, J. G. A. *The Machiavellian moment: Florentine political thought and the Atlantic republican tradition.* Princeton, N.J., 1975.
Poynter, J. R. *Society and pauperism: English ideas on poor relief, 1795–1834.* London & Toronto, 1969.
Radzinowicz, Leon. *A history of English criminal law and its administration from 1750.* 4 vols. London, 1948–68.
Robbins, Caroline. *The eighteenth-century commonwealthman: studies in the transmission, development and circumstance of English liberal thought from the restoration of Charles II until the war with the Thirteen Colonies.* 2nd edn. New York, 1968.
Rogers, James E. Thorold. *A history of agriculture and prices in England.* 7 vols. Oxford, 1866–1902.
Rogers, Nicholas. 'Aristocratic clientage, trade and independency: popular politics in pre-radical Westminster', *Past & Present*, no. 61 (1973), 70-106.
Ross, Dorothy. 'Class privilege in seventeenth-century England', *History*, XXVIII (1943), 148-55.
Schwoerer, Lois G. *'No standing armies!': the anti-army ideology in seventeenth-century England.* Baltimore & London, 1974.
Scouller, R. E. *The armies of Queen Anne.* Oxford, 1966.
Shaw, A. G. L. *Convicts and colonies: a study of penal transportation from Great Britain and Ireland to Australia and other parts of the British Empire.* London, 1966.
Speck, W. A. 'Conflict in society', *Britain after the glorious revolution, 1689–1714.* Ed. Geoffrey Holmes. London, 1969.
   'Social status in late Stuart England', *Past & Present*, no. 34 (1966), 127-9.
Stephen, Sir James Fitzjames. *A history of the criminal law of England.* 3 vols. London, 1883.

Stephen, Sir Leslie, and Lee, Sir Sidney, eds. *Dictionary of National Biography.* 22 vols. London, 1959–60.

Stern, Walter M. 'The bread crisis in Britain, 1795–96', *Economica*, n.s., XXXI (1964), 168-87.

Stevenson, John. 'Food riots in England, 1792–1818', *Popular protest and public order: six studies in British history, 1790–1920.* Ed. John Stevenson and R. Quinault. London, 1974.

Stirling, A. M. W. *Coke of Norfolk and his friends.* 2 vols. London & New York, 1912.

Stone, Lawrence. 'Social mobility in England, 1500–1700', *Past & Present*, no. 33 (1966), 16-55.

Strutt, Joseph. *The sports and pastimes of the people of England.* New edn. London, 1841.

Taylor, Basil. *Stubbs.* London, 1971.

Thompson, E. P. *The making of the English working class.* London, 1963.
　'The moral economy of the English crowd in the eighteenth century', *Past & Present*, no. 50 (1971), 76-136.
　'Patrician society, plebian culture', *Journal of Social History,* VII (1973–4), 382-405.
　Whigs and hunters: the origin of the Black Act. New York, 1975.

Thompson F. M. L. *English landed society in the nineteenth century.* London, 1963.

Thomson, Gladys Scott. *Life in a noble household, 1614–1700.* London, 1937.

Trevelyan, G. M. *England under Queen Anne.* 3 vols. London, 1930–4.

Turberville, A. S., ed. *Johnson's England.* 2 vols. Oxford, 1933.

Twiss, Horace. *The public and private life of Lord Chancellor Eldon with selections from his correspondence.* 2nd edn. 3 vols. London, 1884.

Viner, Jacob. 'Man's economic status', *Man versus society in eighteenth-century Britain.* Ed. James L. Clifford. Cambridge, 1968.

Wake, Joan. *The Brudenells of Deene.* London, 1953.

Walker, J. W. *Wakefield: its history and people.* 3rd edn. 2 vols. Wakefield, 1967.

Webb, Sidney, and Webb, Beatrice. *English local government*. New edn. 11 vols. London, 1963.

Western, J. R. *The English militia in the eighteenth century: the story of a political issue, 1660–1802.* London & Toronto, 1965.
　Monarchy and revolution: the English state in the 1680s. London, 1972.

Whitaker, W. B. *The eighteenth-century English Sunday: a study of Sunday observance from 1677 to 1837.* London, 1940.

Widnell, H. E. R. *The Beaulieu record.* N.p., 1973.

Wilson, Charles. *England's apprenticeship, 1603–1763.* London, 1965.

Wingfield-Stratford, Esmé. *The lords of Cobham Hall.* London, 1959.
　The squire and his relations. London, 1956.

Witcombe, D. T. *Charles II and the cavalier house of commons, 1663–1674.* Manchester, 1966.

Wrigley, E. A. 'A simple model of London's importance in changing English society and economy, 1650–1750', *Past & Present*, no. 37 (1967), pp. 44-86.

Zagorin, Perez. *The court and the country: the beginning of the English revolution.* New York, 1969.

III. Unpublished theses

Cook, P. J. 'Property and prerogative in game: the legal background to the English game and forest laws'. Ph.D. thesis, University of Birmingham, 1975.

Landau, Norma. 'Gentry and gentlemen: the justices of the peace, 1680–1760'. Ph.D. thesis, University of California, Berkeley, 1974.

Pollock, Norman H. 'The English game laws in the nineteenth century'. Ph.D. thesis, John Hopkins University, 1968.

Rogers, Nicholas. 'London politics from Walpole to Pitt: patriotism and independency in an era of commercial imperialism, 1738–63'. Ph.D. thesis, University of Toronto, 1975.

Index